Cloud Native Microservices Cookbook

Master the art of microservices in the cloud with over 100 practical recipes

Varun Yadav

www.bpbonline.com

First Edition 2024

ISBN: 978-93-55519-603

LIMITS OF LIABILITY AND DISCLAIMER OF WARRANTY

Distributors:

BPB PUBLICATIONS
20, Ansari Road, Darya Ganj
New Delhi-110002
Ph: 23254990/23254991

DECCAN AGENCIES
4-3-329, Bank Street,
Hyderabad-500195
Ph: 24756967/24756400

MICRO MEDIA
Shop No. 5, Mahendra Chambers,
150 DN Rd. Next to Capital Cinema,
V.T. (C.S.T.) Station, MUMBAI-400 001
Ph: 22078296/22078297

To View Complete BPB Publications Catalogue Scan the QR Code:

Published by Manish Jain for BPB Publications, 20 Ansari Road, Darya Ganj, New Delhi-110002 and Printed by him at Manipal Technologies, Manipal

www.bpbonline.com

Dedicated to

My beloved parents:

Krishan Kumar Yadav

and

Manju Yadav

Your nurturing guidance and unwavering support have shaped me into the person I am today. With your love and wisdom, you have empowered me to confidently navigate life's journey and make conscientious decisions. Thank you for providing me with a foundation to stand tall and pursue my dreams.

And to my loving wife:

Neha Yadav

Your enduring companionship and intense faith in my abilities have served as my steadfast source of strength and inspiration. I express my deepest gratitude for being my pillar of support and my greatest source of joy.

About the Author

Varun Yadav, a seasoned Computer Science Engineer with nearly two decades of rich expertise spanning Enterprise Architecture, Solution Architecture, Cloud Computing, Microservices, and DevOps. Combining technical acumen with strategic vision, he holds an MBA in Information Management and Strategy, complemented by a Post Graduate Diploma in AI and Machine Learning. With a career deeply rooted in the BFSI domain, Varun has been a driving force behind innovation, actively participating in Proof of Concepts (POCs), leading Idea Generation initiatives, and igniting creativity in Hackathons. Notably, Varun believes in leading by example, having successfully helmed large-scale teams through intricate projects and endeavors. With an unwavering commitment to staying ahead of the curve in technology, he embodies a blend of expertise and foresight, consistently delivering transformative solutions that redefine industry standards. Whether forging innovative approaches or fostering collaborative environments, he stands as a beacon of excellence, guiding teams toward unparalleled success in the ever-evolving landscape of technology.

About the Reviewers

- **Kumar Gaurav**, with over 12 years of experience in software engineering, is currently serving as an Architect at LTI-Mindtree, where he leads digital transformation initiatives. Specializing in open-source solutions and cloud-native technologies, he ensures the implementation of industry best practices in infrastructure setup, development, deployment, and monitoring for large enterprises. Kumar's expertise encompasses Kubernetes, OpenShift, Docker, Git, Java, Microservices, API Gateway, ESB, WSO2, DevOps MySQL, Linux, tool based development and more.

  Certified in WSO2 & Oracle middleware technologies, Kumar excels in on-premise and cloud-based implementations, with proficiency in Amazon Web Services, Google Cloud, and Oracle Cloud. He has played a pivotal role in end-to-end project implementation and post-implementation support across various domains such as Finance, Railways, Healthcare, Power sector, and Business Intelligence.

  Driven by a passion for innovation and fostering seamless communication between systems, Kumar actively seeks networking and collaboration opportunities within the realm of modern digital architecture.

- **Sumit Baja**j, a seasoned Engineering Leader and Integration Solution Architect with 20 years of rich experience in designing and developing software products to solve complex business problems. A creative problem solver and solution-oriented professional, dedicated to improving business operations and meeting client technical needs. With proven leadership characteristics, he drives enterprise-grade solutions from conception to completion, consistently delivering exceptional project outcomes.

Acknowledgement

I am deeply indebted to my wife, Neha, whose constant backing made it possible for me to dedicate countless hours to the creation of this book. Thank you for your patience, and encouragement, and for being my pillar of strength throughout this journey. Your love and belief in me mean everything.

I extend my sincere gratitude to all my managers who have been more than just colleagues; they have been mentors, guides, and friends. Special thanks to Marul Mehta for his invaluable support and confidence in me during the formative stages of my career, and to Rakesh Mahajan for his encouragement to embark on this writing journey. Your belief in my abilities and encouragement has been instrumental in making this book a reality.

I would also like to express my heartfelt appreciation to BPB Publications for giving me the opportunity to write this book. It has been an honor to collaborate with such a reputable publishing house, and I am grateful for the trust they have placed in me.

Preface

Welcome to the preface of this book, where I am thrilled to share my journey and passion for technology with you. From the very beginning, I have been captivated by the wonders of technology, finding immense joy in seeing my contributions come to life and being used by people. It has been an exhilarating ride dedicating my entire career to crafting and delivering technology solutions, particularly in the BFSI domain.

What drove me to write this book? Well, it is simple. I have always craved the full picture – the complete lifecycle, the entire technology stack. That burning curiosity inspired me to embark on this writing journey. This book is not just a collection of recipes; it is a meticulously planned expedition through the intricate world of designing and architecting microservices from scratch, all the way to harnessing the boundless potential of the cloud.

Think of it as your guide to launching microservices in the cloud – a comprehensive roadmap that covers every aspect, from the nitty-gritty of developing microservices to the intricacies of hosting and administrating them in the cloud. Through real-world insights and practical examples, I aim to demystify the complexities of proficient system architectures, equipping you with the tools and know-how to navigate this exciting terrain with confidence.

Chapter breakdown:

Chapter 1: Microservices and Cloud - Discover the foundational concepts of microservice architecture and cloud elasticity. Delve into the importance of Java frameworks and learn to configure cloud services and setup cloud infra for optimal performance.

Chapter 2: Developing Microservices and Test Cases - Establish a solid foundation for microservice development, starting with environment setup and the API-first approach. Explore practical examples and running code snippets to kickstart your journey.

Chapter 3: Externalize Application Configurations - Learn to externalize application configurations for enhanced flexibility and seamless deployment across different environments. Dive into Spring Cloud Config Server and Spring Actuator for efficient configuration management.

Chapter 4: Implementing Dynamic Services - Explore the need for service discovery and various approaches to achieve seamless communication between dynamically changing microservices.

Chapter 5: Containerization Using Docker - Unlock the agility and efficiency of containerization with Docker. Master the process of wrapping applications in lightweight images and deploying them to AWS ECR.

Chapter 6: Pipeline Automation for CI/CD - Streamline your development process with automated CI/CD pipelines. Discover best practices for code quality checks, test case execution, and security assessments.

Chapter 7: Microservices Orchestration - Centralize control and management of containerized applications with microservices orchestration. Learn to set up orchestrators, fetch from registries, and scale your applications seamlessly.

Chapter 8: Auto Scalability, High Availability, and Disaster Recovery - Ensure high availability and scalability of your applications in the AWS cloud. Explore strategies for disaster recovery and handle scale-out and scale-in events effectively.

Chapter 9: Cloud Security - Prioritize security considerations for your microservices in the cloud. Discover techniques to safeguard your applications using available cloud security offerings.

Chapter 10: Observability - Gain insights into the internal state of your applications with observability. Learn to set up logs, metrics, and tracing for better understanding and critical observations about the application behavior.

Chapter 11: Infrastructure Automation with IaC - Simplify infrastructure setup with Infrastructure as Code (IaC). Explore automation techniques for creating and managing infrastructure across different environments.

So, buckle up, dear reader, as we embark on this thrilling adventure together. Let us dive deep into the world of microservices and cloud technologies, and uncover the secrets to building robust, scalable solutions that stand the test of time.

Happy reading and hands-on exploring!

Code Bundle and Coloured Images

Please follow the link to download the
Code Bundle and the *Coloured Images* of the book:

https://rebrand.ly/gah3typ

The code bundle for the book is also hosted on GitHub at **https://github.com/bpbpublications/Cloud-Native-Microservices-Cookbook**. In case there's an update to the code, it will be updated on the existing GitHub repository.

We have code bundles from our rich catalogue of books and videos available at **https://github.com/bpbpublications**. Check them out!

Errata

We take immense pride in our work at BPB Publications and follow best practices to ensure the accuracy of our content to provide with an indulging reading experience to our subscribers. Our readers are our mirrors, and we use their inputs to reflect and improve upon human errors, if any, that may have occurred during the publishing processes involved. To let us maintain the quality and help us reach out to any readers who might be having difficulties due to any unforeseen errors, please write to us at :

errata@bpbonline.com

Your support, suggestions and feedbacks are highly appreciated by the BPB Publications' Family.

Piracy

If you come across any illegal copies of our works in any form on the internet, we would be grateful if you would provide us with the location address or website name. Please contact us at **business@bpbonline.com** with a link to the material.

If you are interested in becoming an author

If there is a topic that you have expertise in, and you are interested in either writing or contributing to a book, please visit **www.bpbonline.com**. We have worked with thousands of developers and tech professionals, just like you, to help them share their insights with the global tech community. You can make a general application, apply for a specific hot topic that we are recruiting an author for, or submit your own idea.

Reviews

Please leave a review. Once you have read and used this book, why not leave a review on the site that you purchased it from? Potential readers can then see and use your unbiased opinion to make purchase decisions. We at BPB can understand what you think about our products, and our authors can see your feedback on their book. Thank you!

For more information about BPB, please visit **www.bpbonline.com**.

Join our book's Discord space

Join the book's Discord Workspace for Latest updates, Offers, Tech happenings around the world, New Release and Sessions with the Authors:

https://discord.bpbonline.com

Table of Contents

Chapter 1
Microservices and Cloud

Introduction

This is an era in which all greenfield application developments are done using microservice architecture, and going cloud is the strategic direction every organization is moving towards.

In this chapter, we will learn the importance of microservice architecture and how cloud elasticity is the go-to technology for leveraging the maximum benefits out of a microservice and the importance of Java frameworks in building enterprise grade microservices.

Structure

In this chapter, we will discuss following topics:

- Importance of microservices
- Importance of cloud
- Using the Java programming language
- Java frameworks for microservices
- Configuring cloud services

Objectives

By the end of this chapter, we will learn the benefits of developing an application using microservice architecture compared to a monolithic architecture, as well as the features provided by cloud infrastructure and how they overcome the challenges that are present in the on-premise deployments. We will also learn the importance of Java as a programming language for developing enterprise grade software applications, the Java frameworks available in the market for developing microservices and why Spring Boot is the most preferred option amongst them. In the end, we will learn how to configure different AWS services that will be required to begin the development of the microservices discussed in detail in later chapters of this book.

Importance of microservices

Microservices have evolved to overcome the issues and challenges faced by the monolithic applications, be it in any phase of the software development lifecycle, development, testing, build, deployment, or maintenance. Although microservices require some extra efforts, they provide many advantages in the larger extent.

The word **micro** means granular, that is, breaking the complete large requirement into small parts and then developing, building, and deploying them as services independent of each other, eventually orchestrating them in tandem to fulfill the complete business requirement. Here, granularity is a subjective term and how granular a service should be, is dependent on case-to-case basis and on the actual business functionality. In most of the cases, the functionality that is subject to change together in the future, should be part of the same microservice.

Figure 1.1 illustrates the difference between a monolithic application and microservices:

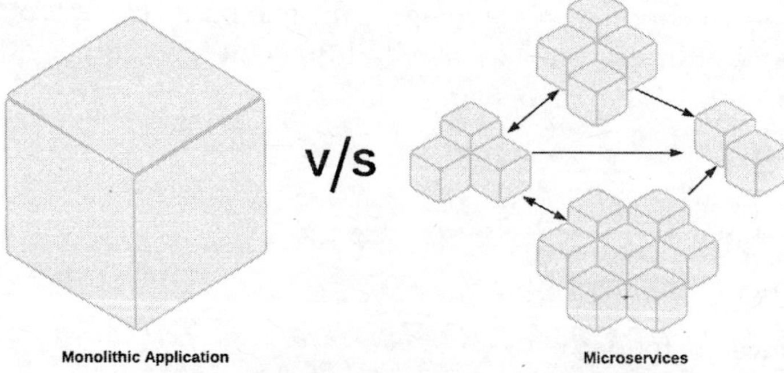

Figure 1.1*: Monolithic versus Microservices*

The benefits of developing an application using a microservice architecture compared with the overwork that needs to be done in different phases of **software delivery life cycle (SDLC)**, are explained as follows.

Development

The benefits and overwork in the development phase are as follows.

Benefits:

- Every microservice can be developed independently of each other.
- Different teams can work together to develop different microservices.
- If required, the microservices can be developed using different technology stacks.

Overwork:

- Multiple code repositories are to be created and maintained, one for each microservice.

Testing

The benefits and overwork in the testing phase are as follows:

Benefits:

- Every microservice can be independently tested by the testing team.
- Test cases can be easily created, since the scope of a microservice is limited compared to the complete functionality.

Overwork:

- Separate integration tests are to be created to test the overall business functionality.
- Multiple test environments might have to be created, if required.

Deployment

The benefits and overwork in the deployment phase are as follows:

Benefits:

- Build pipelines are simple and can be created independently for each microservice.
- Can leverage container and cloud infrastructure.
- **Independent Infrastructure as Code** (**IaC**) scripts can be created, which are simple and can reuse common templates.

Overwork:

- Microservices need to be carefully version controlled to resolve the interdependence on each other.

- Complex orchestration is required to build coordination between multiple microservices.

Management

The benefits and overwork in the management phase are as follows:

Benefits:

- Individual microservices can be upgraded or modified without impacting other services.
- Easier to debug and troubleshoot.
- Application health can be monitored at a microservice level.

Overwork:

- As more than one instance of each microservice can be live at a time, there is a need for complex observability patterns to get the complete insight of the whole application.

Additional advantages of application development using microservice architecture are:

- The design is highly scalable, and more microservices can be easily added later if required.
- Faster time-to-market as microservices are be independently developed, tested, and deployed and the activities can be done in parallel.
- A microservice can be shared with different business modules, which makes it reusable.
- An individual microservice can be scaled in case of heavy load, without impacting others, which has a straight cost and performance benefit.

Thus, the benefits of a microservice architecture are huge compared to the overwork that is required to be done.

It is crucial to acknowledge that adopting a microservices architecture introduces new complexities. Communication between microservices becomes paramount, necessitating the implementation of robust and efficient mechanisms such as REST, gRPC APIs or message queues. Monitoring and managing the entire ecosystem of microservices demand more sophisticated tools and strategies such as service mesh In conclusion, the microservices architecture is a powerful paradigm that addresses the limitations of monolithic applications. It promotes flexibility, scalability, and agility in software development. While it does present additional challenges, the benefits it provides, especially in handling large and complex systems, make it a preferred choice for modern application development.

Importance of cloud

Going cloud is the new norm; every agile company is either migrating their applications to cloud or building new applications in a cloud native way. Adopting cloud allows the enterprises to focus on their core competencies or businesses without bothering about any of the following:

- Hardware infrastructure
- Software licenses
- Security
- Patching
- Backups
- Disaster recovery, and so on.

Everything is taken care of by the cloud provider.

Apart from offloading the preceding tedious and tardy activities from the shoulders of an enterprise, cloud infrastructure provides them with the flexibility to choose from various options of compute and services, depending on their business needs and workloads. In return, enterprises also save costs, as they are only paying for services as per their usage, and there is no need to incur huge costs during off business hours or at the time of lean workloads.

There are multiple cloud providers in the market. Following are the ones that have majority of the market share:

- Amazon Web Services
- Microsoft Azure
- Google Cloud
- Oracle Cloud

Figure 1.2 features some of the cloud provider options:

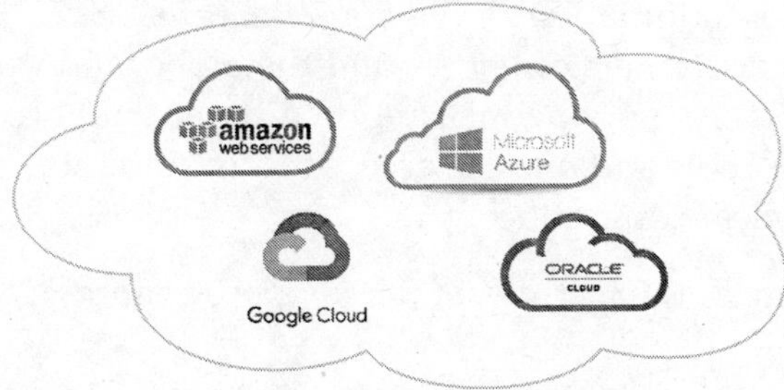

Figure 1.2: *Cloud providers*

The complete benefits of a microservice architecture cannot be achieved without leveraging the dynamics of cloud computing. Real time scalability with zero down time is the key to horizontally scale a microservice, depending on the current load and many other configurable parameters. Cloud provides the infrastructure to scale as many instances of a microservice as required, and provides a way for the load to achieve the maximum utilization of resources, while also being uniformly distributed. All the microservices and their instances are run in a secure and independent environment, but controlled via central orchestration service, such that they can communicate with each other without knowing each other's actual physical location. The same service is also responsible for starting or stopping an instance of a microservice, as per the configured rules.

Cloud also provides services that support **Open Container Initiative** (**OCI**) specifications, particularly the Runtime Specification, that involves downloading an OCI image, and unpacking it into an OCI runtime filesystem bundle, and then finally running it using an OCI runtime. So, that means that any image built as per the OCI Image Specification can be run in the cloud by leveraging such services provided by the cloud. In other words, applications bundled as Docker image (which follows OCI specification) can be run very easily in the cloud environments.

Security is a point which is of outmost importance for any enterprise grade software application and a lot of resources are spent to make an application full proof from security perspective in a typical on-premise installation. Cloud provides lot of built-in components that can be easily bundled into the application architecture, whether it is secured access to the application, stopping hacking or denial-of-service attack, encryption of data both at rest or in transit, auditing of activities performed; there are services that can be directly used. Security concerns can be easily mitigated by picking up and configuring the right security services made available by the cloud providers.

Cloud-native microservices are microservices that are specifically made to exist in the cloud and leverage its dynamics to provide better flexibility, efficiency, and cost optimization.

Using the Java programming language

Java has been an enterprise grade programming language for more than two decades and has proven to be the best for developing big and highly complex software. The language has evolved a lot from its initial days, has great features and is also quite easy to learn. There are too many practitioners of Java round the globe, and this led to a lot of material getting accumulated freely over the internet on different nuances of programming. A lot of support is freely available and one can access this information anytime, from anywhere, whenever stuck or to clear some concepts.

Figure 1.3 features some of the features of the Java programming language:

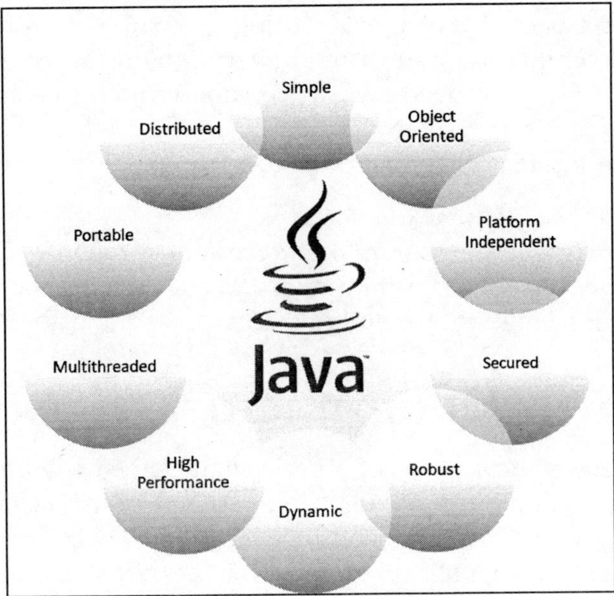

Figure 1.3: Java features

Apart from the standard packages that are available with the **Java Development Kit (JDK)**, there are numerous open-source projects run by different communities such as Apache, Spring, JBoss, and so on, and are available for developers to provide aide in building complex applications and for resolving challenging technical issues.

The complete application development ecosystem is full of tools that are required for the software development written in Java programming language. Pick any application paradigm or SDLC phase and there will be tools written in Java.

Figure 1.4 features some of the tools written in Java:

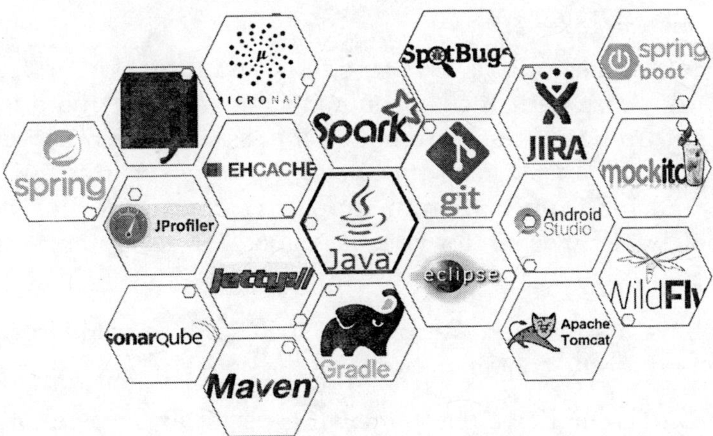

Figure 1.4: Tools written in Java

The other important aspect of Java is that during its complete evolution, it has majorly remained backward compatible, and there are very few instances where an upgrade or feature enhancement creates concerns with the code written in earlier versions. This is very important from an enterprise application perspective where frequent code changes are not at all possible and require the software to be up to date with the latest features and security fixes.

There are other languages in the market that have some or all the features that Java has, but the depth of support from the community, and such a long history make it the most preferred programming language for building enterprise grade applications.

Java frameworks for microservices

Framework is a platform or collection of libraries with some predefined rules to speed up the software development process. While using a framework, the code needs to follow its defined coding patterns and, in a way, it also governs the way code is written. Along with the governance, a lot of functionality is provided out of the box by the frameworks, which makes software development simpler and less prone to errors.

Microservice frameworks are frameworks created specifically for developing microservices. Multiple frameworks for microservices have been developed by different communities, by leveraging the Java programming language. Some of them are matured, some are new and some are very light weight. Here are the details of a few:

- **Spring Boot** is a framework created on top of Spring framework, and is the most matured and tested Java framework for production ready microservices, with enormous support available over the internet. Moreover, the collection of libraries available for Spring Boot is huge; whether it is security, cloud native development kits, data handling, integration with UI or middle-tier, testing, observability, or any other software intricacy, there will be a choice for library selection while working on Spring Boot framework.

- **Micronaut** framework is very modern and uses lot of features of Spring framework. Micronaut focuses on reducing memory footprint and providing quick start up time, which are both very essential for microservices, from both cost and performance perspective. Being very new, the framework is not matured and not much documentation or support is available for it. The framework has lot of potential, however, for now, it is good for developing small microservices compared to anything of enterprise grade.

- **Quarkus** is a full-stack framework specifically created for optimizing Java applications for the container world.

- **Dropwizard** is a light weight framework specifically created for developing REST services, and is based on popular libraries such as `Jetty`, `Jackson`, and `Jersey`.

- **Vert.x** is developed by Eclipse; it is also a light weight framework and majorly focuses on developing reactive microservices. It provides a toolset that can be used to build custom independent components which can be integrated or embedded in Spring framework if required.

Considering the pros and cons on different frameworks, it is not wrong to say that Spring Boot is by far the most preferred Java framework for developing enterprise grade microservices or applications. Microservices developed as part of this book will be based on Spring Boot framework.

Configuring cloud services

The cloud-native microservices developed as part of this book will leverage **Amazon Web Services** (**AWS**) as a cloud provider and will be using AWS cloud services as part of microservices development.

To begin using AWS, a valid account needs to be created with AWS and is assumed to already exist before starting with the development. There are few initial steps that needs to be carried out, and the process is described in the subsequent recipes.

Recipe 1: Installing AWS command line interface

Amazon Web Services Command Line Interface (**AWS CLI**) is an open-source tool offered by the cloud provider, to interact with its services using command-line shell. Though AWS Management Console **graphic user interface** (**GUI**) is convenient and very intuitive, it becomes challenging if an AWS environment needs to be created multiple times or needs replication. Command line is very practical in such scenarios, as commands can be scripted and run as many times as required.

Installing AWS CLI on Windows

Run the following command on command prompt:

```
msiexec.exe /i https://awscli.amazonaws.com/AWSCLIV2.msi
```

This will open the installer which can be navigated to install AWS CLI on windows, as shown in *Figure 1.5*:

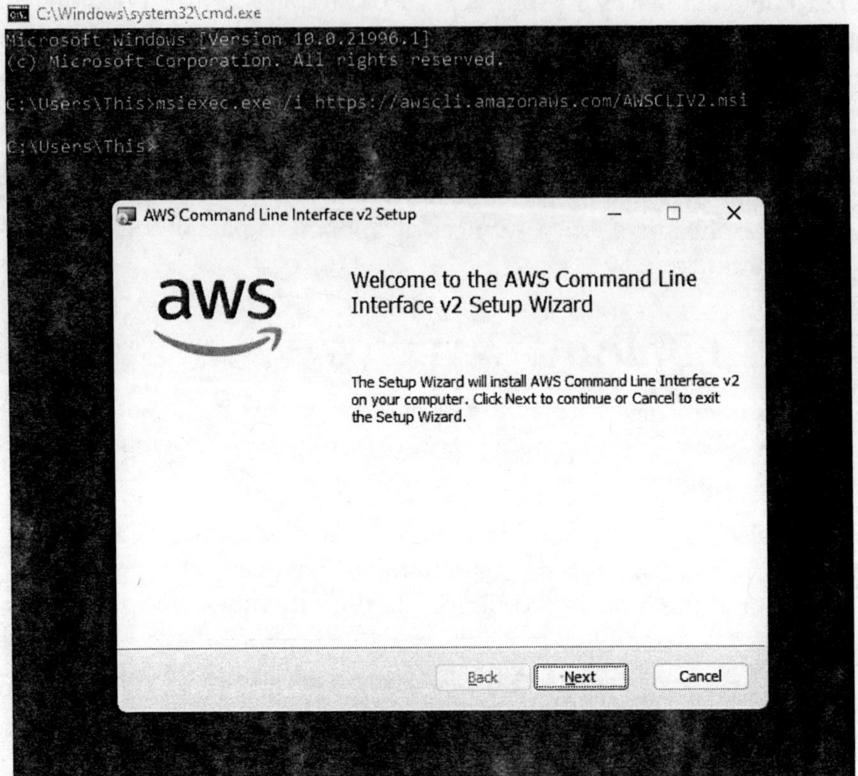

Figure 1.5*: Installing AWS CLI on Windows*

Installed version can be checked by running the following command on the Command Prompt:

```
aws -version
```

The output would be:

```
aws-cli/2.8.7 Python/3.9.11 Windows/10 exe/AMD64 prompt/off
```

Installing AWS CLI on Linux

Run the following command on Linux shell:

```
curl "https://awscli.amazonaws.com/awscli-exe-linux-x86_64.zip" -o
"awscliv2.zip"
unzip awscliv2.zip
sudo ./aws/install
```

It is a combination of three commands which downloads the package, unzips it, and finally installs it, as shown in *Figure 1.6*:

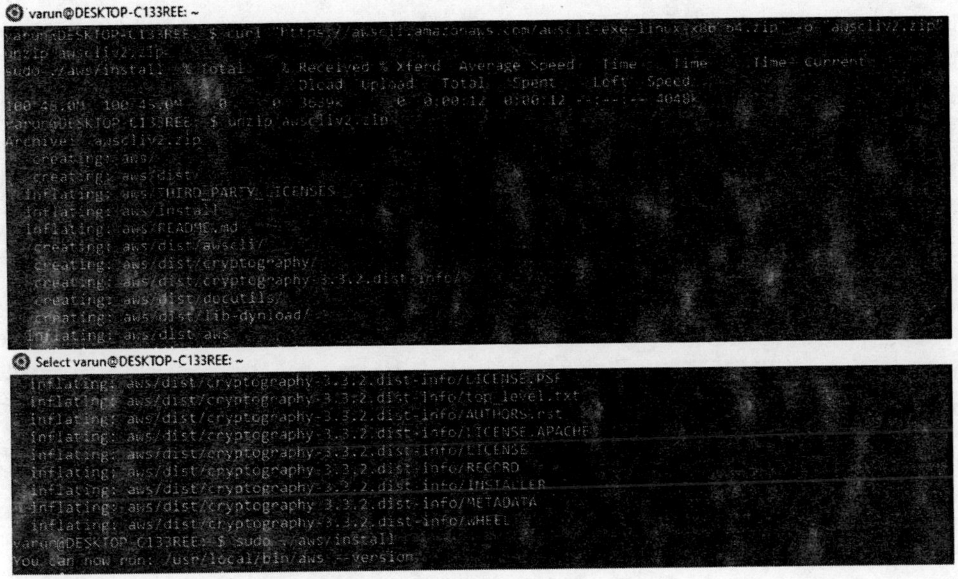

Figure 1.6: Installing AWS CLI on Linux

Installed version can be checked by running the below command on the shell:

```
aws -version
```

The output would be:

```
aws-cli/2.8.7 Python/3.9.11 Linux/5.10.102.1-microsoft-standard-WSL2 exe/
x86_64.ubuntu.20 prompt/off
```

Installing AWS CLI on MacOS

Run the following command on Mac shell:

```
curl "https://awscli.amazonaws.com/AWSCLIV2.pkg" -o "AWSCLIV2.pkg"
sudo installer -pkg AWSCLIV2.pkg -target /
```

The first command downloads the package and the file name to which it needs to written to, this is specified using the **-o** option. The second command runs the MacOS installer program to install the downloaded package at the desired target location. Refer to *Figure 1.7* for reference:

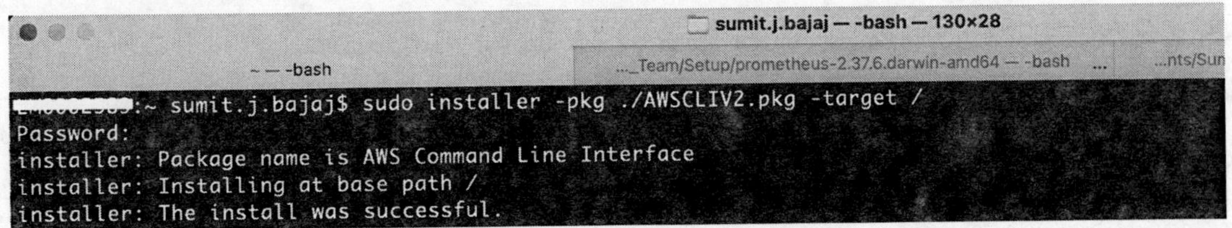

Figure 1.7: Installing AWS CLI on MacOS

Installed version can be checked by running the below command on the shell:

```
aws -version
```

The output would be:

```
aws-cli/2.10.0 Python/3.11.2 Darwin/18.7.0 botocore/2.4.5
```

Recipe 2: Creating IAM admin user

Identity and Access Management (**IAM**) is a user or an entity that is used to interact with AWS. As per AWS guidelines, it is never a good practice to use or share AWS root account's credentials for any configuration or provisioning, because if they are compromised, then the security of the whole application is at big risk. Instead, multiple IAM users are created and are given required privileges; the least required privilege principle is followed, which means that the minimum privilege that is required for the work is given to the IAM user responsible for it. Identity and Access Management will be discussed in detail in the *Cloud Security* chapter.

An admin user will have different credentials than the AWS account and has administrative privileges. This user will be used to create further entities in the AWS account.

Steps to create an admin user

Follow the given steps to create an admin user:

1. Login to the AWS Management Console and search IAM or type in the following URL: **https://console.aws.amazon.com/iam/**.
2. Enable the **Access key – Programmatic access** checkbox. It generates **Access**, and **Secret** keys that can be used to access this user programmatically.
3. Follow the UI to provide username and password.
4. Grant administrative permissions by attaching a predefined **Administrator Access policy**. The JSON of the policy that grants administrative access, that is, allow all:

```
{
    "Version": "2012-10-17",
    "Statement": [
        {
            "Effect": "Allow",
            "Action": "*",
            "Resource": "*"
        }
    ]
}
```

5. It is to be noted that the auto generated **Access** and **Secret** keys, and the IAM user sign-in URL for the above account will be required while login to AWS .

Recipe 3: Configuring IAM admin user in the AWS CLI

User credentials need to be configured in AWS CLI, which internally maintains it in the form of profiles. User credentials can be easily configured using the following command:

```
aws configure
```

Figure 1.8 illustrates the configuration of the admin user in AWS CLI:

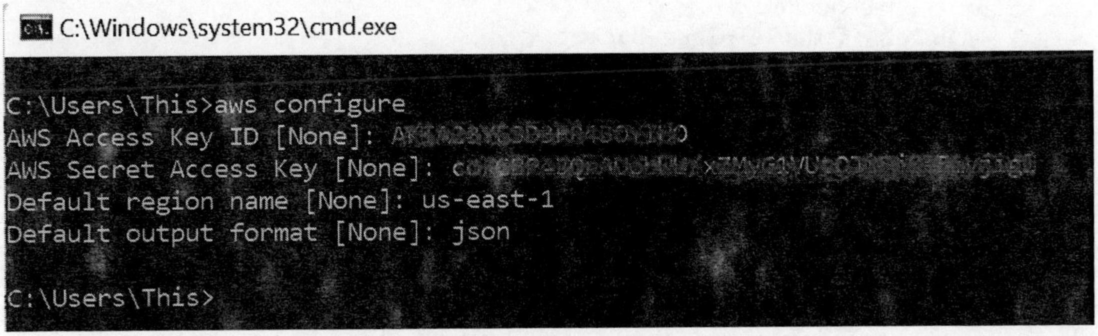

```
C:\Windows\system32\cmd.exe

C:\Users\This>aws configure
AWS Access Key ID [None]:
AWS Secret Access Key [None]:
Default region name [None]: us-east-1
Default output format [None]: json

C:\Users\This>
```

Figure 1.8: Configuring admin user in AWS CLI

Once AWS CLI is configured, all the commands that will be run using this AWS CLI will run using the configured admin user. The default profile is used while executing the AWS CLI command if no specific profile is passed in the command.

Recipe 4: Creating an S3 bucket

Amazon Simple Storage Service (**Amazon S3**) is a storage service in AWS which is used to store data in the form of objects within a bucket. As the microservices that will be created as part of this book require to store data in S3, please find the following ways that can be used to create an S3 bucket in AWS.

Creating an S3 bucket using AWS Management Console

Follow the given steps to create an S3 bucket via AWS S3 Management Console:

1. Login to the AWS Management Console and search S3 or type in the following URL:

   https://console.aws.amazon.com/s3/.

2. Click on the **Create bucket** option, and it will open a self-explanatory form.

3. Fill in all the required details.

   Bucket name: **fs-marketplace-bucket**

4. Click **Create bucket** again.

That is it, the S3 bucket will be created.

Creating an S3 bucket using AWS CLI

AWS CLI provides all possible functionality for creating an S3 bucket as is possible via GUI console. For simplicity of understanding, the bare minimum options have been provided in the create bucket command.

```
aws s3api create-bucket \
        --bucket fs-marketplace-bucket \
        --acl private \
        --region us-east-1
```

Here,

- **bucket** is the bucket name.
- **acl** is the access control list.
- **region** is the region in which bucket needs to be created. If not passed, default region configured in the AWS CLI will be used.

Output:

```
{
    "Location": "/fs-marketplace-bucket"
}
```

Figure 1.9 illustrates the output of the **create-bucket** command:

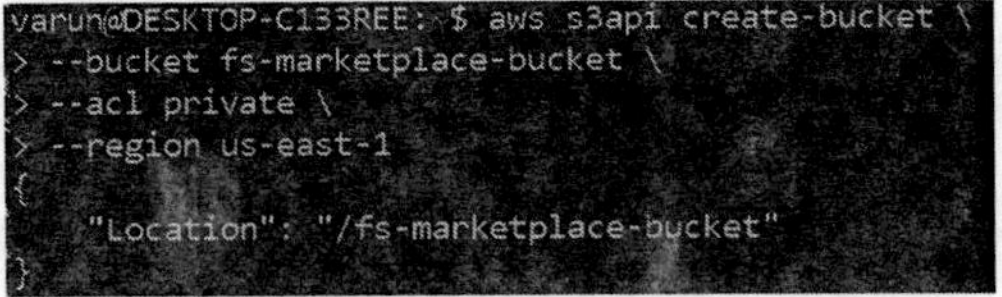

Figure 1.9: Output of create bucket command

As the admin IAM user has been configured in the AWS CLI, the bucket has been created in the AWS account that the IAM user is part of. Moreover, as the bucket has been created using the very same IAM user, this user has access to this private bucket.

The following command can be used to validate whether the bucket has been created successfully or not. It prints the list of all the buckets that are visible to the configured IAM user.

```
aws s3api list-buckets
```

Refer to *Figure 1.10* for an illustration of the same:

```
arun@DESKTOP-C13SREE: $ aws s3api list-buckets
{
    "Buckets": [
        {
            "Name": "fs-marketplace-bucket",
            "CreationDate": "2022-11-07T07:42:12+00:00"
        }
    ],
    "Owner": {
        "DisplayName": "yadavvarun",
        "ID": "[illegible]3"
    }
}
```

***Figure 1.10**: List of visible S3 buckets on AWS CLI*

An S3 bucket has been created with a name **`fs-marketplace-bucket`**. The same can also be validated using AWS S3 console, as shown in *Figure 1.11*:

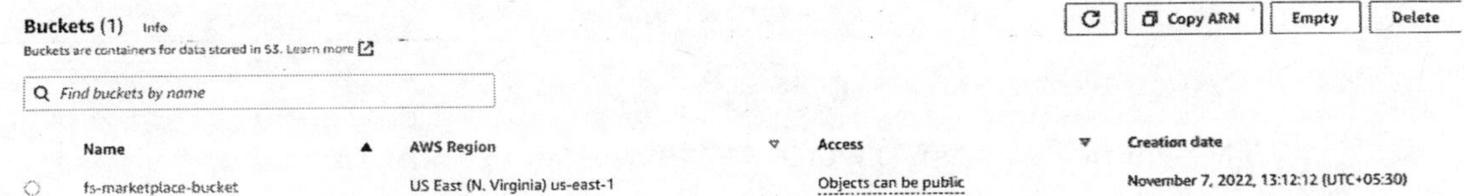

***Figure 1.11**: List of visible S3 buckets on AWS Management Console*

Recipe 5: Creating Postgres DB

AWS RDS is a fully managed **Relational Database Service** provided by Amazon Web Services. There are multiple engine types available to choose from, as part of an RDS service – MySQL, MariaDB, PostgresSQL, Oracle, Microsoft SQL Server, and Amazon Aurora.

PostgresSQL service is to be configured for development of microservices that will be showcased in the following chapter. Free tier is selected from the available templates, there are a lot of configurations related to the performance and high availability of the database, but they will be discussed in detail in later chapter.

Creating a PostgresSQL database using AWS Management Console

Follow the given steps to create an PostgresSQL database via AWS S3 Management Console:

1. Login to the AWS Management Console and search RDS or type in the following URL: **https://console.aws.amazon.com/rds/**.
2. Click **Create database**, and this opens a self-explanatory form.
    a. Postgres DB, this micro service is for hands on purpose, so go with free tier one.
    b. Go with latest version of Postgres, default version will auto appear on drop down.
    c. Go with default configuration of instance configuration.
    d. Go with default storage configuration.
3. Fill in all the required details:
    a. Engine type: **`PostgresSQL`**
    b. Templates: **`Free tier`**
    c. DB instance identifier: **`fs-marketplace`**
    d. Master username: **`postgres`**
    e. Master username password: **`secret11`**
    f. Public access: **`Yes`**
4. Click **Create database** again.

That is it! Free tier PostgresSQL database will be created. The name of database is `fs-marketplace`.

Creating a PostgresSQL database using AWS CLI

AWS CLI is a powerful tool that can be used to create RDS Postgres database, using a single command. All possible configurations are possible via command CLI as well; the bare minimum values have been passed for simplicity. For the rest of the options, the default option will be picked up by the AWS engine:

```
aws rds create-db-instance \
     --db-instance-identifier fs-marketplace \
     --db-instance-class db.t3.micro \
     --allocated-storage 20 \
     --engine postgres \
     --master-username postgres \
     --master-user-password secret11 \
     --port 5432 \
```

```
--publicly-accessible \
--region us-east-1 \
--output json
```

Here:

- **db-instance-identifier** is the database identifier name.
- **db-instance-class** is the compute and memory class.
- **allocated-storage** is the allocated storage in GBs.
- **engine** is an engine type supported by RDS.
- **master-username** is the master username.
- **master-user-password** is the password of master username, and it should be at least 8 characters.
- **port** is the port on which the database will be running.
- **publicly-accessible** is a Boolean value to make database publicly accessible or not.
- **region** is the AWS region, in which the database instance will be created.
- **output** is the output format of the command.

Output:


```
{
    "DBInstance": {
        "DBInstanceIdentifier": "fs-marketplace",
        "DBInstanceClass": "db.t3.micro",
        "Engine": "postgres",
        "DBInstanceStatus": "creating",
        "MasterUsername": "postgres",
        "AllocatedStorage": 20,
        "PreferredBackupWindow": "03:31-04:01",
        "BackupRetentionPeriod": 1,
        "DBSecurityGroups": [],
        "VpcSecurityGroups": [
            {
                "VpcSecurityGroupId": "sg-06eae19abc4de7696",
                "Status": "active"
            }
        ],
        "DBParameterGroups": [
            {
                "DBParameterGroupName": "default.postgres13",
                "ParameterApplyStatus": "in-sync"
            }
        ],
```

```
        "DBSubnetGroup": {
            "DBSubnetGroupName": "default",
            "DBSubnetGroupDescription": "default",
            "VpcId": "vpc-0d98694f904b3983b",
            "SubnetGroupStatus": "Complete",
            "Subnets": [
:...skipping...
```

The output of the AWS CLI command shows that the command has been accepted and database instance status is **"creating"**.

It takes a few minutes for the database instance to be available for access. The following command can be used to validate whether the database instance has been created successfully or not. It prints the details in the JSON format of the provided database:

```
aws rds describe-db-instances --db-instance-identifier fs-marketplace
```

Refer to *Figure 1.12* for details of the provided DB instance identifier:

Figure 1.12: *Details of the provided DB instance identifier*

The endpoint details mentioned in the output JSON are important as they will be used later for connecting to the database:

```
"Endpoint": {
            "Address": "fs-marketplace.cbgzpif7rd3e.us-east-1.rds.ama-
zonaws.com",
            "Port": 5432,
            "HostedZoneId": "Z2R2ITUGPM61AM"
        }
```

Conclusion

In this chapter, initial cloud tools and services that will be used for developing the microservices have been configured, starting with AWS CLI, followed by creating IAM user, S3 bucket and PostgresSQL database instance.

In the next chapter, we will learn initial steps for setting up the development environment. As services are being integrated with each other to achieve common functionality thus it is imperative that they should follow standard schema definition, which helps them to abide by keeping the contract in place with API first approach using OpenAPI Specification. As part of the chapter, we will develop couple of microservices for Financial Services Marketplace application following the API-first approach, using Spring Boot Java framework along with unit test cases and, in the end, showcase the interservice communication between the two microservices.

Points to remember

- How granular a microservice should be developed, depends a lot on the business requirement from both functional and non-functional perspectives.
- When used wisely, cloud infrastructure saves lot of cost compared to the on-premise infrastructure, assuming all the overhead costs have been considered.
- AWS has the highest market share of the overall cloud services market, followed by Microsoft Azure.
- First version of Spring on which Spring Boot is built, was released way back in 2004.
- AWS S3 bucket names are not bound to an account or a region, all S3 buckets globally need to have a unique name.

Questions

1. What makes Micronaut run an application with faster boot time with reduced memory foot print, compared to Spring Boot?
2. What is the compile time of the Micronaut application compared to the Spring Boot application?
3. In which region the RDS database will be created if no region is passed in the AWS CLI command?
4. How access is granted of an AWS service to another AWS service?

Join our book's Discord space

Join the book's Discord Workspace for Latest updates, Offers, Tech happenings around the world, New Release and Sessions with the Authors:

https://discord.bpbonline.com

CHAPTER 2
Developing Microservices and Test Cases

Introduction

The last chapter documented why Spring Boot is the preferred Java framework for developing enterprise grade microservices. We also configured the few initial AWS tools and services beginning with AWS CLI, IAM user, S3 bucket and RDS Postgres database.

In this chapter, we will begin with describing the application that will be built as part of this book, followed by setting up the development environment, walk through the API-first approach for developing microservices, define and develop microservices along with unit test cases, and in the end, enhance the code to show interservice communication.

Structure

In this chapter, we will discuss following topics:

- Application description
- Development environment setup
- Version control system
- API-first approach
- Developing microservices

Objectives

By the end of this chapter, we will learn what steps need to be followed for configuring the development environment including creation of maven projects, establishing database connection, and so on, before beginning the development of microservices, using Spring Boot framework. Next, we will understand the concept of API-first approach, followed by developing the microservices for our application, and creating unit tests for them. In the end, we will enhance the code to show interservice communication, execute the microservices and finally push the code to the Git repositories.

Application description

The application developed in the book mimics an enterprise-level financial service marketplace application, where two microservices will be developed with both being hosted separately. The first microservice accepts the customer's request for a financial product, such as a car loan, home loan, medical insurance, car insurance, mutual funds, or any investment option. It then stores this information in a relational database like Postgres for that customer.

After this, the first service invokes the second service, which will accept the customer details along with the enquiry that has been done, and then broadcasts this information to all the financial service providers who have registered as partner in that marketplace.

The information can be broadcasted using a real time streaming service such as Apache Kafka or updating these details in shared S3 bucket, which can be read by vendors as and when required.

Development environment setup

To commence the process of developing a Java application, the first essential task is configuring your preferred **integrated development environment** (**IDE**). This could encompass a range of options, such as IntelliJ IDEA, Visual Studio, or Eclipse. Throughout this book, we will be using Eclipse IDE for all Java coding examples. However, readers are encouraged to select an IDE that suits their preferences, as all the code references provided in this book are independent of the specific IDE chosen.

As part of the environment setup, the following needs to be completed:

1. Workspace in Eclipse with two Maven projects.
2. Creating `fs-marketplace` database connection.

Recipe 6: Creating Maven projects

Create a new workspace in Eclipse. All the related projects will be created in the same workspace. The next step is to create two Maven projects for the two microservices that need to be developed. It is better to give same group ID to both the projects as that signifies that the projects are interrelated, provide meaningful artifact ids, as they, along with the version, forms the name of the executable JAR.

The two Maven projects that are created are:

- Customer Enquiry
- Enquiry Broadcast

Customer Enquiry

The code for generated **pom.xml** is as follows:

```
<project xmlns="http://maven.apache.org/POM/4.0.0" xmlns:xsi="http://www.w3.org/2001/XMLSchema-instance" xsi:schemaLocation="http://maven.apache.org/POM/4.0.0 https://maven.apache.org/xsd/maven-4.0.0.xsd">
<modelVersion>4.0.0</modelVersion>
<groupId>com.fsm</groupId>
<artifactId>customer-enquiry</artifactId>
<version>0.0.1-SNAPSHOT</version>
<name>Customer Enquiry</name>
<description>Service collects and persists customer enquiry details</description>
</project>
```

Enquiry Broadcast

The code for generated **pom.xml** is as follows:

```
<project xmlns="http://maven.apache.org/POM/4.0.0" xmlns:xsi="http://www.w3.org/2001/XMLSchema-instance" xsi:schemaLocation="http://maven.apache.org/POM/4.0.0 https://maven.apache.org/xsd/maven-4.0.0.xsd">
<modelVersion>4.0.0</modelVersion>
<groupId>com.fsm</groupId>
<artifactId>enquiry-broadcast</artifactId>
<version>0.0.1-SNAPSHOT</version>
<name>Enquiry Broadcast</name>
<description>Service broadcast customer enquiry details to registered financial services providers</description>
</project>
```

In this scenario, both projects share a common group ID, which is **`com.fsm`**. For the projects **Customer Enquiry** and **Enquiry Broadcast**, the artifact IDs are set as **`customer-enquiry`** and **`enquiry-broadcast`**, respectively.

Recipe 7: Enhance pom.xml files

Currently the projects are blank and to begin required Spring Boot dependencies, properties and plugins need to be added in the **`pom.xml`** files.

Customer Enquiry

The updated code for the **`pom.xml`** is as follows:

```
<project xmlns="http://maven.apache.org/POM/4.0.0" xmlns:xsi="http://www.w3.org/2001/XMLSchema-instance" xsi:schemaLocation="http://maven.apache.org/POM/4.0.0 https://maven.apache.org/xsd/maven-4.0.0.xsd">
 <modelVersion>4.0.0</modelVersion>
 <groupId>com.fsm</groupId>
 <artifactId>customer-enquiry</artifactId>
 <version>0.0.1-SNAPSHOT</version>
 <name>Customer Enquiry</name>
 <description>Service collects and persists customer enquiry details</description>

 <parent>
  <groupId>org.springframework.boot</groupId>
  <artifactId>spring-boot-starter-parent</artifactId>
  <version>3.1.3</version>
 </parent>

 <properties>
  <java.version>17</java.version>
 </properties>

 <dependencies>
  <dependency>
   <groupId>org.springframework.boot</groupId>
   <artifactId>spring-boot-starter-web</artifactId>
```

```
    </dependency>
  </dependencies>

  <build>
    <plugins>
      <plugin>
        <groupId>org.springframework.boot</groupId>
        <artifactId>spring-boot-maven-plugin</artifactId>
        <executions>
          <execution>
            <id>repackage</id>
          </execution>
        </executions>
      </plugin>

      <plugin>
        <groupId>org.apache.maven.plugins</groupId>
        <artifactId>maven-compiler-plugin</artifactId>
        <configuration>
          <compilerVersion>${java.version}</compilerVersion>
          <source>${java.version}</source>
          <target>${java.version}</target>
          <encoding>UTF-8</encoding>
          <!—prevents endPosTable exception for maven compile -->
          <useIncrementalCompilation>false</useIncrementalCompilation>
        </configuration>
      </plugin>
    </plugins>
  </build>

</project>
```

Enquiry Broadcast

The updated code for the **`pom.xml`** is as follows:

```
<project xml"s="http://maven.apache.org/POM/4.".0" xmlns:x"i="http://www.w3.org/2001/XMLSchema-insta"ce" xsi:schemaLocati"n="http://maven.apache.org/POM/4.0.0 https://maven.apache.org/xsd/maven-4.0.0."sd">
 <modelVersion>4.0.0</modelVersion>
 <groupId>com.fsm</groupId>
 <artifactId>enquiry-broadcast</artifactId>
 <version>0.0.1-SNAPSHOT</version>
 <name>Enquiry Broadcast</name>
 <description>Service broadcast customer enquiry details to registered financial services providers</description>

 <parent>
  <groupId>org.springframework.boot</groupId>
  <artifactId>spring-boot-starter-parent</artifactId>
  <version>3.1.3</version>
 </parent>

 <properties>
  <java.version>17</java.version>
 </properties>

 <dependencies>
  <dependency>
   <groupId>org.springframework.boot</groupId>
   <artifactId>spring-boot-starter-web</artifactId>
  </dependency>
 </dependencies>

 <build>
  <plugins>
   <plugin>
```

```
        <groupId>org.springframework.boot</groupId>
        <artifactId>spring-boot-maven-plugin</artifactId>
        <executions>
         <execution>
          <id>repackage</id>
         </execution>
        </executions>
      </plugin>

      <plugin>
        <groupId>org.apache.maven.plugins</groupId>
        <artifactId>maven-compiler-plugin</artifactId>
        <configuration>
         <compilerVersion>${java.version}</compilerVersion>
         <source>${java.version}</source>
         <target>${java.version}</target>
         <encoding>UTF-8</encoding>
        --- prevents endPosTable exception for maven compile -->
         <useIncrementalCompilation>false</useIncrementalCompilation>
        </configuration>
      </plugin>
     </plugins>
   </build>

 </project>
```

The description and usage of the tags is documented in *Table 2.1*:

Tag	Description
<parent>	Determines the parent for the current project and its value **spring-boot-starter-parent** makes our project a Spring Boot project and provides default configurations that are required for this application.
<properties>	It is used to define any inherited or custom property to be used in the project. Here, the property **java.version** is used to define the Java compiler version to be used for the project. Although the default value of spring boot starter is 1.8, the value can be overridden using this property value.

Tag	Description
<dependency>	The tag is used to include any dependency in the project. If no version is mentioned along with **groupId** and **artifactId**, then the version configured by the starter parent will be included. Here, **spring-boot-starter-web** is responsible for including all the web application related artifacts to the project.
<plugin>	The tag is used to add any plugins to our project. maven-compiler-**plugin** is used to compile the source code of the project, and it can also be configured to use a particular version of the Java compiler.

***Table 2.1**: Description of maven tags*

Recipe 8: Creating Spring Boot application class

It is a Java class with the **@SpringBootApplication** annotation and is a main class for a Spring Boot application. It has a **main** method that calls the **SpringApplication.run()** method. The **@SpringBootApplication** annotation encapsulates the **@SpringBootConfiguration**, **@EnableAutoConfiguration**, and **@ComponentScan** annotations with their default attributes.

This Java class needs to be invoked to start the application. It internally launches the application server on the configured port and runs the application on top of it.

Here is a more detailed explanation of the annotations involved:

@SpringBootConfiguration: This annotation indicates that the class is a Spring Boot configuration class.

@EnableAutoConfiguration: This annotation enables Spring Boot's auto-configuration mechanism. This means that Spring Boot will automatically configure the application based on the dependencies that are present in the class path.

@ComponentScan: This annotation tells Spring Boot to scan the package where the class is located for components. Components are classes that can be auto-configured by Spring Boot.

The Java class needs to be present in both applications.

Customer Enquiry

The code for **CustomerEnquiryApplication.java** is as follows:

```
package com.fsm.customerenquiry;

import org.springframework.boot.SpringApplication;
```

```
import org.springframework.boot.autoconfigure.SpringBootApplication;

@SpringBootApplication
public class CustomerEnquiryApplication {

  public static void main(String[] args) {
    SpringApplication.run(CustomerEnquiryApplication.class, args);
  }
}
```

Enquiry Broadcast

The code for **EnquiryBroadcastApplication.java** is as follows:

```
package com.fsm.enquirybroadcast;

import org.springframework.boot.SpringApplication;
import org.springframework.boot.autoconfigure.SpringBootApplication;

@SpringBootApplication
public class EnquiryBroadcastApplication {

  public static void main(String[] args) {
    SpringApplication.run(EnquiryBroadcastApplication.class, args);
  }
}
```

Running applications

To execute Spring Boot applications from an IDE, simply run the **CustomerEnquiryApplication.java** and **EnquiryBroadcastApplication.java** files as Java applications. The applications will start accordingly.

Kindly follow the below steps in Eclipse IDE:

1. Open the project in Eclipse.
2. In the **Project Explorer**, right-click on the **CustomerEnquiryApplication.java** file and select **Run As | Java Application**.
3. Repeat step 2 for the **EnquiryBroadcastApplication.java** file.

Figure 2.1 shows the output generated on console for both the applications. It shows the logs generated on running **CustomerEnquiryApplication.java**:

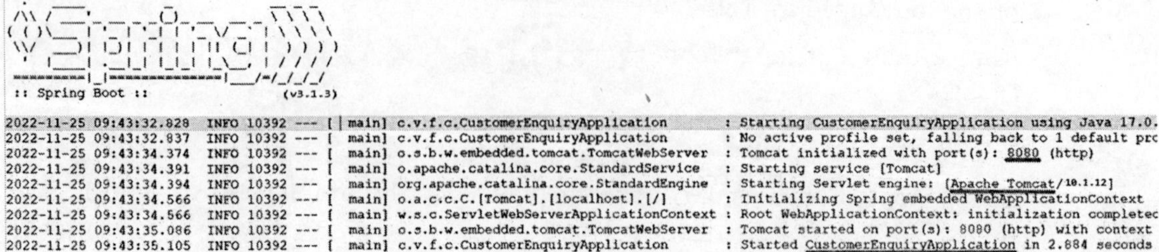

Figure 2.1: *Console output of running CustomerEnquiryApplication.java*

It is quite evident from the logs, that on running the application, Spring Boot first internally launches **Tomcat** engine on port **8080**, which is the default port and then starts the application on top of it.

Refer to *Figure 2.2* for the logs generated on running **EnquiryBroadcastApplication.java**:

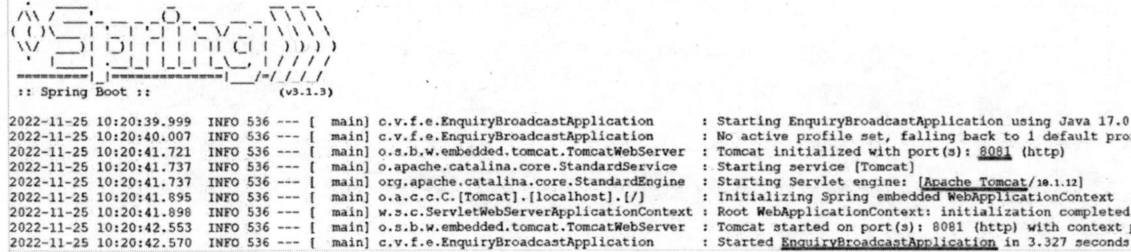

Figure 2.2: *Console output of running EnquiryBroadcastApplication.java*

Since more than one server cannot be started on the same port on same machine, the preceding logs show that the **EnquiryBroadcastApplication** has been started on a **Tomcat** engine initialized with port **8081**. This was done by using the **server.port** property. By default, Spring Boot loads all the properties from the **application.properties** file located in the resources folder. Therefore, before running **EnquiryBroadcastApplication.java**, create an **application.properties** file in the **src/main/resources** folder and add the following property:

```
server.port=8081
```

This will tell Spring Boot to start the **EnquiryBroadcastApplication** on port **8081**.

The skeleton code for both the applications has been created. Later on, in the chapter, it will be enhanced to build and expose the functionalities as APIs.

Recipe 9: Connecting RDS PostgressSQL instance

PostgresSQL database instance has been created in AWS and the credentials for connecting the same, also documented in *Chapter 1, Configuring Cloud Services* are:

```
Username: postgres
Password: secret11
Address: fs-marketplace.cbgzpif7rd3e.us-east-1.rds.amazonaws.com
Port: 5432
```

PostgreSQL can be accessed using multiple clients, but **pgAdmin** is the most popular and feature-rich open-source administration and development tool for PostgreSQL. It is used to maintain the database, run SQL scripts, and create database tables.

To create a connection in **pgAdmin**, click on the **Add New Server** button and provide the required details, such as the hostname, port, database name, username, and password. Then, click on the **Save** button. If there are no errors, the server will be added to the pgAdmin tool.

Here are the steps in more detail:

1. Open **pgAdmin**.
2. Click on the **Servers** node in the tree view.
3. Right-click and select **Add New Server**.
4. In the **Connection** tab, enter the following information:
   a. **Hostname**: The address of the PostgreSQL server.
   b. **Port**: The port number of the PostgreSQL server.
   c. **Database Name**: The name of the database you want to connect to.
   d. **Username**: The username for the PostgreSQL database.
   e. **Password**: The password for the PostgreSQL database.
5. Click on the **Save** button.

If there are no errors, the server will be added to the **pgAdmin** tool. You can then connect to the database and start working with it.

Refer to *Figure 2.3* to view the properties of **`financial-service-marketplace`** database server:

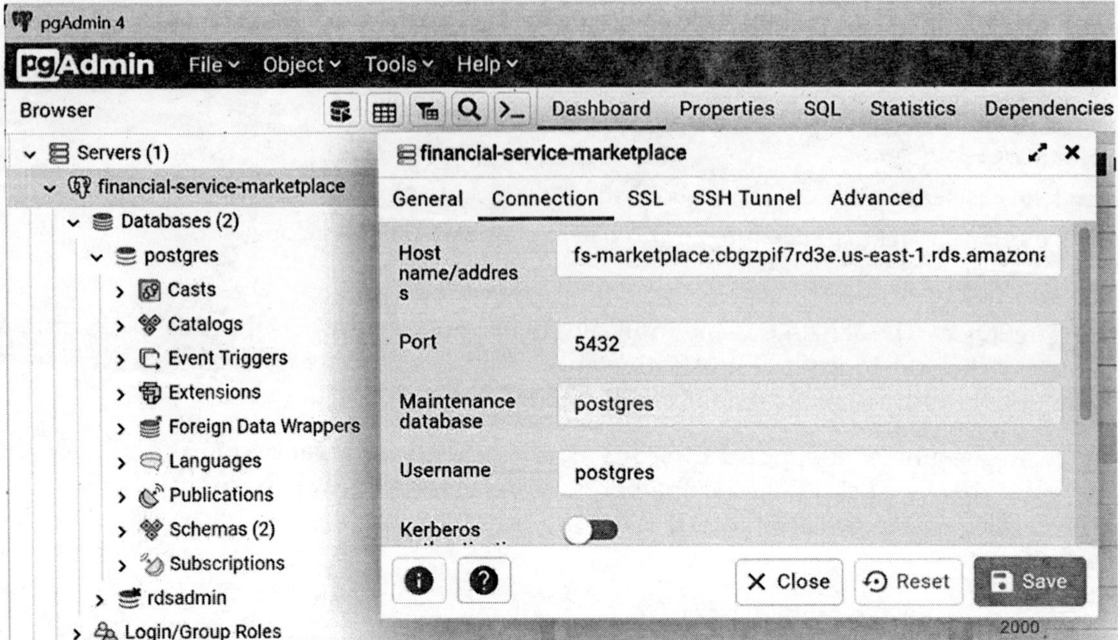

Figure 2.3: pgAdmin tool view of added PostgresSQL database server

Once the server is added and connection is created, the tool's user interface is quite intuitive to manage the database instance and perform database operations.

Recipe 10: Creating database schemas

Conceptually, microservices should have their data in separate database instances and the reason is that, if a particular microservice's database needs to scale, it can be independently scaled without impacting the other databases. For practical purposes, considering the costs involved and scale of the application, data can reside in the same database instance but needs to have separate schemas created for the respective microservices.

SQL queries for creating schemas for both the microservices, as follows.

Customer Enquiry

The following SQL query will create a schema with the name **`customer_enquiry`**:

```
CREATE SCHEMA IF NOT EXISTS customer_enquiry
    AUTHORIZATION postgres;

COMMENT ON SCHEMA customer_enquiry
    IS 'Schema for Customer Enquiry service';
```

Enquiry Broadcast

The following SQL query will create a schema with the name **enquiry_broadcast**:

```
CREATE SCHEMA IF NOT EXISTS enquiry_broadcast
    AUTHORIZATION postgres;

COMMENT ON SCHEMA enquiry_broadcast
    IS 'Schema for Enquiry Broadcast service';
```

Both the preceding schemas are accessible via **postgres** user.

Version control systems

For enterprises that are in a business of creating software, the application code is part of their intellectual property and needs to be protected in all ways. Code repositories not only mitigate the risk of losing the code by keeping it safe and secure, but also help in collaboration amongst multiple developers and keeping the code version controlled. There are two categories of code repositories or version-controlled systems:

- **Centralized version control system**: In these systems, code repository is centrally located and all the developers have its client installed on their local machines. The code resides in the central repository and developers **checkout** on their local machines using the client tool, work on that code and then **check-in** to the central repository. In there, it merges with the latest version of the code. There are multiple implementations of it but the most prominent one in the market is **SVN**, also known as **Apache Subversion** or just **Subversion**.

- **Distributed version control system**: In these systems, there is a public repository and each developer creates a copy of that repository locally on his machine via a process called cloning. Once the code is present on the developer's local machine, the person will work on his local copy, do multiple changes to it, and finally push his changes from his local repository to the public repository. Once that is done, the changes will be available to all other developers as well. The biggest advantage of a **distributed version control system** (**DVCS**) is that it works even in situations where there is no connectivity. Developers can still commit changes to their local repository, version control them and later push the changes to the public repository when possible. The main competitors in this world are Git and Mercurial.

Considering the benefits and general acceptability, we will be using **Git** as the code repository or version control system for the application.

Recipe 11: Creating and configuring Git repositories

There are multiple providers in the market that support Git repository, such as GitLab, Bitbucket, GitHub, and so on. You can choose any as per your preference, and as part of this book, we will be using **GitLab** as it also offers other features such as code review, bug tracking and more, and has a built-in continuous integration and continuous deployment system that allows to build, test, and deploy code in no time.

Steps that need to be followed are as follows:

1. Create an account on GitLab.
2. Create a group with the name **Financial Service Marketplace**. This is created, to group together repositories for both the microservices.
3. Under the earlier created group, create two blank projects with the names **Customer Enquiry** and **Enquiry Broadcast**.

Figure 2.4 illustrates the group and projects created using GitLab UI:

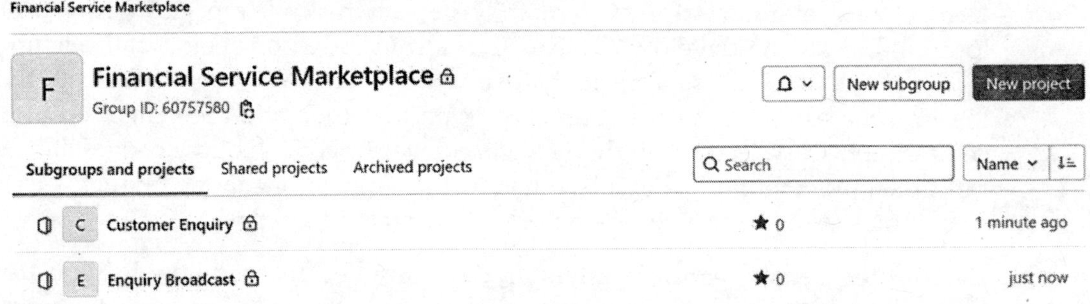

Figure 2.4*: GitLab UI – projects Customer Enquiry and Enquiry Broadcast under Financial Service Marketplace group*

Once the projects are created in GitLab, the existing Maven projects need to be pushed to GitLab.

Install a Git client on the local machine, which will be used to manage the local Git repository and communicate with the public repository. As part of this book, **Git BASH** (Git client for Windows) is the one that will be using to manage the Git repositories. Git client can be installed in Linux and MacOS via command line interface and can be used directly via shell / terminal. Before beginning, Git needs to be configured. Run the following commands on the Git BASH terminal:

```
git config -global user.email "you@example.com"
git config -global user.name "Your Name"
```

There are project and class files that are not part of the code and needs to be ignored while committing the code in the repository. For this, create a file with the name **`.gitignore`** in both the maven projects Customer Enquiry and Enquiry Broadcast with the following mentioned contents:

```
.classpath
.project
target
.settings
```

This file will direct Git not to include any files or folder with the names mentioned. The file also supports wild characters if required.

Once the files have been created, we are good to push the existing maven projects into the public GitLab repositories respectively.

Customer Enquiry

Open Git BASH and change directory to the local Maven project Customer Enquiry and run the following commands in the mentioned order:

```
git init
git add .
git commit -m "Initial Commit"
git remote add source https://yadavvarun1@gitlab.com/financial-service-marketplace/customer-enquiry.git
git push -u -f source master
```

Here,

- **`init`** initializes an empty Git repository, creates a **`.git`** folder in Customer Enquiry directory.
- **`add .`** adds all the changes in the working directory to the staging area.
- **`commit`** commits the changes in local repository with provided message **`"Initial Commit"`**.
- **`remote add`** provides the local Git repo with GitLab URL in which **`yadavvarun1`** is the GitLab user name, and **`customer-enquiry`** is the remote git repository.
- **`push`** pushes the code to the remote Git repository. It requires password for the authentication for the first time.

Figure 2.5 illustrates the output of the Git commands for Customer Enquiry project:

Figure 2.5: Output of Git commands for Customer Enquiry project

Enquiry Broadcast

Open Git BASH and change directory to the local maven project Enquiry Broadcast and run the following commands in the mentioned order:

```
git init
git add .
git commit -m "Initial Commit"
git remote add source https://yadavvarun1@gitlab.com/financial-service-marketplace/enquiry-broadcast.git
git push -u -f source master
```

Here,

- **`init`** initializes an empty Git repository, creates a **`.git`** folder in Enquiry Broadcast directory.
- **`add .`** adds all the changes in the working directory to the staging area.
- **`commit`** commits the changes in local repository with provided message **`"Initial Commit"`**.
- **`remote add`** provides the local Git repo with GitLab URL in which **`yadavvarun1`** is the GitLab user name, **`enquiry-broadcast`** is the remote git repository.
- **`push`** pushes the code to the remote Git repository. It requires password for the authentication for the first time.

Figure 2.6 illustrates the output of the Git commands for Enquiry Broadcast project:

***Figure 2.6**: Output of Git commands for Enquiry Broadcast project*

Create merge request

Earlier, the default name of the GitLab repository was **`master`** but now, on discussion with the developer community, it has been changed to **`main`**. The preceding commands have pushed the changes to the **`master`** branch in the remote repository, and a **Merge request** needs to be raised to merge changes from the **`master`** branch to the **`main`** branch.

Figure 2.7 illustrates the two branches created in a remote Git repository:

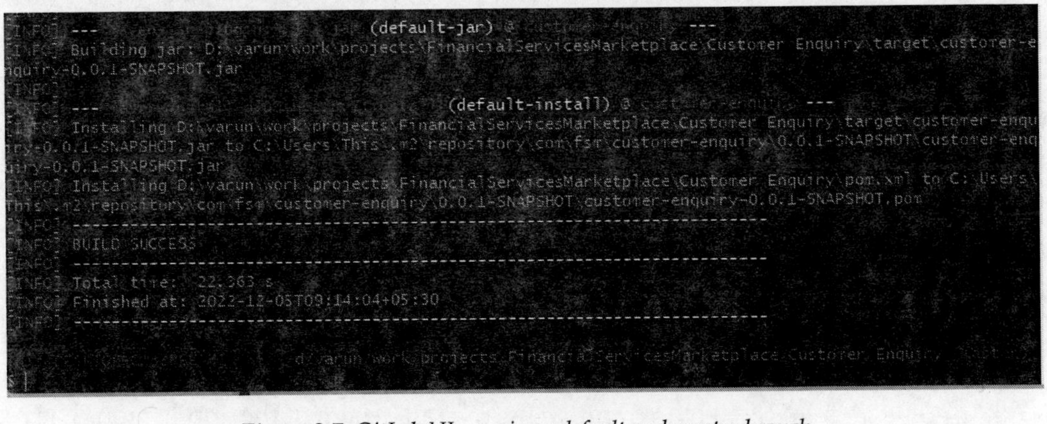

***Figure 2.7**: GitLab UI – main or default and master branch*

Merge requests are assigned to a reviewer who ensures that only the valid changes are merged into the `main` branch. To do this, create a **Merge request** for each project to merge the changes from the `master` branch to the `main` branch. Once the reviewer has approved the merge request, you can accept it to make the changes. Eventually, there will be only one branch, the `main` branch.

Here is a more detailed explanation of the steps involved:

1. Create a **Merge request** for respective branches in the project.
2. In the merge request, specify the changes that you want to merge from the `master` branch to the `main` branch.
3. Assign the merge request to a reviewer.
4. The reviewer will review the changes and approve or reject the merge request.
5. If the reviewer approves the merge request, you can accept it.
6. Once the merge request is accepted, the changes will be merged into the `main` branch.

API-first approach

The API-first approach focuses on the interfaces that an application will use to interact with the outside world. This could include how developers build and test the application, or how a third-party system communicates with it. The design of the API should be user-friendly, consistent, and backward compatible whenever possible. It should also be easy to adopt and compatible with other systems.

The API-first approach is particularly important in the microservices world. In fact, it is essential for realizing the benefits of microservices-based applications. To achieve this, a common API specification language must be used. The most widely used API specification language in the industry is OpenAPI Specification, which was originally called **Swagger Specification**.

The idea is to have developers spend time designing the interfaces first, and then implement the functionality and expose it through those interfaces. These interfaces are like contracts: As long as they remain the same, other parties do not need to worry about the internal workings of the application.

Advantages of API-first approach

The benefits of API-first approach are as follows:

- **Improved design**: This approach helps developers to think about the interfaces early on, that can help to improve the overall design of the application. The reason behind the statement is that; the interfaces are essentially the contracts between the application and the outside world, and if they are not well-designed, it can lead to problems down the road.

- **Increased consistency**: This approach can help to improve the consistency of the application by ensuring that all the interfaces are designed in a consistent way. This makes it easier for developers to understand and work with the application, and it also makes it easier to maintain the application over time.
- **Enhanced maintainability**: This approach can help to improve the maintainability of the application by making it easier to add new features or change existing features. This is because the interfaces are well-defined and documented, so developers can easily understand how to interact with them.
- **Improved interoperability**: This approach can help to improve the interoperability of the application by making it easier for other systems to communicate with it. This is because the interfaces are clearly specified and documented, so other systems can easily understand how to interact with them.
- **Increased developer productivity**: This approach can help to increase developer productivity by providing a clear and concise definition of the application's interfaces. This can help developers to get started quickly and easily, and it can also help them to avoid making mistakes.
- **Independent upgrades**: As the contract remains constant and backward compatible, no change is required to be done in peripheral systems and it provides flexibility for applying bug fixes and upgrading the application.
- **Faster time to market**: Different teams can develop and test their services independently and in parallel, as they only need to simulate the peripheral service, based on the contract that has been published by the other team. Once that is done, both the teams can test the complete flow, even without the presence of the other full-fledged services.

Developing microservices

API-first approach, as mentioned previously, will be taken for developing the microservices. It will initially focus on the designing and development of the interfaces that will be used to interact with the microservices. Before the actual coding of microservices begins, a few database tables need to be created, which will be used internally for CRUD operations.

Recipe 12: Creating database tables

As described earlier, **pgAdmin** is to be used for creating database tables corresponding to the database schemas **`customer_enquiry`** and **`enquiry_broadcast`**. Open **pgAdmin**, connect to the **financial-service-marketplace** database, open its **Query Tool**, and execute the following queries:

Customer Enquiry

Table **User** is to be used to store the information about the application users. The SQL script to create **User table** is as follows:

```
CREATE TABLE IF NOT EXISTS customer_enquiry."user"
(
    user_id serial NOT NULL,
    user_name character varying(50) NOT NULL,
    user_customer_id integer,
    created_date date NOT NULL DEFAULT CURRENT_DATE,
    created_by character varying(50) NOT NULL,
    CONSTRAINT user_pf PRIMARY KEY (user_id),
    CONSTRAINT user_uk1 UNIQUE (user_name),
    CONSTRAINT user_fk2 FOREIGN KEY (created_by)
        REFERENCES customer_enquiry."user" (user_name) MATCH SIMPLE
        ON UPDATE NO ACTION
        ON DELETE NO ACTION
        NOT VALID
);
```

Table **Customer** is to be used to store the information about the customers sending enquiry to the application. The SQL script to create **Customer table** is as follows:

```
CREATE TABLE IF NOT EXISTS customer_enquiry.customer
(
    customer_id serial NOT NULL,
    customer_name character varying(50) NOT NULL,
    customer_gender character(1),
    customer_dob date,
    created_date date NOT NULL DEFAULT CURRENT_DATE,
    created_by character varying NOT NULL,
    CONSTRAINT customer_pk PRIMARY KEY (customer_id),
    CONSTRAINT customer_fk1 FOREIGN KEY (created_by)
```

```
        REFERENCES customer_enquiry."user" (user_name) MATCH SIMPLE
        ON UPDATE NO ACTION
        ON DELETE NO ACTION
        NOT VALID
);
```

Table **Enquiry** is to be used to store the information about the enquiries done by different customers. The SQL script to create **Enquiry table** is as follows:

```
CREATE TABLE IF NOT EXISTS customer_enquiry.enquiry
(
    enquiry_id serial NOT NULL,
    enquiry_customer_id integer NOT NULL,
    enquiry_about character(5) NOT NULL,
    created_date date NOT NULL DEFAULT CURRENT_DATE,
    created_by character varying(50) NOT NULL,
    CONSTRAINT enquiry_pkey PRIMARY KEY (enquiry_id),
    CONSTRAINT enquiry_fk1 FOREIGN KEY (created_by)
        REFERENCES customer_enquiry."user" (user_name) MATCH SIMPLE
        ON UPDATE NO ACTION
        ON DELETE NO ACTION
        NOT VALID,
    CONSTRAINT enquiry_fk2 FOREIGN KEY (enquiry_customer_id)
       REFERENCES customer_enquiry.customer (customer_id) MATCH SIMPLE
        ON UPDATE NO ACTION
        ON DELETE NO ACTION
        NOT VALID
);
```

The SQL script to add foreign constraint in **User table** is as follows:

```
ALTER TABLE IF EXISTS customer_enquiry."user"
    ADD CONSTRAINT user_fk1 FOREIGN KEY (user_customer_id)
    REFERENCES customer_enquiry.customer (customer_id) MATCH SIMPLE
    ON UPDATE NO ACTION
    ON DELETE NO ACTION
    NOT VALID;
```

The SQL script to insert core data is as follows:

```
INSERT INTO customer_enquiry.user(
 user_name, created_by)
 VALUES ('system', 'system');
```

The script is used to create a super admin user for the service. This user can be used to create other admin users, which can further create users from different customers.

The SQL script to insert test data is as follows:

```
INSERT INTO customer_enquiry.customer(
 customer_name, customer_gender, customer_dob, created_by)
 VALUES ('John Paul', 'M', TO_DATE('19850101','YYYYMMDD'), 'system');

INSERT INTO customer_enquiry.customer(
 customer_name, customer_gender, customer_dob, created_by)
 VALUES ('Angela Ray', 'F', TO_DATE('19910202','YYYYMMDD'), 'system');
```

Enquiry Broadcast

Table **Failed_Request_S3** is to be used to persist requests that have been failed to broadcast to the S3 bucket. The SQL script to create **Failed_Request_S3** table is as follows:

```
CREATE TABLE enquiry_broadcast.failed_request_s3
(
    failed_request_s3_id serial NOT NULL,
    failed_request_s3_customer_id integer NOT NULL,
    failed_request_s3_enquiry_about character(5) NOT NULL,
    failed_request_s3_date date NOT NULL,
    failed_request_s3_success_date date,
    created_date date NOT NULL DEFAULT CURRENT_DATE,
    PRIMARY KEY (failed_request_s3_id)
);
```

Recipe 13: Developing Customer Enquiry service

The service is responsible for accepting an enquiry from customer, persisting it in the database table and then sending the information to the broadcast service. Additionally, the service will maintain the customer and user information in which a customer can also be a user in the system. Follow the below steps for creating the service:

1. Adding dependency
2. Adding application.properties
3. Creating RESTController
4. Defining financial products
5. Creating service classes
6. Creating entity classes
7. Creating repositories
8. Code compilation

Adding dependency

The following dependencies need to be added in the **`pom.xml`** file:

```
<dependency>
    <groupId>org.springframework.boot</groupId>
    <artifactId>spring-boot-starter-data-jpa</artifactId>
</dependency>
```

The **`dependency`** will provide JPA functionality to the service; this is required as the service needs to perform database CRUD operations.

```
<dependency>
    <groupId>org.postgresql</groupId>
    <artifactId>postgresql</artifactId>
    <scope>runtime</scope>
</dependency>
```

Since the service requires AWS PostgreSQL RDS as its database provider, the preceding dependency will provide the necessary JAR files (JARs) to establish connections and execute queries on the PostgreSQL database.

Adding application.properties

By default, Spring Boot loads the configurations from a properties file **`application.properties`**. The required file needs to be created under **`src/main/resources`** folder with the following configurations.

`application.properties`

```
spring.datasource.url=jdbc:postgresql://fs-marketplace.cbgzpif7rd3e.us-
east-1.rds.amazonaws.com:5432/postgres
```

```
spring.datasource.username=postgres
spring.datasource.password=secret11
spring.jpa.properties.hibernate.default_schema=customer_enquiry

spring.jpa.show-sql=true
spring.jpa.properties.hibernate.format_sql=true
```

The configurations are set up to supply credentials for establishing a connection to the PostgreSQL database and for displaying and formatting SQL statements on the console.

Creating RESTController

Classes with **@RestController** annotation are used to expose an interface that is used to communicate with the service from the external world. As per API-first approach, this is the first thing that needs to be designed and developed. Once the contract is built, the functionality can be added later.

EnquiryPortalController.java

```java
package com.fsm.customerenquiry.controller;

import java.util.List;
import java.util.stream.Collectors;

import org.springframework.beans.factory.annotation.Autowired;
import org.springframework.http.MediaType;
import org.springframework.web.bind.annotation.GetMapping;
import org.springframework.web.bind.annotation.PostMapping;
import org.springframework.web.bind.annotation.RequestMapping;
import org.springframework.web.bind.annotation.RequestParam;
import org.springframework.web.bind.annotation.RestController;

import com.fasterxml.jackson.databind.JsonNode;
import com.fasterxml.jackson.databind.node.JsonNodeFactory;
import com.fsm.customerenquiry.entity.Customer;
import com.fsm.customerenquiry.service.CustomerService;
import com.fsm.customerenquiry.service.EnquiryService;

@RestController
```

```
@RequestMapping(value = "/", produces = { MediaType.APPLICATION_JSON_VALUE })
public class EnquiryPortalController {

 @Autowired
 private CustomerService customerService;

 @Autowired
 private EnquiryService enquiryService;

 @GetMapping(path = "/customers")
 public List<Customer> getCustomers() {
  return customerService.getCustomers();
 }

 @GetMapping(path = "/fproducts")
 public List<JsonNode> getFinancialProducts() {
  return enquiryService.getFinancialProducts().stream()
     .map(product -> JsonNodeFactory.instance.objectNode().put("name", product.name())
       .put("code", product.getCode()).put("description", product.getDescription()))
     .collect(Collectors.toList());
 }

 @PostMapping(path = "/enquiry")
 public boolean enquiry(@RequestParam("customerId") int customerId,
   @RequestParam("financialProductName") String financialProductName) {
  try {
   enquiryService.customerEnquiry(customerId, financialProductName);
   return true;
  } catch (Exception e) {
   return false;
  }
```

```
  }
}
```

In the preceding class, three REST APIs have been exposed:

1. First, for getting the customers detail and
2. Second, to posts a customer enquiry
3. The third, API is being used to return the details of financial products supported by the application.

Defining financial products

Ideally, financial products that are supported by the system should be maintained in the database. However, for simplicity's sake, they are defined in an enumeration using the following file.

FinancialProduct.java

```
package com.fsm.customerenquiry;

import java.util.Arrays;
import java.util.List;

public enum FinancialProduct {

 CAR_LOAN("CLOAN", "Loan for buying cars"),
 HOME_LOAN("HLOAN", "Loan for buying insurance"),
 HEALTH_INSURANCE("HINSU", "Health insurance"),
 MEDICAL_INSURANCE("MINSU", "Medical insurance");

 private String code;
 private String description;

 private FinancialProduct(String code, String description) {
  this.code = code;
  this.description = description;
 }

```

```
  public String getCode() {
   return code;
  }

  public String getDescription() {
   return description;
  }

  public static FinancialProduct getFinancialProductFromName(String financialProductName) {
   FinancialProduct fiancialProduct = null;
   for (FinancialProduct fp : FinancialProduct.values()) {
    if (fp.name().equals(financialProductName))
     fiancialProduct = fp;
   }

   if (fiancialProduct == null)
    throw new RuntimeException("Unsupported Financial Product");

   return fiancialProduct;
  }

  public static List<FinancialProduct> getFinancialProducts() {
   return Arrays.asList(FinancialProduct.values());
  }
}
```

Creating service classes

Service class provide underlying business functionality for the controllers; they may internally use JPA repositories to communicate with the database. **`@Service`** annotation is used to make a java object a service. The code for the service classes are as follows:

`CustomerService.java`

```
package com.fsm.customerenquiry.service;

```

```
import java.util.List;

import org.springframework.beans.factory.annotation.Autowired;
import org.springframework.stereotype.Service;

import com.fsm.customerenquiry.entity.Customer;
import com.fsm.customerenquiry.repository.CustomerRepository;

@Service
public class CustomerService {

 @Autowired
 CustomerRepository customerRepository;

 public List<Customer>getCustomers(){
  return customerRepository.findAll();
 }
}
```

EnquiryService.java

```
package com.fsm.customerenquiry.service;

import java.util.Calendar;
import java.util.Date;
import java.util.List;

import org.springframework.beans.factory.annotation.Autowired;
import org.springframework.stereotype.Service;

import com.fsm.customerenquiry.FinancialProduct;
import com.fsm.customerenquiry.entity.Customer;
import com.fsm.customerenquiry.entity.Enquiry;
import com.fsm.customerenquiry.repository.EnquiryRepository;

```

```
@Service
public class EnquiryService {

 @Autowired
 EnquiryRepository enquiryRepository;

 public void customerEnquiry(int customerId, String financialProductName) {
  Date requestDate = Calendar.getInstance().getTime();
  persistEnquiry(customerId, financialProductName, requestDate);
  broadcastEnquiry(customerId, financialProductName, requestDate);
 }

 public List<FinancialProduct> getFinancialProducts() {
  return FinancialProduct.getFinancialProducts();
 }

 private void persistEnquiry(int customerId, String financialProductName, Date requestDate) {
  Enquiry enquiry = new Enquiry();
  Customer customer = new Customer(customerId);
  enquiry.setCustomer(customer);
  enquiry.setEnquiryAbout(FinancialProduct.getFinancialProductFromName(financialProductName).getCode());
  enquiry.setCreatedBy("system");
  enquiry.setCreatedDate(requestDate);

  enquiryRepository.save(enquiry);
 }

 private void broadcastEnquiry(int customerId, String financialProductName, Date requestDate) {
 // Coding for calling broadcast enquiry microservice
 }
}
```

CustomerService is responsible for customer related operations. Currently, it is just fetching a list of customers detail, but it can be enhanced to provide comprehensive customer related business functionality. **EnquiryService** is responsible for enquiry related operations. In the preceding code, it is persisting the customer enquiry in the database.

Creating entity classes

These are JPA entities corresponding to database tables and can be generated using a **JPA** tool with a connection to the underlying database. The JPA entities corresponding to each database table is as follows:

User.java

```
package com.fsm.customerenquiry.entity;

import java.io.Serializable;
import java.util.Date;

import jakarta.persistence.Column;
import jakarta.persistence.Entity;
import jakarta.persistence.GeneratedValue;
import jakarta.persistence.GenerationType;
import jakarta.persistence.Id;
import jakarta.persistence.NamedQuery;
import jakarta.persistence.SequenceGenerator;
import jakarta.persistence.Temporal;
import jakarta.persistence.TemporalType;

/**
 * The persistent class for the user database table.
 *
 */
@Entity
@NamedQuery(name = "User.findAll", query = "SELECT u FROM User u")
public class User implements Serializable {
 private static final long serialVersionUID = 1L;

```

```
@Id
 @SequenceGenerator(name = "USER_USERID_GENERATOR", sequenceName =
"USER_USER_ID_SEQ", allocationSize = 1)
 @GeneratedValue(strategy = GenerationType.SEQUENCE, generator =
"USER_USERID_GENERATOR")
@Column(name = "user_id")
private Integer userId;

@Column(name = "created_by")
private String createdBy;

@Temporal(TemporalType.DATE)
@Column(name = "created_date")
private Date createdDate;

@Column(name = "user_customer_id")
private Integer userCustomerId;

@Column(name = "user_name")
private String userName;

public User() {
}
}
```

Customer.java

```
package com.fsm.customerenquiry.entity;

import java.io.Serializable;
import java.util.Date;
import java.util.List;

import jakarta.persistence.Column;
import jakarta.persistence.Entity;
import jakarta.persistence.GeneratedValue;
```

```
import jakarta.persistence.GenerationType;
import jakarta.persistence.Id;
import jakarta.persistence.NamedQuery;
import jakarta.persistence.OneToMany;
import jakarta.persistence.SequenceGenerator;
import jakarta.persistence.Temporal;
import jakarta.persistence.TemporalType;

/**
 * The persistent class for the customer database table.
 *
 */
@Entity
@NamedQuery(name = "Customer.findAll", query = "SELECT c FROM Customer c")
public class Customer implements Serializable {
 private static final long serialVersionUID = 1L;

 @Id
 @SequenceGenerator(name = "CUSTOMER_CUSTOMERID_GENERATOR", sequenceName = "CUSTOMER_CUSTOMER_ID_SEQ", allocationSize = 1)
 @GeneratedValue(strategy = GenerationType.SEQUENCE, generator = "CUSTOMER_CUSTOMERID_GENERATOR")
 @Column(name = "customer_id")
 private Integer customerId;

 @Column(name = "created_by")
 private String createdBy;

 @Temporal(TemporalType.DATE)
 @Column(name = "created_date")
 private Date createdDate;

 @Temporal(TemporalType.DATE)
```

```
@Column(name = "customer_dob")
private Date customerDob;

@Column(name = "customer_gender")
private String customerGender;

@Column(name = "customer_name")
private String customerName;

// bi-directional many-to-one association to Enquiry
@OneToMany(mappedBy = "customer")
private List<Enquiry> enquiries;

public Customer() {
}

public List<Enquiry> getEnquiries() {
 return this.enquiries;
}

public void setEnquiries(List<Enquiry> enquiries) {
 this.enquiries = enquiries;
}

public Enquiry addEnquiry(Enquiry enquiry) {
 getEnquiries().add(enquiry);
 enquiry.setCustomer(this);

 return enquiry;
}

public Enquiry removeEnquiry(Enquiry enquiry) {
 getEnquiries().remove(enquiry);
```

```
    enquiry.setCustomer(null);

    return enquiry;
  }
}
```

Enquiry.java

```
package com.fsm.customerenquiry.entity;

import java.io.Serializable;
import java.util.Date;

import jakarta.persistence.Column;
import jakarta.persistence.Entity;
import jakarta.persistence.FetchType;
import jakarta.persistence.GeneratedValue;
import jakarta.persistence.GenerationType;
import jakarta.persistence.Id;
import jakarta.persistence.JoinColumn;
import jakarta.persistence.ManyToOne;
import jakarta.persistence.NamedQuery;
import jakarta.persistence.SequenceGenerator;
import jakarta.persistence.Temporal;
import jakarta.persistence.TemporalType;

/**
 * The persistent class for the enquiry database table.
 *
 */
@Entity
@NamedQuery(name = "Enquiry.findAll", query = "SELECT e FROM Enquiry
e")
public class Enquiry implements Serializable {
  private static final long serialVersionUID = 1L;
```

```

    @Id
    @SequenceGenerator(name = "ENQUIRY_ENQUIRYID_GENERATOR",
  sequenceName = "ENQUIRY_ENQUIRY_ID_SEQ", allocationSize = 1)
    @GeneratedValue(strategy = GenerationType.SEQUENCE, generator =
  "ENQUIRY_ENQUIRYID_GENERATOR")
    @Column(name = "enquiry_id")
    private Integer enquiryId;

    @Column(name = "created_by")
    private String createdBy;

    @Temporal(TemporalType.DATE)
    @Column(name = "created_date")
    private Date createdDate;

    @Column(name = "enquiry_about")
    private String enquiryAbout;

    // bi-directional many-to-one association to Customer
    @ManyToOne(fetch = FetchType.LAZY)
    @JoinColumn(name = "enquiry_customer_id")
    private Customer customer;

    public Enquiry() {
    }
}
```

Note: Setters and Getters from the above entity classes have been removed to optimize the code.

The JPA entity classes are nothing but serializable POJOs responsible for holding data and represents an object in the database. Also, remember to use the correct namespace, the recent Java versions use **`jakarta`** namespace instead of **`javax`**.

Creating repositories

Repository classes are responsible for querying the underlying database. Entity classes are used as a data transfer object to-and-fro between application and the database. These are interfaces and are annotated with **`@Repository`** annotation. The repositories that have been created, corresponding to customer and enquiry tables, are as follows:

`CustomerRepository.java`

```
package com.fsm.customerenquiry.repository;

import org.springframework.data.jpa.repository.JpaRepository;
import org.springframework.stereotype.Repository;

import com.fsm.customerenquiry.entity.Customer;

@Repository
public interface CustomerRepository extends JpaRepository<Customer, Integer> {
}
```

`EnquiryRepository.java`

```
package com.fsm.customerenquiry.repository;

import org.springframework.data.jpa.repository.JpaRepository;
import org.springframework.stereotype.Repository;

import com.fsm.customerenquiry.entity.Enquiry;

@Repository
public interface EnquiryRepository extends JpaRepository<Enquiry, Integer> {
}
```

Code compilation

To compile the code, follow the below steps:

1. Open the Git BASH client.
2. Navigate to the project directory where **`pom.xml`** exists.
3. Run the below Maven command:
   `mvn clean install`

Figure 2.8 illustrates the final output of the **maven** command for Customer Enquiry project:

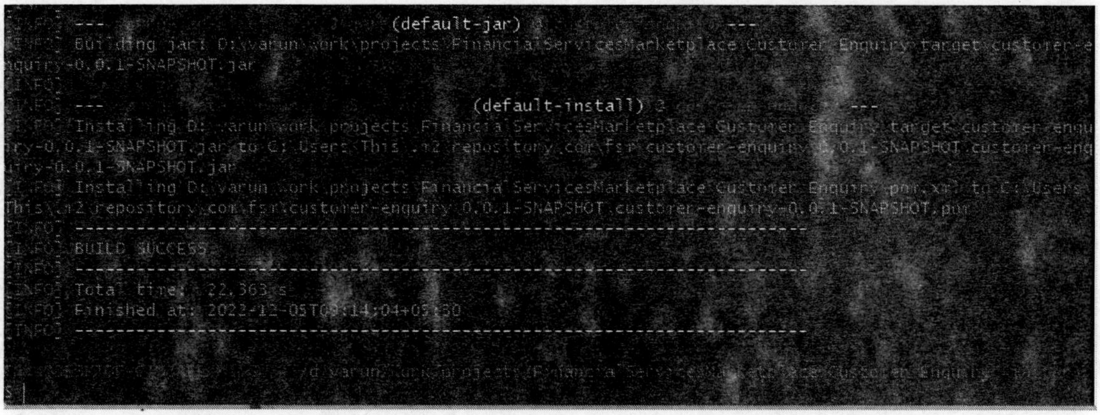

***Figure 2.8**: Success message of mvn clean install for Customer Enquiry project*

Recipe 14: Developing Enquiry Broadcast service

The service is responsible for broadcasting the customer enquiries to AWS S3 and real time streaming systems such as Apache Kafka. The service exposes an endpoint that will be used by Customer Enquiry service to send details of customer enquiries to this service. Follow the below steps for creating the service:

- Adding dependency
- Appending application.properties
- Creating RESTController
- Creating config class
- Creating service class
- Creating entity class
- Creating repositories
- Code compilation

Adding dependency

The following dependencies need to be added in the **pom.xml** file:

```
<!-- https://mvnrepository.com/artifact/com.amazonaws/aws-java-sdk-s3
-->
<dependency>
    <groupId>com.amazonaws</groupId>
```

```
        <artifactId>aws-java-sdk-s3</artifactId>
        <version>1.12.353</version>
</dependency>
```

The **dependency** will provide libraries to communicate with the Amazon S3 service. Additionally, it is necessary to include the **spring-boot-starter-data-jpa** and **postgresql** dependencies. This is because this service requires the capability to perform CRUD operations to store failed requests in the database for later retry attempts.

Appending application.properties

Configuration for spring **datasource** needs to be added for database connectivity.

application.properties

```
server.port = 8081

spring.datasource.url=jdbc:postgresql://fs-marketplace.cbgzpif7rd3e.us-east-1.rds.amazonaws.com:5432/postgres
spring.datasource.username=postgres
spring.datasource.password=secret11
spring.jpa.properties.hibernate.default_schema=enquiry_broadcast
```

The configurations are same as with the Customer Enquiry service, with only difference of the default schema. In this case, the default schema is **enquiry_broadcast**.

Creating RESTController

The following class defines an interface for the outside world for connectivity to Enquiry Broadcast service:

BroadcastController.java

```
package com.fsm.enquirybroadcast.controller;

import java.util.Date;

import org.springframework.beans.factory.annotation.Autowired;
import org.springframework.format.annotation.DateTimeFormat;
import org.springframework.http.MediaType;
import org.springframework.web.bind.annotation.PostMapping;
import org.springframework.web.bind.annotation.RequestMapping;
```

```
import org.springframework.web.bind.annotation.RequestParam;
import org.springframework.web.bind.annotation.RestController;

import com.fsm.enquirybroadcast.service.BroadcastService;

@RestController
@RequestMapping(value = "/", produces = { MediaType.APPLICATION_JSON_VALUE })
public class BroadcastController {

 @Autowired
 BroadcastService broadcastService;

 @PostMapping(path = "/broadcast")
 public boolean enquiryBroadcast(@RequestParam("customerId") int customerId,
   @RequestParam("financialProduct") String financialProduct,
   @RequestParam("requestDate") @DateTimeFormat(pattern = "yyyyMMdd") Date requestDate) {

  return broadcastService.broadcast(customerId, financialProduct, requestDate);

 }
}
```

Creating config class

Config classes are annotated with **@Configuration** annotation and responsible for generating Spring Beans using the methods that are annotated with **@Bean** annotation.

BroadcastConfig.java

```
package com.fsm.enquirybroadcast;

import org.springframework.context.annotation.Bean;
import org.springframework.context.annotation.Configuration;
```

```
import com.amazonaws.auth.AWSCredentials;
import com.amazonaws.auth.AWSStaticCredentialsProvider;
import com.amazonaws.auth.BasicAWSCredentials;
import com.amazonaws.regions.Regions;
import com.amazonaws.services.s3.AmazonS3;
import com.amazonaws.services.s3.AmazonS3ClientBuilder;
@Configuration
public class BroadcastConfig {
 @Bean
 public AmazonS3 AmazonS3() {
    AWSCredentials credentials = new BasicAWSCredentials("<access key>","<secret key>");
  AmazonS3 s3client = AmazonS3ClientBuilder.standard()
      .withCredentials(new AWSStaticCredentialsProvider(credentials)).withRegion(Regions.US_EAST_1).build();
  return s3client;
 }
}
```

The class creates a bean for **AmazonS3** using **Secret Key** and **Access Key** on server startup, so that it can be injected in the service class for putting objects in the S3 bucket.

Creating service class

The following service has one method for broadcasting the details to AWS S3 (implemented) and another for Kafka Topic (to be implemented).

BroadcastService.java

```
package com.fsm.enquirybroadcast.service;
import java.io.ByteArrayInputStream;
```

```
import java.text.DateFormat;
import java.text.SimpleDateFormat;
import java.time.LocalTime;
import java.util.Calendar;
import java.util.Date;
import java.util.HashMap;
import java.util.Map;

import org.springframework.beans.factory.annotation.Autowired;
import org.springframework.stereotype.Service;

import com.amazonaws.services.s3.AmazonS3;
import com.amazonaws.services.s3.model.ObjectMetadata;
import com.fsm.enquirybroadcast.entity.FailedRequestS3;
import com.fsm.enquirybroadcast.repository.FailedRequestS3Repository;

@Service
public class BroadcastService {

    public static final DateFormat DATE_FORMAT = new SimpleDateFormat("yyyyMMdd");

    @Autowired
    private AmazonS3 s3Client;

    @Autowired
    private FailedRequestS3Repository failedRequestS3Repository;

    private String bucketName = "fs-marketplace-bucket";

    // Map maintains financial product codes corresponding to their names
    private Map<String, String> financialProductMap;

```

```
 public boolean broadcast(int customerId, String financialProduct, Date requestDate) {
  boolean isSuccess = true;

  if (!BroadcastToS3(customerId, financialProduct, requestDate))
   isSuccess = false;

  if (!BroadcastToTopic(customerId, financialProduct, requestDate))
   isSuccess = false;

  if (!isSuccess) // Persist the request in DB for retry
   persistRequest(customerId, financialProduct, requestDate);

  return isSuccess;
 }

 private boolean BroadcastToS3(int customerId, String financialProduct, Date requestDate) {

  try {

   // File is created in a requested date folder
   // File name is financial product requested appended with current time
   String fileName = DATE_FORMAT.format(requestDate) + "/" + financialProduct + "-" + LocalTime.now() + ".txt";

   // Content of file is customer id '|' separated with financial product enquired
   String data = "CustomerID:" + customerId + "|FinancialProduct:" + financialProduct;

   ObjectMetadata meta = new ObjectMetadata();
   meta.setContentLength(data.length());

```

```
  s3Client.putObject(bucketName, fileName, new ByteArrayInputStream(data.
getBytes()), meta);

  } catch (Exception e) {
   e.printStackTrace();
   return false;
  }

  return true;
 }

private boolean BroadcastToTopic(int customerId, String financialProduct,
Date requestDate) {
  return true;
 }

 private void persistRequest(int customerId, String financialProduct,
Date requestDate) {

  if (financialProductMap == null) {
   financialProductMap = new HashMap<>();
   populateFinanicalProducts(financialProductMap);
  }

  FailedRequestS3 failedRequestS3 = new FailedRequestS3();
  failedRequestS3.setFailedRequestS3CustomerId(customerId);
   failedRequestS3.setFailedRequestS3EnquiryAbout(financialProductMap.
get(financialProduct));
  failedRequestS3.setFailedRequestS3Date(requestDate);
  failedRequestS3.setCreatedDate(Calendar.getInstance().getTime());

  failedRequestS3Repository.save(failedRequestS3);
 }

```

```
 private void populateFinanicalProducts(Map<String, String>
financialProductMap) {

  financialProductMap.put("CAR_LOAN", "CLOAN");
  financialProductMap.put("HOME_LOAN", "HLOAN");
  financialProductMap.put("HEALTH_INSURANCE", "HINSU");
  financialProductMap.put("MEDICAL_INSURANCE", "MINSU");
 }
}
```

Creating entity class

The following entity class is being created for persisting the requests that are failed to broadcast to the S3 bucket. The persisted requests are later picked again for broadcasting.

FailedRequestS3.java

```
package com.fsm.enquirybroadcast.entity;

import java.io.Serializable;
import java.util.Date;

import jakarta.persistence.Column;
import jakarta.persistence.Entity;
import jakarta.persistence.GeneratedValue;
import jakarta.persistence.GenerationType;
import jakarta.persistence.Id;
import jakarta.persistence.NamedQuery;
import jakarta.persistence.SequenceGenerator;
import jakarta.persistence.Table;
import jakarta.persistence.Temporal;
import jakarta.persistence.TemporalType;

/**
 * The persistent class for the failed_request_s3 database table.
 *
 */
@Entity
```

```
@Table(name = "failed_request_s3")
@NamedQuery(name = "FailedRequestS3.findAll", query = "SELECT f FROM FailedRequestS3 f")
public class FailedRequestS3 implements Serializable {
 private static final long serialVersionUID = 1L;

 @Id
 @SequenceGenerator(name = "FAILED_REQUEST_S3_FAILEDREQUESTS3ID_GENERATOR", sequenceName = "FAILED_REQUEST_S3_FAILED_REQUEST_S3_ID_SEQ", allocationSize = 1)
 @GeneratedValue(strategy = GenerationType.SEQUENCE, generator = "FAILED_REQUEST_S3_FAILEDREQUESTS3ID_GENERATOR")
 @Column(name = "failed_request_s3_id")
 private Integer failedRequestS3Id;

 @Temporal(TemporalType.DATE)
 @Column(name = "created_date")
 private Date createdDate;

 @Column(name = "failed_request_s3_customer_id")
 private Integer failedRequestS3CustomerId;

 @Temporal(TemporalType.DATE)
 @Column(name = "failed_request_s3_date")
 private Date failedRequestS3Date;

 @Column(name = "failed_request_s3_enquiry_about")
 private String failedRequestS3EnquiryAbout;

 @Temporal(TemporalType.DATE)
 @Column(name = "failed_request_s3_success_date")
 private Date failedRequestS3SuccessDate;

 public FailedRequestS3() {
 }
}
```

Note: Setters and Getters from the above entity classes have been removed to optimize the code.

Creating repositories

In this section, we will learn how to create repositories:

`FailedRequestS3Repository.java`

```
package com.fsm.enquirybroadcast.repository;

import org.springframework.data.jpa.repository.JpaRepository;
import org.springframework.stereotype.Repository;

import com.fsm.enquirybroadcast.entity.FailedRequestS3;

@Repository
public interface FailedRequestS3Repository extends
JpaRepository<FailedRequestS3, Integer> {
}
```

Code compilation

To compile the code, follow the below steps:

1. Open the Git BASH client.
2. Navigate to the project directory where **`pom.xml`** exists.
3. Run the below Maven command
   `mvn clean install`

Figure 2.9 illustrates the final output of the **`maven`** command for Enquiry Broadcast project:

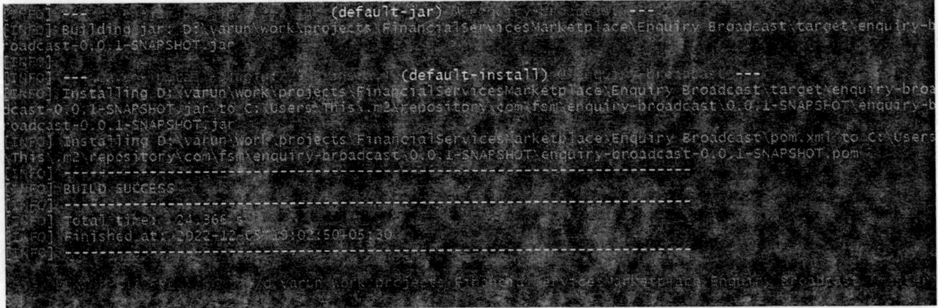

***Figure 2.9:** Success message of mvn clean install for Enquiry Broadcast project*

Recipe 15: Creating unit test cases

Unit tests serve as an effective means to ensure that the intended functionality of the code does not break even when new code is added or modifications are made to the existing code. This becomes particularly crucial as multiple developers may work on a portion of the code in the future to introduce enhancements or address bugs, often without a comprehensive understanding of the entire functionality. Unit tests play a critical role in preserving the stability of the behavior; if a unit test fails, it serves as an alert that something within the code is incorrect.

From Spring Boot version 2.2.x, it has a support for Junit 5 and are loaded as part of **spring-boot-starter-test**. As part of this book, unit tests are written using **Junit 5** libraries.

Adding dependency

The following dependencies need to be added in the **pom.xml** file of both the projects Customer Enquiry and Enquiry Broadcast:

```
<dependency>
  <groupId>org.springframework.boot</groupId>
  <artifactId>spring-boot-starter-test</artifactId>
  <scope>test</scope>
</dependency>
```

The **dependency** will make sure all the unit test JARs are available for the test scope and will not be part of the compiled executable JAR.

Writing test classes

The test classes are created under the folder **src/test/java** of projects Customer Enquiry and Enquiry Broadcast respectively.

CustomerServiceTests.java

```
package com.fsm.customerenquiry;

import static org.assertj.core.api.Assertions.assertThat;

import java.util.ArrayList;
import java.util.List;

import org.junit.jupiter.api.BeforeEach;
```

```
import org.junit.jupiter.api.Test;
import org.mockito.Mockito;
import org.springframework.beans.factory.annotation.Autowired;
import org.springframework.boot.test.context.SpringBootTest;
import org.springframework.boot.test.context.TestConfiguration;
import org.springframework.boot.test.mock.mockito.MockBean;
import org.springframework.context.annotation.Bean;

import com.fsm.customerenquiry.entity.Customer;
import com.fsm.customerenquiry.repository.CustomerRepository;
import com.fsm.customerenquiry.service.CustomerService;

@SpringBootTest(properties = "spring.main.allow-bean-definition-
overriding=true")
public class CustomerServiceTests {

 @TestConfiguration
 static class CustomerServiceTestContextConfiguration {
  @Bean
  public CustomerService customerService() {
   return new CustomerService();
  }
 }

 @Autowired
 private CustomerService customerService;

 @MockBean
 private CustomerRepository customerRepository;

 @BeforeEach
 public void setUp() {

  List<Customer> customerList = new ArrayList<>();
```

```
    customerList.add(new Customer(1));
    customerList.add(new Customer(2));

   Mockito.when(customerRepository.findAll()).thenReturn(customerList);
  }

  @Test
  public void customersShouldBeFound() {
    List<Customer> customerList = customerService.getCustomers();
    assertThat(customerList.size()).isEqualTo(2);
  }
}
```

EnquiryServiceTests.java

```
package com.fsm.customerenquiry;

import static org.junit.jupiter.api.Assertions.assertThrows;
import static org.mockito.ArgumentMatchers.any;

import org.junit.jupiter.api.BeforeEach;
import org.junit.jupiter.api.Test;
import org.mockito.Mockito;
import org.springframework.beans.factory.annotation.Autowired;
import org.springframework.boot.test.context.SpringBootTest;
import org.springframework.boot.test.context.TestConfiguration;
import org.springframework.boot.test.mock.mockito.MockBean;
import org.springframework.context.annotation.Bean;

import com.fsm.customerenquiry.entity.Enquiry;
import com.fsm.customerenquiry.repository.EnquiryRepository;
import com.fsm.customerenquiry.service.EnquiryService;

@SpringBootTest(properties = "spring.main.allow-bean-definition-over-
riding=true")
```

```
public class EnquiryServiceTests {

  @TestConfiguration
  static class EnquiryServiceTestContextConfiguration {
   @Bean
   public EnquiryService enquiryService() {
    return new EnquiryService();
   }
  }

  @Autowired
  private EnquiryService enquiryService;

  @MockBean
  private EnquiryRepository enquiryRepository;

  @BeforeEach
  public void setUp() {
   Mockito.when(enquiryRepository.save(any(Enquiry.class))).thenReturn(null);
  }

  @Test
  public void whenInvalidFinancialProductCode_thenEnquiryShouldNotBeSaved() {
   assertThrows(RuntimeException.class, () -> enquiryService.customerEnquiry(1, "XXXX"));
  }
}
```

BroadcastServiceTests.java

```
package com.fsm.enquirybroadcast;

import static org.assertj.core.api.Assertions.assertThat;
import static org.mockito.ArgumentMatchers.any;
```

```
import java.io.InputStream;
import java.util.Calendar;

import org.junit.jupiter.api.BeforeEach;
import org.junit.jupiter.api.Test;
import org.mockito.Mockito;
import org.springframework.beans.factory.annotation.Autowired;
import org.springframework.boot.test.context.SpringBootTest;
import org.springframework.boot.test.context.TestConfiguration;
import org.springframework.boot.test.mock.mockito.MockBean;
import org.springframework.context.annotation.Bean;

import com.amazonaws.services.s3.AmazonS3;
import com.amazonaws.services.s3.model.ObjectMetadata;
import com.fsm.enquirybroadcast.service.BroadcastService;

@SpringBootTest(properties = "spring.main.allow-bean-definition-
overriding=true")
public class BroadcastServiceTests {

 @TestConfiguration
 static class EnquiryServiceTestContextConfiguration {
  @Bean
  public BroadcastService broadcastService() {
   return new BroadcastService();
  }
 }

 @Autowired
 private BroadcastService broadcastService;

 @MockBean
 private AmazonS3 s3Client;
```

```

    @BeforeEach
    public void setUp() {
        Mockito.when(s3Client.putObject(any(String.class), any(String.class), any(InputStream.class),
        any(ObjectMetadata.class))).thenThrow(RuntimeException.class);
    }

    @Test
    public void whenAWSServiceThrowsException_thenFalseShouldBeReturned() {
        assertThat(broadcastService.broadcast(1, "HOME_LOAN", Calendar.getInstance().getTime())).isEqualTo(false);
    }
}
```

The intent of unit tests is to test a particular functionality and not load the complete Spring context, the actual heavy-duty objects such as JPA repositories and AwazonS3 are mocked to make them light and perform the intended operation.

Maven **clean install** command internally fires all the unit tests by default and in case of any failure, the job halts with a failure message.

Recipe 16: Enhancing microservices for interservice communication

In practical scenarios, services often need to interact with one another to fulfil business functions. In this specific example, the **Customer Enquiry** microservice must communicate with the **Broadcast Enquiry** microservice to broadcast messages, making them accessible to vendors. Also, the Enquiry Broadcast microservice must call the APIs exposed by the **Customer Enquiry** microservice to retrieve information about available financial products.

There are multiple approaches to consume a REST API in Spring. Spring provides two main implementations for this purpose: **RestTemplate** and **WebClient**. RestTemplate is a synchronous and blocking method, whereas WebClient is asynchronous and non-blocking. It utilizes the reactive programming paradigm in its implementation, offering flexibility and efficiency in handling asynchronous operations.

Adding dependency

The following dependencies need to be added in the **pom.xml** file of both the projects Customer Enquiry and Enquiry Broadcast:

```
<dependency>
 <groupId>org.springframework.boot</groupId>
 <artifactId>spring-boot-starter-webflux</artifactId>
</dependency>
```

Service changes

`EnquiryService` of Customer Enquiry microservice needs to be enhanced to call REST API exposed by Broadcast Enquiry microservice.

`EnquiryService.java`

```
private void broadcastEnquiry(int customerId, String financialProductName, Date requestDate) {

  WebClient client = WebClient.builder().baseUrl("http://localhost:8081")
     .defaultHeader(HttpHeaders.CONTENT_TYPE, MediaType.APPLICATION_JSON_VALUE).build();

  try {
   oolean success = client.post()
      .uri(uriBuilder -> uriBuilder.path("/broadcast/").queryParam("customerId", customerId)
        .queryParam("financialProduct", financialProductName)
        .queryParam("requestDate", DATE_FORMAT.format(requestDate)).build())
      .retrieve().bodyToMono(Boolean.class).block();

   if (success)
    System.out.println("Enquiry has been sent for broadcasting");

  } catch (Exception e) {
   System.out.println("Enquiry has not been sent for broadcasting");
   e.printStackTrace();
   throw e;
  }
 }
```

BroadcastService of Enquiry Broadcast microservice needs to be enhanced to call REST API exposed by Customer Enquiry microservice.

BroadcastService.java

```
private void populateFinanicalProducts(Map<String, String> financialProductMap) {

  WebClient client = WebClient.builder().baseUrl("http://localhost:8080")
      .defaultHeader(HttpHeaders.CONTENT_TYPE, MediaType.APPLICATION_JSON_VALUE).build();

  try {
    List<Map<String, String>> financialProducts = client.get()
      .uri(uriBuilder -> uriBuilder.path("/fproducts/").build()).retrieve().bodyToMono(List.class)
      .block();

    for (Map<String, String> fpMap : financialProducts) {
      String name = null;
      String code = null;
      for (Entry<String, String> entry : fpMap.entrySet()) {
       if ("name".equals(entry.getKey())) {
        name = entry.getValue();
       } else if ("code".equals(entry.getKey())) {
        code = entry.getValue();
       }
      }
      financialProductMap.put(name, code);
    }
  } catch (Exception e) {
    System.out.println("Failed loading financial products");
    e.printStackTrace();
    throw e;
  }
}
```

Recipe 17: Running the application

For the complete business functionality, both the services need to be started. The microservices will communicate with each other to complete the business journey. The intended positive flow is:

1. The customer enquiries about a financial product using Customer Enquiry microservice.
2. The microservices persists the customer enquiry in a database table.
3. After persisting, Customer Enquiry microservice calls a REST API of Enquiry Broadcast microservice.
4. Broadcast Enquiry microservice then creates a request string and puts this object on the Amazon S3 bucket.

The result of the compilation of code using `mvn clean install` command is the creation of the executable jars for both the microservices. The jars are available in the **`target`** folder of the respective project. The names of the executable jars are **`customer-enquiry-0.0.1-SNAPSHOT.jar`** and **`enquiry-broadcast-0.0.1-SNAPSHOT.jar`**.

Run the following command to start the microservices:

```
java -jar customer-enquiry-0.0.1-SNAPSHOT.jar
java -jar enquiry-broadcast-0.0.1-SNAPSHOT.jar
```

Once the microservices are running, there are multiple ways to call a REST service. As part of this book, **Postman** tool has been used for calling the APIs.

Figure 2.10 illustrates a scenario where customer with Id equal to **1**, has enquired for financial product **HOME_LOAN** and the response from API call is **true**:

***Figure 2.10**: Postman tool view of calling a REST API*

The following SQL query can be used to validate whether the enquiry has been persisted in the database or not:

```
select * from customer_enquiry.enquiry;
```

Figure 2.11 illustrates that the request of customer with id **1** has been persisted in the table:

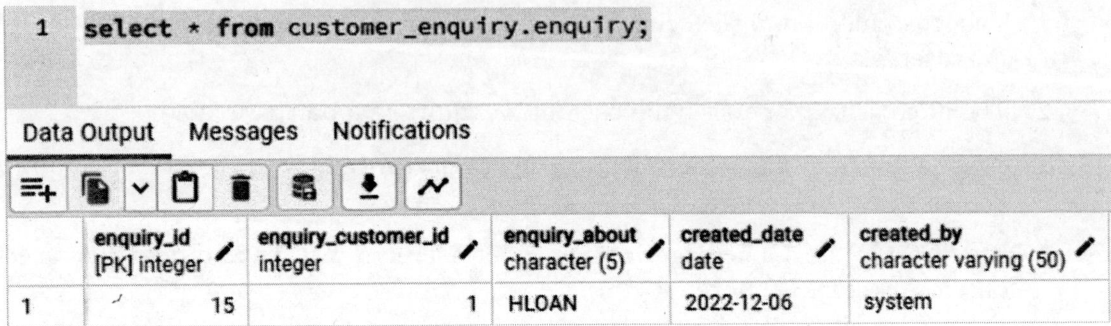

Figure 2.11: *Output of SQL to select all rows from enquiry table*

The following queries can be run on AWS CLI to validate whether a file has been created on the Amazon S3 bucket or not:

```
aws s3 ls s3://fs-marketplace-bucket --recursive --human-readable
```

Output:

```
2022-12-06 02:34:17    39 Bytes 20221206/HOME_LOAN-02:34:17.011.txt
```

Figure 2.12 illustrates that the intended file has been created in the S3 bucket:

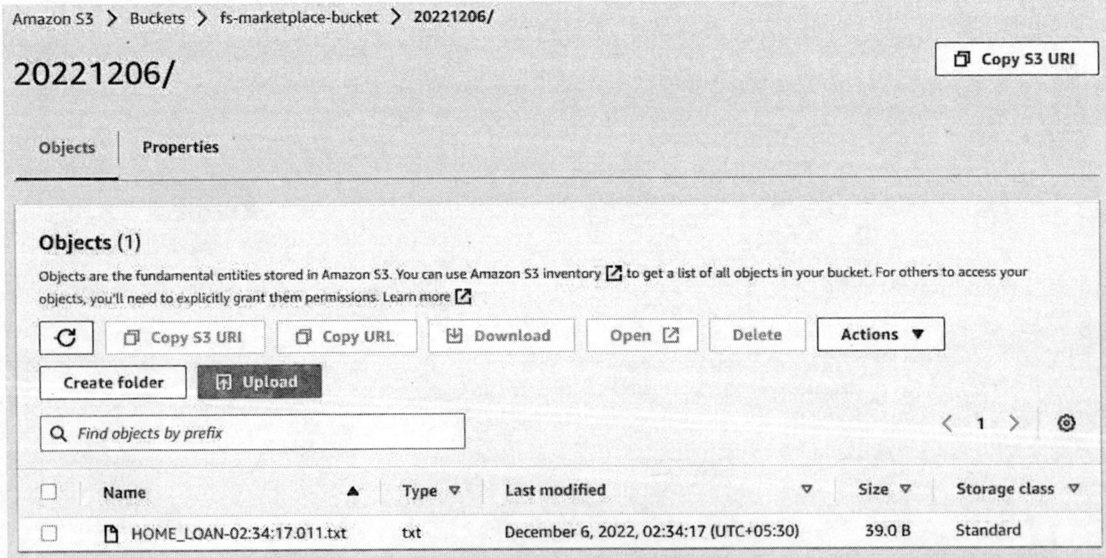

Figure 2.12: *File created under current date folder 20221206*

Recipe 18: Pushing the code to Git repositories

Once the application has been tested and all looks correct, the changes should be pushed to the remote Git repository. The following commands need to be run for both the projects Customer Enquiry and Enquiry Broadcast.

Open Git BASH and from the local maven project folder for both the projects Customer Enquiry and Enquiry Broadcast, run the following commands in the mentioned order:

```
git branch -m chapter2
git add .
git commit -m "Chapter 2 - APIs implemented"
git push -u -f source chapter2
```

The local **`git branch`** has been changed to **`chapter2`** and then the code has been pushed to the remote repository. Source has already been set while setting the version control system. In GitLab, the UI merge requests are created to review and merge the code from **`chapter2`** branch to **`main`** branch. Branch **`chapter2`** will remain in the local repository and can be used for reference later, if required.

Conclusion

In this chapter, we have learnt the steps that need to be followed to set the Spring Boot development environment, along with configuring the version control system Git. API-first approach has been discussed followed by actual microservices development, using this approach. To support the continuous development, unit test cases have been written and microservices have been enhanced to perform interservice communication. In the end, we learnt running the microservices and validating that their behavior is as intended and finally all #the changed code has been pushed to the version control system Git.

In the next chapter, we will explore methods for eliminating hardcoded values within the application and moving them to properties files. Furthermore, we will delve into the process of externalizing these configurations. Additionally, we will learn about **Spring Cloud Config Server** and its utilization for running applications with version-controlled configurations.

Points to remember

- It is not possible for multiple applications to run simultaneously on the same port of a single host machine. Therefore, in this chapter, both microservices are being configured to run on distinct ports (**`8080`** and **`8081`**) to avoid conflicts. This is good from development environments perspective, but in production, the applications will be running in their individual Docker containers (to be discussed in later chapters), in which, there will be no such restrictions. In fact, it is advisable to run them on the same port for easy configurability.

- API-first is a great way for microservices development but it has a prerequisite: requirements need to be clear before beginning with the API design, or else, there will be changes in the interfaces and will have an impact on the other microservices defeating the purpose of API-first approach.
- Unit test cases should be written such that they should cover the complete business requirement. Moreover, it should execute fast enough so that the overall build time of the application should not have a negative impact on other processes.

Questions

1. In microservice design, why is it advisable for each microservice to have their own individual database?
2. While writing unit test case for a particular component, there is no need to call the surrounding components. How can the actual behavior of the surrounding components be mimicked? What is this process called?
3. What are the different ways or design patterns that are used to reflect the changes of one microservice into the other microservices?

Join our book's Discord space

Join the book's Discord Workspace for Latest updates, Offers, Tech happenings around the world, New Release and Sessions with the Authors:

https://discord.bpbonline.com

CHAPTER 3
Externalize Application Configurations

Introduction

The last chapter documented the points that need to be considered before setting the development environment and then provided a step-by-step approach in building the two microservices. It discussed topics ranging from designing the interfaces using API-first approach, to developing all the required components, including unit test cases and finally pushing the code changes to a remote Git repository to version control them, and making them accessible to other developers.

In this chapter, we will begin with discussing the configuration and its importance in defining the application behavior. We will also talk about the powerful concept of externalizing the configurations, so that an application can work in different environments in a hassle-free manner. In the end, we will document the steps to create a Spring Cloud Config Server and enhance the microservices to fetch configurations from this server.

Structure

In this chapter, we will discuss following topics:

- Application configuration
- Externalizing configurations

- Spring Cloud Config Server
- Version controlled configurations
- Secured configurations
- Dynamic configurations

Objectives

By the end of this chapter, we will learn different ways to externalize a configuration in a Spring Boot application, and will know the steps that need to be followed in creating a Spring Cloud Config Server. We will also understand how a Spring Cloud Config Server can be used to pick configurations that are version controlled in a Git repository, combined with secrets fetched from a Vault. Finally, we will enhance the code to retrieve the configurations during the runtime without the need of application restart.

Application configuration

In the previous chapter, we have done few entries in the **`application.properties`** file under the resources folder of both the projects. The entries are nothing but the configurations that have been done to connect to the database and the port on which the application should be running. Passing these values via configurations instead of hardcoding them in the code, makes sure that by just modifying the configurations, a different database or a server port can be used to run the application without recompiling the code.

@Value annotation

The application contains significant amount of business logic that is parameterized and gets executed on the values of certain parameters, and normally, the setting of these parameters is part of the day zero setup. Parameterizing the business logic provides the advantage of using the same application, with a common codebase, for multiple clients who may have varied business requirements. This way, a lot of maintenance effort is saved. Moreover, all the changes go in a single code line which reduces testing, upgrades, and patching efforts.

To support this parameter configuration, Spring Boot has a feature using which values can be easily assigned to the parameters using the annotation **`@Value`**. It is only about setting these values in the properties file, and values gets automatically assigned to the required parameter. Later in this chapter, we will also see how these values can be externalized, so that for the same client, if a parameter needs to have different values as per the environment, then that can be done without modifying or altering the day zero setup.

Recipe 19: Using @Value to inject value as a parameter

There could be a requirement for any implementation of Customer Enquiry microservice in which no broadcasting of the enquiries is required, but instead of that, there should be some other business flow that needs to be kicked in. For example, an email needs to be sent to the central operations team and so on. This is a good use case to control the application based on a parameter.

Adding a property

A new property needs to be added in **application.properties** file of Customer Enquiry microservice using the following code:

```
enquiry.broadcast.enabled=Y
```

The value of this property will be used to configure whether the application should broadcast the enquiries done by the customers or not. Here, the value **Y** is being assigned to this property.

Using the property

EnquiryService of Customer Enquiry microservice is to be enhanced to use the **enquiry.broadcast.enabled** property, as follows:

EnquiryService.java

```
// Package declaration and import statements

@Service
public class EnquiryService {
@Value("${enquiry.broadcast.enabled}")
String broadcastEnabled;

// Existing business logic

 public void customerEnquiry(int customerId, String financialProductName) {
 // Existing business logic

  if ("Y".equalsIgnoreCase(broadcastEnabled)){
```

```
        broadcastEnquiry(customerId, financialProductName, requestDate);
      }
    }
    // Existing business Logic
}
```

Here, global variable **broadcastEnabled** is being annotated with **@Value**, which is linked to the property **enquiry.broadcast.enabled**. Thus, whatever value is being set for the property, is assigned to the variable. The logic has been added to call the broadcast enquiry only in case the value of variable **broadcastEnabled** is set to **Y**.

Profile configuration files

Spring also supports profile specific configuration files, which means that different properties files such as **application-dev.properties**, **application-test.properties**, **application-prod.properties**, and so on, can be created as per the profiles **dev**, **test**, **prod**, and so on, where names of the profiles can be anything. However, in practical terms, profiles are created as per the different environments the application needs to run. By default, all the properties will be picked up from **application.properties** and profile specific properties files, and in case of any conflict, the profile specific properties file is given preference.

Recipe 20: Using profile specific properties

For a use case where development teams do not need to invoke broadcast enquiry microservice, a development specific profile needs to be created, for which the property controlling the broadcast of enquiry is set such that Broadcast Enquiry microservice is not invoked.

Creating application-dev.properties

To make this work, an **application-dev.properties** file will be created in the resource folder of Customer Enquiry microservice, and properties which need to be set differently for development work are set accordingly. Refer to the following details:

application-dev.properties

```
enquiry.broadcast.enabled=N
```

Activating profile

There are different ways to activate a particular profile as part of running the application: It can be done programmatically; by setting it in **application.properties** or by setting it via environment variables. The most clean and easiest way here, is to set it via JVM system parameter. Run the application along with the following JVM argument and the **`dev`** profile will be set for that running instance, as shown:

```
-Dspring.profiles.active=dev
```

When an active Spring profile such as dev is set then, Spring Boot follows a property resolution hierarchy. It reads the properties from both **`application.properties`** and **`application-dev.properties`**. In this hierarchy, the more specific properties file, **`application-dev.properties`**, takes precedence. Therefore, values defined in **`application-dev.properties`** override those in **`application.properties`**.

Externalizing configurations

In practical scenarios, a lot of configurations do need to be changed even for a particular application environment. To accommodate this dynamic nature, Spring Boot offers a built-in feature that allows all properties to be externalized whenever required. Externalization of properties means that their value can be set externally without necessarily being part of the code line, though it is better to have a default value. There are multiple ways to externalize the properties, and common ways to achieve this are as follows:

- External configuration files
- Environment variables
- Command line arguments

For setting value of passwords and other secrets, applications are ideally integrated with **Vaults** or other similar applications such as **Amazon Secret Manager**, and so on. which are responsible for keeping the confidential information safe from the external world. Integration with a vault is documented later in this chapter.

External configuration files

By default, Spring also looks for configurations in a property file located alongside the application JAR. When the application is launched with an **`application.properties`** file in the same directory, these external configurations take precedence over the values defined within the JAR's properties file. This allows for easy externalization and customization of application configurations without altering the packaged JAR.

Recipe 21: Using external configuration file

In our application, there are two independent microservices and they can be running anywhere. Thus, the location of Broadcast Enquiry microservice should not be hard coded inside Customer Enquiry microservice, and instead should be parameterized so that the location can be modified as per the requirement.

Parameterizing location of Broadcast Enquiry microservice

Enhance Customer Enquiry microservices to parameterize the location of Broadcast Enquiry microservice. Refer to the following code:

application.properties

```
# Existing properties
enquiry.broadcast.baseurl=http://localhost:8081
```

EnquiryService.java

```
// Package declaration and import statements
@Service
public class EnquiryService {

// Existing business logic
 @Value("${enquiry.broadcast.baseurl}")
 String broadcastBaseUrl;

public void customerEnquiry(int customerId, String financialProductName) {
// Existing business logic
}

private void broadcastEnquiry(int customerId, String financialProductName, Date requestDate) {
   WebClient client = WebClient.builder().baseUrl(broadcastBaseUrl).defaultHeader(HttpHeaders.CONTENT_TYPE, MediaType.APPLICATION_JSON_VALUE).build();

  // Existing business logic
  }
}
```

Externalizing Broadcast Enquiry location

Another **`application.properties`** needs to be created adjacent to the application **`jar`**, which overrides the value defined in the application **`jar`**.

```
├── application.properties
└── customer-enquiry-0.0.1-SNAPSHOT.jar
0 directories, 2 files
```

Execute the following command to start the microservice:

```
java -jar customer-enquiry-0.0.1-SNAPSHOT.jar
```

The configuration value defined in the external property file gets the preference over the one defined inside the `jar` file.

Environment variables

Configurations can be defined as environment variables, and Spring boot application will set values of properties using those environment variables.

Recipe 22: Using environment variables

Run the following command to set the properties as environment variables:

On Windows

```
set enquiry.broadcast.baseurl=http://localhost:8084
```

On Linux

```
export enquiry.broadcast.baseurl=http://localhost:8084
```

Once the environment variable is set, run the following command to start the microservice:

```
java -jar customer-enquiry-0.0.1-SNAPSHOT.jar
```

The environment variable gets the preference over the one defined in the external properties file.

Command line arguments

Configurations can directly be passed to the application via command line, and the Spring boot application will set values of properties using those command line arguments.

Recipe 23: Using command line arguments

Run the following command to start the microservice:

```
java -jar customer-enquiry-0.0.1-SNAPSHOT.jar -
enquiry.broadcast.baseurl=http://localhost:8083
```

Here, the property **`enquiry.broadcast.baseurl`** is passed as an argument while running the application via command line. It gets preference over the value defined in the environment variables.

Configuration override order

The preference in which properties are loaded are as follows:

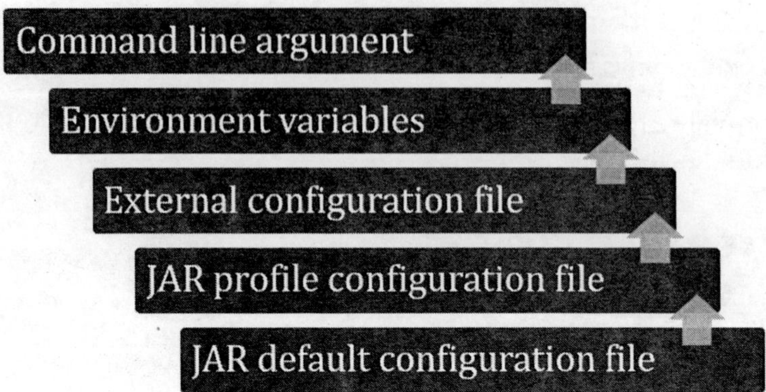

***Figure 3.1**: Configuration preference order*

The above order is in increasing order of precedency bottom-up where **`application.properties`** inside the **`jar`**, has the least precedence and property value passed via command line argument has the highest precedence.

Version controlled configurations

As we have seen in previous section, it is not difficult to pass the configuration value to the Spring Configuration. There are multiple ways to perform the same, but none of them is handy in controlling the configuration values passed to the application.

In real and practical application development, configurations are equally important to the code and needs to be version controlled so the changes to them can be easily tracked. To resolve this issue, Spring has something called **Spring Cloud Config Server** which is nothing but set of HTTP APIs running on top of a backend storage. The backend storage is pluggable but for all practical reasons, Git repository is commonly used across the industry.

Recipe 24: Creating Spring Cloud Config Server

It is used as a central place to manage configurations for all the application servers/ microservices and for different environments.

The steps required to set up a Spring Cloud Config Server backed by a Git repository for version controlling the configurations are provided here. Once done, a separate Git repository should be created, and the code changes for Config Server should be pushed to this Git repository, for keeping it version controlled.

Configure server Maven project

Create a new Maven project using the eclipse IDE with a name **Config Server**.

The code for **pom.xml** is as follows:

```
<project xmlns="http://maven.apache.org/POM/4.0.0" xmlns:xsi="http://www.w3.org/2001/XMLSchema-instance" xsi:schemaLocation="http://maven.apache.org/POM/4.0.0 https://maven.apache.org/xsd/maven-4.0.0.xsd">
  <modelVersion>4.0.0</modelVersion>
  <groupId>com.fsm</groupId>
  <artifactId>config-server</artifactId>
  <version>0.0.1-SNAPSHOT</version>
  <name>Configuration Server</name>
  <description>Configuration Server for Financial Services Marketplace microservices </description>

  <parent>
  <groupId>org.springframework.boot</groupId>
  <artifactId>spring-boot-starter-parent</artifactId>
  <version>3.1.3</version>
  </parent>

 <properties>
  <java.version>17</java.version>
  <spring-cloud.version>2022.0.3</spring-cloud.version>
 </properties>

 <dependencyManagement>
    <dependencies>
         <dependency>
             <groupId>org.springframework.cloud</groupId>
             <artifactId>spring-cloud-dependencies</artifactId>
             <version>${spring-cloud.version}</version>
             <type>pom</type>
             <scope>import</scope>
```

```
            </dependency>
        </dependencies>
    </dependencyManagement>

    <dependencies>
        <dependency>
            <groupId>org.springframework.boot</groupId>
            <artifactId>spring-boot-starter-security</artifactId>
        </dependency>
        <dependency>
            <groupId>org.springframework.cloud</groupId>
            <artifactId>spring-cloud-starter-config</artifactId>
        </dependency>
        <dependency>
            <groupId>org.springframework.cloud</groupId>
            <artifactId>spring-cloud-config-server</artifactId>
        </dependency>
    </dependencies>

<build>
  <plugins>
   <plugin>
    <groupId>org.springframework.boot</groupId>
    <artifactId>spring-boot-maven-plugin</artifactId>
    <executions>
     <execution>
      <id>repackage</id>
     </execution>
    </executions>
   </plugin>
   <plugin>
    <groupId>org.apache.maven.plugins</groupId>
    <artifactId>maven-compiler-plugin</artifactId>
```

```
      <configuration>
        <compilerVersion>${java.version}</compilerVersion>
        <source>${java.version}</source>
        <target>${java.version}</target>
        <encoding>UTF-8</encoding>
        <useIncrementalCompilation>false</useIncrementalCompilation>
      </configuration>
    </plugin>
  </plugins>
</build>

</project>
```

Creating server application class

Create an application Java class that needs to be invoked in order to start the application. Furthermore, it internally launches the application server on the configured port and runs the Config Server on top of it.

The code for **ConfigSeverApplication.java** is as follows:

```
package com.fsm.configserver;

import org.springframework.boot.SpringApplication;
import org.springframework.boot.autoconfigure.SpringBootApplication;
import org.springframework.cloud.config.server.EnableConfigServer;

@SpringBootApplication
@EnableConfigServer
public class ConfigSeverApplication {

  public static void main(String[] args) {
    SpringApplication.run(ConfigSeverApplication.class, args);
  }
}
```

Here, the annotation **@EnableConfigServer** is responsible for making this application act like a Config Server.

Creating configuration Git repository

Create a Git repository with a name **FSM Configurations** to maintain the configurations. The repository will be used to track all the changes done in the configurations and will help in version controlling them.

The format of creating the properties inside the Git repository is as follows:
`{application}-{profile}.properties`

Here,

- `application` is the name of the application or microservice.
- `profile` is the name of the profile for that application. Different files can be created for different profiles of an application.

Figure 3.2 features Git repository structure for storing configurations:

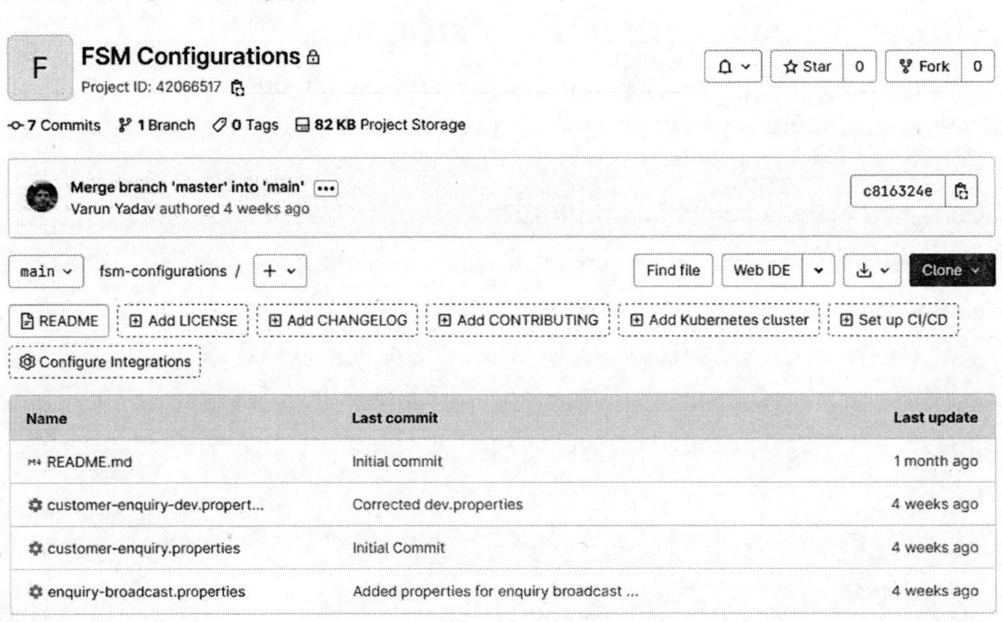

***Figure 3.2:** FSM configurations Git repository*

In the preceding figure, we created three property files in the Git repository corresponding to the two projects Customer Enquiry and Enquiry Broadcast, and they are as follows:

- Customer Enquiry
    - `customer-enquiry.properties`
    - `customer-enquiry-dev.properties`

- Enquiry Broadcast
  - o **enquiry-broadcast.properties**

The contents of the property files are exactly the same as what has been in their projects. The property files will be fetched from the Config Server and the desired configurations are then used in the corresponding applications.

Point Config Server to configuration Git Repository

The configuration server must be modified to specify the source from which it should retrieve the property files. This is again a configuration that needs to be done inside Config Server's application properties.

Create **application.properties** in the resources folder of Config Server with the required details. Refer to the following code:

```
server.port=8888
spring.cloud.config.server.git.uri=https://gitlab.com/financial-service-
marketplace/fsm-configurations
spring.cloud.config.server.git.username=yadavvarun1
spring.cloud.config.server.git.password=*****
spring.cloud.config.server.git.clone-on-start=true
spring.security.user.name=fsmConfigAdmin
spring.security.user.password=password
```

Here,

- **spring.cloud.config.server.git.uri** is the URI of the Git repository.
- **spring.cloud.config.server.git.username** is the username to be used for accessing the Git repository.
- **spring.cloud.config.server.git.password** is the password of the corresponding user for accessing Git repository.
- **spring.cloud.config.server.git.clone-on-start** property defines whether to clone the repository on server startup or not, if the property is set to true and there is some error in connecting to the Git repository then the server will not start.
- **spring.security.user.name** and **spring.security.user.password** are the username and password for Spring Config Server, respectively. Whatever username and password are set here, need to be passed in the request from respective microservices, for connecting to the Config Server.

Values of all the preceding properties should be configurable and could be passed during the run time.

Accessing configurations

Configurations can be accessed from the Config Server, using the following Git-backed configuration API.

`http://{hostname}:{port}/{application}/{profile}[/{label}`

Here,

- **`hostname`** is the name of the hostname where Config Server is running.
- **`port`** is the port on which Config Server is running.
- **`application`** is the name of the application for which configuration needs to be fetched.
- **`profile`** is the profile for which configuration needs to be fetched.
- **`label`** is optional and refers to a Git branch.

Example 1:

http://localhost:8888/customer-enquiry/dev

Output:


```
{
  "name":"customer-enquiry",
  "profiles":[
    "dev"
  ],
  "label":null,
  "version":"89648457a855bad5c3f1cec0ffac73eda781ffc2",
  "state":null,
  "propertySources":[
    {
      "name":"https://gitlab.com/financial-service-marketplace/fsm-
configurations/customer-enquiry-dev.properties",
      "source":{
        "enquiry.broadcast.enabled":"N"
      }
    },
    {
      "name":"https://gitlab.com/financial-service-marketplace/fsm-
configurations/customer-enquiry.properties",
      "source":{
```

```
        "spring.datasource.url":"jdbc:postgresql://fs-marketplace.
cbgzpif7rd3e.us-east-1.rds.amazonaws.com:5432/postgres",
        "spring.datasource.username":"postgres",
        "spring.datasource.password":"secret11",
        "spring.jpa.properties.hibernate.default_schema":"customer_
enquiry",
        "spring.jpa.show-sql":"true",
        "spring.jpa.properties.hibernate.format_sql":"true",
        "enquiry.broadcast.enabled":"Y",
        "enquiry.broadcast.baseurl":"http://localhost:8081"
      }
    }
  ]
}
```


The response is in the JSON format, containing properties and their values for both **dev** and default **profiles**.

Example 2:

http://localhost:8888/enquiry-broadcast/default

Output:


```
{
  "name":"enquiry-broadcast",
  "profiles":[
    "default"
  ],
  "label":null,
  "version":"89648457a855bad5c3f1cec0ffac73eda781ffc2",
  "state":null,
  "propertySources":[
    {
      "name":"https://gitlab.com/financial-service-marketplace/fsm-configura-
tions/enquiry-broadcast.properties",
      "source":{
        "server.port":"8081",
        "spring.datasource.url":"jdbc:postgresql://fs-marketplace.cbgzpi-
f7rd3e.us-east-1.rds.amazonaws.com:5432/postgres",
        "spring.datasource.username":"postgres",
        "spring.datasource.password":"secret11",
        "spring.jpa.properties.hibernate.default_schema":"enquiry_broad-
cast",
        "customer.enquiry.baseurl":"http://localhost:8080"
      }
```

```
    }
  ]
}
```

As the profile passed in the API is the default profile, the response only contains the properties from the default configuration file, that is, **enquiry-broadcast.properties**.

Config server details in microservices

Both the microservices need to connect to the Spring Cloud Config Server. For this, the microservices need to be enhanced to have a feature to connect to the Spring Cloud Config Server and this is done by adding the following **dependency** in the respective **pom** files.

Pom.xml

```
<properties>
     <spring-cloud.version>2022.0.3</spring-cloud.version>
</properties>

<dependencyManagement>
   <dependencies>
         <dependency>
              <groupId>org.springframework.cloud</groupId>
              <artifactId>spring-cloud-dependencies</artifactId>
              <version>${spring-cloud.version}</version>
              <type>pom</type>
              <scope>import</scope>
         </dependency>
   </dependencies>
</dependencyManagement>
<dependency>
      <groupId>org.springframework.cloud</groupId>
      <artifactId>spring-cloud-starter-config</artifactId>
</dependency>
```

Here, the **DependencyManagement** tag makes sure that the compatible version of the Spring Cloud Starter Config is being added. The **dependency** needs to be added in both Customer Enquiry and Enquiry Broadcast microservices.

Moreover, both the microservices Customer Enquiry and Enquiry Broadcast needs to know the details to connect to the Config Server for fetching the required configurations. These are again configured in the **application.properties** of the respective microservices. The previous configurations are now redundant as the same has been moved to Git repository. Now there is no need to have profile specific property file inside the applications.

```
Customer Enquiry: application.properties

spring.application.name=customer-enquiry
spring.config.import=configserver:http://localhost:8888
spring.cloud.config.username=fsmConfigAdmin
spring.cloud.config.password=password

Enquiry Broadcast: application.properties

spring.application.name=enquiry-broadcast
spring.config.import=configserver:http://localhost:8888
spring.cloud.config.username=fsmConfigAdmin
spring.cloud.config.password=password
```

Here,

- **spring.application.name** is the name of the application the particular property is part of, and this is the same name with which the configuration file has been created under the Git repository.
- **spring.config.import** is the URI where the Spring Config Server is running.
- **spring.security.user.name** and **spring.security.user.password** are username and password respectively, for accessing the Spring Config Server.

Again, values of all the preceding properties are not required to be hard coded in the application but can be passed on at run time, as discussed earlier in this chapter.

During the microservices startup the following events takes place:

1. Connect to the Spring Cloud Config Server
2. Fetch all configuration values via API
3. Pass the values to the microservices
4. Application bootstrapping

Secured configurations

Using Git repository as SCM (Source code management) tool for Config Server as backend is an ideal way to version control the configurations and it even supports encryption for storing secrets and other sensitive information. However, many organizations refrain from storing the passwords and certificates in Git repositories due to security reasons. To save us from this, **Vault** comes into the picture.

Vault is a software tool designed for securely storing secrets in an encrypted manner. Access to these secrets is protected by a master password or other authentication methods. Several implementations provide this functionality, including Secret Server, CyberArk, BeyondTrust, and HashiCorp Vault. Among these, **HashiCorp Vault** is the most widely adopted and renowned solution in the industry.

Recipe 25: Integrating with HashiCorp Vault

Spring offers a library designed for seamless integration with Vault, enabling the enhancement of the Spring Config Server by incorporating a composite repository that combines both Git and Vault repositories. The properties returned by the Config Server will be a composition of properties stored in both Git repository and HashiCorp Vault. In this case, all the properties except database credentials will be fetched from the Git repo, and value of database username and password which is a secret, will be fetched from the Vault. Values from Vault gets a precedence over values from Git, while fetching the property values from the Config Server.

Before enhancing the application, let us first setup an instance of HashiCorp Vault.

Setting up a Vault

Follow the below steps to install HashiCorp Vault in your Windows/Linux machine:

1. Download the package from the Vault official website.
2. The package is downloaded as a zip archive.
3. Unzip the package
4. Vault runs on a single binary named **`vault`**
5. Add the **`vault`** binary to system **`PATH`** variable as per your operating system configuration.

Once installed, try running the following command to verify that it has been successfully installed:

```
vault
```

If **vault** is accessible, then it will display the available commands for the Vault. Refer to *Figure 3.3* for the list of commands available for a Vault:

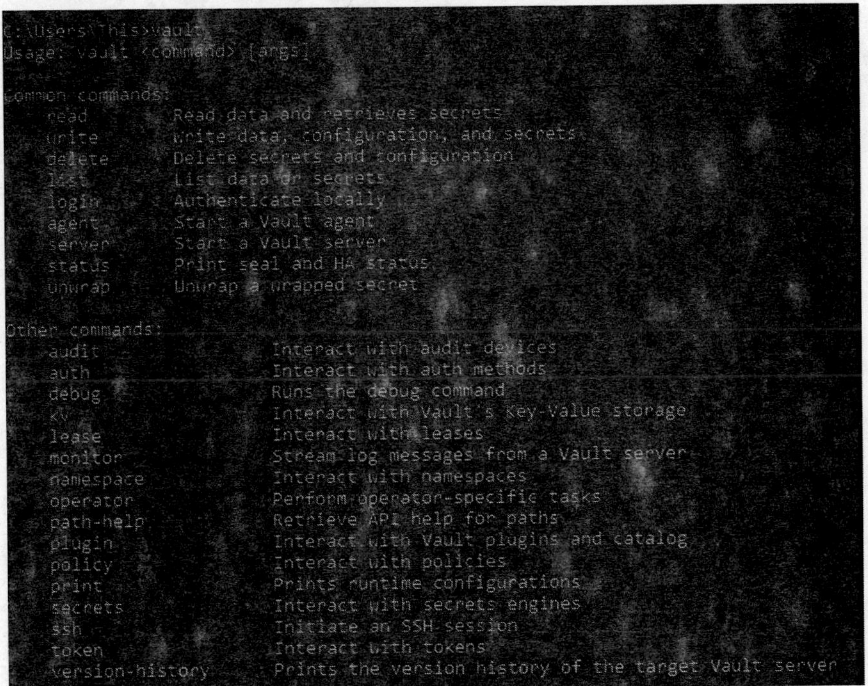

Figure 3.3: Output of vault command

The Vault server needs to be started to proceed, and from development perspective, **dev** mode should be used. Using HashiCorp Vault in production requires a separate license. For starting the Vault server with the dev profile, run the following command:

```
vault server -dev -dev-root-token-id="00000000-0000-0000-0000-000000000000"
```

Here,

- **dev** is a mode in which the server needs to be started. In this mode, Vault runs in-memory and starts unsealed.
- **dev-root-token-id** sets the token that needs to be used to access the Vault. It is not recommended to use simple tokens in the production environments.

Output:

```
WARNING! Dev mode is enabled! In this mode, Vault runs entirely in-memory
and starts unsealed with a single unseal key. The root token is already
authenticated to the CLI, so you can immediately begin using Vault.
```

```
You may need to set the following environment variables:

PowerShell:
    $env:VAULT_ADDR="http://127.0.0.1:8200"
cmd.exe:
    set VAULT_ADDR=http://127.0.0.1:8200

The unseal key and root token are displayed below in case you want to
seal/unseal the Vault or re-authenticate.

Unseal Key: ChuSffS0sE/CG2J6wa2NORPAWiASAVz9W+c3XswXS+s=
Root Token: 00000000-0000-0000-0000-000000000000

Development mode should NOT be used in production installations!
```

The preceding output confirms that the Vault server is running in the **dev** mode and can be accessed using the provided URL and token. Run the following commands in a separate Command Prompt, before Vault is being accessed to store and retrieve passwords:

```
set VAULT_ADDR=http://127.0.0.1:8200
vault status
```

Refer to *Figure 3.4* for the output of the preceding commands:

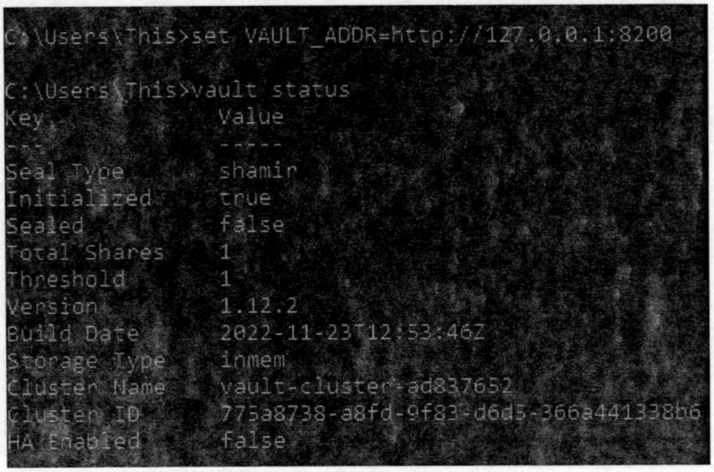

```
C:\Users\This>set VAULT_ADDR=http://127.0.0.1:8200

C:\Users\This>vault status
Key             Value
---             -----
Seal Type       shamir
Initialized     true
Sealed          false
Total Shares    1
Threshold       1
Version         1.12.2
Build Date      2022-11-23T12:53:46Z
Storage Type    inmem
Cluster Name    vault-cluster-ad837652
Cluster ID      775a8738-a8fd-9f83-d6d5-366a441338b6
HA Enabled      false
```

Figure 3.4: Output of vault status command

Storing secrets in a Vault

Secrets in the Vault are stored at different paths, run the following command to get a list preconfigured paths in the Vault:

`vault secrets list`

Refer to *Figure 3.5* for the list of paths configured in the Vault:

```
C:\Users\This>vault secrets list
Path          Type         Accessor              Description
----          ----         --------              -----------
cubbyhole/    cubbyhole    cubbyhole_109e779d    per-token private secret storage
identity/     identity     identity_eb887965     identity store
secret/       kv           kv_25ba9059           key/value secret storage
sys/          system       system_8cd7efca       system endpoints used for control, policy and debugging
```

***Figure 3.5**: Output of vault secret list command*

Here, **`secret/`** is a path that stores secrets in **Key Value** pair. It is also possible to enable a custom path if required. Run the following command to store secrets in **`vault`** at path **`secret/`** in the form of **Key** and **Values**:

```
vault kv put secret/customer-enquiry spring.datasource.username=postgres
spring.datasource.password=secret11
```

Here,

- **`customer-enquiry`** is the name set in the property **`spring.application.name`** of the application that will be accessing the Config Server for the configurations.

It can be verified that the secrets have been stored successfully by fetching them using the following command:

`vault kv get secret/customer-enquiry`

Refer to *Figure 3.6* for the secrets stored at the path **`secret/customer-enquiry`**:

```
C:\Users\This>vault kv get secret/customer-enquiry
======== Secret Path ========
secret/data/customer-enquiry

======= Metadata =======
Key                Value
---                -----
created_time       2023-02-03T07:25:16.6323993Z
custom_metadata    <nil>
deletion_time      n/a
destroyed          false
version            9

=============== Data ===============
Key                           Value
---                           -----
spring.datasource.password    secret11
spring.datasource.username    postgres
```

***Figure 3.6**: Secrets stored in the Vault*

Config Server with composite backend

Currently, the backend system for our Config Server is a Git repository, and it needs to be enhanced to have a composite backend comprising of both Git and Vault, so that the properties returned by the Config Server is a union of both properties from Git and Vault.

Enhance Spring Config Server to add a dependency in its **pom.xml** file to support Vault.

```
<dependency>
        <groupId>org.springframework.vault</groupId>
        <artifactId>spring-vault-core</artifactId>
</dependency>
```

Once **dependency** has been added, Config Server needs to be made aware of the Vault by providing all the required vault property values to it.

Application.properties

```
# Existing config server properties
spring.cloud.config.server.vault.port:8200
spring.cloud.config.server.vault.host:127.0.0.1
spring.cloud.config.server.vault.scheme:http
spring.cloud.config.server.vault.authentication:TOKEN
spring.cloud.config.server.vault.token:00000000-0000-0000-0000-000000000000
spring.cloud.config.server.vault.kv-version:2

spring.profiles.active=git,vault
```

Setting the active profile to both **git** and **vault** makes sure that Config Server uses both Git repository and Vault, as a backend for returning the configurations.

In production environments, the value of token should not be hardcoded but needs to be passed as an environment variable.

Using the same URL pattern as discussed in the previous recipe to access the configuration, we have:

http://localhost:8888/customer-enquiry/default

Output:

```
{
  "name":"customer-enquiry",
  "profiles":[
    "default"
  ],
  "label":null,
```

```
  "version":null,
  "state":null,
  "propertySources":[
    {
      "name":"vault:customer-enquiry",
      "source":{
        "spring.datasource.password":"secret11",
        "spring.datasource.username":"postgres"
      }
    },
    {
      "name":"https://gitlab.com/financial-service-marketplace/fsm-configura-
tions/customer-enquiry.properties",
      "source":{
        "spring.datasource.url":"jdbc:postgresql://fs-marketplace.cbgzpi-
f7rd3e.us-east-1.rds.amazonaws.com:5432/postgres",
        "spring.datasource.username":"",
        "spring.datasource.password":"",
       "spring.jpa.properties.hibernate.default_schema":"customer_enquiry",
        "spring.jpa.show-sql":"true",
        "spring.jpa.properties.hibernate.format_sql":"true",
        "enquiry.broadcast.enabled":"Y",
        "enquiry.broadcast.baseurl":"http://localhost:8081"
      }
    }
  ]
}
```


In this case, the database credentials have been set to null in the property files and their values will be picked from the Vault secrets.

Refer to *Figure 3.7* to understand use of Config Server in securing and version controlling configurations:

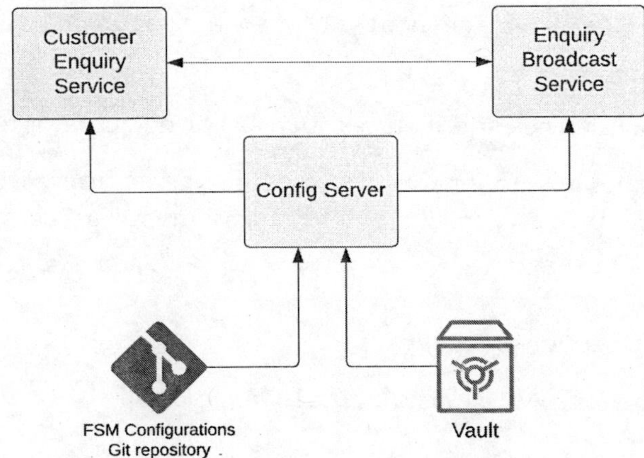

Figure 3.7: *Config Server with composite registry comprising of Git and Vault*

Dynamic configurations

Updating the configurations during the runtime helps applications to run without downtime. The concept is so powerful that the application can refresh its configurations with latest changes done in any of the properties outside the run context.

Recipe 26: Updating configurations at runtime

In our application design, microservices fetch the configurations from the Spring Config Server, which internally fetches the configurations from the Git repository and Vault. By default, Spring Config Server updates the local copies of all the properties as soon as there is any change in the property files on the Git repository or a secret in a Vault. This means that the only change that is required to be done is at the microservices end to refresh its properties from the Config Server, once the new values of the properties have been committed in the Git repository or updated in the Vault.

Configuring Spring Actuator

The Spring Actuator is mainly used for monitoring the overall health of the application. It has different predefined endpoints for different purposes, and will be discussed in detail, later on in the book. The endpoint that is important here is **`/refresh`**, which reloads all Environment property sources and publishes an event **`EnvironmentChangeEvent`**, which means that the environment has changed.

Microservices need to be enhanced. Add the following dependency in their **`pom.xml`** files:

`pom.xml`

```
<dependency>
      <groupId>org.springframework.boot</groupId>
      <artifactId>spring-boot-starter-actuator</artifactId>
</dependency>
```

The preceding dependencies add features such as spring actuator to the application.

The endpoint **`/refresh`** is not enabled by default, and so, there is a need to enable it by setting the following property in Customer Enquiry microservice:

`application.properties`

```
# Existing config server properties

management.endpoints.web.exposure.include=refresh
```

Using @RefreshScope

Spring cloud has an annotation **@RefreshScope**, that when used on a component, changes its default scope from singleton to refresh. If the scope is refresh and **EnvironmentChangeEvent** occurs, Spring clears its internal cache for that component and re-instantiates it with the latest configuration values.

To use **@RefreshScope**, the following dependency needs to be added to the Customer Enquiry microservice:

pom.xml

```
<dependency>
        <groupId>org.springframework.cloud</groupId>
        <artifactId>spring-cloud-starter</artifactId>
</dependency>
```

Here, the version mentioned is the one that is compatible with the corresponding Spring Boot version.

Now, the **EnquiryService** of Customer Enquiry microservice needs to be enhanced to use **@RefreshScope** annotation.

EnquiryService.java

```
// Package declaration and import statements

@Service
@RefreshScope
public class EnquiryService {

// Existing business logic
}
```

Using this annotation, the scope of **EnquiryService** has been changed from default singleton to refresh. The component will be re-instantiated every time on the environment change event, if there is any change in the value of corresponding properties referred from the given component. This is important as it protects the component to be recreated just because an event has been raised, as it only makes sense to do it if there is change in any of the configurations.

Validating the solution

To validate that the value of a property is being updated at run time, let us add an interface in Customer Enquiry microservice to return the values of the properties used in it.

`EnquiryPortalController.java`

```
// Package declaration and import statements

public class EnquiryPortalController {

// Existing business logic

  @GetMapping(path = "/config")
  public String getConfigurations() {
   return JsonNodeFactory.instance.objectNode()
       .put("enquiry.broadcast.enabled", enquiryService.getBroadcastEnabled())
         .put("enquiry.broadcast.baseurl", enquiryService.getBroadcastBaseUrl()).toString();
  }
}
```

The preceding interface returns the current values of the properties **`enquiry.broadcast.enabled`** and **`enquiry.broadcast.baseurl`** in the microservice.

Start the Config Server and then Enquiry Service microservice. Do a Get call to the following API, and it will return the values of the of the properties **`enquiry.broadcast.enabled`** and **`enquiry.broadcast.baseurl`**.

API Request URL:

http://localhost:8080/config

Response:

```
{
  "enquiry.broadcast.enabled":"Y",
  "enquiry.broadcast.baseurl":"http://localhost:8081"
}
```

Now, update the value of the property **`enquiry.broadcast.enabled`** to **`N`** in **`customer-enquiry.properties`** of Git repository **FSM Configurations**. As soon as the changes get merged in the `main` branch, they will be picked up by the Config Server. Do a Post call to the following refresh API of the actuator.

Actuator API:

http://localhost:8080/actuator/refresh

API Response:

```
[
    "config.client.version",
    "enquiry.broadcast.enabled"
]
```

The response shows that the property **`enquiry.broadcast.enabled`** has been updated and its value has been refreshed in the microservice. This can be validated by again running the following API:

API Request URL:

http://localhost:8080/config

API Response:

```
{
  "enquiry.broadcast.enabled":"N",
  "enquiry.broadcast.baseurl":"http://localhost:8081"
}
```

Hence validated that the value of the property has been updated in the microservice without restarting the application or any down time.

Conclusion

In this chapter, we have learnt the use of configurations in the application and different ways to externalize them and their order of preference. We also learnt how configurations can be version controlled in a Git repository and accessed via a Config Server. To maintain the secrecy of secrets, HashiCorp Vault has been installed, and Config Server has been enhanced to use it as a composite backend along with a Git repository. In the end, we learned how configuration values can be updated during the run without restarting the application.

In the next chapter, we will learn the ways to implement dynamic lookout of services and different ways of service discovery.

Points to remember

- Configuration files can also assign values to properties using environment variables and support default values in case no value is being set for that environment variable.
- Value for accessing vault should always be passed as an environment variable in production systems.
- A Config Server is not necessary to access a Vault, and if required, an application can directly communicate with the Vault server to fetch secrets.
- To support high availability, there should always be more than one instance of Config Server running, and to support this, backend system should be centrally located like a Git repository or a Vault but not local file systems.

Questions

1. What will happen on starting an application if the Config Server is not available? How can the situation be prevented?
2. What is the way to configure profile specific properties in a Vault?
3. Can variables defined in beans with explicit singleton scope and assigned values using configurations be refreshed on the fly?
4. How does an Actuator refresh work, in case of multi-node environment?

Join our book's Discord space

Join the book's Discord Workspace for Latest updates, Offers, Tech happenings around the world, New Release and Sessions with the Authors:

https://discord.bpbonline.com

CHAPTER 4

Implementing Dynamic Services

Introduction

The previous chapter covered the application configuration and different ways to externalize them. It also explained the steps required to secure and version control the externalized configuration using **Spring Cloud Config Server** and eventually talked about updating the configurations on the fly without restarting the application or microservice.

In this chapter, we will begin with discussing dynamic services and the need of service discovery in the world of microservices. Then we will discuss different types of service discoveries with examples, along with their pros and cons, and in the end, we will explain different patterns of service registry and which one to use when.

Structure

In this chapter, we will discuss following topics:

- Importance of service discovery
- Service discovery patterns
    - o Client-side service discovery
    - o Server-side service discovery

- Client-side versus server-side service discovery
- Service registration patterns
  - o Self-registration
  - o Third-party registration

Objectives

By the end of this chapter, we will learn about dynamism in the world of microservices and how the concept of service discovery comes as a saviour in resolving the concerns raised because of this dynamic nature of microservices. Next, we will get to know the different ways of implementing service discovery, that is, client-side and server-side discovery and along the way, we will enhance our solution **Financial Service Marketplace** to implement ways of service discovery. In the end, we will differentiate between the service discovery patterns and talk about options for doing service registration.

Importance of service discovery

Service discovery is a crucial aspect in the world of microservices architecture. In a microservices environment, where applications are broken down into small, independently deployable services that communicate with each other, the challenge arises of how to locate and communicate with these services effectively, especially as they can be dynamically deployed and scaled. One way is to wire the locations of the service to be communicated via configurations but that is old fashioned and not practical in modern microservice architectures.

Service discovery addresses this challenge by providing a mechanism for services to register themselves when they start up and to discover the location of other services within the same network. This allows services to communicate with each other without hardcoding IP addresses or endpoints, which can become cumbersome and error-prone as the number of services grows and their locations change.

The main components of a service discovery system are:

- **Service registry:** This is a centralized database or repository where services register themselves along with their network location and other relevant metadata. The registry keeps track of which services are currently available and their corresponding locations.
- **Service registrar:** Each service instance (running container or virtual machine) is responsible for registering itself with the service registry upon startup. It provides information about its service name, IP address, port, and potentially other metadata.

- **Service discovery client:** Any service that wants to communicate with another service queries the service registry to obtain the necessary information about the location (IP and port) of the desired service. The client can periodically refresh this information to stay up-to-date.
- **Load balancing:** Service discovery often goes hand-in-hand with load balancing. When there are multiple instances of a service available, a load balancer can distribute incoming requests across these instances to ensure optimal resource utilization and responsiveness.

Refer to *Figure 4.1* to understand dynamic discovery of services:

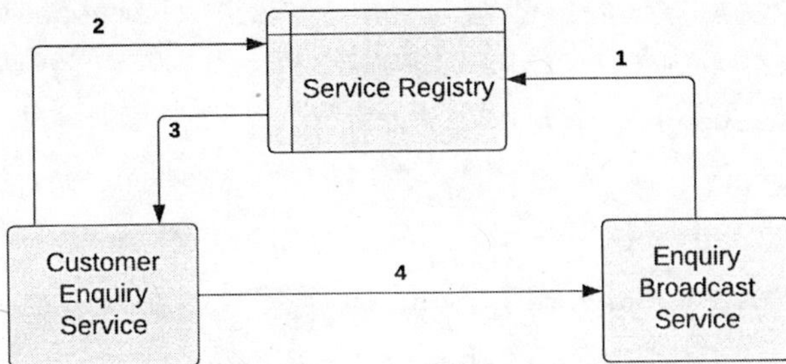

***Figure 4.1**: Customer Enquiry Service is using Service Registry to discover Enquiry Broadcast Service*

The details of steps that are performed for dynamic service discovery are as follows:

1. On startup, Enquiry Broadcast service registers itself with service registry by sharing its location.
2. Before invoking Enquiry Broadcast service, Customer Enquiry service contacts the service registry for the location of Enquiry Broadcast service.
3. Service registry searches for the location of Enquiry Broadcast service in its internal storage and returns it to Customer Enquiry service.
4. On getting the location, Customer Enquiry service invokes the Enquiry Broadcast service.

Thus, service registry is an important part of dynamic service discovery. There are several popular service discovery tools and technologies, including Netflix Eureka, Consul, and Zookeeper. These tools allow for automatic registration and de-registration of services, making it easier for developers to manage their microservice-based applications. The following recipe is on creating a discovery registry using Netflix Eureka.

Recipe 27: Creating discovery server

Spring Cloud does come with an implementation of a discovery server and it is called **Spring Cloud Eureka Server**. The steps required to setup a Spring Cloud Discovery Server that acts as a service registry for the application, are given below. Once done, a separate Git repository should be created, and the code changes for discovery server should be pushed to this Git repository for keeping it version controlled.

Configure server Maven project

Create a new Maven project using the eclipse IDE with a name **Discovery Server**.

The code for **pom.xml** is as follows:

```
<project xmlns="http://maven.apache.org/POM/4.0.0" xmlns:xsi="http://www.w3.org/2001/XMLSchema-instance" xsi:schemaLocation="http://maven.apache.org/POM/4.0.0 https://maven.apache.org/xsd/maven-4.0.0.xsd">
  <modelVersion>4.0.0</modelVersion>
  <groupId>com.fsm</groupId>
  <artifactId>discovery-server</artifactId>
  <version>0.0.1-SNAPSHOT</version>
  <name>Discovery Server</name>
  <description>Discovery Server for Financial Service Marketplace application</description>
  <parent>
     <groupId>org.springframework.boot</groupId>
     <artifactId>spring-boot-starter-parent</artifactId>
  <version>3.1.3</version>
  </parent>
  <properties>
     <java.version>17</java.version>
     <spring-cloud.version>2022.0.3</spring-cloud.version>
  </properties>
  <dependencyManagement>
   <dependencies>
         <dependency>
               <groupId>org.springframework.cloud</groupId>
```

```
                <artifactId>spring-cloud-dependencies</artifactId>
                <version>${spring-cloud.version}</version>
                <type>pom</type>
                <scope>import</scope>
            </dependency>
        </dependencies>
    </dependencyManagement>

     <dependencies>
   <dependency>
       <groupId>org.springframework.cloud</groupId>
        <artifactId>spring-cloud-starter-netflix-eureka-server</artifactId>
   </dependency>
     </dependencies>

     <build>
    <plugins>
     <plugin>
      <groupId>org.springframework.boot</groupId>
      <artifactId>spring-boot-maven-plugin</artifactId>
      <executions>
       <execution>
        <id>repackage</id>
       </execution>
      </executions>
     </plugin>
     <plugin>
      <groupId>org.apache.maven.plugins</groupId>
      <artifactId>maven-compiler-plugin</artifactId>
      <configuration>
       <compilerVersion>${java.version}</compilerVersion>
       <source>${java.version}</source>
       <target>${java.version}</target>
```

```
                <encoding>UTF-8</encoding>
                <useIncrementalCompilation>false</useIncrementalCompilation>
            </configuration>
        </plugin>
    </plugins>
</build>

</project>
```

Here, the latest version of Spring Boot, that is **3.1.3** is being used with Java version **17** and the compatible Spring Cloud dependencies. The dependency **spring-cloud-starter-gateway** makes this application act as a gateway server. The dependency **spring-cloud-starter-netflix-eureka-server** is responsible for providing all the required artifacts for creating a discovery server.

Creating server application class

Create an application Java class that needs to be invoked for starting the application, and it internally launches the application server on the configured port and runs the discovery server on top of it.

DiscoveryServerApplication.java

```
package com.fsm.servicediscovery;

import org.springframework.boot.SpringApplication;
import org.springframework.boot.autoconfigure.SpringBootApplication;
import org.springframework.cloud.netflix.eureka.server.EnableEurekaServer;

@SpringBootApplication
@EnableEurekaServer
public class DiscoveryServerApplication {

  public static void main(String[] args) {
    SpringApplication.run(DiscoveryServerApplication.class, args);
  }
}
```

Here, the annotation **@EnableEurekaServer** is responsible for making this application act like a discovery server.

Configuring discovery server

Create **`application.properties`** in the resources folder of the discovery server with the following configurations.

`Application.properties`

```
spring.application.name=etflix-eureka-server
server.port=8761
eureka.client.registerWithEureka=false
eureka.client.fetchRegistry=false
```

Here,

- **`server.port`** is the port on which the Eureka server will be running, and **8761** is the default port for Eureka server.
- **`eureka.client.registerWithEureka`** and **`eureka.client.fetchRegistry`** are set to false as Eureka server in itself is also an Eureka client and setting these properties to false will avoid unnecessary errors as there is no need to register a server with itself.

Refer to *Figure 4.2* for the Eureka server dashboard accessible on localhost and port **8761**:

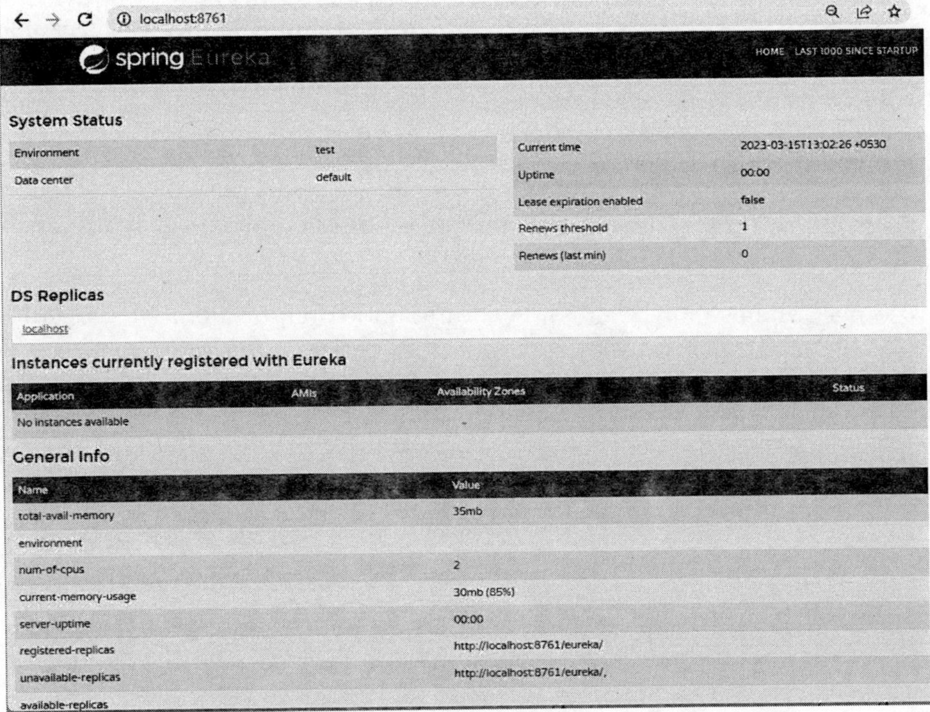

Figure 4.2*: Eureka server with currently no registered services*

Advanced service discovery features also helps to resolve issues such as network failure, service outages, and load balancing. If a service is unavailable, the discovery process can redirect the client to another instance of the same service. This way, service discovery provides resilience and fault tolerance to microservice-based applications, allowing them to continue functioning even in the event of failures.

Service discovery patterns

Service discovery is an essential component of a microservices architecture that enables various services to find and connect with one another. A methodical way to overcoming the difficulty of finding and accessing services in a distributed system, is provided by service discovery patterns. Client-side and server-side discovery are two typical service discovery patterns.

Client-side service discovery

In client-side discovery, each service instance registers itself with a service registry, and clients use the registry to find the needed service. The benefit of this strategy is that customers can select the appropriate service instance based on their unique requirements.

In client-side service discovery, the client oversees deciding which service instance to use, based on the data the service registry provides. To aid clients in making wise decisions, the register may include metadata such as IP addresses, port numbers, and health status. Without the aid of an intermediate such as a load balancer, the client can then communicate directly with the chosen service instance.

Client-side service discovery offers several benefits. By dividing out the burden for service discovery among several clients, it lessens the stress placed on the load balancer. Since clients can select the ideal instance based on their own criteria, it also enables more adaptable routing and load balancing schemes.

But it also necessitates more client-side coding and configuration, which could increase latency if the registry is out-of-date or if service instances are constantly added or removed. Moreover, client-side service discovery tightly bounds the service consuming other services with the service registry as the logic to discover the service needs to be built in each consumer service, irrespective of the programming language and the framework used. Refer to *Figure* 4.3 for the working of client-side service discovery:

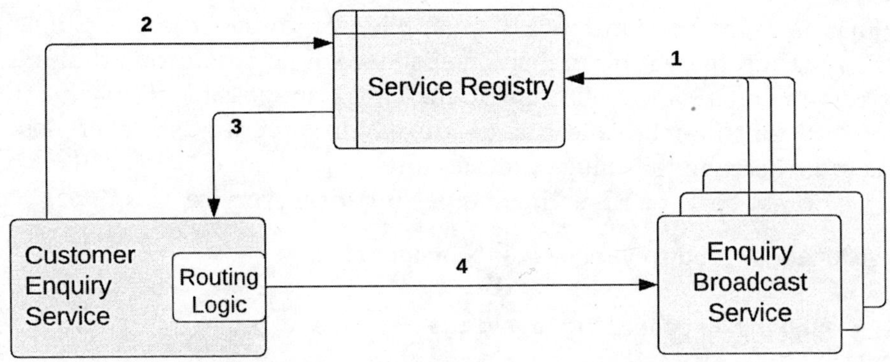

Figure 4.3: *Customer Enquiry Service is using client-side discovery to locate instances of Enquiry Broadcast Service*

In this case, Enquiry Broadcast services registers themselves with the service registry. Customer Enquiry service queries the service registry to get the details of the registered Enquiry Broadcast service instances and then uses the inbuilt load balancing and routing logic to call an instance of Enquiry Broadcast service.

Recipe 28: Client-side discovery using Eureka server

Eureka server as a discovery server has already been created as part of the previous recipe, which will be used for client-side service discovery. Enquiry Broadcast service code will be enhanced so that its instances will register themselves with the Eureka server on startup and Customer Enquiry service code will be enhanced to query the Eureka server to fetch the details of the registered Enquiry Broadcast service instances before invoking one of them.

Registering service with Eureka server

Enquiry Broadcast service needs to register itself with the discovery server that is the Eureka server on startup. This is simply achieved by adding the **spring-cloud-starter-netflix-eureka-client** dependency in the service application. Spring Boot automatically registers the application with the Eureka server on finding this dependency.

Enquiry Broadcast: pom.xml

```
<dependency>
    <groupId>org.springframework.cloud</groupId>
    <artifactId>spring-cloud-starter-netflix-eureka-client</artifactId>
</dependency>
```

We know that more than one instance of an application cannot run on a single port, but in practical scenarios, there is more than one instance of an application running together. If they are running on a same environment, then it is only possible if they are running on different ports. Spring Boot has a feature to auto assign server ports to every instance, and this is achieved by setting the value of server ports to **0**. Changes also needs to be done to configure the Eureka server URL in the Enquiry Broadcast service.

```
FSM Configurations/ enquiry-broadcast.properties

# Existing enquiry broadcast properties
server.port = 0
eureka.client.serviceUrl.defaultZone=http://localhost:8761/eureka
```

Now, on invoking Enquiry Broadcast service, a new instance of the service is started registering itself to the Eureka server.

Refer to *Figure 4.4* for the Eureka server dashboard, to view services registered with the application name:

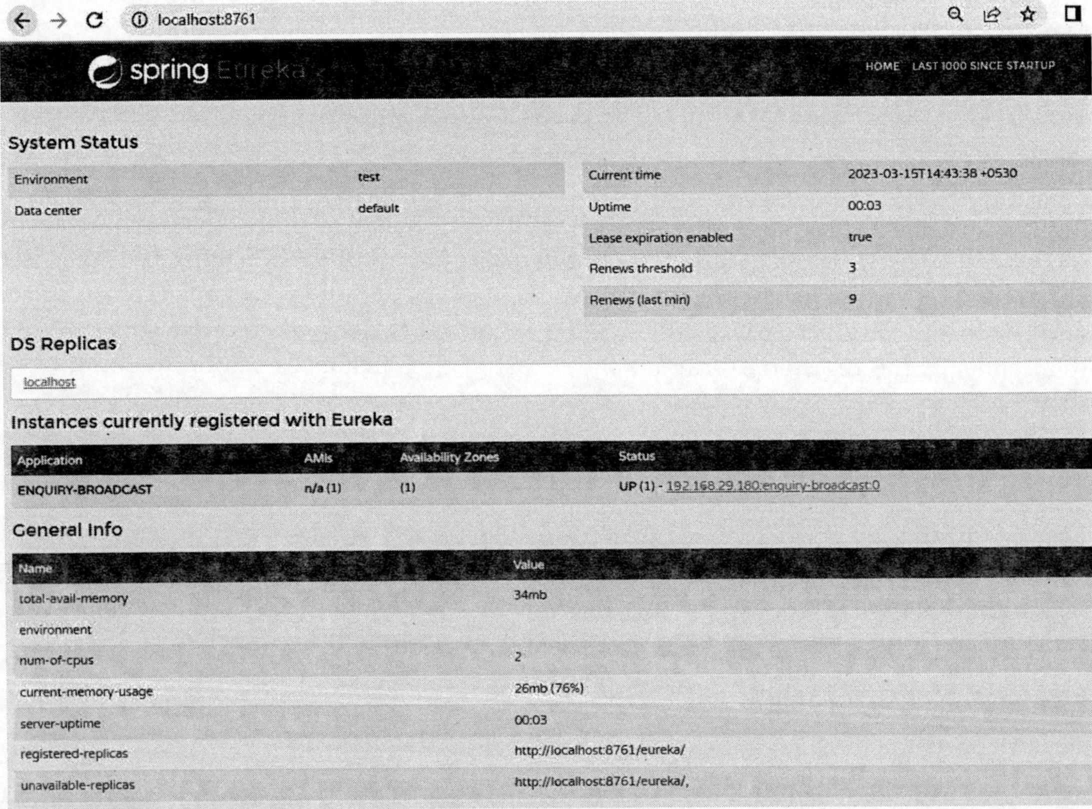

***Figure 4.4**: Eureka Server with application registered with the name ENQUIRY-BROADCAST*

The name with which the application is registered, is same as the name of the application configured in the **application.properties** of that service and it is insensitive to the case.

Service discovery and invocation

Base URL of Enquiry Broadcast service is as of now configured in the Customer Enquiry service. This needs to be modified such that Customer Enquiry service calls the service registry or Eureka server; in our case, to fetch the URL for Enquiry Broadcast service and then use it to invoke the service.

Like Enquiry Broadcast service, **spring-cloud-starter-netflix-eureka-client** needs to be added as a dependency in Customer Enquiry service.

Customer Enquiry: pom.xml

```
<dependency>
    <groupId>org.springframework.cloud</groupId>
    <artifactId>spring-cloud-starter-netflix-eureka-client</artifactId>
</dependency>
```

The application logic needs to be changed to use a **EurekaClient** to fetch the URL for Enquiry Broadcast service.

EnquiryService.java

```
// Package declaration and import statements

@Service
@RefreshScope
public class EnquiryService {

// Existing business logic

  @Value("${enquiry.broadcast.baseurl}")
  String broadcastBaseUrl;

  @Autowired
  EurekaClient discoveryClient;

// Existing business logic
```

```

private void broadcastEnquiry(int customerId, String financialProductName, Date requestDate) {

  String broadcastEnquiryURL= null;

// Static Broadcast Enquiry URL passed as configuration
// broadcastEnquiryURL= broadcastBaseUrl;

  InstanceInfo instance = discoveryClient.getNextServerFromEureka("ENQUIRY-BROADCAST", false);
// Broadcast Enquiry URL using Client-Side discovery
  broadcastEnquiryURL= instance.getHomePageUrl();

  WebClient client = WebClient.builder().baseUrl(broadcastEnquiryURL)
      .defaultHeader(HttpHeaders.CONTENT_TYPE, MediaType.APPLICATION_JSON_VALUE).build();

// Existing business logic
}
```

More matured libraries like Feign and Ribbon can be used in conjunction with a service registry to enhance load balancing capabilities in a microservices architecture. These libraries provide advanced features that simplify and improve the way services discover and interact with each other.

Server-side service discovery

In server-side discovery, each service instance registers itself with a service registry, and clients use a gateway, a load balancer or a proxy server which internally uses the registry to find the needed service and routes the requests to the appropriate service instance. With this approach, service instances self-register with a service registry that the load balancer or gateway keeps an eye on. When a client sends a request, the load balancer receives it and decides which service instance to use, based on numerous factors including load balancing algorithms, health status, or location.

There are various benefits to server-side service discovery. It simplifies the client-side code and lowers the volume of network queries by offloading the client's duty for service discovery. Moreover, it offers a centralized point of control for handling service instances, simplifying system scaling and maintenance.

Server-side service discovery does, however, have some down sides. If the load balancer or gateway malfunctions, it could result in a single point of failure. The configuration and infrastructure needed to set up and maintain the load balancer or gateway are also supplementary and extra overhead. Clients may also experience high response time as sometimes the chosen service instance can occasionally result in subpar performance. Refer to *Figure 4.5* for the working of server-side service discovery:

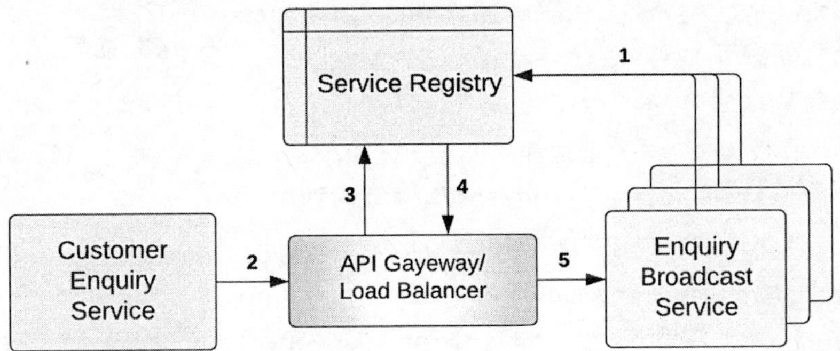

Figure 4.5*: Customer Enquiry service is using Server-Side Discovery to locate instances of Enquiry Broadcast service*

In this case, instances of Enquiry Broadcast services register themselves with the service registry. Customer Enquiry service queries the API gateway / load balancer which internally queries the server registry to get the details of the registered Enquiry Broadcast service instances and then uses the inbuilt load balancing and routing logic to call an instance of Enquiry Broadcast service. It is clear from the diagram itself that the number of hops increases in case of the server-side discovery compared to client-side discovery pattern.

Recipe 29: Creating gateway server

Spring Cloud Gateway is a lightweight, developer-friendly gateway built on top of Spring Framework 5, Spring Boot 2, and Project Reactor; and it is free and open-source. It provides a dynamic and flexible way to route, filter, and manage traffic between different services in your microservices ecosystem. Spring Cloud Gateway acts as an entry point for all incoming requests, allowing you to implement various cross-cutting concerns such as security, rate limiting, load balancing, and more in a centralized manner. Spring Cloud Gateway has other built-in filters available, such as routing, logging, rate limiting, and authentication and to achieve sophisticated routing and security needs, developers can modify and link these filters. Moreover, it provides non-blocking I/O, which makes it perfect for high-traffic, low-latency scenarios. It also supports reactive programming.

It supports server-side discovery by acting as a single point for all the requests and it dynamically finds the called service by querying a service registry which in this case, is Eureka server, where all the other services are registering themselves on their startup. Once done, a separate Git repository should be created, and the code changes for gateway server should be pushed to this Git repository for keeping it version controlled.

Configure server Maven project

Create a new Maven project using the eclipse IDE with a name **`Gateway Server`**.

The code for **`pom.xml`** is as follows:

```
<project xmlns="http://maven.apache.org/POM/4.0.0" xmlns:xsi="http://www.w3.org/2001/XMLSchema-instance" xsi:schemaLocation="http://maven.apache.org/POM/4.0.0 https://maven.apache.org/xsd/maven-4.0.0.xsd">
  <modelVersion>4.0.0</modelVersion>
  <groupId>com.fsm</groupId>
  <artifactId>gateway-server</artifactId>
  <version>0.0.1-SNAPSHOT</version>
  <name>Gateway Service</name>
   <description>Proxy Server for Server-Side Service Discovery</description>

  <parent>
      <groupId>org.springframework.boot</groupId>
      <artifactId>spring-boot-starter-parent</artifactId>
      <version>3.1.3</version>
  </parent>

  <properties>
      <java.version>17</java.version>
      <spring-cloud.version>2022.0.3</spring-cloud.version>
  </properties>

  <dependencyManagement>
   <dependencies>
        <dependency>
            <groupId>org.springframework.cloud</groupId>
            <artifactId>spring-cloud-dependencies</artifactId>
            <version>${spring-cloud.version}</version>
            <type>pom</type>
            <scope>import</scope>
```

```
            </dependency>
        </dependencies>
    </dependencyManagement>

    <dependencies>
   <dependency>
        <groupId>org.springframework.cloud</groupId>
        <artifactId>spring-cloud-starter-netflix-eureka-client</artifactId>
   </dependency>
   <dependency>
          <groupId>org.springframework.cloud</groupId>
        <artifactId>spring-cloud-starter-gateway</artifactId>
   </dependency>
     </dependencies>

      <build>
    <plugins>
     <plugin>
      <groupId>org.springframework.boot</groupId>
      <artifactId>spring-boot-maven-plugin</artifactId>
      <executions>
       <execution>
        <id>repackage</id>
       </execution>
      </executions>
     </plugin>
     <plugin>
      <groupId>org.apache.maven.plugins</groupId>
      <artifactId>maven-compiler-plugin</artifactId>
      <configuration>
       <compilerVersion>${java.version}</compilerVersion>
       <source>${java.version}</source>
       <target>${java.version}</target>
       <encoding>UTF-8</encoding>
```

```
        <useIncrementalCompilation>false</useIncrementalCompilation>
      </configuration>
    </plugin>
  </plugins>
 </build>
</project>
```

Here, the latest version of Spring Boot, that is **3.1.3** is being used with Java version **17** and the compatible Spring Cloud dependencies. The dependency **spring-cloud-starter-gateway** makes this application act as a gateway server. The dependency **spring-cloud-starter-netflix-eureka-client** is responsible for providing all the required artifacts for creating a discovery client as it needs to connect to the discovery server.

Create server application class

Create an application Java class that needs to be invoked for starting the application, and it internally launches the application server on the configured port and runs the gateway server on top of it.

GatewayServerApplication.java

```
package com.fsm.servicediscovery;

import org.springframework.boot.SpringApplication;
import org.springframework.boot.autoconfigure.SpringBootApplication;
import org.springframework.cloud.client.discovery.EnableDiscoveryClient;

@SpringBootApplication
@EnableDiscoveryClient
public class GatewayServerApplication {

 public static void main(String[] args) {
  SpringApplication.run(GatewayServerApplication.class, args);
 }
}
```

Configuring routing configuration

There are multiple ways in which a gateway server can be used, but in this case, it needs to perform service discovery by querying the discovery server. So, for that, routing mechanism needs to be configured using the following class:

RoutingConfiguration.java

```
package com.fsm.servicediscovery;

import org.springframework.cloud.gateway.route.RouteLocator;
import org.springframework.cloud.gateway.route.builder.
RouteLocatorBuilder;
import org.springframework.context.annotation.Bean;
import org.springframework.context.annotation.Configuration;

@Configuration
public class RoutingConfiguration {

  @Bean
  public RouteLocator configureRoute(RouteLocatorBuilder builder) {
     return builder.routes().route("broadcastId", r -> r.path("/broad-
cast/**").uri("lb://enquiry-broadcast"))
        .build();
  }
}
```

Here, a configuration has been setup such that for any requests with defined path (/**broadcast/****), need to be queried to the configured discovery server and requests need to be routed to the response from that discovery server. The preceding configuration is done programmatically but is also possible to do via properties file.

The gateway server can also be enhanced with add-on complex logic for filtering the requests, load balancing, and so on, which makes it very useful while implementing microservice architecture.

Configuring gateway server

Create **application.properties** in the resources folder of the gateway server with the following configurations.

Application.properties

```
server.port=8085
spring.application.name=gateway-server

eureka.client.serviceUrl.defaultZone=http://localhost:8761/eureka
```

Here,

- **server.port** is the port on which the gateway server will be running.
- **eureka.client.serviceUrl.defaultZone** makes gateway server know the URL for the Eureka server that is the service registry.

In conclusion, Spring Cloud Gateway offers a cutting-edge and scalable method for developing gateway services in a microservices architecture. It is a well-liked option among developers and companies wishing to implement cloud-native technologies because to its simplicity, flexibility, and extensibility.

Recipe 30: Server-side discovery using Spring Cloud Gateway

Enquiry Broadcast service as shown in the client-side discovery, is already registering itself with the service registry that is the discovery server. Moreover, as part of the previous recipe, Spring Cloud Gateway server has been created which acts as an API gateway and is responsible for the service discovery by querying the service registry. Thus, Customer Enquiry microservice needs to be enhanced to point to the gateway server while calling Enquiry Broadcast service and all work is then done by the gateway server regarding the discovery of the service and calling that service.

Configuring gateway server URL

The Customer Enquiry service needs to know the location of the gateway server which is configured in the properties of Customer Enquiry microservice as follows:

FSM Configurations/ customer-enquiry.properties

```
# Existing customer enquiry properties
gateway.service.url=http://localhost:8085
```

The property will be accessed in the application code in the subsequent section, though the value is hardcoded but can always be passed at runtime using multiple ways as discussed in the previous chapter, that is *Externalize Application Configuration*.

Gateway server invocation and service discovery

Like the way the base URL of Enquiry Broadcast service was initially passed as a configuration, the URL for the gateway server needs to be passed to the Customer Enquiry service.

EnquiryService.java

```
// Package declaration and import statements

```

```java
@Service
@RefreshScope
public class EnquiryService {

// Existing business logic

@Value("${enquiry.broadcast.baseurl}")
private String broadcastBaseUrl;

// @Autowired
// EurekaClient discoveryClient;

 @Value("${gateway.service.url}")
 private String gatewayServiceUrl;

// Existing business logic

private void broadcastEnquiry(int customerId, String financialProductName, Date requestDate) {

   String broadcastEnquiryURL = null;

//  Static Broadcast Enquiry URL passed as configuration
//  broadcastEnquiryURL = broadcastBaseUrl;

//  InstanceInfo instance = discoveryClient.getNextServerFromEureka("ENQUIRY-BROADCAST", false);
//  Broadcast Enquiry URL using Client-Side discovery
//  broadcastEnquiryURL = instance.getHomePageUrl();

//  Broadcast Enquiry URL using Server-Side discovery
   broadcastEnquiryURL = gatewayServiceUrl;

   WebClient client = WebClient.builder().baseUrl(broadcastEnquiryURL)
```

```
        .defaultHeader(HttpHeaders.CONTENT_TYPE, MediaType.APPLICATION_JSON_VALUE).build();

// Existing business Logic
}
```

While invoking Enquiry Broadcast service, Customer Enquiry service calls the gateway server and then all the work of discovering the exact location of the Enquiry Broadcast service and invoking, is responsibility of the gateway server.

Client-side versus server-side service discovery

The previous sections explained the working of both client-side and server-side service discovery patterns. In this section, we will be explaining the key differences between the two based on engineering aspects that play an important role in the lifecycle of a software application:

- **Responsibility**: In client-side service discovery, it is up to the client to find and choose the right service instance; in server-side service discovery, it is up to a load balancer or gateway to direct traffic to the right service instance.
- **Configuration**: In contrast to server-side service discovery, which involves more infrastructure and configuration to set up and maintain the load balancer or gateway, client-side service discovery involves more client-side programming.
- **Flexibility**: Client-side service discovery gives users the ability to choose the best service instance for their needs. However, server-side service discovery offers less freedom because the load balancer or gateway chooses the instance based on its own standards.
- **Failure resilience**: Client-side service discovery has the potential to be more resilient to failures because clients can continue to communicate with active service instances even if the registry is momentarily down, whereas server-side service discovery may result in the creation of a single point of failure if the load balancer or gateway malfunctions.
- **Scalability**: Server-side service discovery has the potential to be more scalable because a load balancer or gateway can handle a huge volume of requests and distribute them among several service instances.
- **Security**: Server-side service discovery can offer higher levels of security since a load balancer or gateway can enforce authentication and authorization rules and shield service instances from direct client access.
- **Complexity**: Client-side service discovery can make the client-side code more complex, whereas server-side service discovery can make the infrastructure and configuration more complex.

- **Network traffic**: Server-side service discovery offloads this burden to the load balancer or gateway, but client-side service discovery generates higher network traffic since clients must query the service registry to discover service instances.
- **Latency**: Server-side service discovery can result in lower latency because the load balancer can choose the quickest and nearest instance. Client-side service discovery can result in higher latency if the registry is out-of-date or if service instances are regularly added or withdrawn.
- **Monitoring**: Since the load balancer or gateway can gather and analyse information about the traffic and performance of the service instances, server-side service discovery can offer greater monitoring and management capabilities.

Considering the preceding key differences on the variety of software engineering aspects, the industry majorly has more implementations of server-side service discovery compared to the other one.

Service registration patterns

As we have seen in the previous section, service registry is an important part of the whole service discovery. Microservices design uses the service registration to enable dynamic and automatic discovery of service instances. The service registry keeps an up-to-date list of all service instances that are available, as well as their metadata, which other services can use to find and connect with them.

There are two different ways of service registration:

- **Self-registration**: In the self-registration pattern, each service instance is responsible for registering itself with the service registry upon startup. This approach gives each service control over its registration process and allows it to provide metadata about its capabilities and properties.
- **Third-party registration:** In the third-party registration pattern, a separate component is responsible for registering and deregistering service instances with the service registry. The service instances delegate this responsibility to the third-party component.

Self-registration

This is a registration pattern that we have discussed in the previous sections and have also seen the code for its implementation. In this, each service instance is responsible for registering itself with a service registry, service instances can transmit a heartbeat to the service registry as a failsafe to let it know they are still online and accessible. The instance can be de-registered if the heartbeat stops, because it means the instance is either offline or not responding. Refer to *Figure 4.6* which illustrates self-registration pattern of services:

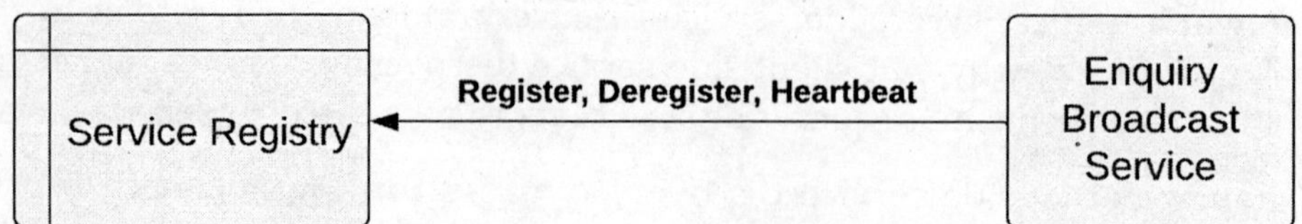

Figure 4.6: *Enquiry Broadcast service is self-registering, deregistering itself with the Service Registry*

Self-registration pattern is straightforward and light weight and does not require any intermediary component, but it couples the service instance with the service registry and requires more code and configuration on the service side and may result in inconsistent or stale registry data.

The strong coupling of services and service registry can be overcome by a different pattern, that is, third-party registration.

Third-party registration

In this registration pattern, a third component known as the service registrar is responsible for registering and deregistering the services. The service registrar polls the deployment environment to keep track of the changes to instances that are currently operating. It logs a newly discovered service instance in its database after discovering it and de-registers them when they get terminated. Refer to *Figure 4.7* which illustrates third-party registration pattern of services:

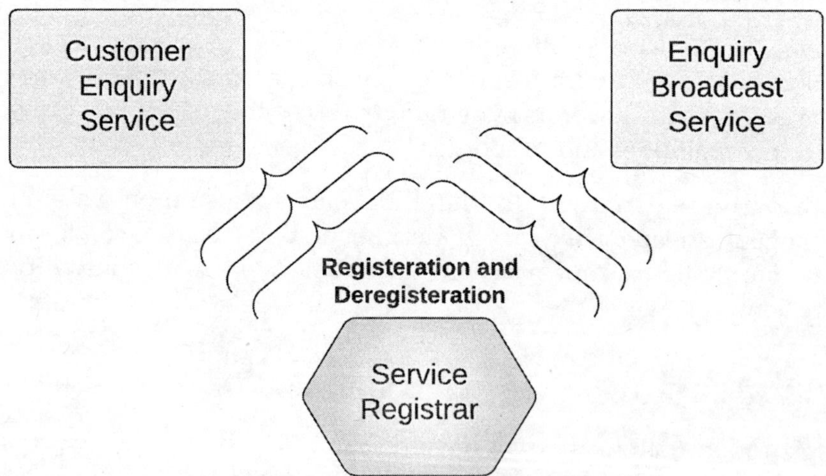

Figure 4.7: *Service Registrar is registering, deregistering the services*

The advantage of this is that the services in this pattern are decoupled with the service registry and are independent of any registration and deregistration logic. However, the third-party service responsible for managing the service registration needs to be part of the deployment environment maintaining lifecycle of all the services.

Container orchestration platforms such as Kubernetes, Docker Swarm, Amazon ECS, and so on, are using third-party registration pattern; the service registry and discovery features are embedded into these orchestration technologies. Services are automatically registered and exposed as Kubernetes services or Docker services and the platforms also offer load balancing, scalability, and failover functionalities.

The reason of decoupling of services with each other and service registry is a primary reason the industry is majorly going with third-party registration patterns for complex applications comprising of multiple microservices and using container orchestrators *(discussed later in the book)* for the microservices deployment, both on cloud and on-premises environments. For simpler applications, there is no requirement for getting into the complexity of using a container orchestrator. Hence, self-registration is an ideal option in such scenarios.

Conclusion

In this chapter, we have learnt the importance of service discovery for the independent implementation of services, talked about both design patterns of service discovery that is client-side service discovery and server-side service discovery, and the differences between the two from the software engineering parameters perspective. Later, we discussed service registration patterns which is an important prerequisite for the service discovery. In the end, we explained why third-party service registration pattern is the preferred option in the industry over self-registration.

In the next chapter, we will learn about containers and how a service can be containerized using Docker containers, which is a prerequisite for running them using orchestrator platforms.

Points to remember

- Service registries and gateway servers need to be managed and deployed separately, adding to the complexity of the overall application.
- Both client-side and server-side service discovery implementations do have a flexibility of addon functionalities such as load balancing, filtering, circuit breaker, and so on, using other corresponding libraries.
- Though container orchestrator platforms do simplify things from the service discovery and managing service lifecycle, they come with their own installation and management complexities and requires a different set of expertise.

Questions

1. How to handle scenarios in client-side service discovery in which service registry is down because of some unexpected reason and may take few minutes to be back?
2. What will happen if the gateway server or load balancer stops responding in case of a server-side service discovery? How to handle such scenarios in the design?
3. How do third-party registrar services get to know about availability and unavailability of a service?

Join our book's Discord space

Join the book's Discord Workspace for Latest updates, Offers, Tech happenings around the world, New Release and Sessions with the Authors:

https://discord.bpbonline.com

CHAPTER 5
Containerization Using Docker

Introduction

The previous chapter explained the need of service discovery in the world of microservices, the two service discovery patterns and different ways to implement them. It also talked about the service registration patterns and explained why complex applications with multiple microservices prefer container orchestration platforms such as Kubernetes, Docker Swarm, and so on, which internally implement third party service registration pattern.

In this chapter, we will pick up where we left off in the last one and delve into the **Open Container Initiative** (**OCI**) for applications. We will explore its advantages and discuss how Docker, as an OCI-compliant solution, can assist us in achieving the same. We will walk through with the steps involved in containerizing an application using Docker, starting with installing Docker, building Docker images, and finally running them. In the end, we will push the Docker images to an image registry.

Structure

In this chapter, we will discuss following topics:

- Introduction to containers
- Open Container Initiative

- Docker
- Installing Docker
- Building Docker images
- Running Docker images
- Pushing Docker images to image registry

Objectives

The objective of this chapter is to understand the concept of application containerization and the utilization of Docker for this purpose. This entails Docker installation, understanding different components and the containerization of three microservices: Customer Enquiry, Enquiry Broadcast, and Config Server applications. Finally, we will execute these microservices as Docker containers and push them to an image registry.

Introduction to containers

Containers, as the name suggests, is a bundle of small components grouped together so that collectively they constitute a fully functional entity. The idea was inspired by shipping containers, which are boxes with standardized dimensions and a surrounding system that is used to transport goods globally. The same crane, ship, train, truck, and so on, can transport any shipping container as they work on the boxes regardless of what is inside them. They are designed to perform a specific job and this makes the automation possible, leading to increased reliability and cost reductions.

In the software world, the problem that containers solved is the uncertainty around running the code when it is shipped from one environment to another. Prior to the introduction of containers, when the code is moved from developer's machine to staging server or from staging server to the production environment, it often fails because of environmental differences. Even though code is packaged in boxes as `jar` files for the java code, or other package files for a different programming language so that transfer of code from one environment to another is seamless, there are still chances of failure, as the code also has dependencies beyond the shipped package, for example, system libraries and so on.

Containers solve this problem as it is a standalone executable package that contains all the code, libraries, and dependencies required to run a piece of software. No matter the underlying infrastructure or host system, containers offer an isolated runtime environment that guarantees the software will operate in the same way. With containers, the process of transferring containers from a developer's machine to a testing environment or a production server becomes hassle-free.

Recently, containers have become a popular technology, especially when used with microservices architecture. The construction of small, modular, independently deployable services that integrate to form a bigger application is the focus of the microservices architecture and containers offer a uniform and effective approach to bundle and deliver these services.

Containerization platforms such as Docker Swarm, Kubernetes, and so on, are used to generate and orchestrate containers. These tools offer a means of creating, deploying, and managing containers on large scale. Containerization enables better agility and quicker release cycles by enabling the independent development and deployment of each microservice. Moreover, containers allow for horizontal scaling, which enables numerous instances of a service to be started or stopped as necessary to manage shifting traffic or demand levels. Refer to *Figure 5.1* to imagine the structure of containers in the software world:

***Figure 5.1**: Group of containers*

In general, containers have emerged as a crucial piece of technology for contemporary software development, majorly in the context of microservices architecture. Containers enable improved agility, scalability, and reliability in the development and deployment of microservices-based systems by offering a uniform and effective method for packaging, bundling, and deploying software.

Open Container Initiative

From **opencontainer.org**, the Open Container Initiative is an open governance structure for the express purpose of creating open industry standards around container formats and runtimes. Established in June 2015 by Docker and other leaders in the container industry, the OCI currently contains three specifications: Runtime specification (`runtime-spec`), image specification (`image-spec`) and distribution specification (`distribution-spec`).

The objective of this initiative is to establish a consistent standard that all vendors can embrace, ensuring that containerized applications are not tied to any specific platform, thereby enabling interoperability and portability. OCI's specifications are crafted in a way that permits the utilization of various container formats and runtime environments.

The OCI Image Format Specification (**https://github.com/opencontainers/image-spec**) strictly defines the requirements for an OCI image (container image), which consists of a manifest, an optional image index, a set of filesystem layers, and a configuration. The schema for OCI image components is fully supported by the APIs defined in the OCI distribution specification.

The OCI Runtime Specification (**https://github.com/opencontainers/runtime-spec**) defines how to properly run a container **Filesystem Bundle** which fully adheres to the OCI image format specification. The OCI runtime specification is relevant to the OCI distribution specification as they both support OCI images, and that container runtimes use the APIs defined in the OCI distribution specification to fetch pre-built container images and run them.

The OCI Distribution Specification (**https://github.com/opencontainers/distribution-spec**) is also designed to adhere to the OCI image format specification and provide standard APIs, which can be used by OCI runtimes to work on OCI images.

Using these standards developers can build containers using tools and can deploy them on any of the platforms both supporting OCI specifications. This enables greater flexibility in deploying container-based applications across different cloud providers and on-premise environments.

There are multiple products available in the market that support the OCI specifications, such as:

- **Docker**: Docker was one of the founding members of the OCI and continues to support its specifications. Docker provides a container runtime engine (**`runc`**) and a suite of tools for building, distributing, and managing containers that conform to the OCI specification.
- **Buildah**: Buildah is a tool for building OCI-compliant container images. It allows users to build images using either the same syntax that is used by Docker or via a command-line interface, and produces images that conform to the OCI image specification.
- **BuildKit**: It is merely an optimized version of Docker's build engine.
- **Amazon ECS**: Amazon Elastic Container Service is a managed service provided by AWS that supports OCI runtime specification and can be used to run any OCI compliant image as a container.
- **Kubernetes**: Kubernetes or K8s is a popular container orchestration platform that supports the OCI image specification. It provides a container runtime environment and a set of tools for deploying and managing containers' life cycle. It is also available for on-premises environments.
- **Podman**: Podman is a lightweight container runtime environment that supports the OCI image specification. Podman provides a command-line interface for managing containers and images that conform to the OCI specifications.

- **Docker Hub**: Powered by Docker, Docker Hub is the world's largest library and community for container images.
- **Amazon ECR**: Amazon Elastic Container Registry is compliant with OCI distribution specification and provides an API to support pushing and pulling of OCI specific images.
- **CRI-O**: CRI-O is a lightweight container runtime specifically designed for Kubernetes. It adheres to OCI standards and is used by Kubernetes to run containers.
- **rkt**: rkt (pronounced rocket) is a container runtime created by CoreOS, which supports OCI standards and focuses on simplicity and security.
- **nerdctl**: nerdctl is a command-line tool for managing OCI containers.
- **skopeo**: skopeo is a tool for copying images between registries.
- **Azure Container Registry**: It is a managed container registry from Microsoft Azure that supports the OCI image format.
- **Google Kubernetes Engine**: GKE is a managed Kubernetes service from Google Cloud Platform that supports the OCI image format and runtime.

Overall, standardizing the container ecosystem and encouraging the use of open standards for container formats and runtime environments are essential goals of the Open Container Initiative. The OCI promotes increased creativity and cooperation in the container ecosystem by offering a standard framework for applications built on containers.

Docker

Docker is one of the founding members of Open Container Initiative and the OCI image standard was formed using the original image format created by Docker. Docker also provided its runtime, **runC**, to the OCI, in order to serve it as the first implementation of the standard.

Docker is a popular containerization platform that enables developers to build, package, and deploy applications as containers. It makes it easier to design and deploy applications in a consistent and repeatable manner by offering a straightforward and effective method for creating and managing containers. Moreover, Docker also offers an ecosystem of tools, plugins and services that expand its capabilities and allow integrations with numerous third parties. It provides container orchestration with **Docker Swarm**, container registry services with **Docker Hub**, and many more. Refer to *Figure 5.2* to get the glimpse of some of the tools and services offered by Docker:

***Figure 5.2:** Docker tools and services*

Docker is comprised of the following important components:

- **runC**: A tool for spawning and running containers based on **Open Containers Initiative** (**OCI**) runtime specification.
- **Containerd**: A daemon that manages the lifecycle of containers on hosts, typically using runC.
- **Docker Engine**: The container engine offered by Docker. Generally, this includes the Docker daemon binary, which needs to be installed on hosts where containers need to run. Docker engine builds on top of **Containerd** which builds on top of **runC**.

Due to the popularity of Docker and the services it offers, application **dockerization** has also been used many times interchangeably with application **containerization**. Overall, Docker has become a critical tool in modern software development, particularly in the context of microservices architecture, where it enables developers to build and deploy small, independently deployable services in a scalable and efficient manner. In the subsequent sections, we will see how an application is containerized using Docker and run as containers.

Installing Docker

Before we can proceed with building Docker images, we need to first install Docker in our environment. Primarily, Docker has been used on Linux environments using Linux Docker Engine but can also be easily installed on Windows and Mac machines using Docker Desktop. Docker Desktop provides **graphical user interface** (**GUI**) that lets one manage the containers, applications, and images directly from the host machine. Docker Desktop is now available for Linux as well.

As previously mentioned, Docker is compatible with Windows but is predominantly used on Linux. Now, let us explore the installation process for Docker on Linux (specifically, Ubuntu 20.04), referred to as Linux Docker Engine, and on Windows using Docker Desktop.

Recipe 31: Installing Linux Docker Engine on Linux

To install the Docker Linux Engine on Ubuntu, please execute the provided commands within the Ubuntu terminal.

Uninstalling old versions

Uninstalling any previous Docker version before installing a fresh install. It is an optional step and is only required if there is already Docker or its supporting components installed on the system.

```
sudo apt-get remove docker docker-engine docker.io containerd runc
```

The output could be that the packages are not previously installed, as also shown in *Figure 5.3*:

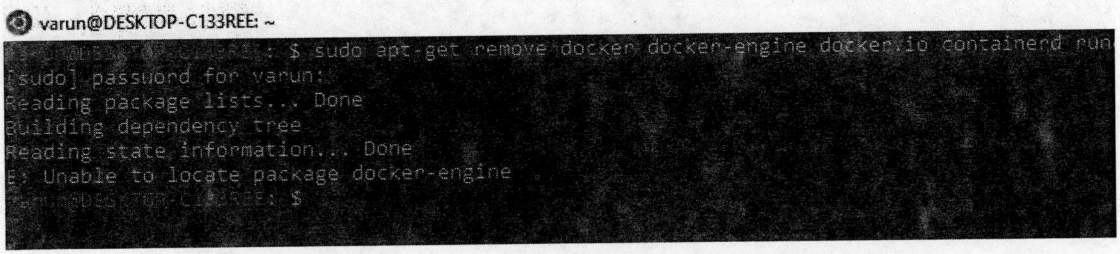

```
varun@DESKTOP-C133REE: ~
$ sudo apt-get remove docker docker-engine docker.io containerd run
[sudo] password for varun:
Reading package lists... Done
Building dependency tree
Reading state information... Done
E: Unable to locate package docker-engine
$
```

Figure 5.3: Output of the remove command of Docker and other components

There could be some containers, volumes or images associated with the previous version that are not automatically removed on uninstallation of Docker and is suggested to clean manually before the fresh installation of Docker.

Setting up the apt repository

There are different ways of installing Docker, either using Docker Desktop, installing it manually or using convenience scripts provided by Docker. But as part of this recipe, we will setup and install Docker Engine from Docker's **apt** repository. Follow the given steps:

1. Update the **apt** package index and install packages to allow **apt** to use a repository over HTTPS:

   ```
   sudo apt-get update
   ```

Depending on the currently installed packages, the output could be as shown in *Figure 5.4*:

```
$ sudo apt-get update
[sudo] password for varun:
Get:1 http://security.ubuntu.com/ubuntu focal-security InRelease [114 kB]
Hit:2 http://archive.ubuntu.com/ubuntu focal InRelease
Get:3 http://archive.ubuntu.com/ubuntu focal-updates InRelease [114 kB]
Get:4 http://security.ubuntu.com/ubuntu focal-security/main amd64 Packages [2049 kB]
Get:5 http://archive.ubuntu.com/ubuntu focal-backports InRelease [108 kB]
Get:6 http://archive.ubuntu.com/ubuntu focal-updates/main amd64 Packages [2430 kB]
Get:7 http://security.ubuntu.com/ubuntu focal-security/main Translation-en [334 kB]
Get:8 http://archive.ubuntu.com/ubuntu focal-updates/main Translation-en [416 kB]
Get:9 http://archive.ubuntu.com/ubuntu focal-updates/main amd64 c-n-f Metadata [16.4 kB]
Get:10 http://archive.ubuntu.com/ubuntu focal-updates/restricted amd64 Packages [1671 kB]
Get:11 http://archive.ubuntu.com/ubuntu focal-updates/restricted Translation-en [235 kB]
Get:12 http://archive.ubuntu.com/ubuntu focal-updates/restricted amd64 c-n-f Metadata [620 B]
Get:13 http://archive.ubuntu.com/ubuntu focal-updates/universe amd64 Packages [1039 kB]
Get:14 http://security.ubuntu.com/ubuntu focal-security/main amd64 c-n-f Metadata [12.5 kB]
Get:15 http://security.ubuntu.com/ubuntu focal-security/restricted amd64 Packages [1561 kB]
Get:16 http://archive.ubuntu.com/ubuntu focal-updates/universe Translation-en [244 kB]
Get:17 http://archive.ubuntu.com/ubuntu focal-updates/universe amd64 c-n-f Metadata [24.0 kB]
Get:18 http://archive.ubuntu.com/ubuntu focal-updates/multiverse amd64 Packages [25.1 kB]
Get:19 http://archive.ubuntu.com/ubuntu focal-updates/multiverse Translation-en [7408 B]
Get:20 http://archive.ubuntu.com/ubuntu focal-updates/multiverse amd64 c-n-f Metadata [592 B]
Get:21 http://archive.ubuntu.com/ubuntu focal-backports/main amd64 Packages [45.7 kB]
Get:22 http://archive.ubuntu.com/ubuntu focal-backports/main amd64 c-n-f Metadata [1420 B]
Get:23 http://archive.ubuntu.com/ubuntu focal-backports/universe amd64 Packages [24.9 kB]
Get:24 http://archive.ubuntu.com/ubuntu focal-backports/universe Translation-en [16.3 kB]
Get:25 http://archive.ubuntu.com/ubuntu focal-backports/universe amd64 c-n-f Metadata [880 B]
Get:26 http://security.ubuntu.com/ubuntu focal-security/restricted Translation-en [220 kB]
Get:27 http://security.ubuntu.com/ubuntu focal-security/restricted amd64 c-n-f Metadata [624 B]
Get:28 http://security.ubuntu.com/ubuntu focal-security/universe amd64 Packages [813 kB]
Get:29 http://security.ubuntu.com/ubuntu focal-security/universe Translation-en [162 kB]
Get:30 http://security.ubuntu.com/ubuntu focal-security/universe amd64 c-n-f Metadata [17.5 kB]
Get:31 http://security.ubuntu.com/ubuntu focal-security/multiverse amd64 Packages [22.9 kB]
Get:32 http://security.ubuntu.com/ubuntu focal-security/multiverse Translation-en [5488 B]
Get:33 http://security.ubuntu.com/ubuntu focal-security/multiverse amd64 c-n-f Metadata [516 B]
Fetched 11.7 MB in 13s (883 kB/s)
Reading package lists... Done
$
```

***Figure 5.4**: Output of the apt-get update command*

```
sudo apt-get install \
    ca-certificates \
    curl \
    gnupg
```

The output would be as shown in the *Figure 5.5*:

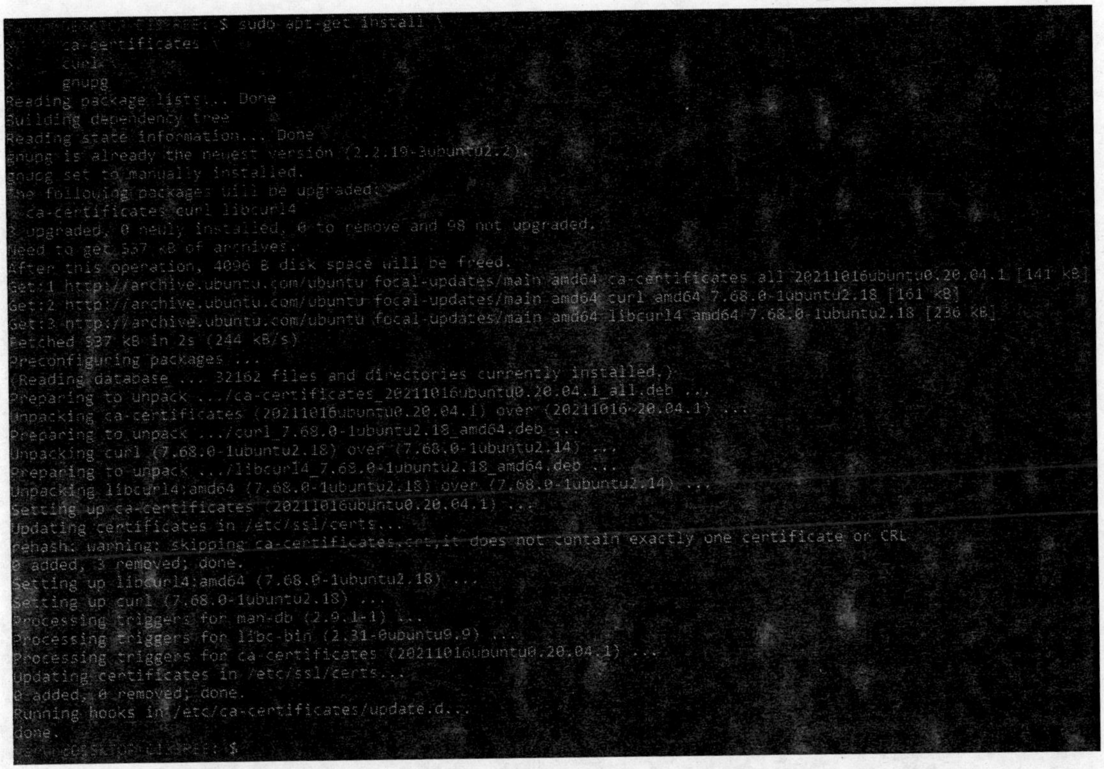

Figure 5.5: Output of the apt-get install ca-certificates command

The certificates are fetched and installed in the system.

2. Adding Docker's official GPG Key:

```
sudo mkdir -m 0755 -p /etc/apt/keyrings
curl -fsSL https://download.docker.com/linux/ubuntu/gpg | sudo gpg
--dearmor -o /etc/apt/keyrings/docker.gpg
```

It will install the key in the mentioned location. It is not a standard but a good practice and lot of software vendors follow it. It validates the integrity of a software package before installation. Maintainer of the package signs each package and makes the public key available, which should be used while installing the software.

3. Run the following command to setup the repository:

```
echo \
    "deb  [arch="$(dpkg  --print-architecture)"  signed-by=/etc/apt/
keyrings/docker.gpg] https://download.docker.com/linux/ubuntu \
  "$(. /etc/os-release && echo "$VERSION_CODENAME")" stable" | \
  sudo tee /etc/apt/sources.list.d/docker.list > /dev/null
```

Missing the above property may lead to unstable repository that can lead to errors such as packages not being available while installing the Docker Engine.

Installing Docker Engine

Before Docker Engine is installed, **apt** package index needs to be updated. Make sure that the read permission is granted for the Docker public key file before updating the package index.

1. Run the following commands to give read permissions and update **apt** package index:

   sudo chmod a+r /etc/apt/keyrings/docker.gpg

   sudo apt-get update

The output would be as shown in the *Figure 5.6*:

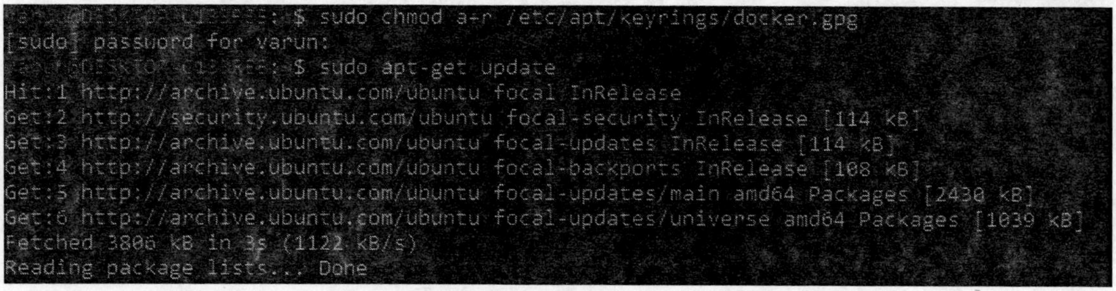

```
$ sudo chmod a+r /etc/apt/keyrings/docker.gpg
[sudo] password for varun:
$ sudo apt-get update
Hit:1 http://archive.ubuntu.com/ubuntu focal InRelease
Get:2 http://security.ubuntu.com/ubuntu focal-security InRelease [114 kB]
Get:3 http://archive.ubuntu.com/ubuntu focal-updates InRelease [114 kB]
Get:4 http://archive.ubuntu.com/ubuntu focal-backports InRelease [108 kB]
Get:5 http://archive.ubuntu.com/ubuntu focal-updates/main amd64 Packages [2430 kB]
Get:6 http://archive.ubuntu.com/ubuntu focal-updates/universe amd64 Packages [1039 kB]
Fetched 3806 kB in 3s (1122 kB/s)
Reading package lists... Done
```

Figure 5.6: Output of the chmod and apt-get update command

2. Installing latest version of Docker Engine, containerd, and Docker compose:

   sudo apt-get install docker-ce docker-ce-cli containerd.io docker-buildx-plugin docker-compose-plugin

If everything goes well as per the above commands, the generated output will look similar to shown in *Figure 5.7*:

Figure 5.7: Output of the apt-get install command for Docker Engine and required components

3. Run the below command to start the Docker daemon:

   ```
   sudo dockerd
   ```

In case of no error, the preceding command starts the Docker daemon in the terminal. Open a new terminal and run the **Hello World** image:

```
sudo docker run hello-world
```

If Docker has been successfully installed, the output is as shown in *Figure 5.8*:

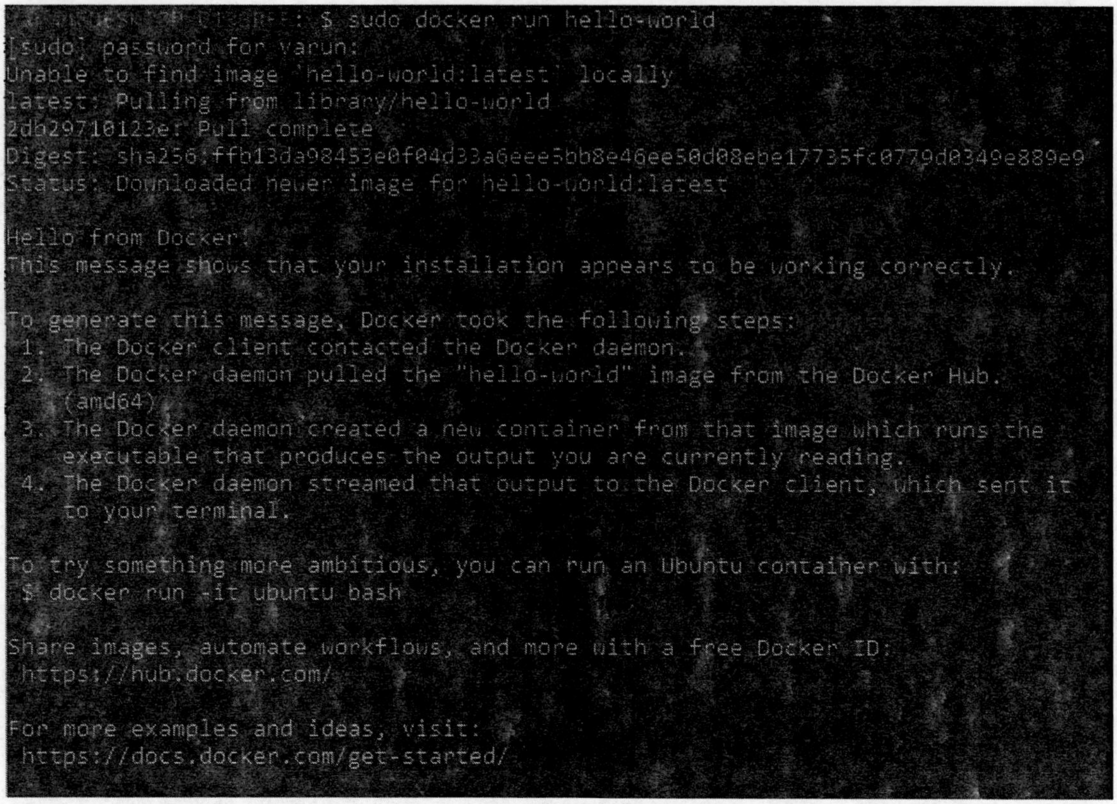

```
$ sudo docker run hello-world
[sudo] password for varun:
Unable to find image 'hello-world:latest' locally
latest: Pulling from library/hello-world
2db29710123e: Pull complete
Digest: sha256:ffb13da98453e0f04d33a6eee5bb8e46ee50d08ebe17735fc0779d0349e889e9
Status: Downloaded newer image for hello-world:latest

Hello from Docker!
This message shows that your installation appears to be working correctly.

To generate this message, Docker took the following steps:
 1. The Docker client contacted the Docker daemon.
 2. The Docker daemon pulled the "hello-world" image from the Docker Hub.
    (amd64)
 3. The Docker daemon created a new container from that image which runs the
    executable that produces the output you are currently reading.
 4. The Docker daemon streamed that output to the Docker client, which sent it
    to your terminal.

To try something more ambitious, you can run an Ubuntu container with:
 $ docker run -it ubuntu bash

Share images, automate workflows, and more with a free Docker ID:
 https://hub.docker.com/

For more examples and ideas, visit:
 https://docs.docker.com/get-started/
```

Figure 5.8: Output of running the docker hello-world image

This output makes sure that the Docker Engine has been successfully installed on the system.

Recipe 32: Installing Docker Desktop on Windows

Before installing Docker Desktop for Windows, download the installer using the link **https://desktop.docker.com/win/main/amd64/Docker Desktop Installer.exe**.

Follow the given steps:

1. Double-click **Docker Desktop Installer.exe** to run the installer.
2. Docker Desktop on Windows can be installed using **Windows Subsystem for Linux** (**WSL 2**) or Hyper-V backend. As part of this recipe, Docker Desktop will be installed using WSL 2 backend. Run the following command in Windows Command Prompt to check the status of current WSL installed:

   ```
   wsl --status
   ```

   Output would be:

```
Default Distribution: Ubuntu
Default Version: 2
```

If the version is 1, run the following commands using Windows Command Prompt as admin:

Update WSL

```
wsl --update
```

Shutdown WSL

```
wsl --shutdown
```

Set the default version to 2 and then restart the machine

```
wsl --set-default-version 2
```

While installing Docker Desktop, make sure to use WSL 2 instead of Hyper-V when prompted for an option.

3. Follow the instructions on the installation wizard to authorize and proceed with the install.
4. On successful installation, click **Close** to complete the process.
5. If the admin account is different than the user account, then the user needs to be added to the **docker-user** group.

Once installed, Docker Desktop can be accessed from installed applications menu in Windows.

Building Docker images

As we know, building Docker images means a process of creating an image which contains all the dependencies including the underlying operating system along with the application that needs to be containerized. Building Docker images require a creation of a file called **Dockerfile**, which is a simple text file with instructions and arguments that Docker can read and create Docker images.

Dockerfile

Dockerfile contains instructions to the Docker daemon that are read as part of the Docker build process. Docker daemon reads the instructions in the Dockerfile in order, and creates a new image layer for each instruction until all the instructions have been read, and eventually creating the final desired image. Each layer represents a change to the file system or configuration of the image. Output of running an instruction which forms a layer on top of the previous layer is a temporary image created for the interim usage. Docker also uses a caching mechanism to speed up the build process. If a layer has already been built, Docker reuses the cached layer instead of rebuilding it. Refer to the *Table 5.1* for important **Dockerfile** instructions and their explanation:

Instruction	Explanation
FROM	The **FROM** instruction is normally the first instruction in a Dockerfile, it specifies the base image to use for the new image. The syntax of the command is: **FROM <image name>:<tag name>**, where tag name is optional.
RUN	A **RUN** instruction is used to run specified commands. The commands are run as part of the image build process. Example: **RUN apt-get update**
WORKDIR	This instruction sets the working directory for subsequent instructions. Any instruction after this like **RUN, COPY,** and so on. will be executed on the set directory. In most of the cases it is the directory where the application code resides. Example: **WORKDIR /usr/app/xyz**
COPY	Copies files and directories from the host machine to the container. The **COPY** instruction is used to add application code and configuration files to the container. **COPY <Source> <Destination>** Example: **COPY application.jar .** This command copies **application.jar** from host machine to the container current directory.
ADD	It is similar to **COPY** with an addon, it also allows downloading files from a URL. Example: **ADD http://abc.com/xyz.txt /use/app**
CMD	Specifies the default command to run when the container starts. The **CMD** instruction is used to specify the main process or command that will be run when the container is started. This command can be overridden by the command passed during Docker run. Example: **CMD echo "Hello World"**

Instruction	Explanation
`ENTRYPOINT`	The `ENTRYPOINT` instruction is used to specify the main process or command that will be run when the container is started. The main difference between `CMD` and `ENTRYPOINT` is that the later will always run. Example: `ENTRYPOINT ["/bin/echo", "Welcome to world of Docker"]`
`ENV`	Sets environment variables in the container.
`EXPOSE`	Used to expose a container port to the outside world. Example: `EXPOSE 8080`

***Table 5.1**: Important Dockerfile instructions with explanations*

Before we get started, the initial step is to select the foundational image for our application container. The base image can be a simple light weight operating system or an operating system with added libraries and packages. Recommendation from Docker is to always use the latest official image of any offerings, so that it has all the vulnerabilities fixed.

Moreover, it is always better to use light base images as they have less memory footprint and takes less time for the container to start. We will be going with Alpine base images to build our Docker images; Alpine is a very light weight Linux operating system. The exact image to be used is **Alpine with Amazon Corretto 17**; Corretto is a binary distribution of the **Open Java Development Kit (OpenJDK)** with long-term support from Amazon. Corretto JDK is very much tuned for running on AWS environments and is very heavily used in the industry.

.dockerignore file

Dockerfile along with a context which is nothing but a set of files located in the specified path or URL, are used for building the image. Files from the context may be copied to the image using the `COPY` command explained in *Table 5.1* and becomes the part of the image. As part of the build process, these files are compressed and copied to the Docker server which can be running on the same machine or on a remote machine. And many times, all files from the context are not required to be part of the image; they are skipped using a file called `.dockerignore`. If this file is present in the `root` directory of the context, the Docker modifies the context to exclude the files and directories that matches with the patterns present in the file. It works similar to the `.gitignore` file that is used while working with Git.

Here is an example of the `.dockerignore` file:

```
# comment
/test*
*/*/*xyz*
log?
```

Here,

- lines starting with the **#** character are ignored; use it for comments
- ***** matches any sequence of non-separator characters
- **?** matches any single non-separator character

If the `.dockerignore` is not present, then it can lead to few concerns:

- **Increased execution time and resources**: Including unnecessary files will increase the compression time as well as add on to network latency, leading to higher build execution time. Moreover, any change in the files that are part of an internal layer of the build process will invalidate the cache and the layer image needs to be built again, adding to execution time and resources.
- **Increased image size**: Dockerfile may have code to copy all files from a folder or a subfolder. Out of these, a few are redundant files and if not ignored, will only increase the size of the docker image.
- **Unintentional secret or source code exposure**: There might be code in the Dockerfile like `COPY`, which copies all the contents of the root folder. If there are files containing secrets or source code, then copying them to Docker image will expose the secrets or the source code.

Third-party registration pattern

As part of containerization, the following application images need to be created:

- Customer Enquiry
- Broadcast Enquiry
- Config Server

You may be wondering why the applications for discovery server and gateway server are not containerized. The reason is that as part of this book, the upcoming recipes will not be based on self-registration and instead focus on **third-party registration** of services about which we touch base in the previous chapter. The pattern does not require coupling between the services and service registry and is advisable for big complex applications containing multiple microservices. Moreover, container orchestration platforms support this pattern and how to configure that will be discussed in the subsequent chapters.

Entry point script

It is a script that is used to invoke the application on container startup and is configured using **ENTRYPOINT** instruction of a Dockerfile. The script is not mandatory for creating container images but very practical to have. A lot of programmatic as well as environment specific configurations such as usage of environment variables, virtual machine configurations, and so on, can be easily done for an application using this script. It can be enhanced to handle graceful shutdown of an application; the concept discussed in the subsequent chapters. The script is a shell script if the base image is Linux operating system and a batch script for Windows.

Recipe 33: Creating entry point scripts

As our application images will be built on Linux based operating system, shell script needs to be created for both the applications Customer Enquiry microservice and Enquiry Broadcast microservice. The file will be part of the code line.

Customer enquiry entry point script

Create a file with the name **CustomerEnquiryEntryPoint.sh** inside the Customer Enquiry application project:

CustomerEnquiryEntryPoint.sh

```
#!/bin/sh

execution_handler(){
 HEAP_OPTS="-Xms${MIN_HEAP_SIZE} -Xmx${MAX_HEAP_SIZE}"
 EXTERNAL_PARAMS="--spring.config.import=${CONFIG_SERVER_URL} --spring.cloud.config.username=${CONFIG_SERVER_USERNAME} --spring.cloud.config.password=${CONFIG_SERVER_PASSWORD} --spring.datasource.username=${DATABASE_USERNAME} --spring.datasource.password=${DATABASE_PASSWORD}"

 if [ ! -d "log" ]; then # If log folder does not exist
  echo "Log folder does not exist, creating it";
  mkdir -p log
 else
  echo "Log folder already exists, deleting contents";
  rm -rf log
  mkdir -p log
```

```
14.    fi
15.    nohup java -jar customer-enquiry.jar ${EXTERNAL_PARAMS} ${HEAP_OPTS} > log/nohup.out &
16. }
17.
18. execution_handler
19. while true
20. do
21.    tail -f log/nohup.out & wait ${!}
22. done
```

Here,

- **Line 1,** the text **`#!/bin/sh`** indicates that the script should be interpreted and executed by the Bourne shell where **`#!`** is called has hashbang and **`/bin/sh`** is the path to the shell interpreter
- **Line 4** contains variables **`MIN_HEAP_SIZE`** and **`MAX_HEAP_SIZE`** and their values are set at the environment level; these variables give the flexibility of providing the heap size parameters on application startup, for example: **`HEAP_OPTS="-Xms256M -Xmx512M"`**.
- **Line 5** contains variables for accessing Config Server and Database. You may notice that database URL is not part of it as it will be fetched from the Config Server.

The shell script can be tested by manually setting the environment variables and running the script file using the following commands:

```
export MIN_HEAP_SIZE=256m
export MAX_HEAP_SIZE=512m
export CONFIG_SERVER_URL=configserver:http://localhost:8888 # URL of Config Server
export CONFIG_SERVER_USERNAME=fsmConfigAdmin
export CONFIG_SERVER_PASSWORD=password
export DATABASE_USERNAME=postgres
export DATABASE_PASSWORD= secret11
sh CustomerEnquiryEntryPoint.sh
```

The last command should start the Customer Enquiry microservice and it creates **`nohup.log`** file under the log folder. Before running the command, make sure that the executable **`jar`** is renamed to **`customer-enquiry.jar`**.

If shell script has been created using Windows, make sure it is converted to Unix format otherwise there may be error identified as **No such file or directory** or **Permission denied**. So, use the following command in Linux to convert the same:

```
dos2unix CustomerEnquiryEntryPoint.sh
```

The output would be:

```
dos2unix: converting file CustomerEnquiryEntryPoint.sh to Unix format...
```

Enquiry Broadcast entry point script

Create a file with the name **`EnquiryBroadcastEntryPoint.sh`** inside the Enquiry Broadcast application project:

`EnquiryBroadcastEntryPoint.sh`

```
#!/bin/sh

execution_handler(){
 HEAP_OPTS="-Xms${MIN_HEAP_SIZE} -Xmx${MAX_HEAP_SIZE}"
 EXTERNAL_PARAMS="--spring.config.import=${CONFIG_SERVER_URL} --spring.cloud.config.username=${CONFIG_SERVER_USERNAME} --spring.cloud.config.password=${CONFIG_SERVER_PASSWORD} --spring.datasource.username=${DATABASE_USERNAME} --spring.datasource.password=${DATABASE_PASSWORD}"

 if [ ! -d "log" ]; then # If log folder does not exist
  echo "Log folder does not exist, creating it";
  mkdir -p log
 else
  echo "Log folder already exists, deleting contents";
  rm -rf log
  mkdir -p log
 fi
 nohup java -jar enquiry-broadcast.jar ${EXTERNAL_PARAMS} ${HEAP_OPTS} > log/nohup.out &
}

execution_handler

```

```
while true
do
 tail -f log/nohup.out & wait ${!}
done
```

It is same as that of Customer Enquiry application. Only the name of executable **jar** file has changed.

Config Server entry point script

Create a file with the name **ConfigServerEntryPoint.sh** inside the Config Server application project.

ConfigServerEntryPoint.sh

```
#!/bin/sh

execution_handler(){
 HEAP_OPTS="-Xms${MIN_HEAP_SIZE} -Xmx${MAX_HEAP_SIZE}"
 EXTERNAL_PARAMS="--spring.profiles.active=${PROFILE} --spring.security.user.name=${CONFIG_SERVER_USERNAME} --spring.security.user.password=${CONFIG_SERVER_PASSWORD} --spring.cloud.config.server.git.password=${GIT_PASSWORD}"

 if [ ! -d "log" ]; then # If Log folder does not exist
  echo "Log folder does not exist, creating it";
  mkdir -p log
 else
  echo "Log folder already exists, deleting contents";
  rm -rf log
  mkdir -p log
 fi

 nohup java -jar config-server.jar ${EXTERNAL_PARAMS} ${HEAP_OPTS} > log/nohup.out &
}

execution_handler
```

```
20. while true
21. do
22.  tail -f log/nohup.out & wait ${!}
23. done
```

Here,

- **Line 5** contains the variables for spring profile, spring security credentials for Config Server and password for accessing Git.
- No Vault related configuration variables have been passed as the only profile that will be activated is Git. Customer Enquiry and Enquiry Broadcast microservices will get the database credentials from environment variables as mentioned in their respective entry point shell scripts.

The shell script can be tested by manually setting the environment variables and running the script file using the following commands:

```
export MIN_HEAP_SIZE=256m
export MAX_HEAP_SIZE=512m
export PROFILE=git
export CONFIG_SERVER_USERNAME=fsmConfigAdmin
export CONFIG_SERVER_PASSWORD=password
export GIT_PASSWORD=*****
sh ConfigServerEntryPoint.sh
```

The logs will be generated in the log folder.

Recipe 34: Creating .dockerignore

In the above section, the importance of the **`.dockerignore`** file was discussed. The file needs to be created in every project, for which the Docker image needs to be built.

Customer Enquiry .dockerignore

Create a file with a name **`.dockerignore`** inside the Customer Enquiry application project:

`.dockerignore`

```
.git
.settings
.classpath
.gitignore
.project
```

```
6. src
7. pom.xml
8. *.md
9. target
10. !target/customer-enquiry*.jar
```

The files matching with the above pattern are ignored from the Docker context. Pay attention to the usage of **!** in line 10; combination of line 9 and 10 ignores all files from the **target** folder except file matching with **customer-enquiry*.jar**.

Similar to Customer Enquiry **.dockerignore** file, create **.dockerignore** files for Enquiry Broadcast and Config Server applications.

Enquiry Broadcast .dockerignore

Create a file with a name **.dockerignore** inside the Enquiry Broadcast application project:

.dockerignore

```
.git
.settings
.classpath
.gitignore
.project
src
pom.xml
target/*
!target/enquiry-broadcast*.jar
```

Enquiry Broadcast .dockerignore

Create a file with a name **.dockerignore** inside the Config Server application project:

.dockerignore

```
.git
.settings
.classpath
.gitignore
.project
src
```

```
pom.xml
target/*
!target/config-server*.jar
```

Recipe 35: Creating Dockerfile

As discussed before, **Dockerfile** is a text file with the set of instructions that is read by Docker daemon to generate Docker image. Also mentioned before, the base image that we will be using for microservices Docker containers is Alpine Corretto 17.

Customer Enquiry Dockerfile

Create a file with the name **Dockerfile** inside the Customer Enquiry application project:

Dockerfile

```
# Base Image
FROM amazoncorretto:17-alpine-jdk

# Create application directory
RUN mkdir customer-enquiry

# Set application directory as work directory
WORKDIR /customer-enquiry

# Create log directory inside customer-enquiry
RUN mkdir log

# Copy last built customer enquiry executable jar to application directory and rename it to customer-enquiry.jar
COPY target/customer-enquiry*.jar customer-enquiry.jar

# Copy entry point script to customer-enquiry
COPY CustomerEnquiryEntryPoint.sh CustomerEnquiryEntryPoint.sh

# Convert entry point script in unix format
RUN dos2unix CustomerEnquiryEntryPoint.sh

```

```
# Give executable permissions on entry point script
RUN chmod +x CustomerEnquiryEntryPoint.sh

# Set the entry point script as ENTRYPOINT
ENTRYPOINT ["/customer-enquiry/CustomerEnquiryEntryPoint.sh"]
```

The Dockerfile will be present in the project folder at root level and expects the customer enquiry application executable to be present in the target folder, which is normally the case as well, **mvn install** command build the jar inside the **target** folder.

Customer Enquiry project structure

Here is the output of the tree command for better understanding of the structure:

```
tree -L 2
```

The output would be:

```
.
├── .classpath
├── .dockerignore
├── .git
├── .gitignore
├── .project
├── .settings
├── CustomerEnquiryEntryPoint.sh
├── Dockerfile
├── README.md
├── pom.xml
├── src
│   ├── main
│   └── test
└── target
    ├── classes
    ├── customer-enquiry-0.0.1-SNAPSHOT.jar
    ├── customer-enquiry-0.0.1-SNAPSHOT.jar.original
    ├── generated-sources
    ├── generated-test-sources
    ├── maven-archiver
    └── test-classes
```

The files that are highlighted are the ones to be used as part of docker build context, and the rest are ignored because of **.dockerignore** file.

Similarly, **Dockerfile** for Enquiry Broadcast and Config Server are to be created.

Enquiry Broadcast Dockerfile

Create a file with the name **Dockerfile** inside the Enquiry Broadcast application project:

Dockerfile

```
# Base Image
FROM amazoncorretto:17-alpine-jdk

# Create application directory
RUN mkdir enquiry-broadcast

# Set application directory as work directory
WORKDIR /enquiry-broadcast

# Create log directory inside enquiry-broadcast
RUN mkdir log

# Copy last built enquiry broadcast executable jar to application directory and rename it to enquiry-broadcast.jar
COPY target/enquiry-broadcast*.jar enquiry-broadcast.jar

# Copy entry point script to enquiry-broadcast
COPY EnquiryBroadcastEntryPoint.sh EnquiryBroadcastEntryPoint.sh

# Convert entry point script in unix format
RUN dos2unix EnquiryBroadcastEntryPoint.sh

# Give executable permissions on entry point script
RUN chmod +x EnquiryBroadcastEntryPoint.sh

# Set the entry point script as ENTRYPOINT
ENTRYPOINT ["/enquiry-broadcast/EnquiryBroadcastEntryPoint.sh"]
```

Config Server Dockerfile

Create a file with the name **Dockerfile** inside the Config Server application project:

Dockerfile

```
# Base Image
FROM amazoncorretto:17-alpine-jdk

# Create application directory
RUN mkdir config-server

# Set application directory as work directory
WORKDIR /config-server

# Create log directory inside config-server
RUN mkdir log

# Copy last built config server executable jar to application directory and rename it to config-server.jar
COPY target/config-server*.jar config-server.jar

# Copy entry point script to config-server
COPY ConfigServerEntryPoint.sh ConfigServerEntryPoint.sh

# Convert entry point script in unix format
RUN dos2unix ConfigServerEntryPoint.sh

# Give executable permissions on entry point script
RUN chmod +x ConfigServerEntryPoint.sh

# Set the entry point script as ENTRYPOINT
ENTRYPOINT ["/config-server/ConfigServerEntryPoint.sh"]
```

Now, once the required files entry point script **.dockerignore** and **Dockerfile** have been created, Docker images can also be created. Please read the next recipe for more details.

Recipe 36: Build Docker image using CLI

Docker image can be created using **Command Line Interface** (**CLI**) by invoking Docker build command, which passes the Docker context to the Docker Engine. Docker Engine goes through instructions written in the Dockerfile to create a Docker image for the application. Before proceeding, make sure that the Docker daemon is running in the background. The docker daemon status can be checked via below commands:

- **`docker info`**
- **`ps -ef | grep dockerd`**

If not up, run the following command as documented in *Recipe 32*:

```
sudo dockerd
```

Building Customer Enquiry Docker image

Once Docker daemon is running in background, run the following command from the location in the file system where Dockerfile is present:

```
sudo docker build . -t customer-enquiry-1.0
```

Here,

- **.** indicates to include all files in the current directory location.
- **`customer-enquiry-1.0`** is the tag to be set for the image. Tags are important for version controlling the image. Tag is of the format **`<repository>:<tag>`**. It is slightly confusing as there is an option to provide a separate value of **`<tag>`** whose default value is **`latest.`** **`<repository>:<tag>`** is sometimes referred to as a tag or name.

The output of the command would be as shown in the *Figure 5.9*:

```
varun@DESKTOP-C133REE:/mnt/d/varun/work/projects/FinancialServicesMarketplace/Customer Enquiry$ sudo docker build . -t customer-enquiry-1.0
[+] Building 3.1s (13/13) FINISHED
 => [internal] load build definition from Dockerfile
 => => transferring dockerfile: 870B
 => [internal] load .dockerignore
 => => transferring context: 144B
 => [internal] load metadata for docker.io/library/amazoncorretto:17-alpine-jdk
 => [1/8] FROM docker.io/library/amazoncorretto:17-alpine-jdk@sha256:7fa638463726cb1646100882b2baafd1b78978007bbfc28cb36a7fb5e9ebe8dd
 => [internal] load build context
 => => transferring context: 140B
 => CACHED [2/8] RUN mkdir customer-enquiry
 => CACHED [3/8] WORKDIR /customer-enquiry
 => CACHED [4/8] RUN mkdir log
 => CACHED [5/8] COPY target/customer-enquiry*.jar customer-enquiry.jar
 => CACHED [6/8] COPY CustomerEnquiryEntryPoint.sh CustomerEnquiryEntryPoint.sh
 => CACHED [7/8] RUN dos2unix CustomerEnquiryEntryPoint.sh
 => CACHED [8/8] RUN chmod +x CustomerEnquiryEntryPoint.sh
 => exporting to image
 => => exporting layers
 => => writing image sha256:26654e567f75ac32b84e3c86848ed6e70db8010178498214660a33b1d0d5924b
 => => naming to docker.io/library/customer-enquiry-1.0
varun@DESKTOP-C133REE:/mnt/d/varun/work/projects/FinancialServicesMarketplace/Customer Enquiry$ _
```

Figure 5.9: Output of the docker build command

The output of the command shows the usage of **.dockerignore** file and creation of interim layered images if not cached, as well as using cached images if available before creating the final image in the end. What is worth noticing is that the 8 steps in the output corresponds to the 8 instructions present in the **Dockerfile**, before setting the **ENTRYPOINT** for the container. The created image is present in the Docker server which can be accessed later for running Docker containers.

Similarly create Docker images for Enquiry Broadcast and Config Server applications.

Building Enquiry Broadcast Docker image

Run the following command from the location in the file system where **Dockerfile** is present:

```
sudo docker build . -t enquiry-broadcast-1.0
```

The command generates the Docker image for Enquiry Broadcast.

Building Config Server Docker image

Run the following command from the location in the file system where **Dockerfile** is present.

```
sudo docker build . -t config-server-1.0
```

The command generates the Docker image for Config Server.

Verifying created Docker images

Run the below query to verify that the Docker images have been created:

```
sudo docker images
```

The output would be:

```
REPOSITORY              TAG       IMAGE ID        CREATED         SIZE
config-server-1.0       latest    7c3426d71328    3 days ago      246MB
enquiry-broadcast-1.0   latest    56cb01e33d52    3 days ago      265MB
customer-enquiry-1.0    latest    5a0a07065bed    4 days ago      263MB
```

As names of all the images are in the output, it implies that the images have been created successfully.

Running Docker images

In the test and production environments, Docker images are run as containers on top of an OCI complaint container orchestrator platform such as AWS ECS, Kubernetes, and so on. This is where the power of containers is realized to its max; new containers are spawned on the fly horizontally scaling the applications as well adding new microservices to the ecosystem.

In development environments, images can be run simply using the following command:

docker run

The command can be run with lot of options, and the ones which are commonly used are documented in the *Table 5.2:*

Option	Usage
--network	Connecting a container to a network. Example: **--network=host** Connects the container to the host machine.
--volume, -v	Mounting a volume. Example: **-v=/mnt/d/input:/app/input** Mounts **/mnt/d/input** from network to **/app/input** of container.
--env, -e	Setting environment variables inside a container. Example: **-e=MIN_HEAP_SIZE=256m** Sets **MIN_HEAP_SIZE** as environment variable.
--workdir, -w	Setting work directory of the container. Example: **--workdir=/app** Sets the work directory as **/app**
--cpus	Assigning number of CPUs to the container. Example **--cpus=2** Assigns 2 CPUs to the container.
--name	Assigning a name to a container **--name=CustomerEnquiry1** Assigns name **CustomerEnquiry1** to the container.

Table 5.2: Commonly used docker run options

Image name needs to be passed as an argument to the **docker run** command to start a container for that image.

Recipe 37: Run Docker image using CLI

Before running Docker images as container, make sure that Docker daemon is running on the host machine. Once it is running, the docker run command can be used to spawn a container. Both the services Customer Enquiry and Enquiry Broadcast has a dependency on Config Server, so run it first before them.

Running Config Server Docker image

We have created an entry point script for Config Server Docker image which will be invoked first on starting the container for the image. As the script requires few environment variables for its execution, they need to be set in container using the options discussed previously for the **`docker run`** command.

Run the following command to start the Docker container for the provided image:

```
sudo docker run --network=host -e MIN_HEAP_SIZE=256m -e MAX_HEAP_SIZE=512m \
-e PROFILE=git \
-e CONFIG_SERVER_USERNAME=fsmConfigAdmin -e CONFIG_SERVER_PASSWORD=password \
-e GIT_PASSWORD=**** \
config-server-1.0:latest
```

Here,

- The value of different environment variables is set using a **`docker run`** option.
- In the last line, name of the image is passed, keyword **`latest`** is the tag name to be used which is optional, and **`latest`** is the default value of the tag.

The command starts a new container and the output would be as shown in *Figure 5.10*:

Figure 5.10: Output of the docker run command

Similarly, containers can be started for Customer Enquiry and Enquiry Broadcast microservices.

Running Customer Enquiry Docker image

Run the following command to start the Docker container for the provided image:

```
sudo docker run --network=host -e MIN_HEAP_SIZE=256m -e MAX_HEAP_SIZE=512m \
-e CONFIG_SERVER_URL=configserver:http://localhost:8888 \
-e CONFIG_SERVER_USERNAME=fsmConfigAdmin -e CONFIG_SERVER_PASSWORD=password \
-e DATABASE_URL=jdbc:postgresql://fs-marketplace.cbgzpif7rd3e.us-east-1.
rds.amazonaws.com:5432/postgres \
```

```
-e DATABASE_USERNAME=postgres -e DATABASE_PASSWORD=secret11 \
customer-enquiry-1.0:latest
```

Running Enquiry Broadcast Docker image

Run the following command to start the Docker container for the provided image:

```
sudo docker run --network=host -e MIN_HEAP_SIZE=256m -e MAX_HEAP_SIZE=512m \
-e CONFIG_SERVER_URL=configserver:http://localhost:8888 \
-e CONFIG_SERVER_USERNAME=fsmConfigAdmin -e CONFIG_SERVER_PASSWORD=password \
-e DATABASE_URL=jdbc:postgresql://fs-marketplace.cbgzpif7rd3e.us-east-1.
rds.amazonaws.com:5432/postgres \
-e DATABASE_USERNAME=postgres -e DATABASE_PASSWORD=secret11 \
enquiry-broadcast-1.0:latest
```

Recipe 38: Entering Docker containers

In this recipe, the three containers have started corresponding to the three applications: Config Server, Customer Enquiry and Enquiry Broadcast.

The running Docker containers can be listed using the following command:

```
sudo docker ps
```

The output would be as shown in *Figure 5.11*:

```
varun@DESKTOP-C133REE: $ sudo docker ps
[sudo] password for varun:
CONTAINER ID   IMAGE                          COMMAND                    CREATED          STATUS
d1684b1907d3   enquiry-broadcast-1.0:latest   "/enquiry-broadcast/…"   18 minutes ago   Up 18 minutes
d1e5df9363f8   customer-enquiry-1.0:latest    "/customer-enquiry/C…"   20 minutes ago   Up 20 minutes
b5862122e451   config-server-1.0:latest       "/config-server/Conf…"   23 minutes ago   Up 23 minutes
```

***Figure 5.11**: Output of the docker ps command*

As they all are running in their separate containers, it is equivalent to say that they are running in their totally separate environments. However, for development purpose, they are currently bound to the same host. If they are not bound to the same host, the ports on which they are running will not interfere with each other, which also means that all microservices and their instances can possibly run on the same port without interference with other.

As shown in *Figure 5.11,* each container is allotted a unique container Id and that can be used to get into the running container's shell using the following command:

```
docker exec -it <container_id> sh
```

Here,

- `-it` is interactive and TTY (Teletype).
- `container_id` is the ID of the target container.

Entering Config Server container

Run the following command to enter the running Config Server container:

```
sudo docker exec -it b5862122e451 sh
```

Here the container id is **b5862122e451**, which is of Config Server application as shown in *Figure 5.11*. The output of the given command would be as shown in *Figure 5.12*:

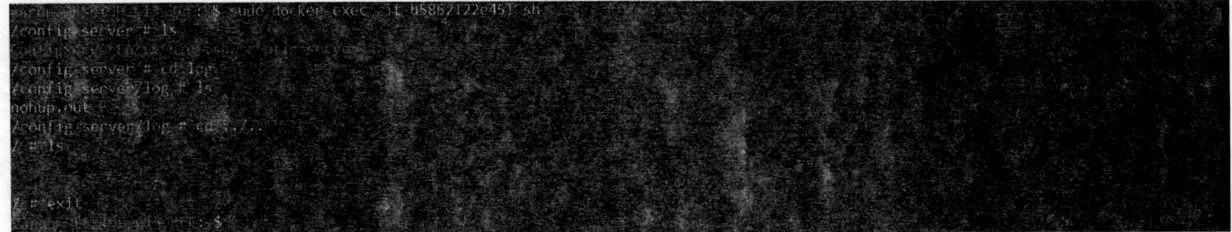

***Figure 5.12**: Getting inside of Docker container of Config Server application*

Once in the docker container's shell, all the commands executed will run in that container until the container is exited using the **exit** command, as also shown as the last command in *Figure 5.12*.

Similarly, the other two containers can be enquired.

Entering Customer Enquiry container

Run the following command to enter the running Config Server container:

```
sudo docker exec -it d1e5df9363f8 sh
```

Here, **d1e5df9363f8** is the container ID of Customer Enquiry container as also shown in the *Figure 5.11*.

Entering Enquiry Broadcast container

Run the following command to enter the running Config Server container:

```
sudo docker exec -it d1684b1907d3 sh
```

Here, **d1684b1907d3** is the container id of Enquiry Broadcast container as also shown in the *Figure 5.11*.

Pushing Docker images to image registry

Image registries complying with OCI standards are used to store and manage OCI images, and there are many implementations of the same, including Docker Hub which is the world's largest library and community for container images. All major cloud providers have their own image registries, such as, Amazon ECR (Elastic Container Registry), Azure Container Registry, Google Cloud Container Registry, Oracle Cloud Registry, and so on.

As part of this book, **Amazon ECR** is the registry that will be used to maintain and store our application images. It is a fully managed image registry powered by Amazon and offers high performance, and furthermore, images can be pushed or pulled easily from anywhere. It is very handy for running the applications inside AWS environments as can be accessed using simple resource-based permissions using AWS IAM.

An AWS account has an ECR private registry and can be accessed using the following URL:

```
https://<aws_account_id>.dkr.ecr.<region>.amazonaws.com
```

Here, `aws_account_id` is the account id of the respective account. One or more repositories can be created in a registry to store images in them. By default, the AWS account has read and write permissions to the repositories in its registry. Docker clients need to authenticate to the private registry before the **`docker push`** and **`docker pull`** commands can be used to push and pull images.

Repository creation strategy

Ideally there should be one repository per image and images need to be version controlled using the tags set for that image. This is not practical majorly for an application that comprises of number of microservices each having its own image, going by the ideal setup there will be number of repositories that needed to be created and maintainer.

Recommended way is to create one repository for the application and then differentiate between the images for different microservices using the tags. This is a smarter way in which the tags are assigned, such that they hold both the name and version of the image. This is the strategy that is being taken and demonstrated next.

Recipe 39: Creating a repository in AWS ECR

An AWS repository can be simply created using both AWS Management Console or via AWS CLI.

Creating repository using AWS Management Console

Follow the given steps to create an AWS repository via AWS S3 Management Console:

1. Login to the AWS Management Console and search ECR or type in the following URL: **https://us-east-1.console.aws.amazon.com/ecr/repositories** The region can be changed as per your preference.
2. Click on the **Create repository** option, and it will open a self-explanatory form.
3. Fill in all the required details.
    a. Repository name: **`fsm-repository`**
4. Click **Create repository** again.

And that is it! an ECR repository will be created.

Creating repository using AWS CLI

A repository in AWS ECR can be created using the following AWS CLI command:

```
aws ecr create-repository \
--repository-name fsm-repository \
--image-scanning-configuration scanOnPush=true \
--region us-east-1
```

Here,

- **`fsm-repository`** is the name of the repository.
- **`scanOnPush`** is a flag if set to **`true`** makes sure the image is scanned for vulnerabilities when pushed.

Output is as shown in the *Figure 5.13*:

```
$ aws ecr create-repository \
pository> --repository-name fsm-repository \
> --image-scanning-configuration scanOnPush=true \
> --region us-east-1
{
    "repository": {
        "repositoryArn": "arn:aws:ecr:us-east-1:746797604555:repository/fsm-repository",
        "registryId": "746797604555",
        "repositoryName": "fsm-repository",
        "repositoryUri": "746797604555.dkr.ecr.us-east-1.amazonaws.com/fsm-repository",
        "createdAt": "2023-04-09T17:36:29+05:30",
        "imageTagMutability": "MUTABLE",
        "imageScanningConfiguration": {
            "scanOnPush": true
        },
        "encryptionConfiguration": {
            "encryptionType": "AES256"
        }
    }
}
```

***Figure 5.13**: Output of AWS create-repository command*

Using the given command, a new repository has been created with the name **`fsm-repository`** and has a unique URI as given:

`746797604555.dkr.ecr.us-east-1.amazonaws.com/fsm-repository`

Recipe 40: Authenticating to ECR

As mentioned, an AWS account has an **Elastic Container Registry** (**ECR**) and Docker clients need to authenticate to it before images can be pushed or pulled from a repository in the registry.

If AWS CLI has been configured to query the AWS account, **`get-login-password`** is the simplest way to fetch the password for accessing ECR, using the following command:

```
aws ecr get-login-password --region <region>
```

The given command is joint with the **`docker login`** command using the pipe separator and the final query would be:

```
aws ecr get-login-password --region <region> | docker login --username AWS
--password-stdin <aws_account_id>.dkr.ecr.<region>.amazonaws.com
```

Here, the username to be used is AWS. Before running the final query, make sure that the docker client user, in this case **`root`**, is part of the docker group. Otherwise, the user needs to be added to the docker group. Once confirmed, run the following query to authenticate your Docker client with the ECR:

```
aws ecr get-login-password --region us-east-1 | sudo docker login --username AWS --password-stdin 746797604555.dkr.ecr.us-east-1.amazonaws.com
```

The output of the query would be:

```
WARNING! Your password will be stored unencrypted in /root/.docker/config.json.
Configure a credential helper to remove this warning. See
https://docs.docker.com/engine/reference/commandline/login/#credentials-store

Login Succeeded
```

After successful login, the Docker client will be able to push and pull the images to and from the ECR repository.

Recipe 41: Pushing images to ECR repository

Before pushing images to a repository, they need to be tagged first with that repository. As tag is a combination of **<repository>:<tag>**, it makes sure that the correct name and version is being used. When an image is pushed with a tag that already exists in the repository, the tag will be assigned to a newly pushed image. A command in the fellow format is being used to tag an image with a repository:

```
sudo docker tag <repository-source>:<tag-source> <repository-target>:<tag-target>
```

Here,

- **<repository-source>:<tag-source>** is the name or tag of the local image that needs to be pushed.
- **<repository-target>** is the name of the target repository.
- **<tag-target>** is the tag of the image in the target repository, which is optional with the default value as **latest**.

Once an image is tagged, it is pushed to the repository using the following command:

```
sudo docker push <repository-target>:<tag-target>
```

Here,

- **<repository-target>** is the target repository.
- **<tag-target>** is the target tag, which is optional with the default value as **latest**.

Pushing Customer Enquiry image

As mentioned, the image needs to be first tagged with the target repository. Run the following command to tag it with the ECR repository:

```
sudo docker tag customer-enquiry-1.0:latest 746797604555.dkr.ecr.us-east-1.
amazonaws.com/fsm-repository:customer-enquiry-1.0
```

Here,

- **`746797604555.dkr.ecr.us-east-1.amazonaws.com/fsm-repository`** is a target repository.
- **`customer-enquiry-1.0`** is a target tag as per the strategy discussed.

After tagging push the image using the following command:

```
sudo docker push 746797604555.dkr.ecr.us-east-1.amazonaws.com/fsm-
repository:customer-enquiry-1.0
```

The output of the commands is as shown in *Figure 5.14*:

Figure 5.14: Output of docker tag and docker push commands

Similarly push other two images to the ECR repository.

Pushing Enquiry Broadcast image

Run the following commands to tag and push the Enquiry Broadcast image to the ECR repository:

```
sudo docker tag enquiry-broadcast-1.0:latest 746797604555.dkr.ecr.us-
east-1.amazonaws.com/fsm-repository:enquiry-broadcast-1.0

sudo docker push 746797604555.dkr.ecr.us-east-1.amazonaws.com/fsm-reposito-
ry:enquiry-broadcast-1.0
```

Pushing Config Server image

Run the following commands to tag and push the Config Server image to the ECR repository:

```
sudo docker tag config-server-1.0:latest 746797604555.dkr.ecr.us-east-1.amazonaws.com/fsm-repository:config-server-1.0

sudo docker push 746797604555.dkr.ecr.us-east-1.amazonaws.com/fsm-repository:config-server-1.0
```

Viewing images in the ECR repository

Login to AWS Management Console to view the images pushed to the ECR repository. Refer to *Figure 5.15* for viewing the three images that have been pushed to the repository **`fsm-repository`**:

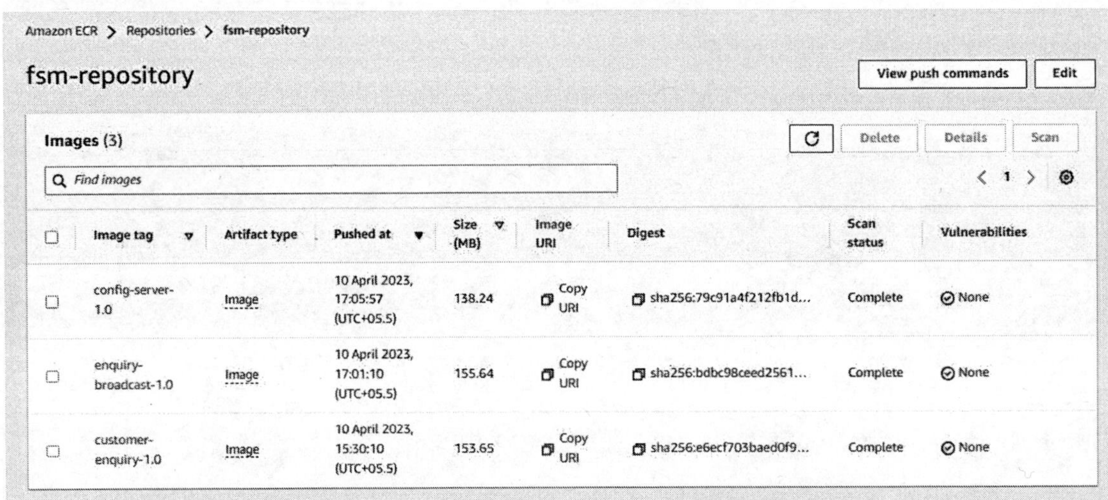

Figure 5.15*: View of ECR repository with three images*

Please notice that the scan status is complete and no vulnerabilities have been found in the images. The scan is done because it has been configured while creating the repository as explained in a previous recipe.

Conclusion

In this chapter, we have learnt the importance of containerization, OCI specifications and different implementations for the same. Step by step approach has been discussed for containerizing an application, starting with installation of Docker Engine, building of Docker images, running images as Docker containers, creation of AWS ECR repository and pushing the images into that repository. Each step has been detailed out with recipes explaining the same using running code examples, that are all linked to the broader application **Financial Service Marketplace**.

In the next chapter, we will learn about **continuous integration (CI)** and build Git pipelines for the automatic integration of the code. It will make sure as soon as the code is committed for an application in the Git repository, an automatic pipeline will be invoked, compile the code into an artifact and create docker images for the same.

Points to remember

- Keep the container images as small as possible. This can be achieved by choosing the base image wisely, removing unnecessary files from the context and only including what is necessary for the application to run.
- Always use environment variables as pass configuration information to a Docker container, such as database connection strings.
- When pushing Docker images to a container registry, make sure to use a secure registry and follow best practices for securing container images.
- Tag Docker images with a version number or other identifier to make it easier to manage and track different versions of the image.

Questions

1. What will happen if there is no **`.dockerignore`** file in the context?
2. Name a few common Docker CLI commands used for managing Docker images and containers.
3. What is a multi-stage build? How is it beneficial?
4. What is the difference between a private and public container registry?
5. How to tag a Docker image before pushing it to a container registry?
6. How is a Docker image shared between a development and production environment?

CHAPTER 6

Pipeline Automation for CI/CD

Introduction

The last chapter detailed out the containerization world, explaining the benefits of containers and the purpose of the **Open Container Initiative** (**OCI**). It also explained the steps involved in containerizing an application, starting from installing Docker, building and running Docker images, and finally pushing them to an image registry. Also, during the course, of the chapter the three microservices that have been developed as part of the *Financial Service Marketplace* application are containerized using Docker.

In this chapter, we will talk about continuous integration and its benefits in software application development. We will explain the development of pipelines used for compiling the code and building artifacts, and ways to automate these pipelines for continuous integration and delivery. As part of this development, we will talk about code quality checks, security checks, test cases, etc. and how they are integrated into the pipelines to improve the overall standard of the artifacts produced.

Structure

In this chapter, we will discuss the following topics:

- Introduction to CI and CD pipelines
- Benefits of CI / CD pipelines

- GitLab CI/CD
- Pipeline terminology
- Building GitLab pipelines
- Scheduling GitLab pipelines

Objectives

By the end of this chapter, we will learn the importance of **continuous integration** (**CI**) and **continuous delivery/deployment (CD)**, and how pipeline automations contribute to it. We will also demonstrate the different steps of a pipeline and how they can be used in automation testing, security testing, automatic code reviews and building. During this chapter, we will build GitLab pipelines for the three microservices: Customer Enquiry, Enquiry Broadcast and Config Server, and automate them for continuous integration and deployment.

Introduction to CI and CD pipelines

Continuous integration and **continuous delivery** (**CI/CD**) is a powerful practice that falls under the DevOps group, a group that is a combination of development and operations teams. CI/CD combines the practices of continuous integration and continuous delivery. CI/CD pipelines have revolutionized the software development and deployment processes, enabling organizations to deliver software faster, more reliably, and with higher quality. These pipelines are the backbone of modern software development, automating various stages of the **software development lifecycle** (**SDLC**) and providing a structured, efficient way to build, test, and deploy applications.

At its core, a CI/CD pipeline is a set of automated workflows and processes that orchestrate the steps required to take code from development to production. The CI part, focuses on the frequent and automated integration of code changes into a shared repository. Developers push code changes to this repository, triggering automated builds and tests to ensure that new code additions do not introduce errors or break existing functionality.

The CD part, continuous delivery and continuous deployment, extends the CI concept by automating the deployment of tested code to various environments, such as staging and production. Continuous Delivery ensures that code is always in a deployable state, allowing for manual approval before deployment to production. Continuous Deployment takes this a step further by automating the release of code to production as soon as it passes all tests.

Benefits of CI/CD pipelines

Continuous integration (**CI**) and **continuous delivery/continuous Deployment** (**CD**) pipelines offer numerous benefits to software development and deployment processes, contributing to faster, more reliable, and higher-quality software delivery. Here are the key benefits of CI and CD pipelines:

- **Automated testing**: CI pipelines automate the process of running tests whenever code changes are made. This ensures that issues and bugs are identified and addressed early in the development process, reducing the cost and effort required for bug fixes later.
- **Rapid feedback**: Developers receive immediate feedback on the quality of their code after each commit, allowing them to quickly address issues and iterate on their work. This accelerates the development cycle.
- **Code quality improvement**: CI encourages best practices such as code reviews, code standards, and code quality checks. As a result, the overall code quality tends to improve over time.
- **Consistency**: CD pipelines ensure that the same deployment process is followed consistently across environments. This minimizes configuration drift and reduces the chances of deployment-related errors.
- **Reduced manual intervention**: CD pipelines automate deployment tasks, reducing the need for manual interventions. This decreases the risk of human errors during deployments.
- **Faster time-to-market**: CD pipelines enable organizations to release new features and updates to users quickly and with confidence. This agility in software delivery can give businesses a competitive edge.
- **Rollback capabilities**: CD pipelines often include automated rollback procedures. If an issue is detected in a production release, the pipeline can automatically roll back to the previous stable version, minimizing downtime and user impact.
- **Resource efficiency**: Automation of repetitive tasks and testing processes reduces the time and resources required for manual intervention, allowing teams to focus on more strategic and creative aspects of development.
- **Enhanced collaboration**: CI/CD practices promote collaboration among development, testing, and operations teams. They encourage shared responsibility for the entire software delivery process.
- **Increased reliability**: CD pipelines ensure that only thoroughly tested and validated code changes are deployed to production. This results in more stable and reliable applications.

- **Improved security**: Security checks and scans can be integrated into CI/CD pipelines to detect vulnerabilities and security issues early in the development process, reducing security risks.
- **Traceability and auditability**: CI/CD pipelines provide a detailed audit trail of code changes, tests, and deployments, which is valuable for compliance, troubleshooting, and accountability.
- **Scalability**: CI/CD pipelines are scalable and can handle the increased workload as development and deployment processes grow in complexity.
- **Cost savings**: By catching and addressing issues early in development, CI/CD pipelines help reduce the cost of fixing bugs and issues in production.

CI/CD pipelines significantly enhance the software development and deployment lifecycle by automating processes, ensuring code quality, accelerating delivery, and minimizing risks. These practices have become essential in modern software development and are widely adopted in DevOps and agile methodologies.

GitLab CI/CD

There is a wide range of CI/CD pipeline tools available, each with its own strengths and use cases. Some popular CI/CD tools include Jenkins, Travis CI, CircleCI, TeamCity, and GitLab CI/CD. These tools offer features like automated testing, deployment, integration with version control systems, and the ability to define and execute complex workflows. Amongst all of them, GitLab is the most robust and comprehensive platform and best suits for our use case. Here are some reasons why one should consider using GitLab for CI/CD:

- **Built-in version control**: GitLab includes a version control system (Git) as part of its platform, eliminating the need for external repositories. This cohesiveness provides a unified environment for code management, collaboration, and CI/CD.
- **Diverse ecosystem**: GitLab CI/CD integrates with a wide range of tools and services, allowing users to customize and extend their CI/CD pipelines as needed. This flexibility accommodates various technology stacks and deployment targets.
- **Community and support**: GitLab has a thriving community and offers both open-source and enterprise versions. Users can access documentation, forums, and professional support options.

Apart from the above mentioned, there are many other good reasons for the adoption of GitLab as a CI/ CD tool. Whether for a small development team or a large enterprise, GitLab's flexibility and feature set make it a valuable tool for achieving DevOps and CI/ CD goals.

Pipeline terminology

Before starting with CI/CD on GitLab, one should be aware of the common terminology used in the process.

.gitlab-ci.yml file

The **`.gitlab-ci.yml`** file, often referred to as the GitLab CI/CD configuration file, is a YAML file used by GitLab's built-in CI/CD pipeline system and is located at the root of the project. The file defines the stages, jobs, and tasks required to automate the testing, building, and deployment of code within a GitLab project. It is a crucial component for setting up and customizing CI/CD pipelines in GitLab, allowing developers to specify how their code should be processed and deployed when changes are pushed to the repository. The content of the file includes instructions for defining variables, specifying Runners (execution environments), and managing the entire CI/CD workflow, making it a central piece for automating software delivery processes.

Runners

GitLab Runners are lightweight, autonomous agents that run jobs in your GitLab CI/CD pipelines. These Runners can execute tasks such as building, testing, and deploying code. They can be hosted on various platforms, including cloud instances, on-premises servers, or even on developer workstations. Runners are essential for the automation and parallel execution of CI/CD jobs and play a vital role in scaling and optimizing your software development and delivery processes within GitLab.

Jobs

In GitLab CI/CD pipelines, jobs are individual tasks defined in the **`.gitlab-ci.yml`** file that specify a set of commands or scripts to be executed. Each job represents a discrete unit of work, such as building an application, running tests, or deploying code.

Stages

Stages group jobs together based on their logical order in the pipeline. Stages represent different phases of the CI/CD process, such as **`build`**, **`test`**, **`deploy`**, and **`cleanup`**. By organizing jobs into stages, one can ensure that tasks are executed sequentially and efficiently, with dependencies between jobs and stages clearly defined. This allows for greater control and automation in the CI/CD pipelines, enhancing the reliability and consistency of the software delivery process.

Building GitLab pipelines

As part of this chapter, GitLab CI/CD pipelines will be created for the three microservices: **Config Server**, **Customer Enquiry**, and **Enquiry Broadcast**. The only prerequisites for building pipelines are a GitLab project and a maintainer or owner role for the project. The projects of the above three microservices are already in GitLab, so we are good to go.

The next thing is to make sure that the **Runners** are available and registered with the project. It can be skipped if we are fine to use the shared Runners provided by GitLab. As part of this chapter, the GitLab Runners are to be used for running pipelines.

Recipe 42: Creating a .gitlab-ci.yml file

The `.gitlab-ci.yml` file is to be created at the root of the project in the repository. The file can be created in the file system and then pushed to the repository, or the pipeline editor provided by GitLab can be leveraged for the same. Follow the following steps to create a `.gitlab-ci.yml` file:

1. Login to the GitLab console and select the project for which the file needs to be created.

2. Select the branch and click + and then **New file**, refer to *Figure 6.1* for reference:

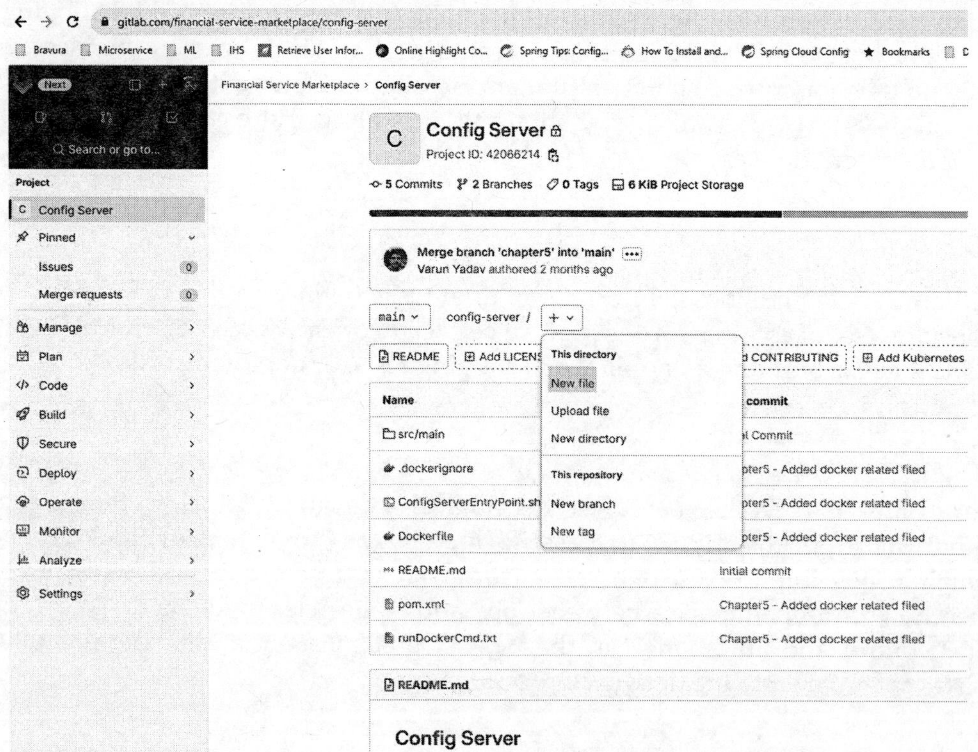

Figure 6.1: Creating a new file in the config server main branch

3. Paste the following code in the file editor:

```
stages:     # List of stages for jobs and their order of execution
  - build
  - test
  - deploy

build-job:
  stage: build  # The job runs in the `build` stage
  script:
    - date
    - echo "Project '$CI_PROJECT_PATH'"
    - echo "Brach '$CI_COMMIT_BRANCH'"
    - echo "Running '$CI_JOB_NAME' job under '$CI_JOB_STAGE' stage."
    - echo "The job is responsible for building the artifact."
  after_script:
    - echo "Job '$CI_JOB_NAME' is $CI_JOB_STATUS"

test1-job:
  stage: test
  script:
    - echo "Running '$CI_JOB_NAME' job under '$CI_JOB_STAGE' stage."
    - echo "The job is responsible for testing the artifact."

test2-job:
  stage: test
  script:
    - echo "Running '$CI_JOB_NAME' job under '$CI_JOB_STAGE' stage."
    - echo "The job is responsible for testing and allows failures."
  allow_failure: true

deploy-prod:
```

```
31.    stage: deploy
32.    script:
33.        - echo "Running '$CI_JOB_NAME' job under '$CI_JOB_STAGE' stage."
34.        - echo "The job will be responsible for deploying artifact"
35.    environment: production
```

Here,

- **`build-job`**, **`test1-job`**, **`test2-job`**, and **`deploy-prod`** are the four jobs.
- The jobs are grouped into three stages: **`build`**, **`test`** and **`deploy`**.
- The stages run in the order they are defined in the stages, as coded in lines *1-4*.
- If there is more than one job in a stage, they can run in parallel. If a job fails, the whole stage is marked as fail and the jobs from the subsequent stages do not start, unless the job that failed allows failure.
- **`allows_failure`**: It is set to true for jobs that can fail sometimes and we do not want the pipeline to halt because of this failure.
- The keywords starting with **`$`** are variables, the variables used in the above code are all predefined variables and their descriptions are documented in *Table 6.1*:

Variable name	Description
`CI_PROJECT_PATH`	Project name along with the project namespace
`CI_COMMIT_BRANCH`	Name of the commit branch
`CI_JOB_NAME`	Name of the job
`CI_JOB_STAGE`	Name of the job's stage
`CI_JOB_STATUS`	Status of the job: success, failed or cancelled

***Table 6.1**: Predefined variables with their descriptions*

Apart from using predefined variables Gitlab also has the provision to create custom global and job level variables:

- The commands mentioned under the script run in a sequence for a job.
- GitLab checks out the code in each job before executing the scripts.
- **`echo`** command displays the text in the UI when a job is viewed.
- The commands mentioned under **`after_script`** run in the end for a job.
- **`environment`** keyword defines and determines the environment to which the artifact is to be deployed. GitLab tracks what is being deployed to which environment.

4. Enter a commit message and click **Commit changes** to create the file.

Currently the file just has a skeleton defined for the pipeline, in the subsequent recipes the stages and jobs will be enhanced with the logic to build the Docker images for the corresponding microservice, tested and pushed to the Amazon **Elastic Container Registry (ECR)**.

Recipe 43: Viewing pipeline execution

As soon as the changes are committed to the Git repository the pipeline gets triggered and runs the jobs defined in the **`.gitlab-ci.yml`** file. The pipelines can be accessed from the **Pipelines** link on the left menu, refer to *Figure 6.2*:

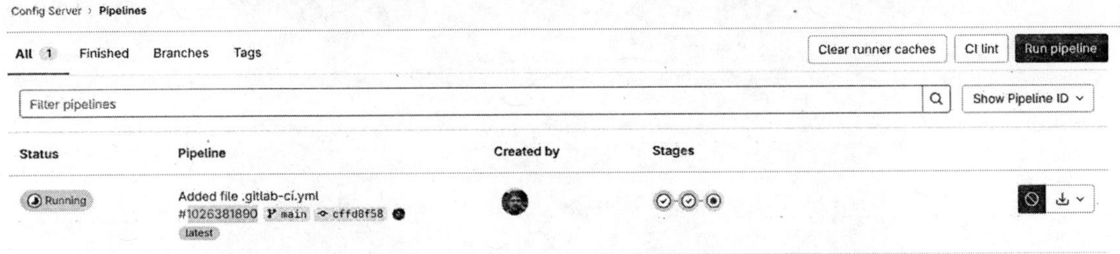

Figure 6.2: Pipeline running on committing the changes to the Git repository

Click on the pipeline id to view the visual representation of the pipeline execution. Refer to *Figure 6.3* to view the pipeline comprised of three stages, with the build and deploy stages having one job each and the test stage having two jobs that ran in parallel:

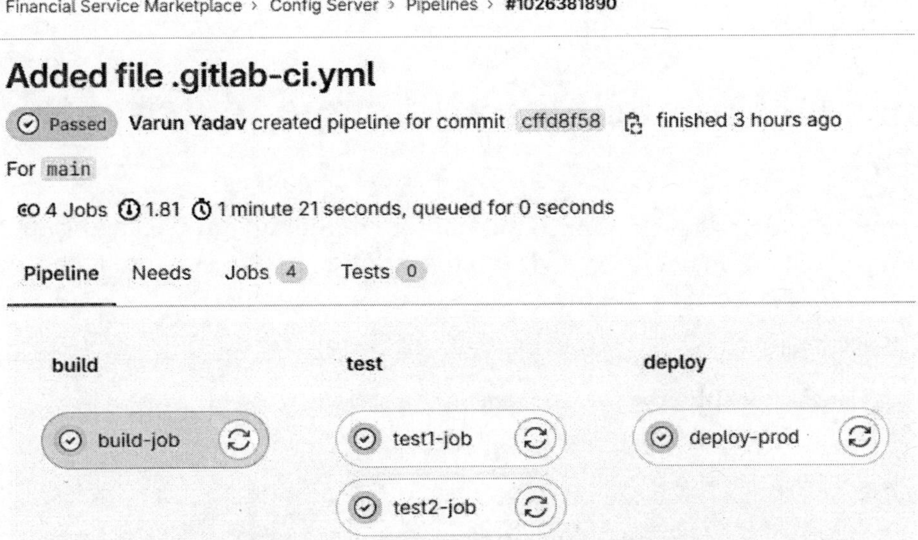

Figure 6.3: Pipeline visual representation

Click on one of the jobs, for example **build-job**, to view the details for that job, refer to *Figure 6.4* for reference, the text provided as an input to the **echo** command is visible on the job detail UI screen:

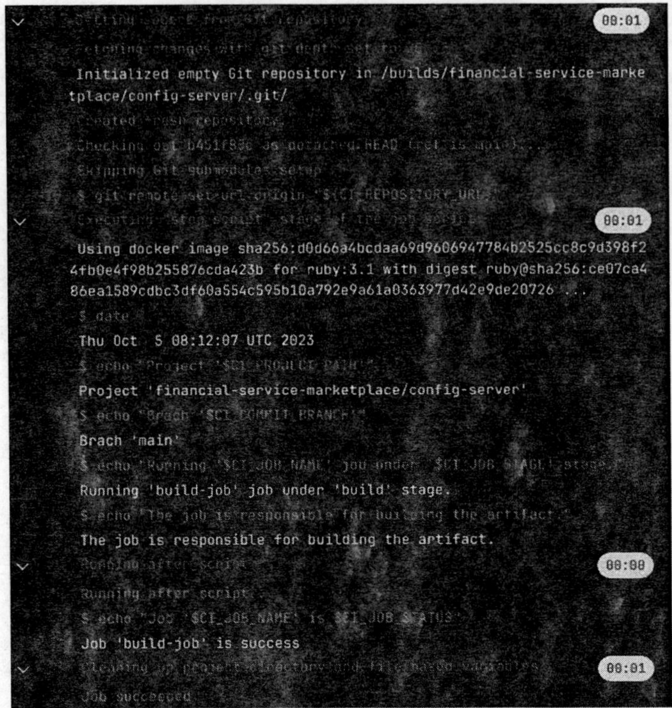

***Figure 6.4**: Pipeline's build-job details*

The skeleton CI/CD pipeline is up and running.

Recipe 44: Enhancing build stage to generate artifact

The microservices are Maven applications so for compiling and packaging the code the Runners need to have maven along with all the required packages. Update the build job in the **.gitlab-ci.yml** code as follows:

```
build-job:
  stage: build
  image: maven:3.8.4-openjdk-17
  script:
    - echo "Project '$CI_PROJECT_PATH'"
    - echo "Brach '$CI_COMMIT_BRANCH'"
```

```
7.        - echo "Running '$CI_JOB_NAME' job under '$CI_JOB_STAGE' stage."
8.        - echo "The job is responsible for building the artifact."
9.        - mvn package
10.     artifacts:
11.       paths:
12.         - target/config-server*.jar
13.       expire_in: 1 day
```

Here,

- *Line 3* of the code directs GitLab to use maven image with JDK 17 to be used for compiling the code.
- *Line 9* is a maven command that compiles the maven Spring boot code to generate the artifact in the **`target`** folder. As a part of this script, all the unit tests get executed making sure the new changes are not breaking any existing logic.
- **`artifacts`** define the artifacts if any are generated as part of the job. The artifacts can be accessed by the subsequent stages in the pipeline or can be downloaded from the UI if required.
- **`paths`** define the files and directories to be added to the artifacts. The paths are relative to the project repository.
- **`expire_in`** is being used to set the expiry time limit for the artifacts.

Refer to *Figure 6.5* for the details of the execution of the build job:

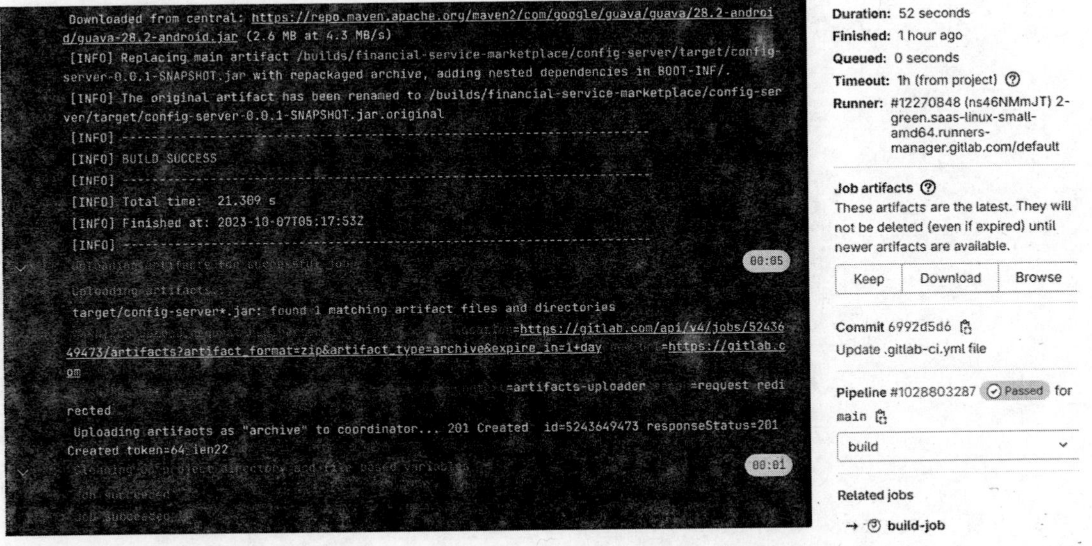

Figure 6.5: build-job generating and saving the Spring boot jar as an artifact

Recipe 45: Adding a stage to generate Docker image of the artifact

Once the code artifact has been generated in the previous stage, the next step is to generate the Docker image of the artifact. Update **`.gitlab-ci.yml`** code to add **`dockerize`** stage after the **`build`** stage as follows:

```
1. stages:   # List of stages for jobs and their order of execution
2.   - build
3.   - dockerize
4.   - test
5.   - deploy
6.
7. variables:
8.   IMAGE_VERSION: '1.0'
9.
10. dockeriz-job:
11.   stage: dockerize
12.   image: docker:latest
13.   services:
14.     - docker:dind
15.   script:
16.     - docker build . -t config-server-$IMAGE_VERSION
17.     - mkdir image
18.       - docker save config-server-$IMAGE_VERSION > image/config-server-$IMAGE_VERSION.tar
19.   artifacts:
20.     paths:
21.       - image
22.     expire_in: 1 hour
```

Here,

- *Line 3* shows a new stage **`dockerize`** has been added, which gets executed after the **`build`** stage.
- *Line 7-8* adds a new global variable **`IMAGE_VERSION`** used to control the versioning of the Docker image. Currently, the value is hardcoded but the logic can be built to dynamically assign this value.

- *Line 12* directs GitLab to use the Docker image.
- **`services`** section at *Line 13* defines any services that needs to be started before running the scripts.
- *Line 14* is used to start the **`docker-in-docker`** service. This is required because the runner itself runs as a Docker image.
- *Line 18* saves the Docker image as a **`tar`** file in the **`image`** directory, so that it can be added to an artifact and used in subsequent stages.

On execution, the **`dockerize-job`** runs the Docker **`build`** command inside the project checked-out folder. The folder contains the *Dockerfile* referenced by the command and the other prerequisite files **`.dockerignore`** and **`ConfigServerEntryPoint.sh`**. Moreover, config server jar used for building the Docker image is available in the **`target`** folder as an outcome of the execution of the previous **`build`** stage.

The script in *Line 16* builds the Docker image as per the contents of the *Dockerfile*. The name of the image is created by appending the value set in the variable **`IMAGE_VERSION`** with **`config-server`**. Refer to *Figure 6.6* for the details of the execution of the **`dockerize`** job:

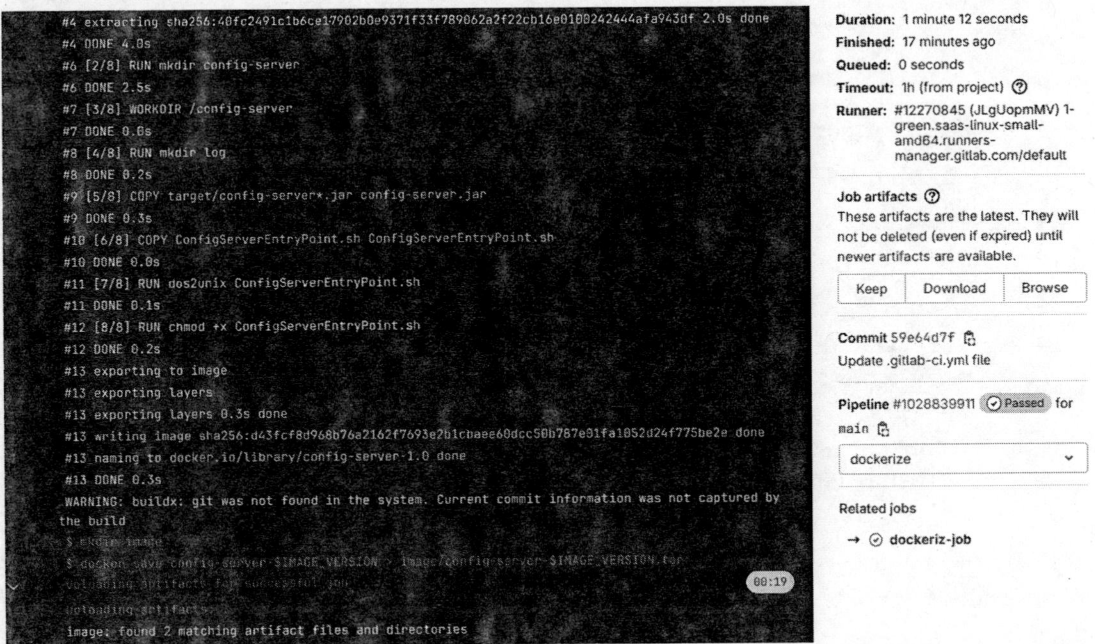

Figure 6.6: dockerize-job creating Docker image of the Spring boot artifact

Recipe 46: Enhancing test stage to test the Docker image

The Docker image needs to be tested before it can be pushed to the Amazon ECR. The test stage needs to be enhanced so that required tests can be done on the Docker image to get a surety that nothing majorly fails once the image is deployed. Any number of test jobs can be added to the stage for better test coverage. As part of this recipe to test Docker image is running fine, the image is started as a Docker container, and then the Actuator health URLs are accessed to check whether the Config Server is up or not. Update the test job in the **.gitlab-ci.yml** code as follows:

```
test1-job:
  stage: test
  variables:
    HEALTH_RESPONSE: ''
    STATUS: ''
  image: docker:latest
  services:
    - docker:dind
  before_script:
    - apk add --no-cache curl jq
  script:
    - echo "Running '$CI_JOB_NAME' job under '$CI_JOB_STAGE' stage."
    - echo "The job is responsible for testing the artifact."
    - docker load -i image/config-server-$IMAGE_VERSION.tar
    - docker run -d --network=host -e MIN_HEAP_SIZE=256m -e MAX_HEAP_SIZE=512m -e PROFILE=git -e CONFIG_SERVER_USERNAME=fsmConfigAdmin -e CONFIG_SERVER_PASSWORD=password -e GIT_PASSWORD=**** config-server-$IMAGE_VERSION:latest
    - sleep 15
    - HEALTH_RESPONSE=$(curl -s -X GET http://docker:8888/Actuator/health/)
    - echo "Health response is $HEALTH_RESPONSE"
    - STATUS=$(echo "$HEALTH_RESPONSE" | jq -r '.status')
    - echo "Health status is $STATUS"
    - |
      if [ "$STATUS" != "UP" ]; then
        echo "Status is not UP. Failing the pipeline."
```

```
24.         exit 1
25.     fi
```

Here,

- *Line 3-5* adds local variables to the job, the variables are to be used in the scripts for storing and accessing the Actuator health parameter.
- Commands mentioned under **`before_script`** are run before executing the scripts.
- *Line 10* adds the **`curl`** and **`jq`** packages on the Docker container. The packages are used to fetch and parse the response from the Actuator URL.
- *Line 14* loads the image generated as an artifact in the previous **`dockerize`** stage.
- *Line 15* runs the image as a detached Docker container.
- **`sleep`** halts the job for the mentioned time in seconds before executing the next command. This is done to make sure the container gets enough time to get started.
- *Lines 17-19* call the Actuator URL and stores the application health status is the **`STATUS`** variable. Note that instead of localhost in the URL Docker has been used, this is because when using the **`docker-in-docker`** service hostname is to be accessed via **`docker`** keyword.
- *Lines 21-25* show a multi-line command which has an **`If`** condition to fail the job if the status of the application is not **`UP`**. Any non-zero exit code is considered as a failure.

Refer to *Figure 6.7* for the details of the execution of the test job:

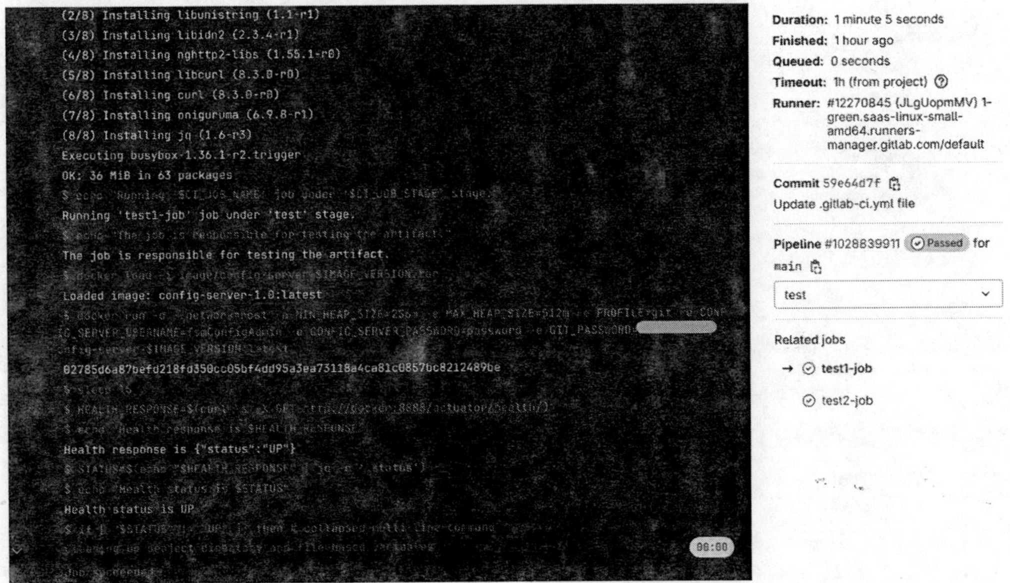

Figure 6.7: test-job1 testing Docker image by accessing the health status of the application

Recipe 47: Enhancing deploy stage to push the Docker image to Amazon ECR

Once the Docker image has passed the testing stage, it is safe to deploy that image in the UAT or production environments. As part of this recipe, in the deployment stage the Docker image will be pushed to the configured **AWS ECR (Elastic Container Registry)**. But before pushing anything to ECR authentication needs to be established between GitLab and AWS ECR, for this create an IAM user in AWS with the required privileges by attaching the following policy and note down its access key and secret key of the user:

AmazonEC2ContainerRegistryFullAccess: Security credentials need to be protected from direct access, for the same GitLab has a mechanism of CI/CD variables. These variables can be set at the project level or can be set at the group level and inherited in projects. These variables are injected in every pipeline run and can be used same as global variables. To set these variables, go to **Settings | CI/CD** and configure the values for the following variables:

- **`AWS_ACCESS_KEY_ID`**
- **`AWS_SECRET_ACCESS_KEY`**
- **`AWS_ACCOUNT_ID`**
- **`AWS_DEFAULT_REGION`**

Refer to *Figure 6.8* for reference:

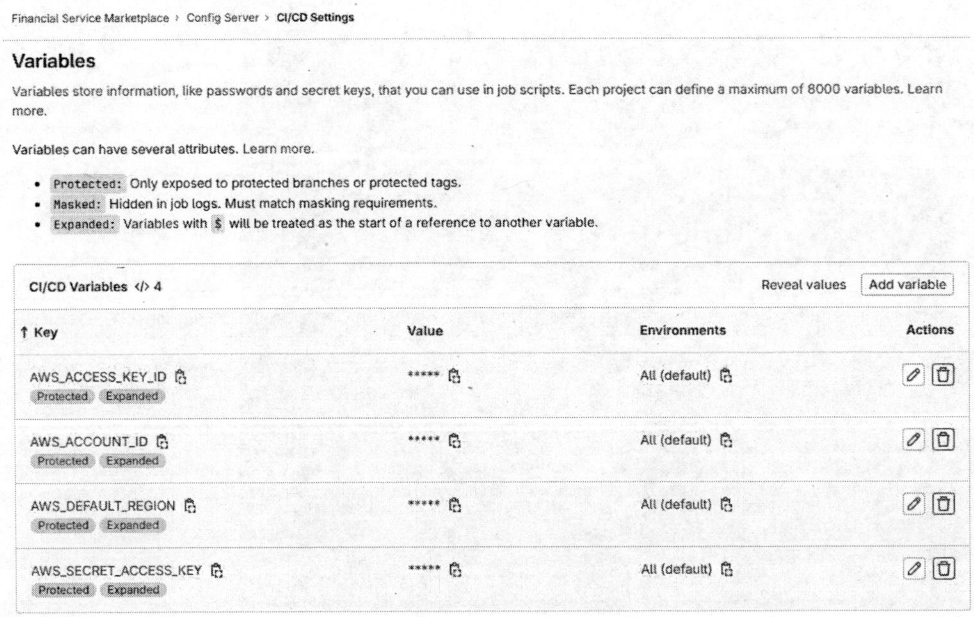

Financial Service Marketplace › Config Server › **CI/CD Settings**

Variables

Variables store information, like passwords and secret keys, that you can use in job scripts. Each project can define a maximum of 8000 variables. Learn more.

Variables can have several attributes. Learn more.

- `Protected:` Only exposed to protected branches or protected tags.
- `Masked:` Hidden in job logs. Must match masking requirements.
- `Expanded:` Variables with `$` will be treated as the start of a reference to another variable.

CI/CD Variables </> 4 Reveal values Add variable

↑ Key	Value	Environments	Actions
AWS_ACCESS_KEY_ID Protected Expanded	*****	All (default)	
AWS_ACCOUNT_ID Protected Expanded	*****	All (default)	
AWS_DEFAULT_REGION Protected Expanded	*****	All (default)	
AWS_SECRET_ACCESS_KEY Protected Expanded	*****	All (default)	

Figure 6.8: *CI/CD variables configured for Config Server project*

Update the deploy job in the **.gitlab-ci.yml** code as follows:

```
1.  deploy-prod:
2.    stage: deploy
3.    image: docker:latest
4.    services:
5.      - docker:dind
6.    variables:
7.        AWS_ECR_REGISTRY:  $AWS_ACCOUNT_ID.dkr.ecr.$AWS_DEFAULT_REGION.
    amazonaws.com
8.      AWS_ECR_FSM_REPO: $AWS_ECR_REGISTRY/fsm-repository
9.    before_script:
10.     - apk add -no-cache py3-pip
11.     - pip install awscli
12.   script:
13.     - echo "Running '$CI_JOB_NAME' job under '$CI_JOB_STAGE' stage."
14.     - echo "The job will be responsible for deploying artifact"
15.     - docker load -i image/config-server-$IMAGE_VERSION.tar
16.     - aws ecr get-login-password | docker login --username AWS --pass-
    word-stdin $AWS_ECR_REGISTRY
17.     - docker tag config-server-$IMAGE_VERSION:latest $AWS_ECR_FSM_RE-
    PO:config-server-$IMAGE_VERSION
18.     - docker push $AWS_ECR_FSM_REPO:config-server-$IMAGE_VERSION
19.   environment: production
```

Here,

- *Line 7* creates a local variable to store the location of the ECR registry by using the combination of GitLab CI/CD variables.
- *Line 10* adds the **py3-pip** package to the Docker container. The packages are used to install **awscli** later in *Line 11*.
- *Line 16* establishes an authentication between the Docker container running in GitLab and AWS ECR. It internally uses the CI/CD variables **AWS_ACCESS_KEY_ID** and **AWS_SECRET_ACCESS_KEY** for authentication.
- *Line 17* tags the image with the target repository.
- *Line 18* pushes the image to the target repository.

Refer to *Figure 6.9* for the details of the execution of the deployment job:

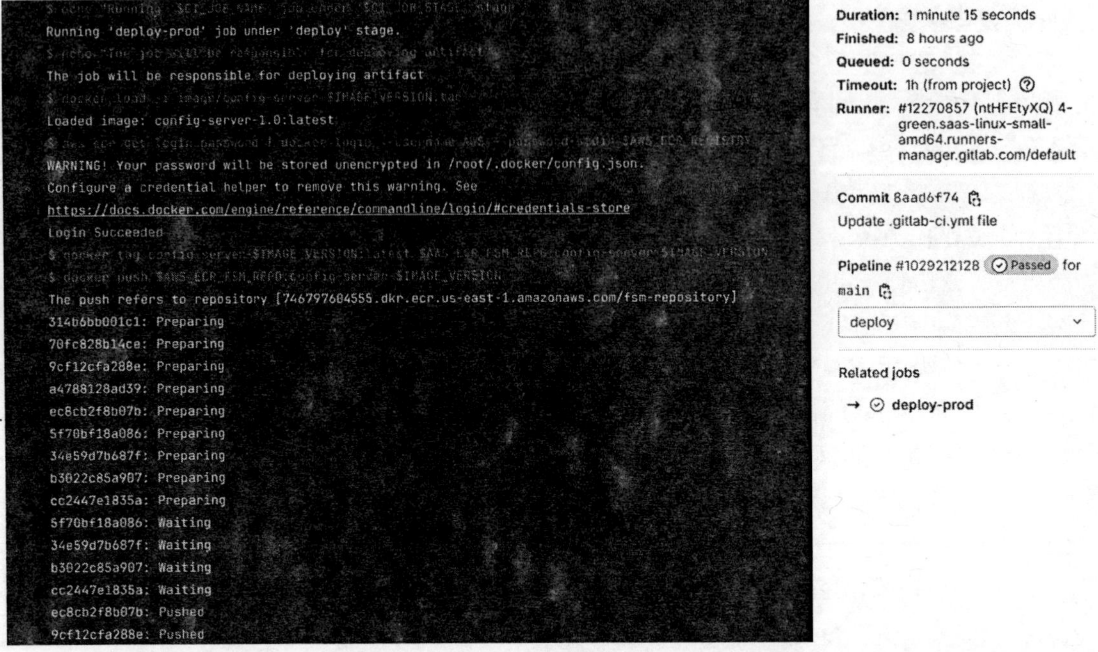

***Figure 6.9**: deploy-job pushing the Docker image to AWS ECR after successful authentication*

Recipe 48: Adding rules in the deployment job to only execute the job conditionally

By default, the pipeline gets triggered every time anything is committed or merged in the repository. Pushing Docker images as part of the deployment job should only be done in a predefined interval, preferably in overnight builds and not in every pipeline run. This saves a lot of unnecessary resource wastage and keeps the production environment releases more controlled. Update the deploy job in the **`.gitlab-ci.yml`** code as follows, so that it does not get executed in every pipeline run:

```
deploy-prod:
  stage: deploy
  image: docker:latest
  services:
    - docker:dind
  variables:
    # Existing Logic
  before_script:
```

```
9.       # Existing Logic
10.    script:
11.      # Existing Logic
12.    environment: production
13.    rules:
14.      - if: $CI_PIPELINE_SOURCE == 'merge_request_event'
15.        when: never # Do not run if the pipeline source is a merge request
16.      - if: $CI_PIPELINE_SOURCE == 'push'
17.        when: never # Do not run if the pipeline source is a push
18.      - when: on_success
19.          # Run in case of other instances like pipelines scheduled
```

Here,

- **`CI_PIPELINE_SOURCE`** is a predefined variable which holds the value of the source of the pipeline execution and can have possible values like **`push`**, **`web`**, **`schedule`**, **`api`**, **`external`**, **`chat`**, **`webide`**, **`merge_request_event`**, **`external_pull_request_event`**, **`parent_pipeline`**.
- *Line 14-18* directs GitLab to only add the job in the pipeline if the source of pipeline execution is not a merge request event nor a push event.

Linting

Linting is a process of maintaining code quality, consistency, and adherence to coding standards within a software project. It can be added as a stage in the GitLab pipeline, which is primarily responsible for analyzing the source code for potential issues, code style violations, and programming errors, and it often employs specialized tools and linters to accomplish these tasks. Linting is a critical practice in modern software development, as it helps catch and rectify issues early in the development process, reducing the chances of bugs and enhancing code maintainability.

The linting stage acts as an early warning system, allowing developers to address issues promptly before they become more complex and costly to resolve. It promotes coding best practices, consistent coding standards, and adherence to project-specific guidelines, ultimately leading to higher-quality code and improved maintainability. By incorporating linting into the CI/CD pipeline, development teams can streamline their code review processes, reduce manual effort in code quality assessment, and ensure that the software they deliver is both robust and aligned with industry best practices.

Recipe 49: Adding a linting stage to check code style violations

The linting stage typically involves running static analysis tools and linters tailored to the language's specific requirements. For Java projects, tools like **Checkstyle**, **PMD**, and **SpotBugs** are commonly used. Checkstyle enforces coding style and formatting rules, PMD identifies potential code quality issues and anti-patterns, and SpotBugs detects bugs and performance issues through bytecode analysis. When integrated into the CI/CD pipeline, these tools automatically scan the codebase for violations, generate detailed reports, and highlight areas that require attention. Update **`.gitlab-ci.yml`** code to add the *lint* stage before the *build* stage as follows:

```
1. stages:   # List of stages for jobs and their order of execution
2.   - lint
3.   - build
4.   - dockerize
5.   - test
6.   - deploy
7.
8. lint-job:
9.   stage: lint
10.   variables:
11.     CHECKSTYLE_VERSION: "3.3.0"
12.   image: maven:3.8.4-openjdk-17
13.   script:
14.       - mvn org.apache.maven.plugins:maven-checkstyle-plugin:$CHECKSTYLE_VERSION:checkstyle
15.   artifacts:
16.     paths:
17.       - target/checkstyle-result.xml
18.     expire_in: 1 day
```

Here,

- *Line 2* shows a new stage **`dockerize`** has been added which gets executed before any other stage.
- *Line 14* runs the check style plugin on the code.

- *Line 17* adds the results of the check style run in the artifacts, which can be downloaded for evaluation.

Refer to *Figure 6.10* for the details of the execution of the linting job:

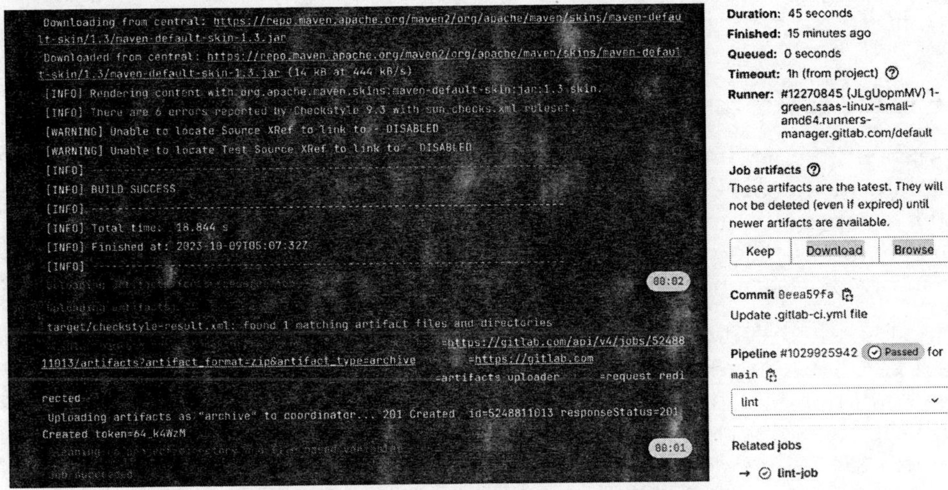

***Figure 6.10**: lint-job checks for code style violations*

The artifacts can be either downloaded and can be browsed in the GitLab UI. Click the **Browse** button to view the artifacts, refer to *Figure 6.11* for reference:

Passed **Job #5248811013** in pipeline **#1029925942** for 0eea59fa from main by **Varun Yadav** 24 minutes ago

Artifacts / target — Download artifacts archive

Name	**Size**
..	
checkstyle-result.xml	1.34 KiB

This XML file does not appear to have any style information associated with it. The document tree is shown below.

```
▾<checkstyle version="9.3">
  ▾<file name="/builds/financial-service-marketplace/config-server/src/main/java/com/fsm/configserver/ConfigSeverApplication.java">
     <error line="1" severity="error" message="Missing package-info.java file."
     source="com.puppycrawl.tools.checkstyle.checks.javadoc.JavadocPackageCheck"/>
     <error line="7" column="1" severity="error" message="Utility classes should not have a public or default
     constructor." source="com.puppycrawl.tools.checkstyle.checks.design.HideUtilityClassConstructorCheck"/>
     <error line="11" column="1" severity="error" message="File contains tab characters (this is the first
     instance)." source="com.puppycrawl.tools.checkstyle.checks.whitespace.FileTabCharacterCheck"/>
     <error line="11" column="9" severity="error" message="Missing a Javadoc comment."
     source="com.puppycrawl.tools.checkstyle.checks.javadoc.MissingJavadocMethodCheck"/>
     <error line="11" column="33" severity="error" message="Parameter args should be final."
     source="com.puppycrawl.tools.checkstyle.checks.FinalParametersCheck"/>
   </file>
  ▾<file name="/builds/financial-service-marketplace/config-server/src/main/resources/application.properties">
     <error line="1" severity="error" message="File does not end with a newline."
     source="com.puppycrawl.tools.checkstyle.checks.NewlineAtEndOfFileCheck"/>
   </file>
</checkstyle>
```

***Figure 6.11**: Check style violations*

As part of the SDLC the violations highlighted above need to be addressed in the subsequent code changes. Similarly, PMD and SpotBugs can be added and run in the same linting job.

Note: All the above steps need to be repeated for all the microservices in their corresponding Git projects.

Scheduling GitLab pipelines

GitLab's scheduled pipelines are a powerful feature that allows to automate and schedule the execution of the CI/CD pipelines at specific times or on predefined intervals. This capability is especially useful for tasks like periodic testing, security scans, or regular deployments. Scheduled pipelines are a fundamental part of GitLab's automation suite, offering improved efficiency and reliability in software development workflows.

With GitLab's scheduled pipelines, one can set up recurring jobs to run on a schedule, making it easier to maintain the codebase's health and security. For example, one can schedule daily builds and tests to catch regressions early, perform regular vulnerability scans to keep the software secure, or automate the deployment of updates to a staging environment for testing. This automation not only saves time but also ensures that crucial tasks are consistently executed, reducing the risk of human error. Whether working on a small project or managing a complex software pipeline, GitLab's scheduled pipelines are a valuable tool for streamlining the CI/CD processes and ensuring the reliability of the software releases.

Recipe 50: Scheduling a GitLab pipeline

Gitlab supports scheduling of the pipelines using its GUI. Pipeline can be scheduled using a **`cron`** syntax.

The **`cron`** syntax is a standardized way to represent time and date intervals, commonly used in Unix-like operating systems for scheduling tasks. A **`cron`** expression consists of five fields, each separated by a space, representing the minute, hour, day of the month, month, and day of the week, in that order. Additionally, there is an optional sixth field for the year, which is rarely used. Here is a breakdown of the **`cron`** syntax:

```
* *  * * * *

| | | | | |

| | | | | └── Year (optional)

| | | | └────── Day of the week (0 - 6, Sunday to Saturday; or use names)

| | | └──────── Month (1 - 12 or use names)

| | └────────── Day of the month (1 - 31)

| └──────────── Hour (0 - 23)

└────────────── Minute (0 - 59)
```

Go to the GitLab UI left menu and click **Build | Pipeline** schedules to open the pipeline schedule UI screen. Set the description of the schedule along with the interval pattern, target repository branch and the preferred time zone, refer to *Figure 6.12* for reference:

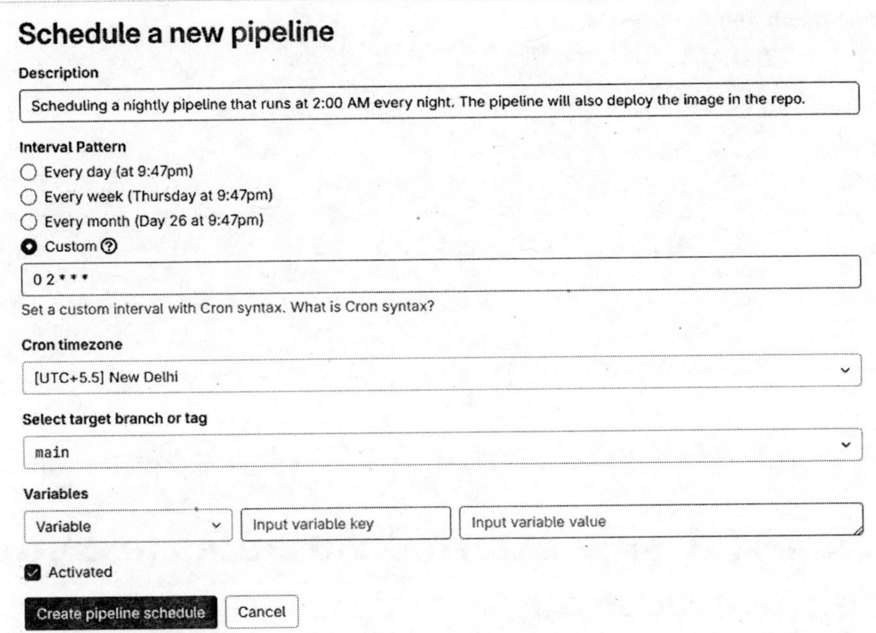

Figure 6.12: Scheduling a GitLab pipeline

Here, the **`cron`** syntax used against *Interval Pattern* is, **`0 2 * * *`**, which indicates the job to run at 2 AM daily. Input variables can be added per schedule to conditionally execute the pipeline jobs.

Click **Create pipeline schedule** to create a schedule, refer to *Figure 6.13* to view scheduled pipelines:

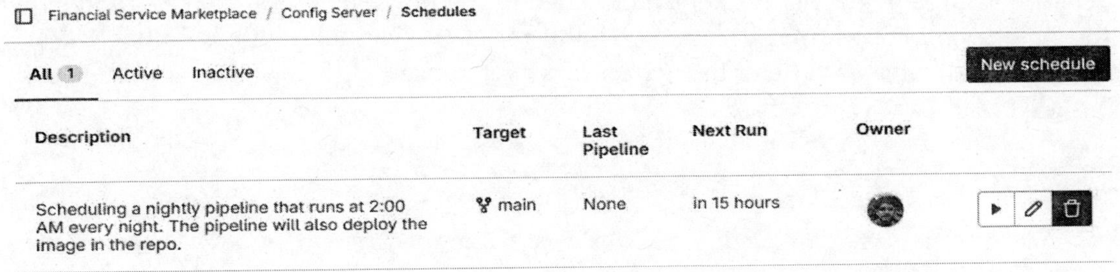

Figure 6.13: Viewing scheduled pipelines

Like other trigger events the pipeline runs for scheduled pipelines are visible under **Build | Pipelines**. Refer to *Figure 6.14* to validate the run for a scheduled pipeline:

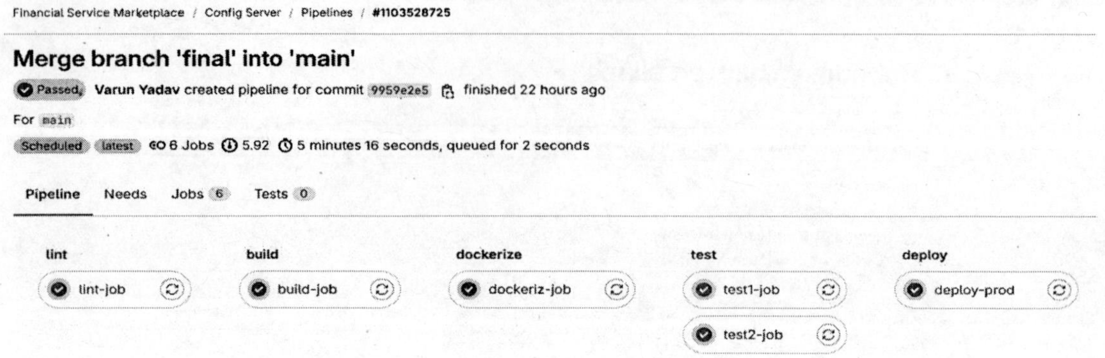

Figure 6.14: *Run of a scheduled pipeline*

Note: A label scheduled has been stamped along with the pipeline run.

Recipe 51: Using external variables to control pipeline execution

Many times, there is a requirement to frequently check quality of the code and validate that there are no compilation issues raised as part of new code commits. For this it is wise to run the linting and build stages of the pipeline frequently without going through the heavy process of dockerizing and testing the code.

It can be achieved by scheduling a pipeline to run frequently, say every 30 mins and using the variables that can be injected as part of scheduling to control the flow of pipeline to only run the **`lint`** and **`build`** stages and skipping the rest.

Schedule a pipeline using the steps mentioned in the previous recipe, make sure to enter the *Interval Pattern* as **`*/30 * * * *`**, and inject the variable with key **`CHECK_CODE_QUALITY`** and value as **`Y`**. Refer to *Figure 6.15* for reference:

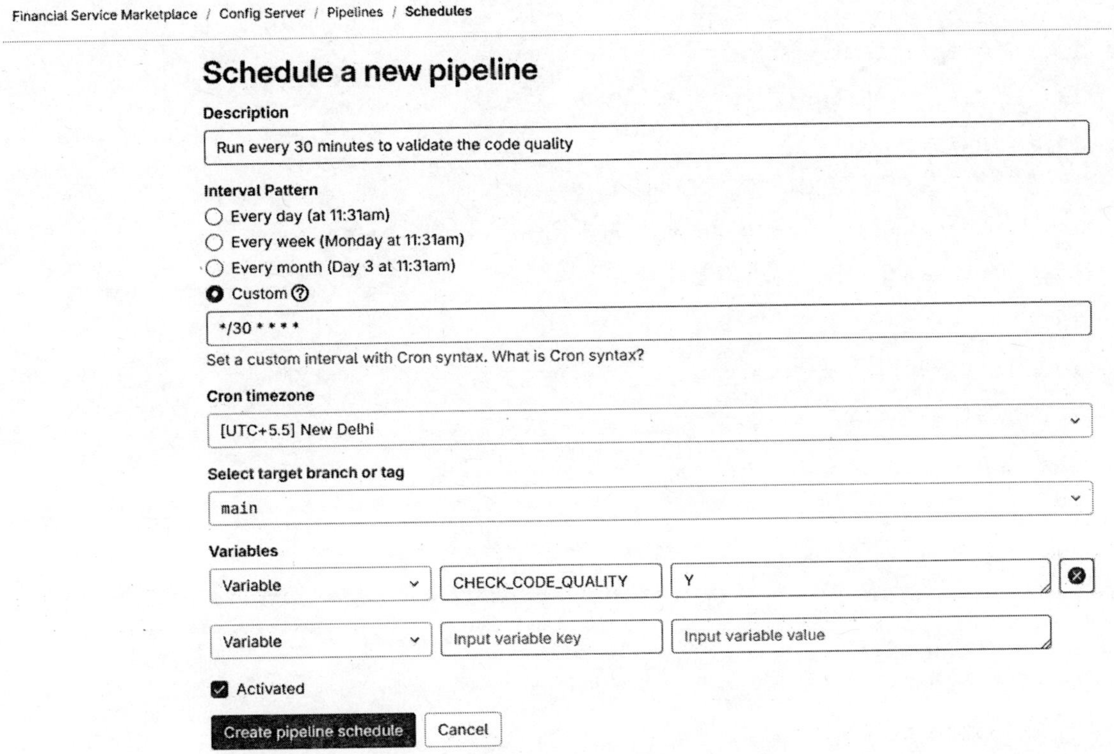

***Figure 6.15**: Scheduling a GitLab pipeline with injected variable*

`.gitlab-ci.yml` file needs to be enhanced for the stages which are to be skipped as part of pipeline runs for the above schedule. The logic needs to be embedded for pipeline stages: **`dockerize`**, **`test`** and **`deploy`** using the variable **`CHECK_CODE_QUALITY`** which is being set as part of the pipeline runs. Update the jobs for the stages **`dockerize`**, **`test`** and **`deploy`** in the **`.gitlab-ci.yml`** code as follows:

```
# No change in the existing logic for lint-job and build-job

dockeriz-job:
  stage: dockerize
  #Existing logic for dockerize-job
  rules:
    - if: $CHECK_CODE_QUALITY == 'Y'
      when: never # Do not run if checking code quality
    - when: on_success

```

```
test1-job:
  stage: test
  #Existing logic for test1-job
  rules:
    - if: $CHECK_CODE_QUALITY == 'Y'
      when: never # Do not run if checking code quality
    - when: on_success

test2-job:
  stage: test
  #Existing logic for test2-job
  rules:
    - if: $CHECK_CODE_QUALITY == 'Y'
      when: never # Do not run if checking code quality
    - when: on_success

deploy-prod:
  stage: deploy
  #Existing logic for deploy-prod
  rules:
    - if: $CI_PIPELINE_SOURCE == 'merge_request_event'
      when: never # Do not run if the pipeline source is a merge request
    - if: $CI_PIPELINE_SOURCE == 'push'
      when: never # Do not run if the pipeline source is push command
    - if: $CHECK_CODE_QUALITY == 'Y'
      when: never # Do not run if checking code quality
    - when: on_success
```

The above code is making sure not to run a job if the value of variable **CODE_CHECK_QUALITY** is set to **Y**. For the above scheduled runs only jobs corresponding to **lint** and **build** stages will run as visible in *Figure 6.16*:

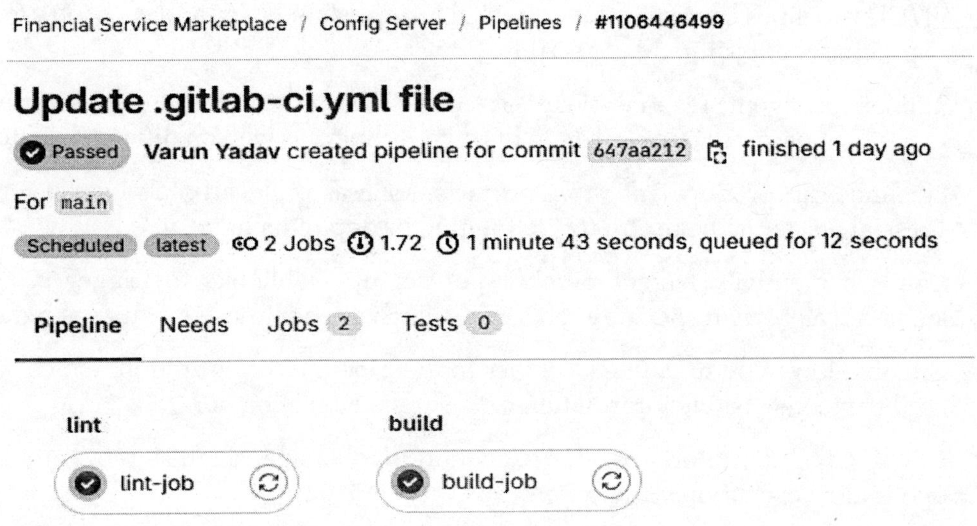

Figure 6.16: Pipeline execution only runs lint and build jobs

Conclusion

In this chapter, we have got a comprehensive understanding of the CI/CD pipelines and the pivotal role they play in modern software development. They are the backbone of an agile and efficient development process, automating critical tasks like code integration, testing, and deployment. The benefits of CI/CD are numerous, ranging from faster time-to-market and improved code quality to reduced manual intervention and enhanced collaboration among development teams. In the context of GitLab, a leading DevOps platform, this chapter delved into the practical aspects of building a CI/CD pipeline. GitLab simplifies the pipeline creation process with its intuitive **`.gitlab-ci.yml`** configuration, offering flexibility, scalability, and integration with various tools. By following the best practices and examples provided, readers can harness the power of GitLab CI/CD to streamline their software development workflows, deliver higher-quality code, and ultimately drive innovation in their projects.

In the next chapter, we will learn about orchestration platforms and their use in managing multiple microservices, starting from fetching container images from registries, running them as microservices, and maintaining their complete life cycle.

Points to remember

- CI/CD pipelines are tightly integrated with version control systems like Git. Changes pushed to the repository trigger pipeline executions, ensuring that new code is continuously integrated and tested.

- CI/CD pipelines consist of stages, which group related jobs, and each job executes a specific set of commands or scripts.
- Runners are agents responsible for executing jobs in the pipeline. GitLab provides shared Runners, but one can set up his own Runners as well on different platforms.
- Pipelines can produce and store artifacts, such as build artifacts or test reports. These artifacts can be useful for debugging or deployment.
- One can manually trigger pipelines or set up webhooks to trigger pipelines automatically when specific events occur, such as code pushes or merge requests.
- GitLab allows you to define variables in the pipeline configuration, which can be used to store sensitive information or customize job behavior.
- GitLab CI/CD supports parallel execution of jobs, which can significantly speed up pipeline execution for large projects.
- GitLab CI/CD can integrate security scanning tools to automatically check for vulnerabilities and security issues in your code.
- Environments in GitLab allow you to define and manage deployment targets, such as staging or production environments, for your applications.
- GitLab provides built-in monitoring and logging features to track the progress and performance of your pipelines.

Questions

1. Describe the concept of stages and jobs in a GitLab CI/CD pipeline. How are they organized and executed?
2. What is the role of GitLab Runners in the execution of CI/CD pipeline jobs, and how can they be configured?
3. What are artifacts in the context of GitLab CI/CD, and how are they useful in pipeline workflows?
4. What is parallelism in CI/CD pipelines, and how can it improve the efficiency of pipeline execution in GitLab?
5. How do we make sure no confidential information is being made available to the pipeline developers?
6. In what ways can one ensure continuous improvement in GitLab CI/CD pipelines, and what practices should be adopted for optimization?
7. How to schedule a GitLab pipeline so that it runs in every 2 hours?

CHAPTER 7

Microservices Orchestration

Introduction

The last chapter detailed out the continuous integration and delivery and its benefits in software application development. It also talked about the ways of developing automated pipelines for generating continuous build artifacts.

In this chapter, we will talk about orchestration platforms and their use in running microservices. We will demonstrate ways to set up an orchestrator for the microservices, including fetching their OCI images from a registry and running them as a container. We will also show how orchestrator platforms do dynamic service registry as third-party registration. During the course, we will create an **Elastic Container Service** (**ECS**) cluster on AWS, define tasks, deploy, and execute our application microservices.

Structure

In this chapter, we will discuss the following topics:

- Orchestration of microservices
- Benefits of orchestration platforms
- Load balancer
- Amazon Elastic Container Service

- o Amazon ECS cluster
- o AWS Fargate
- o Amazon ECS task definition
- o Amazon ECS service

Objectives

By the end of this chapter, we will learn the use of Orchestrator platforms in supporting enterprise application, which comprises multiple microservices communicating with each other for the end goal. The chapter demonstrates how to configure AWS **Elastic Container Service (ECS)**, which is an orchestrator for running the three application microservices: Customer Enquiry, Enquiry Broadcast, and Config Server. As part of the configuration, Fargate task definitions will be created to fetch microservices docker images from the AWS **Elastic Container Registry (ECR)** registry and execute them as Docker containers.

Orchestration of microservices

Microservices can be developed to take a lot of decisions autonomously, as also described in *Chapter 4, Implementing Dynamic Services*. A lot of logic can be built into microservices itself on handling exception scenarios, addressing performance concerns, and so on. This is referred to as *microservices choreography*, a bottom-up approach where the microservices themselves possess decision-making authority. However, as microservice architecture grows in complexity and scale, it becomes increasingly difficult to manage them using the above technique, and that is when orchestration of microservices becomes handy. Orchestration of microservices is nothing but the management and coordination of multiple microservices within a distributed system.

Microservices orchestration can be very well understood by taking an example of musical orchestra. The most noticeable aspect of an orchestra is how each performer plays an instrument while still maintaining rhythm with the other musicians. The orchestra's conductor oversees controlling the sync between each member. Similarly, in microservice orchestration each microservice is allowed to carry out responsibilities assigned by the orchestrator (conductor). A microservice completes the task and updates on its progress while the orchestrator stores the necessary data in its storage area keeping the complete process in sync.

These platforms have a mechanism to dynamically discover new instances of microservices, internally monitor their performance, and ensure they are working together to deliver the desired functionality. Orchestrator platforms offer a way to horizontally scale a specific microservice in or out according to business requirements, depending on resource usage or predefined rules.

Another important aspect of microservices orchestration is communication between services. Microservices typically communicate using lightweight protocols such as HTTP or gRPC, and orchestration platforms provide a way to manage and optimize this communication. For example, a platform might provide a service mesh architecture that allows for traffic management and monitoring, or a message broker system that enables asynchronous communication between microservices.

There are many orchestration platforms that align with OCI specifications are prevalent in the market, with **Kubernetes (K8s)**, **Amazon Elastic Container Service (ECS)**, **Docker Swarm**, and **OpenShift** being among the most utilized. While Kubernetes stands out as the predominant orchestration platform in the industry, this chapter specifically emphasizes deploying applications on Amazon ECS due to our application's preference for AWS as the primary cloud provider. Despite AWS offering a managed Kubernetes service in Amazon **Elastic Kubernetes Service (EKS)**, the chapter prioritizes Amazon ECS over EKS considering factors such as cost optimization and the application's complexity.

Benefits of orchestration platforms

Orchestration platforms absorb lot of complexities of running multiple microservices and take care of a lot of boiler plate functionalities, which would otherwise may lead to a nightmare if to be done separately. The following are the benefits of using an orchestration platform:

- **Automation**: Orchestration platforms automate various tasks involved in managing microservices, reducing the need for manual intervention and saving time and effort.
- **Scalability**: Orchestration platforms provide mechanisms for scaling microservices up or down based on demand. They allow for easy horizontal scaling by adding or removing instances of microservices as needed.
- **High availability**: Orchestration platforms ensure that microservices are highly available by managing failover, fault tolerance, and load balancing. They can automatically detect and recover from failures to maintain system availability.
- **Service discovery**: Orchestration platforms provide service discovery mechanisms that enable microservices to locate and communicate with each other dynamically, even as the number of instances and their locations change.
- **Resource optimization**: Orchestration platforms optimize resource utilization by dynamically allocating resources to microservices based on their needs. They ensure efficient and optimal utilization of resources such as CPU and memory. This helps in overall cost optimization as well.
- **Fault isolation**: Orchestration platforms isolate faults within microservices, preventing failures in one microservice from impacting the entire system. They can automatically restart failed instances or redirect traffic to healthy instances.

- **Rolling updates**: Orchestration platforms facilitate rolling updates of microservices, allowing for seamless updates without downtime. They can gradually update instances while ensuring the overall system remains operational.
- **Health monitoring**: Orchestration platforms monitor the health and performance of microservices, collecting metrics and providing insights into the state of the system. This enables proactive monitoring and issue resolution.
- **Security**: Orchestration platforms often include security features such as access control, authentication, network security and encryption. They provide a secure environment for managing and running microservices, protecting against unauthorized access and data breaches.
- **DevOps enablement**: Orchestration platforms align with DevOps principles by enabling seamless collaboration between development and operations teams. They support **continuous integration and continuous deployment** (**CI/CD**) pipelines and promote efficient collaboration and automation throughout the software development lifecycle.

The above advantages of orchestration platforms enhance the efficiency, scalability, reliability, and manageability of microservices architecture. This empowers organizations to effectively construct and operate intricate distributed systems.

Load balancer

The load balancer is not a new term for software enthusiasts; it has been used in the industry for a very long time. The primary purpose of using a load balancer is to distribute the incoming traffic amongst a group of servers so that the software can scale horizontally and its performance remains optimum even at the time of peak loads. Common load balancing algorithms are:

- **Least response time**, which determines which server is responding most quickly
- **Round robin**, which evenly cycles through the possible server destinations
- **Weighted round robin**, which enables network administrators to designate weights to servers based on each system's capacity; and
- **Least outstanding request**, which selects servers with the fewest number of queued requests.
- **IP Hash**: The hash of the client's IP address is used to determine which server will handle the request.

There are two major types of load balancers:

- Application Load Balancer
- Network Load Balancer

The major difference between the above types is that an application load balancer works at the application layer that is, on protocols HTTP, HTTPS, and so on, where as a network load balancer works at transport layer that is, on protocols TCP, UDP, and so on.

To support multiple instances of microservices, they need to be running behind a load balancer and as Amazon ECS is the orchestration platform on which the application is to be deployed the ideal choice is to use **AWS Application Load Balancer**.

AWS Application Load Balancer

It automatically distributes your incoming traffic across multiple targets, such as EC2 instances, containers, and IP addresses, in one or more Availability Zones. It monitors the health of its registered targets, and routes traffic only to the healthy targets. They serve as the single point of contact for the client and scale as the incoming traffic changes over time. The application load balancer contains:

- **Listeners**: Listens to the incoming traffic using the configured protocol and port. A minimum of one listener needs to be configured for an application load balancer.
- **Rules**: Listeners comprises of **rules**, they have conditions if met the configured rule action is triggered. By default, a listener gets created with a *default rule* that does not have a condition. If the conditions of none of the listener's rules are met, then the action for the default rule is performed.
- **Target groups**: Group of registered targets, such as an EC2 instance or a container. Health check parameters can be configured for each registered target and requests are only forwarded to as a rule action only if a target is in a healthy state.

Recipe 52: Creating AWS Application Load Balancer

There are multiple ways to create an **Application Load Balancer** (**ALB**), it can be created using AWS CLI, or via AWS Management Console. Using a management console requires a listener to be created as part of ALB creation, which internally requires a Target Group for rule action. That is why it is preferred to create ALB via the management console as part of creating an ECS service, discussed later in the chapter. There is no such restriction while creating an ALB via AWS CLI, listeners and target groups can be added later while creating an ECS service.

Creating Application Load Balancer using AWS CLI

Run the following AWS CLI command to create an AWS Application Load Balancer:

```
aws elbv2 create-load-balancer --name fsm-load-balancer  \
--subnets subnet-05cb20f57875d70eb subnet-0c4370a5045d8c9e7
```

Here,

- **`fsm-load-balancer`** is the name of ALB.
- **`subnet-05cb20f57875d70eb`** and **`subnet-0c4370a5045d8c9e7`** are subnets in different availability zones to which the ALB will rout traffic. Minimum two availability zones and one subnet per availability zone needs are required while creating an ALB.

In the above command, no listener, rule, or target group has been mentioned as an argument, as the details are not yet available.

Output is as shown in *Figure 7.1*:

```
$ aws elbv2 create-load-balancer --name fsm-load-balancer \
> --subnets subnet-05cb20f57875d70eb subnet-0c4370a5045d8c9e7
{
    "LoadBalancers": [
        {
            "LoadBalancerArn": "arn:aws:elasticloadbalancing:us-east-1:746797604555:loadbalancer/app/fsm-l
oad-balancer/f1d95f36f6d5a99e",
            "DNSName": "fsm-load-balancer-1737637159.us-east-1.elb.amazonaws.com",
            "CanonicalHostedZoneId": "Z35SXDOTRQ7X7K",
            "CreatedTime": "2023-07-19T11:38:14.610000+00:00",
            "LoadBalancerName": "fsm-load-balancer",
            "Scheme": "internet-facing",
            "VpcId": "vpc-0d98694f904b3983b",
            "State": {
                "Code": "provisioning"
            },
            "Type": "application",
            "AvailabilityZones": [
                {
                    "ZoneName": "us-east-1a",
                    "SubnetId": "subnet-05cb20f57875d70eb",
                    "LoadBalancerAddresses": []
                },
                {
                    "ZoneName": "us-east-1b",
                    "SubnetId": "subnet-0c4370a5045d8c9e7",
                    "LoadBalancerAddresses": []
                }
            ],
            "SecurityGroups": [
                "sg-06eae19abc4de7696"
            ],
            "IpAddressType": "ipv4"
        }
    ]
}
```

***Figure 7.1**: Output of AWS create-load-balancer command*

ALB is created with a default security group as no security group has been provided as a parameter in the above command. In the above ALB creation command, we have not provided the scheme that defines the accessibility of the load balancer for example public or internal. The default scheme is **internet-facing** and hence out LB has been created with access over the internet. If the requirement is not to use the ALB over the internet, then the scheme needs to be set as **internal** along with private subnets.

Amazon Elastic Container Service

Amazon **Elastic Container Service (ECS)** is an Amazon's fully managed container orchestration service that can be used to deploy, manage, and scale containerized applications effectively. It has a strong integration with the AWS ecosystem and offers a user-friendly method for running container workloads with top-notch security features both locally utilizing Amazon ECS anywhere and in the cloud. Give Amazon ECS a brief description of your application and the resources needed, and it will deploy, monitor, and scale it across a variety of customizable computing alternatives with seamless interfaces to the other supporting AWS services your application requires. Execute system tasks like customizing scaling and capacity rules, as well as monitoring and analyzing data from telemetry and application logs.

Amazon ECS cluster

An individual work item running in an Amazon ECS is called a **task** and though these tasks can be run directly but if a task is required to be run for long, it needs to be wrapped up inside a **service.** A service defines which task and how many instances of that task need to run. Amazon ECS is nothing but a logical grouping of these services and tasks. The cluster comprises certain resources that are used by the services running inside it:

- The infrastructure on which the services need to run and can be any of the following:
    - AWS Cloud Amazon EC2 instance
    - AWS Cloud Serverless infra (AWS Fargate)
    - On-premises VMs or servers
- The network under which the tasks run, may comprise of VPCs and subnets.
- A namespace, is optional and used for communication between services using Service Connect.
- A monitoring option using Amazon CloudWatch container insights that automatically collects, aggregates, and summarizes Amazon ECS metrics and logs.

  So, the first step before running a container in Amazon ECS is to create an Amazon ECS cluster. As part of this book the underlying infrastructure to be used is AWS Fargate which is a serverless option provided by AWS Cloud.

AWS Fargate

AWS Fargate is a serverless compute engine for containers that allows developers to run containers without having to manage the underlying infrastructure. It is included in the offerings of Amazon Elastic Container Service and Amazon Elastic Kubernetes Service, offering a streamlined and effective approach for deploying and overseeing containerized applications. With Fargate, developers can focus on building and deploying their applications without the need to provision or manage the infrastructure that supports them.

One of the key advantages of AWS Fargate is its serverless nature. Users do not need to worry about tasks such as server provisioning, patching, or scaling the underlying infrastructure. Fargate abstracts away the complexities of container orchestration, making it easier for developers to deploy and manage their applications. It allows users to specify the amount of vCPU and memory that their containerized application needs, and AWS Fargate takes care of provisioning the necessary resources.

AWS Fargate is highly scalable, supporting applications that range from a single container to complex, multi-container setups. This scalability is particularly valuable for applications with varying workloads, as Fargate can automatically scale resources up or down based on demand, ensuring optimal performance and cost efficiency.

In terms of security, AWS Fargate provides a secure and isolated environment for running containers. Every task, which is a grouping of containers operating concurrently, is allocated its exclusive kernel runtime. Tasks operate independently, without sharing the underlying infrastructure thus achieving the physical isolation. This isolation helps prevent one task from impacting the security or performance of another.

Recipe 53: Creating Amazon ECS cluster

An Amazon ECS cluster can be simply created using both AWS Management Console or AWS CLI.

Creating ECS cluster using AWS Management Console

Follow the given steps to create an ECS cluster via AWS ECS Management Console:

1. Login to the AWS Management Console and search ECS or type in the following URL: **https://us-east-1.console.aws.amazon.com/ecs/v2/clusters**

   The region can be changed as per your preference.

2. Click on the **Create cluster** option, and it will open a self-explanatory form.

3. Fill in all the required details.

   a. Cluster name: `fsm-ecs-cluster`

   b. Select VPC and choose subnets where tasks need to be run.

   c. Infrastructure: Select **AWS Fargate**

4. Click **Create**.

And that is it! an Amazon ECS cluster will be created.

Creating ECS cluster using AWS CLI

A ECS cluster can be created using the following AWS CLI command:

```
aws ecs create-cluster \
--cluster-name fsm-ecs-cluster \
--capacity-providers FARGATE \
--region us-east-1
```

Here,

- **fsm-ecs-cluster** is the name of the cluster.
- **FARGATE** is the underlying hardware to be used for running the containers.
- **us-east-1** is the region where the cluster is to be created.

Output is as shown in the *Figure 7.2*:

```
$ aws ecs create-cluster \
> --cluster-name fsm-ecs-cluster \
> --capacity-providers FARGATE \
> --region us-east-1
{
    "cluster": {
        "clusterArn": "arn:aws:ecs:us-east-1:746797604555:cluster/fsm-ecs-cluster",
        "clusterName": "fsm-ecs-cluster",
        "status": "ACTIVE",
        "registeredContainerInstancesCount": 0,
        "runningTasksCount": 0,
        "pendingTasksCount": 0,
        "activeServicesCount": 0,
        "statistics": [],
        "tags": [],
        "settings": [
            {
                "name": "containerInsights",
                "value": "disabled"
            }
        ],
        "capacityProviders": [
            "FARGATE"
        ],
        "defaultCapacityProviderStrategy": []
    }
```

Figure 7.2: Output of AWS create-cluster command

Refer to *Figure 7.3* to view the ECS cluster in AWS Admin console:

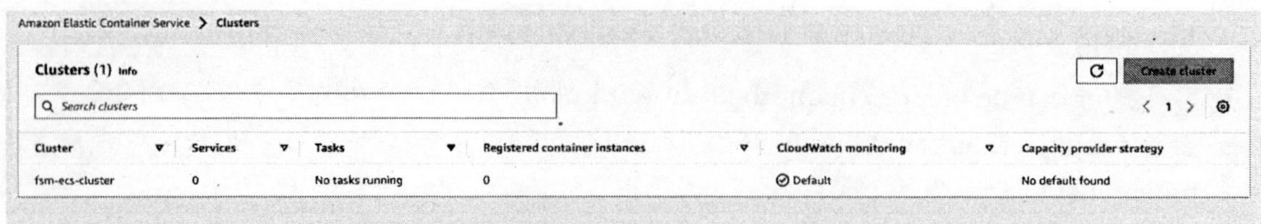

***Figure 7.3:** ECS cluster with the name fsm-ecs-cluster created*

Amazon ECS task definition

As discussed earlier, a task represents a single operational unit within an ECS cluster, and a task definition serves as the explicit definition of such a task. Essentially, it acts as a blueprint detailing what should run, the required configuration, and the way it should operate. It is a text file in JSON format that describes how many containers need to run together along with certain parameters as part of the definition.

Following are some of the parameters that can be specified in a task definition:

- The Docker image to use with each container in the task.
- How much CPU and memory to use with each task or each container within a task.
- The launch type to use, which determines the infrastructure that the tasks are hosted on.
- The networking mode to use for the containers in the task. The options are bridge, host, awsvpc, and none.
- The logging configuration to use for the tasks.
- Whether the task continues to run if the container finishes or fails.
- The command that the container runs when it is started.
- Any data volumes that are used with the containers in the task.
- Task Role ARN, this specifies the **Amazon Resource Name** (**ARN**) of the IAM role used by the task.
- Health Check, used to monitor the health check of the containers. It specifies the parameters like run, interval, and timeout.

A task can comprise more than one container, one main microservice container and other side car container. The side car containers are optional and are normally used for side jobs like shipping the logs to a log aggregator engine, shipping JVM matrices of the main microservice container to a central engine, and so on. All the containers inside a task share resources like CPU, memory, ephemeral storage, and so on.

Recipe 54: Creating Amazon ECS task definitions

In the financial service marketplace application, there are three microservices, Customer Enquiry, Enquiry Broadcast and Config Server. A task definition needs to be created for all three microservices. AWS Management Console supports creation of task definition using the step-by-step GUI screens and via a JSON format.

Creating Config Server ECS task definition

Config Server ECS task definition will be created using step-by-step GUI screens:

1. Login to the AWS Management Console and search ECS or type in the following URL: **https://us-east-1.console.aws.amazon.com/ecs/v2/task-definitions**

   The region can be changed as per your preference.

2. Click on the **Create new task definition** option.

3. Provide details like task definition name, the name and image URL of the containers along with the ports that need to be exposed and any environment variables that need to be passed on container startup and click **Next**. Refer to *Figure 7.4* for reference:

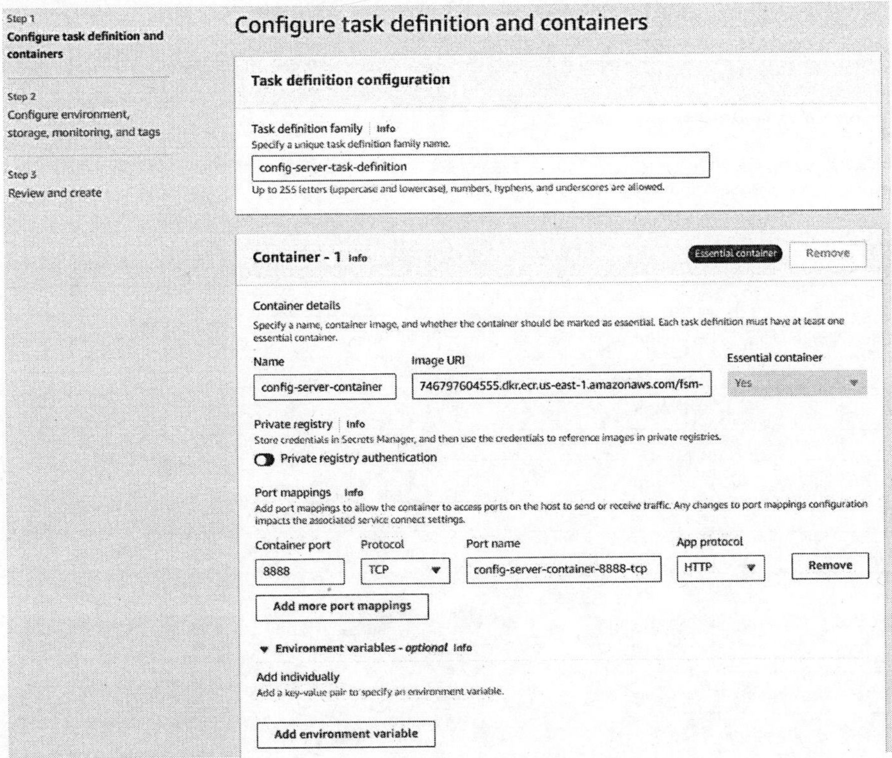

***Figure 7.4:** Creating ECS task definition*

Here,

- **config-server-task-definition** is the name of task definition.
- **config-server-container** is the name of the container.
- **746797604555.dkr.ecr.us-east-1.amazonaws.com/fsm-repository:config-server-1.0** is image URI in the format **repository-url/image:tag**.
- **8888** is the container port as config server microservice runs on port **8888**.

Following environment variables need to be passed to the Config Server microservice:

- **MIN_HEAP_SIZE = 256m**
- **MAX_HEAP_SIZE = 512m**
- **PROFILE = git**
- **CONFIG_SERVER_USERNAME = fsmConfigAdmin**
- **CONFIG_SERVER_PASSWORD = password**
- **GIT_PASSWORD = ****

Refer to *Figure 7.5* for reference, the Figure is in continuation of *Figure 7.4*:

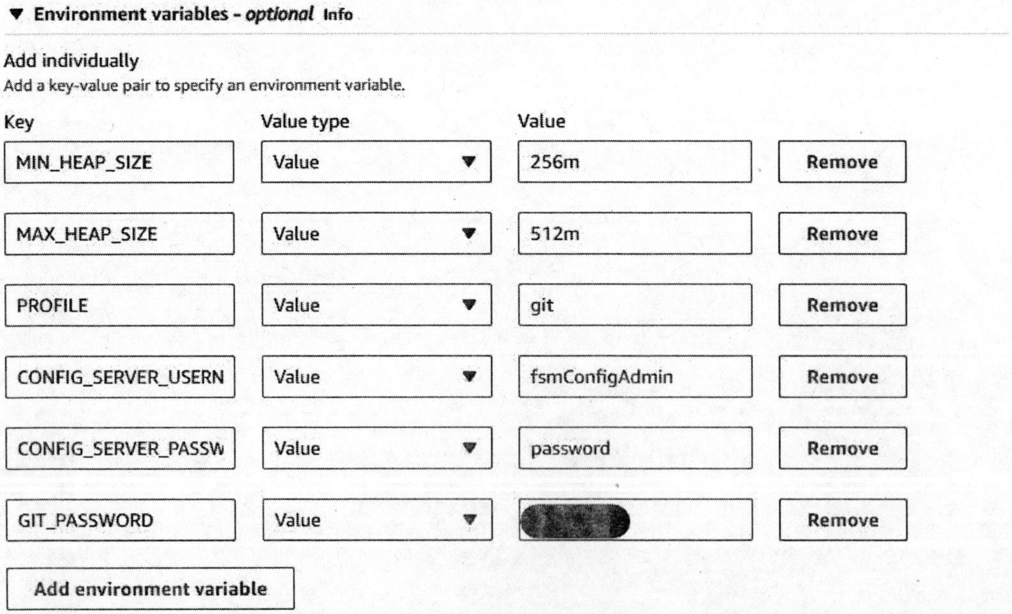

▼ **Environment variables - *optional*** Info

Add individually
Add a key-value pair to specify an environment variable.

Key	Value type	Value	
MIN_HEAP_SIZE	Value ▼	256m	Remove
MAX_HEAP_SIZE	Value ▼	512m	Remove
PROFILE	Value ▼	git	Remove
CONFIG_SERVER_USERN	Value ▼	fsmConfigAdmin	Remove
CONFIG_SERVER_PASSW	Value ▼	password	Remove
GIT_PASSWORD	Value ▼		Remove

Add environment variable

***Figure 7.5**: Adding environment variables for a container*

4. Provide environment as AWS Fargate (selected by default), sizing parameters **CPU** as **1 vCPU** and **Memory** as **2 GB**. Container size is required if there is more than one container part of a task definition and different sizes need to be provided for each of them. Refer to *Figure 7.6* for reference:

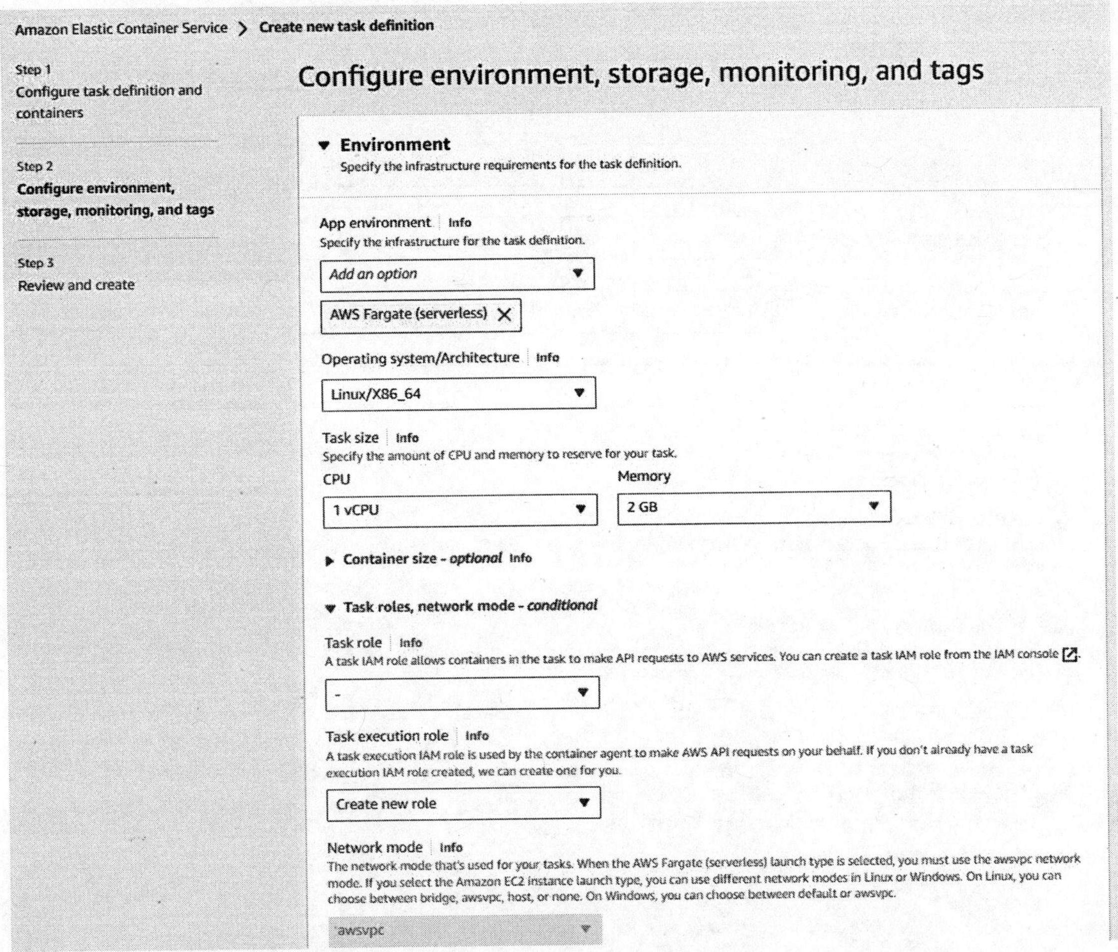

***Figure 7.6:** Configuring environment and sizing details for a task definition*

Make sure network mode is **awsvpc**.

5. A permanent file system like **Amazon Elastic File System** (**EFS**) can be mounted to a task definition. A good use case is if containers need to access a shared file location for a business functionality, or for collecting log files. Leaving it blank as there is no use case for mounting a shared file system.

6. Configure log collection method, this is required logs from the console are not visible as there is no access to containers running as a Fargate service. Moreover, logs written on a container file system will be lost on container shutdown.

Amazon CloudWatch is the preferred option for log collection. Refer to *Figure 7.7* for reference, it is in continuation to *Figure 7.6*:

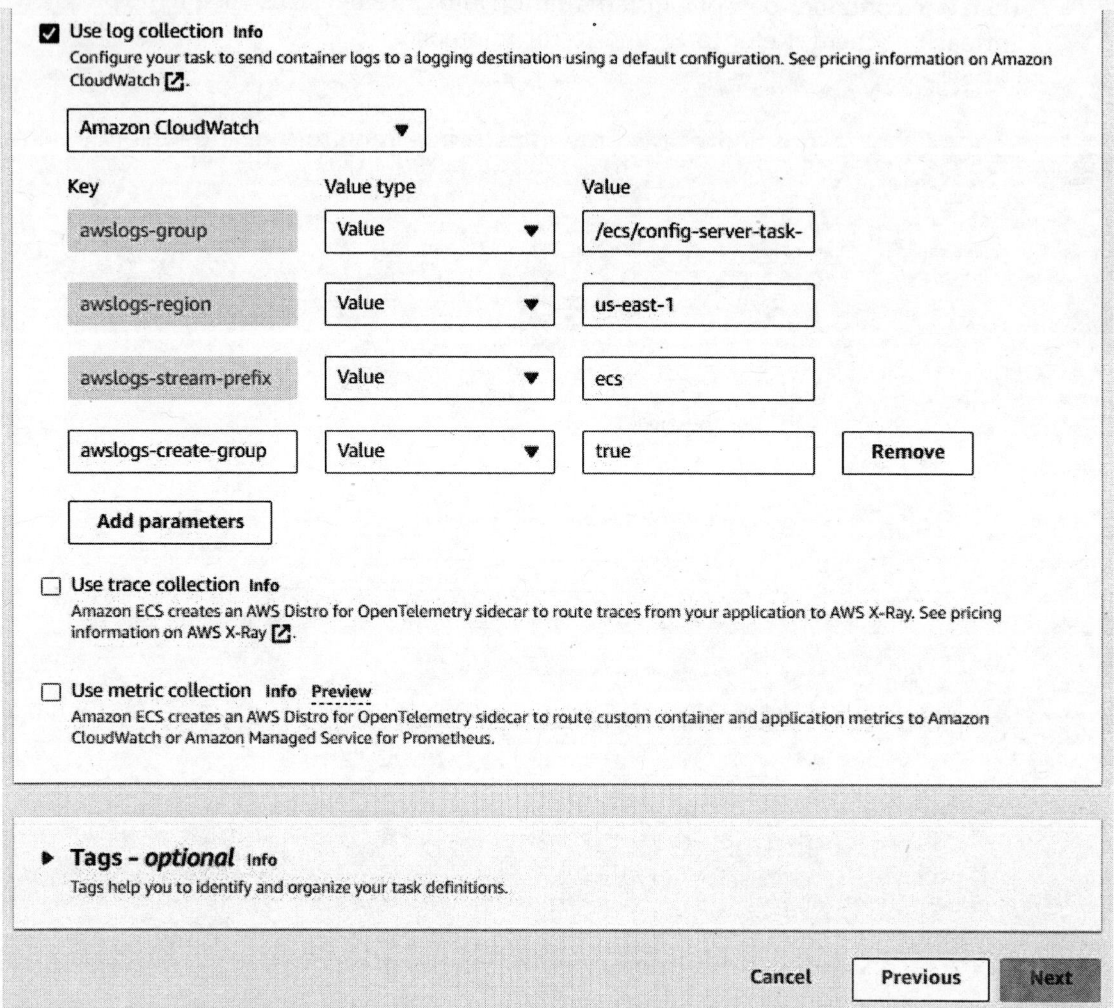

Figure 7.7: Configuring log collection parameters for a task definition

Here,

- `/ecs/config-server-task-definition` is the group under CloudWatch that will hold the logs for this task.

7. Validate all the details and click **Create**. First version of the task definition has been created, any change to a task definition requires a new version needs to be created. Refer to *Figure 7.8* for viewing the newly created task definition:

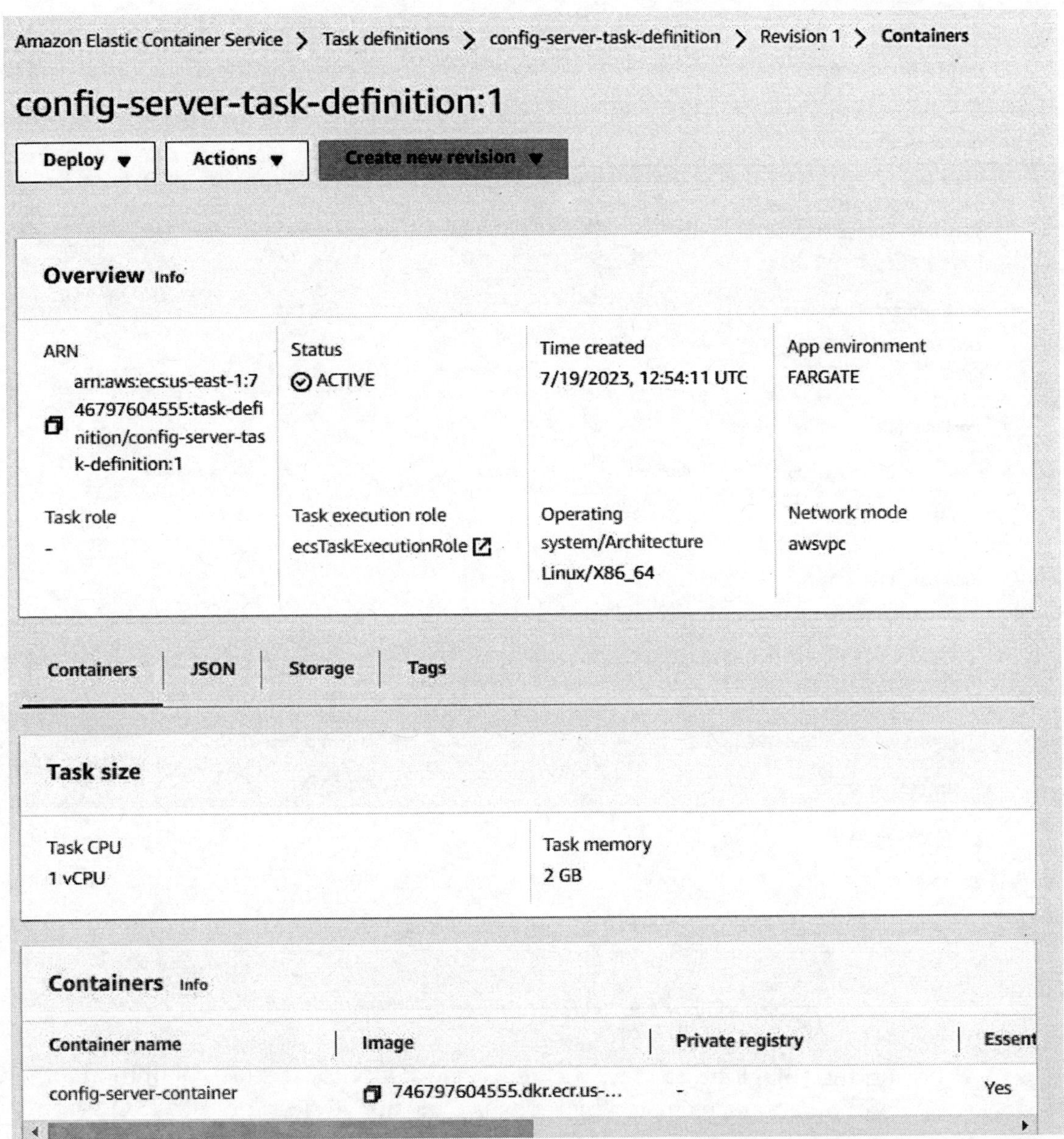

Figure 7.8: config-server-task-definition revision 1 has been created

8. Click on the container link to validate the details for the container details. Refer to *Figure 7.9* for viewing the details of **`config-server-container`**:

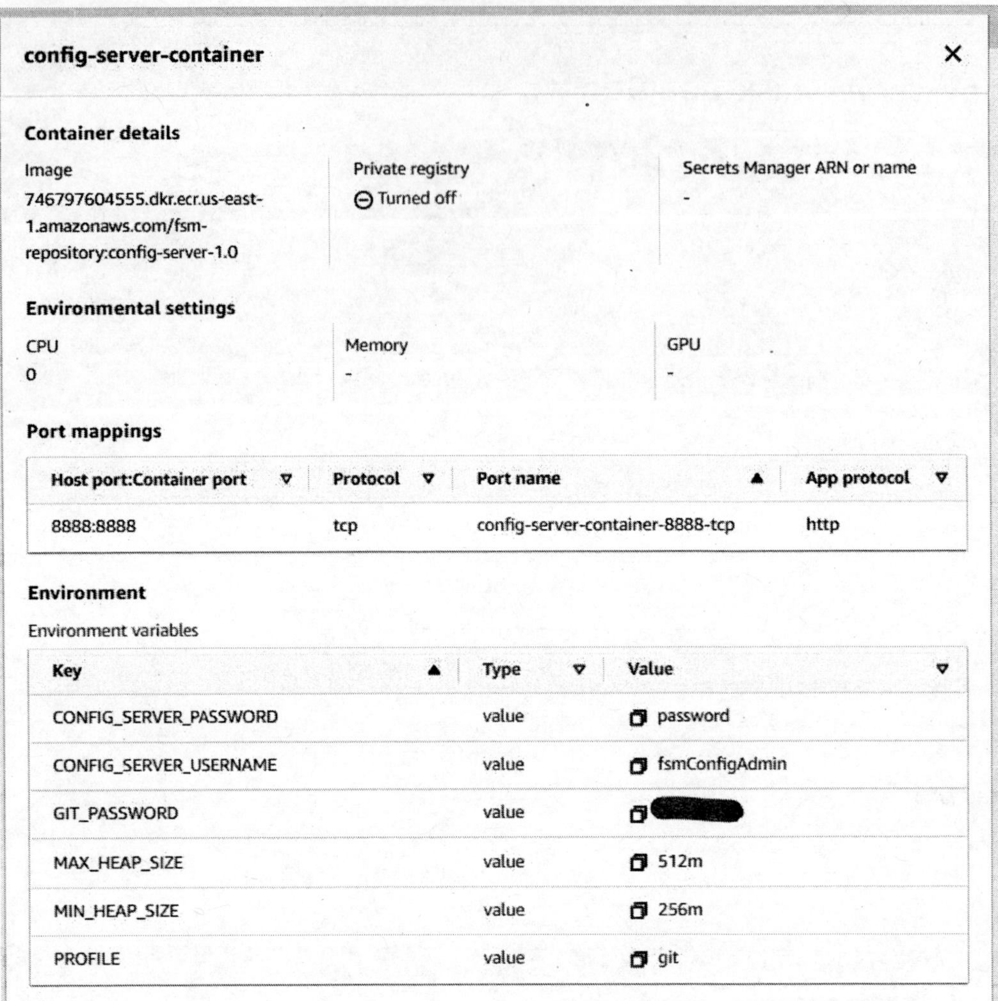

Figure 7.9: config-server-container details

9. Click on the **JSON** tab to view the generated JSON for the task definition, other task definitions can be created by repeating the above steps or with **JSON** option by taking references from the following JSON sections:

```
{
        "taskDefinitionArn":  "arn:aws:ecs:us-east-1:746797604555:task-definition/config-server-task-definition:1",
```

The following section describes the container definitions in the above task definition. As only one container has been created in the task definition, the array of **`containerDefinitions`** only has an entry for container with a name **`config-server-container`** and path of the image to be used for the container:

```
"containerDefinitions": [
    {
        "name": "config-server-container",
        "image": "746797604555.dkr.ecr.us-east-1.amazonaws.com/
fsm-repository:config-server-1.0",
```

The following section defines the port mappings, that is, which port of the container is mapped to which port of the host machine. Here, port 8888 of container is mapped with port 8888 of the host machine:

```
        "portMappings": [
            {
                "name": "config-server-container-8888-tcp",
                "containerPort": 8888,
                "hostPort": 8888,
                "protocol": "tcp",
                "appProtocol": "http"
            }
        ],
```

The following section defines the environment variables and their corresponding value passed to the container, these are the same variables and their values that have been mentioned in above *Figure 7.7* while creating the task definition:

```
        "environment": [
            {
                "name": "GIT_PASSWORD",
                "value": "****"
            },
            {
                "name": "CONFIG_SERVER_PASSWORD",
                "value": "password"
            },
            {
                "name": "PROFILE",
                "value": "git"
            },
            {
                "name": "MIN_HEAP_SIZE",
```

```
                "value": "256m"
            },
            {
                "name": "MAX_HEAP_SIZE",
                "value": "512m"
            },
            {
                "name": "CONFIG_SERVER_USERNAME",
                "value": "fsmConfigAdmin"
            }
        ],
    }
],
```

The following section defines the name of the family the container belongs to, it is used to group different versions of the similar tasks:

```
"family": "config-server-task-definition",
```

The following section defines the networking mode to be used for the containers within the task. The **AWS Virtual Private Cloud** (**VPC**) mode is commonly used in Fargate deployments. In **awsvpc** mode, each task gets its own **elastic network interface** (**ENI**) with a private IP address. This allows containers to communicate over the network as if they were running on the same host. It also provides security benefits by leveraging VPC features like security groups and network ACLs.

```
"networkMode": "awsvpc",
```

The following section defines the task definition revision, which starts with **1** for a new task definition and the status which has been set to **ACTIVE**:

```
"revision": 1,
"status": "ACTIVE",
```

The following section defines the compatible infrastructure requirements for the launch of the tasks. The field helps in defining constraints for where the task can be scheduled:

```
"requiresCompatibilities": [
    "FARGATE"
],
```

The following section defines the CPU and memory assigned to the task when it is executed and also the runtime platform for the task:

```
        "cpu": "1024",
        "memory": "2048",
        "runtimePlatform": {
            "cpuArchitecture": "X86_64",
            "operatingSystemFamily": "LINUX"
        }
    }
```

Creating Customer Enquiry ECS task definition with JSON

Follow the steps for creating the task definition:

1. Log in to the AWS Management Console and search ECS or type in the following URL: **https://us-east-1.console.aws.amazon.com/ecs/v2/task-definitions**.

   The region can be changed as per your preference.

2. Click on the **Create new task definition with JSON** option.

3. Paste the above created JSON and click **Create**.

4. A sample JSON file is displayed as follows:

```
{
    "requiresCompatibilities": [
        "FARGATE"
    ],
    "family": "",
    "containerDefinitions": [
        {
            "name": "",
            "image": "",
            "essential": true
        }
    ],
    "volumes": [],
    "networkMode": "awsvpc",
    "memory": "3 GB",
    "cpu": "1 vCPU",
```

```
    "executionRoleArn": "arn:aws:iam::746797604555:role/
ecsTaskExecutionRole"
}
```

5. Modify **family**, **containerDefinition** and **memory** section as follows, click **Create**:

   Family, the task definition family is a way to group different revisions of a task definition. When one creates a new revision of a task definition, it is associated with a family. The family name remains constant across different revisions, making it easy to organize and manage multiple versions of a task definition that share similar characteristics or functionalities.

   ```
   "family": "customer-enquiry-task-definition"
   ```

   All the versions of this task definition will be grouped with the family name **customer-enquiry-task-definition**.

   Container Definition, taking the reference from above JSON of the task definition **config-server-container** set the details for the container for Customer Enquiry microservice:

```
"containerDefinitions": [
        {
            "name": "customer-enquiry-container",
            "image": "746797604555.dkr.ecr.us-east-1.amazonaws.com/
fsm-repository:customer-enquiry-1.0",
            "cpu": 0,
            "portMappings": [
                {
                    "name": "customer-enquiry-container-8080-tcp",
                    "containerPort": 8080,
                    "hostPort": 8080,
                    "protocol": "tcp",
                    "appProtocol": "http"
                }
            ],
            "essential": true,
            "environment": [
                {
                    "name": "CONFIG_SERVER_USERNAME",
                    "value": "fsmConfigAdmin"
```

```
                },
                {
                    "name": "CONFIG_SERVER_PASSWORD",
                    "value": "password"
                },
                {
                    "name": "CONFIG_SERVER_URL",
                    "value": "configserver:http://fsm-load-
balancer-1737637159.us-east-1.elb.amazonaws.com:8888"
                },
                {
                    "name": "MIN_HEAP_SIZE",
                    "value": "256m"
                },
                {
                    "name": "MAX_HEAP_SIZE",
                    "value": "512m"
                },
                {
                    "name": "DATABASE_URL",
                    "value": "jdbc:postgresql://fs-marketplace.
cbgzpif7rd3e.us-east-1.rds.amazonaws.com:5432/postgres"
                },
                {
                    "name": "DATABASE_USERNAME",
                    "value": "postgres"
                },
                {
                    "name": "DATABASE_PASSWORD",
                    "value": "****"
                }
            ]
        }
    ],
```

Here, name of the container, the path of the image, mapping of container ports and environment variable values are set for a container as part of the task definition.

Note that the environment variable **`CONFIG_SERVER_URL`** has the value as the DNS name of the **application load balancer** (**ALB**) **`fsm-load-balancer`**, this is because config server needs to be accessed via this load balancer.

Memory, set the memory to be allocated to the container when the task is executing.

```
"memory": "2 GB"
```

Here, memory of 2 GB is allocated to the container.

6. First version of the task definition has been created, any change to a task definition requires a new version needs to be created. Refer to *Figure 7.10* for viewing the newly created task definition:

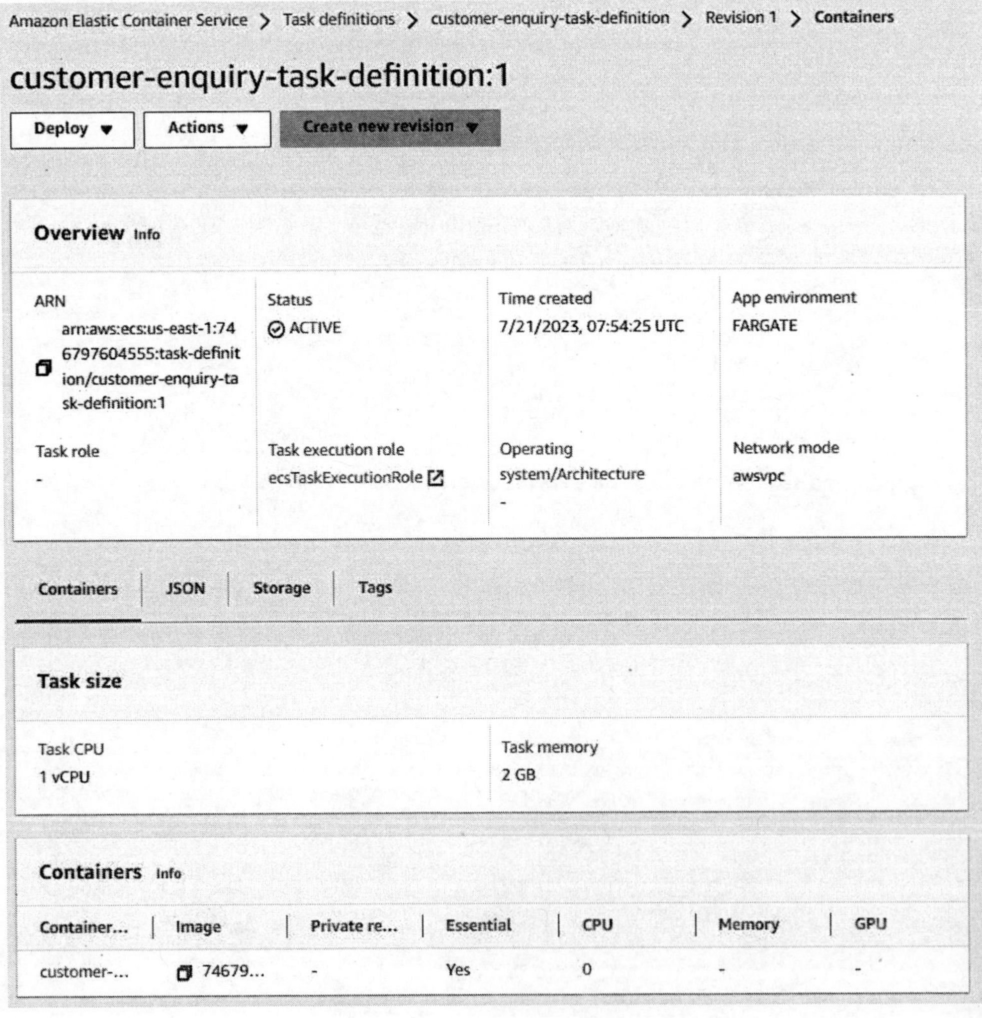

Figure 7.10: customer-enquiry-task-definition revision 1 has been created

Creating Enquiry Broadcast ECS task definition with JSON

Enquiry Broadcast task definition is created very similar to the Customer Enquiry task definition.

Make sure that the application has been configured to run on port 8080, which is the default port for a Spring Boot application.

Refer to *Figure 7.11* to view all three task definitions corresponding to the three microservices that is, Config Server, Customer Enquiry and Enquiry Broadcast:

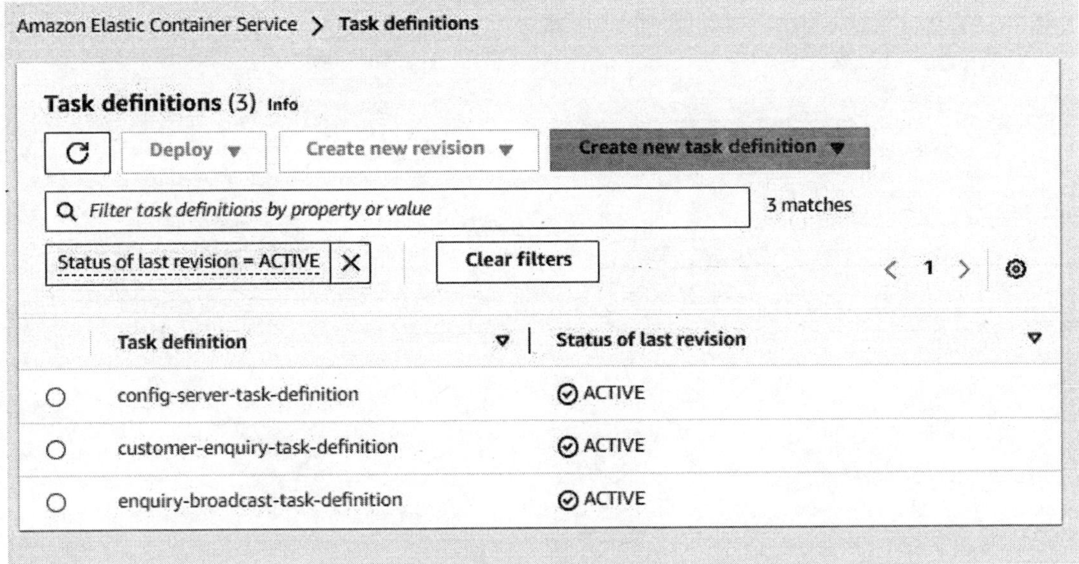

Figure 7.11: Active task definitions

Amazon ECS service

As discussed before, tasks within an ECS cluster that are required to be running for long, need to be wrapped up inside a **service**. If one of tasks fails or stops, the Amazon ECS service scheduler launches another instance of that task definition as its replacement. This helps to maintain the desired number of tasks in a service and provides resiliency to the business application.

Recipe 55: Creating Amazon ECS Services

In the already created ECS cluster `fsm-ecs-cluster`, three services need to be created one for each type definition that has been created in the previous recipe.

Creating Config Server ECS service

Follow the below steps for creating the ECS service:

1. Log in to the AWS Management Console and search ECS or type in the following URL: **https://us-east-1.console.aws.amazon.com/ecs/v2/clusters.**

   The region can be changed as per your preference.

2. Select the cluster **`fsm-ecs-cluster`** and from the below tabs click **Services** and then **Create**. Refer to *Figure 7.12* for reference:

Figure 7.12: Services section of fsm-ecs-cluster

3. In the **Deployment configuration** section provide the following details:

   a. Task definition family: Select **`config-server-task-definition`** from the drop down.

   b. Revision: Select the latest revision or a different one as desired.

   c. Service name: Any logical name, like **`config-service`**.

   d. Desired tasks: The number of instances of the tasks running under this service will be equal to the number mentioned here. While creating the service for the first time it is advisable to mention it as 1, and can be increased later as required.

Refer to *Figure 7.13* for reference:

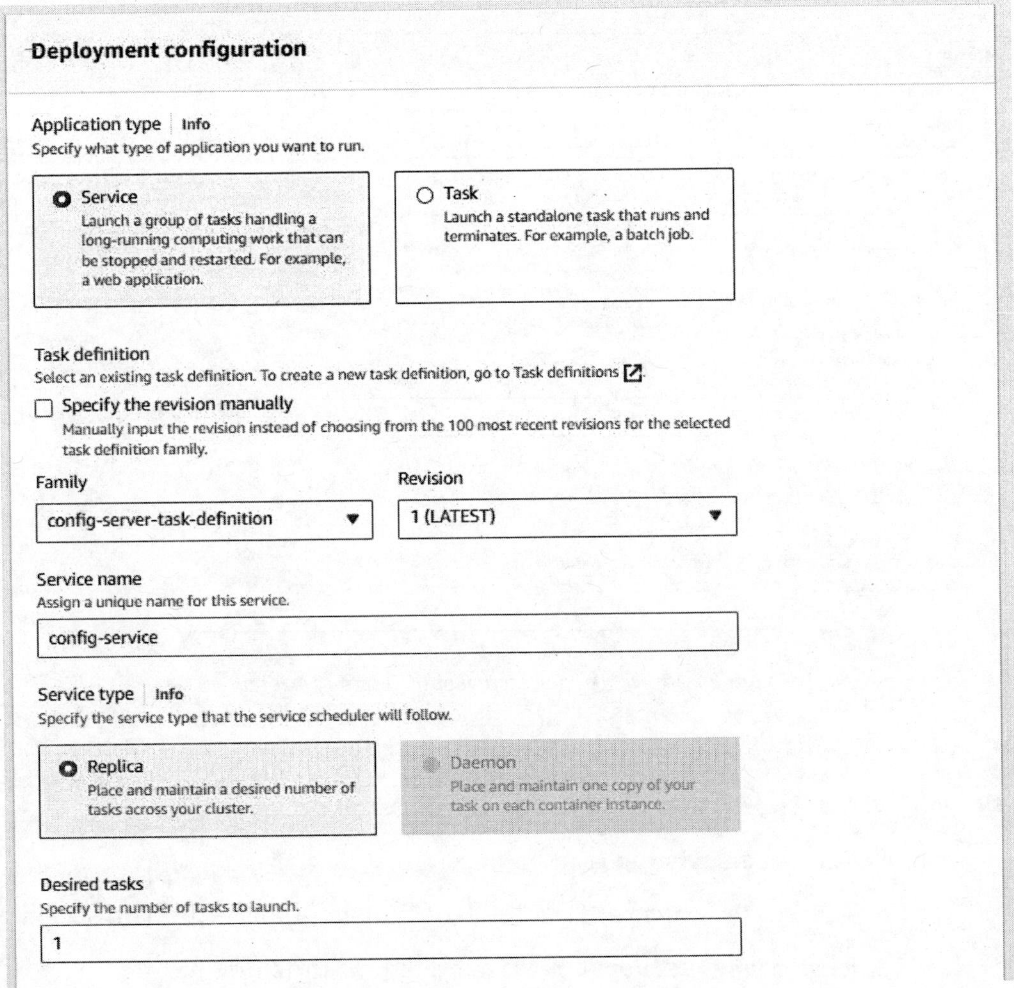

***Figure 7.13**: Deployment configuration section of ECS service creation*

4. In the **Networking** section, choose exclusively the subnets designated for container execution. While it is possible to select all available subnets, it is essential to align with the subnets of AZs specified during ALB creation. If ALB has been configured to be used with only 2 AZs then ensure that subnets of these same two AZs are selected when creating the ECS service. Failure to do so may result in the ALB being unable to redirect traffic to containers in other subnets. Refer to *Figure 7.14* for reference:

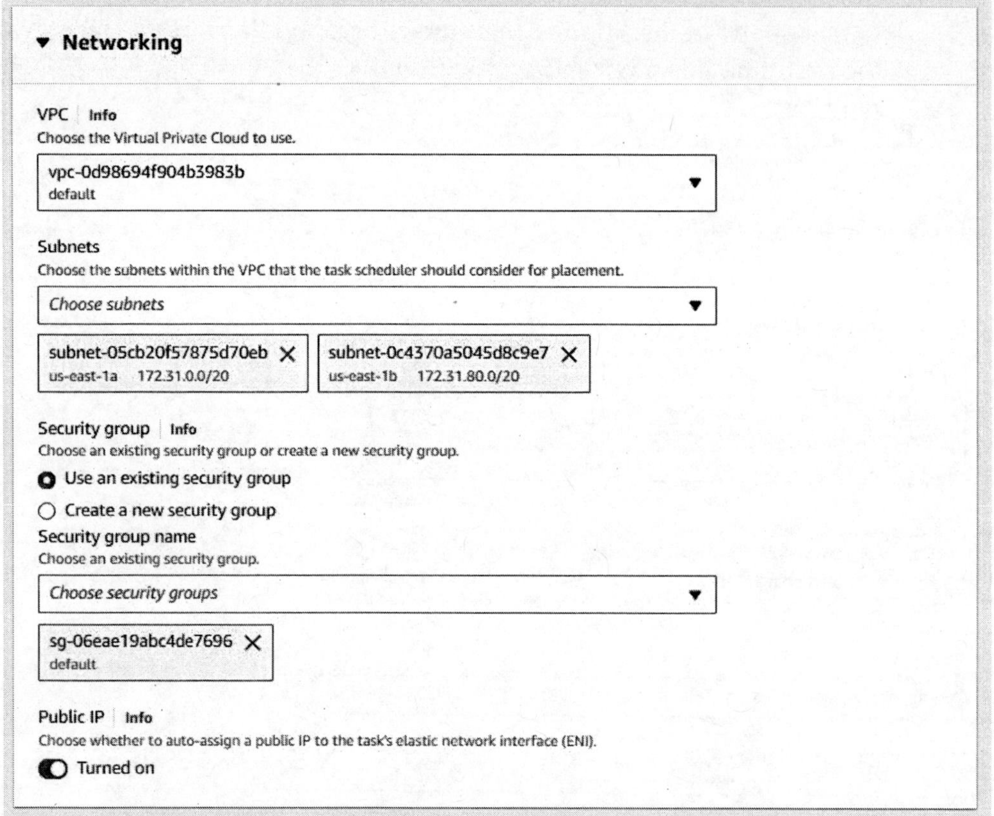

Figure 7.14: *Networking section of ECS service creation*

5. In the **load balancing** section, provide the below details:
   a. Select **Application Load Balancer** from drop down.
   b. Select **Use an existing load balancer.**
   c. Select the load balancer **`fsm-load-balancer`** from the drop down.
   d. Choose **`config-server-container`** from the drop down.
   e. As no listener was attached while creating the load balancer, select **Create new listener** and in the port mention 8888.

As Config Server only needs to be invoked from other internal microservices and not from outside, a separate listener on a different port other than 80 is preferred. Moreover, the config server URL passed as an environment variable in the other two microservice task definitions has the port configured as 8888, **http://fsm-load-balancer-1737637159.us-east-1.elb.amazonaws.com:8888.**

f. Select **Create new target group** and mention the health check URL as **`/actuator/health`**. It is an URL for checking the health check using an actuator which has been preconfigured in the microservices.

   ALB calls this URL on a configured frequency and in case the health check fails the corresponding container is deregistered from the ECS service and the service spawns a new container to replace the unhealthy container.

   Refer to *Figure 7.15* for reference:

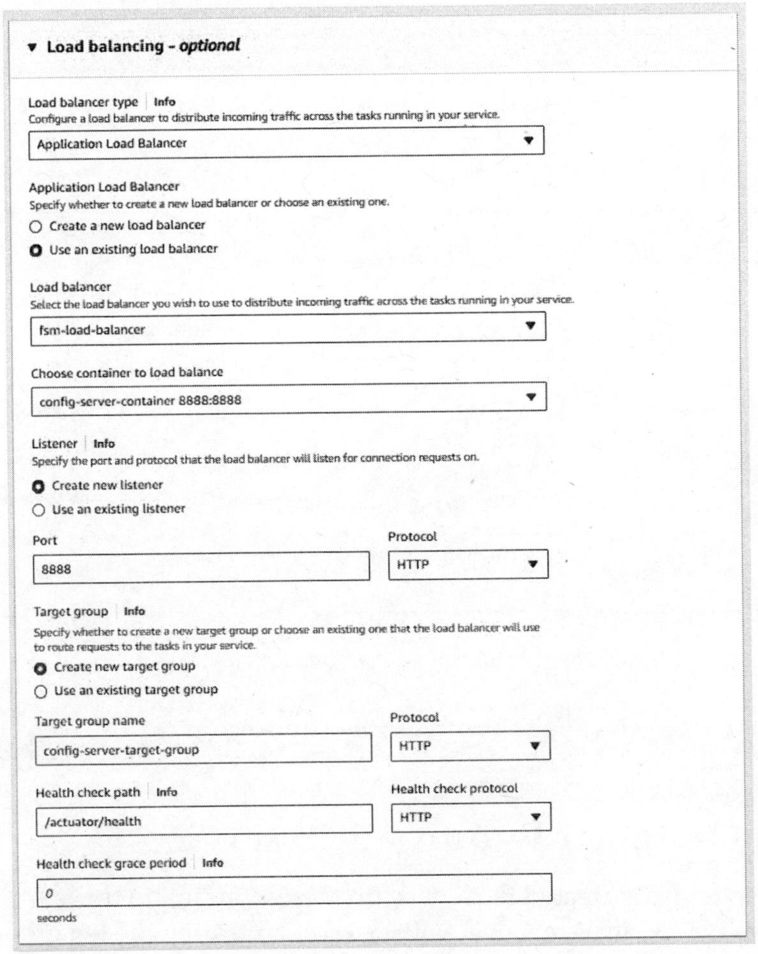

Figure 7.15: Load balancing section of ECS service creation

6. Click **Create** to create the service. It takes few minutes to get the service created, as listener and target group need to be created along the service. Once all is fine the service is started as the desired number of tasks configured is 1 which is more than 0.
7. View the newly created service under **Services** tab of the cluster, refer to *Figure 7.16* for reference:

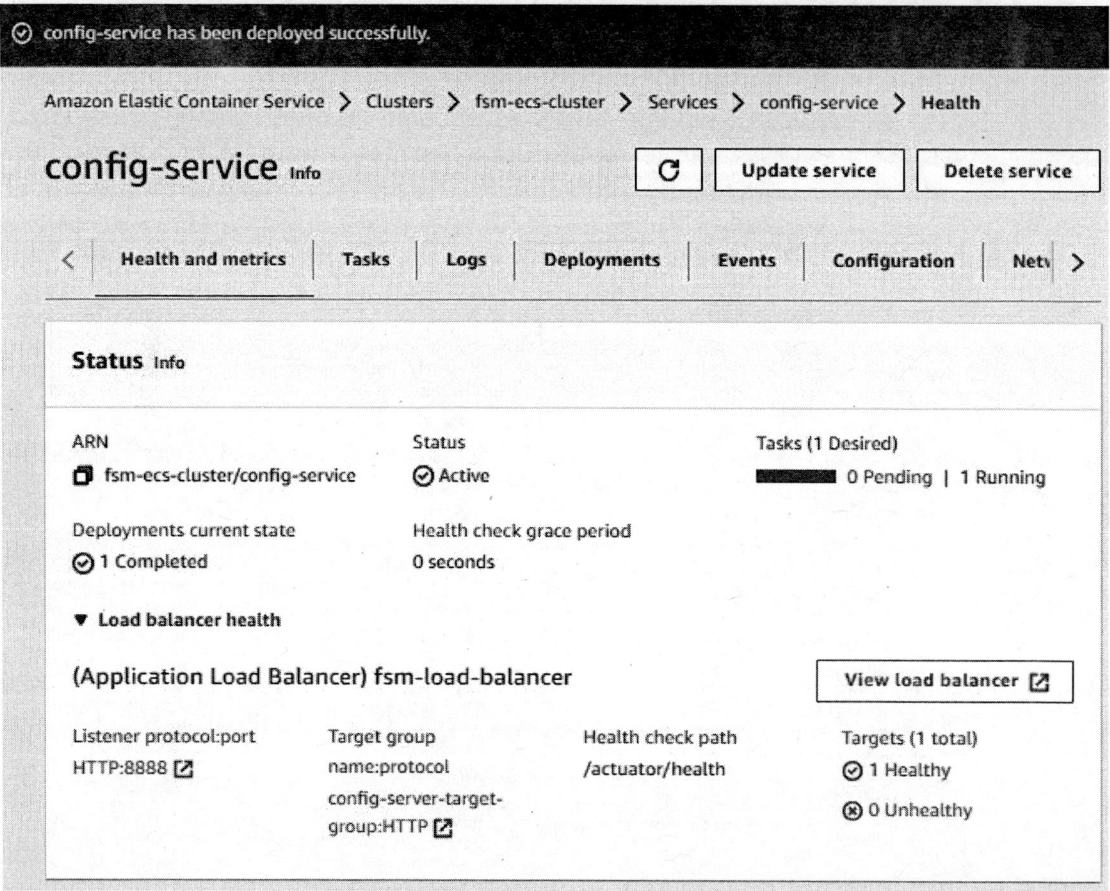

Figure 7.16: config-service and running 1 task

Note: There is no direct way to stop a running service and can be stopped by updating the desired number of tasks to 0.

Creating Customer Enquiry ECS service

Before the ECS service is created the log group corresponding to the task definition needs to be created in the CloudWatch. Follow the steps for creating the log group:

1. Click **Create log group** under CloudWatch.
2. Provide log group name as **`/ecs/customer-enquiry-task-definition`**.
3. Click **Create.**

The log group needs to be created for the Customer Enquiry microservice the **`ecsTaskExecutionRole`** does not have the create log group permission. In the case of Config Server as Task Definition was created via GUI, creating the log group separately was not required.

Customer Enquiry service is to be created in similar way as Config Server service, provide the details accordingly:

1. Task definition family: Select **`customer-enquiry-task-definition`** from the drop down.
2. Service name: Any logical name, like **`customer-enquiry-service`**.
3. Load balancer: **Create new listener** and in the port mention 80. It is a publicly accessed service and in ideal world should be accessed over port 80.
4. Target group name: **`customer-enquiry-target-group`**
5. Health check path: Same as before it is the Actuator default path for example, **`/actuator/health`**.

The newly created service will be up and running, refer to *Figure 7.17* for reference:

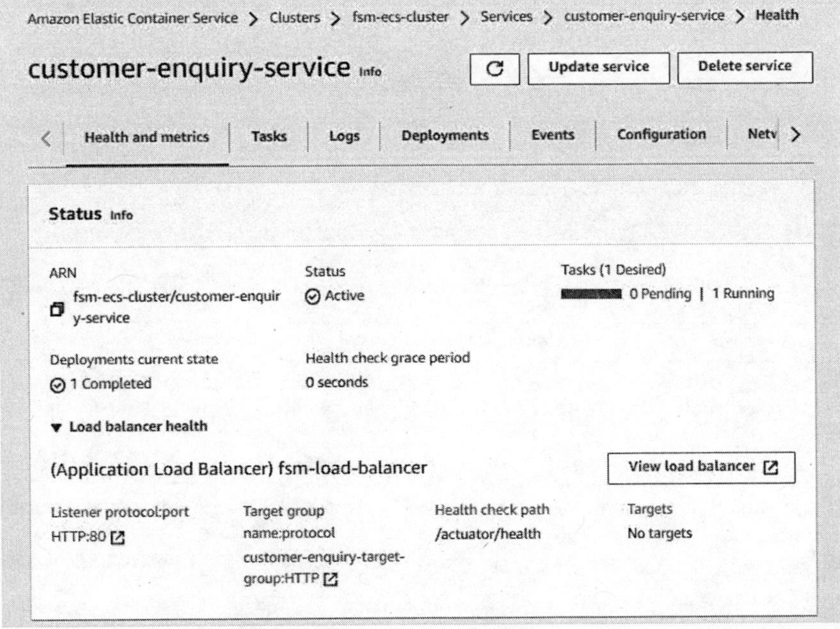

Figure 7.17: *customer-enquiry-service and running 1 task*

Creating Enquiry Broadcast ECS service

The Enquiry Broadcast service is to be created in a very similar way as Customer Enquiry service, the only configuration that is deviating is in the load balancing section.

1. Select the existing listener and from drop down select *80:HTTP*.
2. Path pattern is **`/broadcast`**. This is required as now there are two target groups associated with the load balancer on listener 80 and it needs to know on what condition the traffic needs to be routed to **`enquiry-broadcast-target-group`**.

Refer to *Figure 7.18* for all the three services that have been created:

***Figure 7.18**: Running Amazon ECS services*

Recipe 56: Validating Application Load Balancer details

As part of the creation of Amazon ECS services the Application Load Balancer **`fsm-load-balancer`** has been modified to have two listeners running on port 80 and 8888 for protocol HTTP. The details of the application load balancer can be viewed by clicking **`fsm-load-balancer`** from the **EC2 | Load balancer**. Refer to *Figure 7.19* for reference:

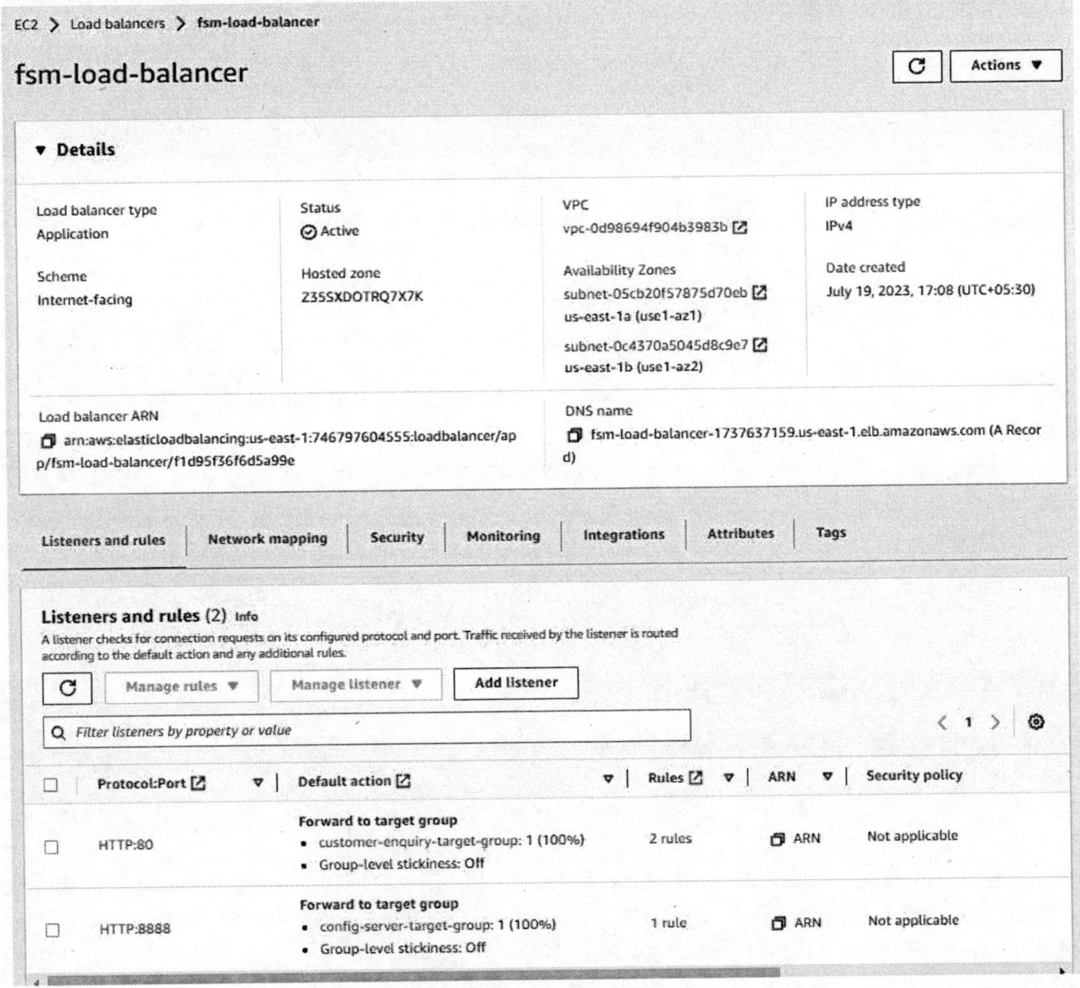

Figure 7.19: fsm-load-balancer details

From the preceding figure there are two listeners configured for the ALB:

- **`HTTP:80`**
- **`HTTP:8888`**

Against listener 1 there are two rules configured, click on the Rules link for listener HTTP:80 to view the rule details. Refer to *Figure 7.20* for reference:

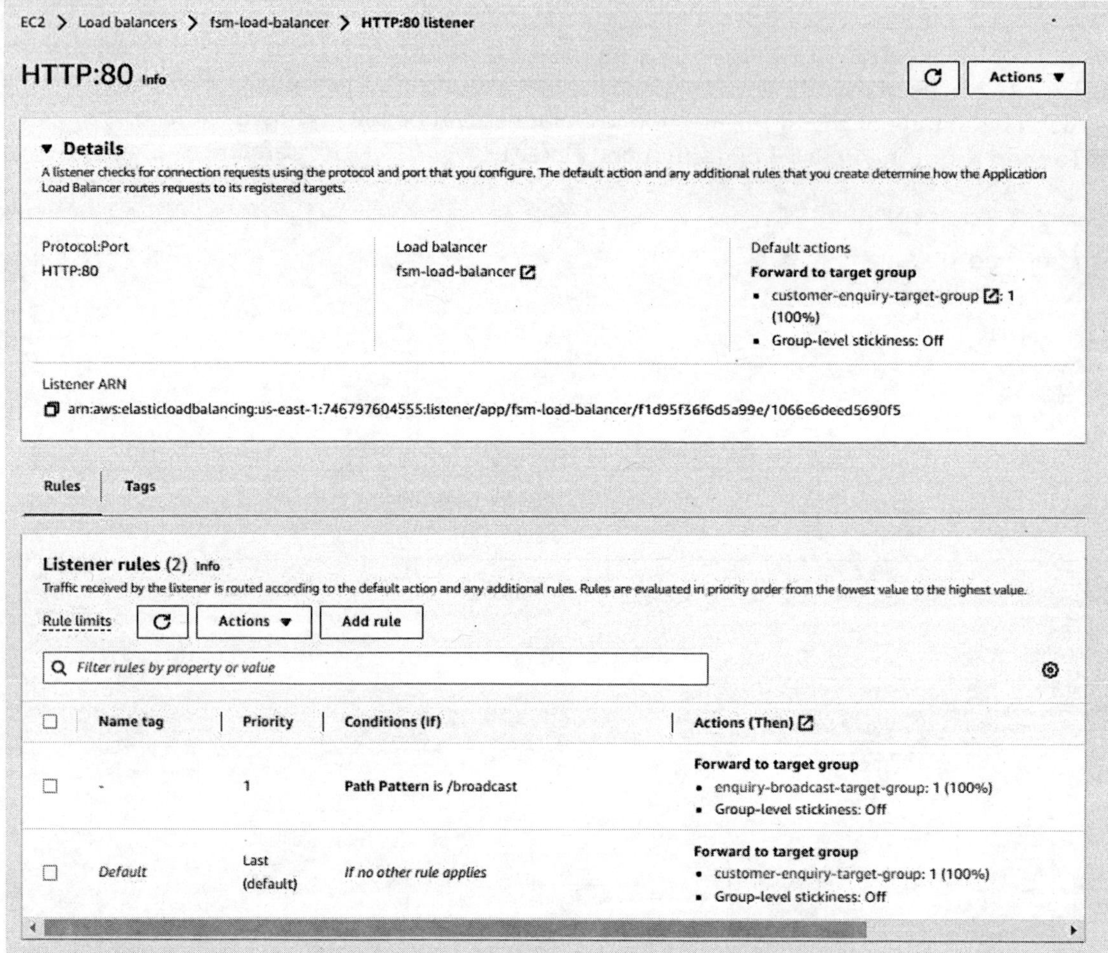

***Figure 7.20:** fsm-load-balancer listener HTTP:80 rules*

The preceding figure validated that listener HTTP:80 will route the traffic to **`enquiry-broadcast-target-group`** if the URL path has a pattern **`/broadcast`**; otherwise, it will route it to **`customer-enquiry-target-group`**. The complete flow can be visualized using *Figure 7.21*:

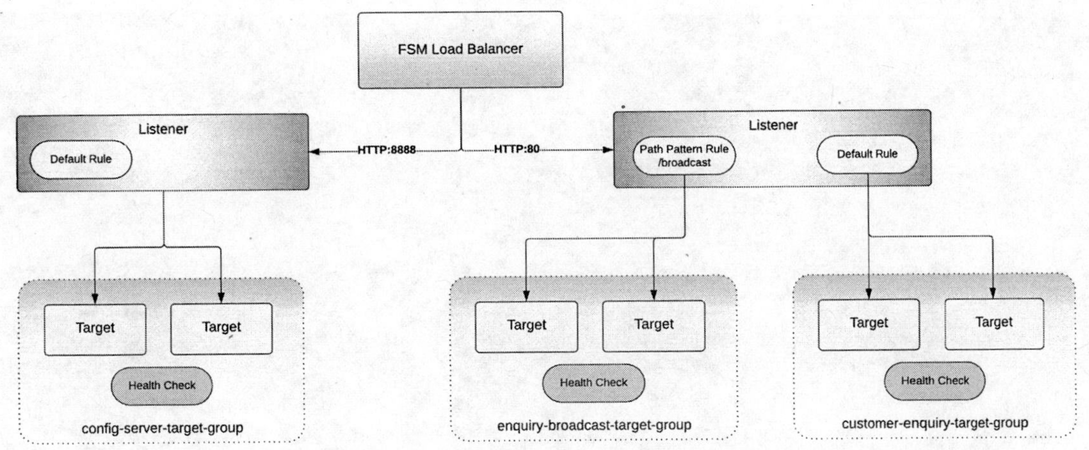

***Figure 7.21:** fsm-load-balancer incoming request flow*

New rules can be added as and when required from the same screen itself. The details can be viewed and updated using the AWS CLI commands as well.

Recipe 57: Creating target group using AWS CLI

Target groups can also be created using CLI, run the following AWS CLI command:

```
aws elbv2 create-target-group --name customer-enquiry-target-group-2
--protocol HTTP --port 80 \
--health-check-path /actuator/health --vpc-id vpc-0d98694f904b3983b --ip-
address-type ipv4
```

Here,

- `protocol` defines the protocol to be used for routing traffic to the targets.
- `port` defines the port on which target receives the traffic.
- `health-check-patch` is the path to be invoked for checking the health of a target.
- `vpc-id` is an identifier for the virtual private cloud.

Output is as shown in *Figure 7.22*:

Figure 7.22: Output of AWS create-target-group command

Recipe 58: Adding an HTTP listener to an ALB with default rule using AWS CLI

Run the following AWS CLI command to attach an HTTP listener to an application load balancer and forwards requests to target group as a default action:

```
aws elbv2 create-listener --load-balancer-arn
arn:aws:elasticloadbalancing:us-east-1:746797604555:loadbalancer/app/fsm-
load-balancer/96acbb6afc91f9db \
--protocol HTTP --port 80  \
--default-actions Type=forward,TargetGroupArn=arn:aws:elasticloadbalan
cing:us-east-1:746797604555:targetgroup/customer-enquiry-target-group-
2/25573e8a098f7a09
```

Here,

- `load-balancer-arn` is the ARN for the load balancer to which the listener is to be added.
- `protocol` defines the protocol to be used for connections from clients to the load balancer. Supported protocols for an ALB are HTTP and HTTPS.
- `port` defines the port on which the load balancer is listening.
- `default-actions` defines an action to be taken for the default rule.
- `Type=forward,TargetGroupArn` means forward the request to the configured target group. The target group ARN has been copied from the output of the `create-target-group` command from the previous recipe.

Output is as shown in *Figure 7.23*:

Figure 7.23: Output of AWS create-listener command

Recipe 59: Adding a conditional rule to a listener

If there is a listener already in place, forwarding the requests to a target group through a default rule, it is possible to augment the setup by introducing an additional rule. This new rule can be configured to route requests to a different target group based on a specified condition. To facilitate this, you may need to create an additional target group if one does not already exist. The command mentioned in the above recipe can be used for the same:

```
aws elbv2 create-target-group --name enquiry-broadcast-target-group-2
--protocol HTTP --port 80 \
--health-check-path /actuator/health --vpc-id vpc-0d98694f904b3983b
```

The above command creates a target group with the name **enquiry-broadcast-target-group-2**.

Once the target group is available, run the below command to add a conditional rule to a listener:

```
aws elbv2 create-rule --listener-arn arn:aws:elasticloadbalancing:us-east-1:746797604555:listener/app/fsm-load-balancer/96acbb6afc91f9db/0aff34d041ea69ed \
--priority 1 --conditions Field=path-pattern,Values='/broadcast' \
--actions Type=forward,TargetGroupArn=arn:aws:elasticloadbalancing:
us-east-1:746797604555:targetgroup/enquiry-broadcast-target-group-2/0799206e52e03a9c
```

Here,

- **listener-arn** is the ARN of the listener to which a rule is to be added.
- **priority** defines the order of rule execution, lower the value the higher the priority.

- **`conditions`** define the criteria when to execute the rule.
- **`Field=path-pattern,Values`** sets the condition to match the request URL path with the defined pattern.
- **`actions`** define an action to be taken for the rule.
- **`Type=forward,TargetGroupArn`** means forward the request to the configured target group. The target group ARN has been copied from the output of the **`create-target-group`** command from the previous recipe.

Output is as shown in *Figure 7.24*:

Figure 7.24: Output of AWS create-rule command

Recipe 60: Validating Application Load Balancer details using AWS CLI

Run the following commands to get insights about a load balancer:

- **`aws elbv2 describe-load-balancers`**
- **`aws elbv2 describe-load-balancer-attributes`**
- **`aws elb2 describe-listeners`**
- **`aws elb2 describe-target-groups`**
- **`aws elb2 describe-rules`**

AWS CLI command to view load balancer:

```
aws elbv2 describe-load-balancers --load-balancer-arns
arn:aws:elasticloadbalancing:us-east-1:746797604555:loadbalancer/app/fsm-
load-balancer/96acbb6afc91f9db
```

AWS CLI command to get load balancer attributes:

```
aws elbv2 describe-load-balancer-attributes --load-balancer-arn
arn:aws:elasticloadbalancing:us-east-1:746797604555:loadbalancer/app/fsm-
load-balancer/96acbb6afc91f9db
```

AWS CLI command to view listeners:

```
aws elbv2 describe-listeners --load-balancer-arn
arn:aws:elasticloadbalancing:us-east-1:746797604555:loadbalancer/app/fsm-
load-balancer/96acbb6afc91f9db
```

AWS CLI command to view target groups:

```
aws elbv2 describe-target-groups --load-balancer-arn
arn:aws:elasticloadbalancing:us-east-1:746797604555:loadbalancer/app/fsm-
load-balancer/96acbb6afc91f9db
```

AWS CLI command to view rules:

```
aws elbv2 describe-rules --listener-arn arn:aws:elasticloadbalancing:us-
east-1:746797604555:listener/app/fsm-load-balancer/96acbb6afc91f9db/0aff34d0
41ea69ed
```

Conclusion

In this chapter, we have learnt benefits of running the application on an orchestration platform and deployed the financial service marketplace microservices on the Amazon ECS orchestrator. We have gone through the step-by-step process of creating every component required for deploying the application on the ECS orchestrator platform. In this demonstration, we illustrated the process by which an orchestrator platform retrieves an image from the registry and deploys it as a container. Additionally, we showcased how services are automatically discovered through the implementation of the third-party service discovery pattern.

In the next chapter, we will learn about the elasticity of cloud detailing on the topics Auto Scalability, High Availability and Disaster Recovery. They are very important for an application to be performant on peak loads along with the optimal usage of the hardware; also makes sure the system is up and running even in the situations of any disaster.

Points to remember

- Implement health checks for microservices to ensure that they are running properly. Orchestration platforms use health checks to determine the availability of service instances and perform necessary actions in case of failures.
- Make sure to only expose the container ports that are required for running the application else it may lead to security concerns.
- Any update to the task definition creates a new version of it and AWS ECS service needs to be updated with the new version for changes to take place.
- There is no direct way to stop an ECS service, for this the desired number of tasks needs to be updated to 0.
- Internal communication between microservices should happed using a private Application Load Balancer.

Questions

1. What is Amazon ECS, and how does it differ from other container orchestration platforms?
2. What are the key components of Amazon ECS?
3. How do you deploy a containerized application on Amazon ECS?
4. How do you handle service discovery in Amazon ECS?
5. What is the difference between Fargate and EC2 launch types in Amazon ECS?
6. Can you explain the process of updating a running task in Amazon ECS?
7. How does Amazon ECS handle load balancing for containerized services?
8. How can you monitor and troubleshoot microservices running on Amazon ECS?
9. What are the different factors in scaling microservices on Amazon ECS?
10. What cost optimization strategies can be considered for microservices orchestration on Amazon ECS?

CHAPTER 8

Auto Scalability, High Availability, and Disaster Recovery

Introduction

The last chapter explained orchestrator platforms and their use in running microservices. It also talked about the step-by-step approach for setting up the Amazon **Elastic Container Service (ECS)** orchestrator on Fargate, showcasing the mechanism of dynamic service registry for the microservices.

In this chapter, we will talk about the ways to leverage the elasticity of the cloud for scaling the application as and when needed. As part of the chapter, we will demonstrate the ways an application needs to handle scale in events. We will show how high availability, which is a key to serve customers continuously without fail, is attained in the cloud environment and how high availability and auto scalability go together. The chapter also talks about the disaster recovery strategy and how it is implemented in the AWS environments.

Structure

In this chapter, we will discuss the following topics:

- Auto scalability
- Handling of scale-in events gracefully
- High availability
- Disaster recovery

Objectives

By the end of this chapter, we will learn the principles, strategies, and best practices for achieving high availability and auto scalability in Amazon ECS environments. By delving into the concepts of horizontal scaling, fault tolerance, and dynamic resource allocation, this chapter aims to equip readers with the knowledge and practical insights needed to design, implement, and manage ECS architectures that seamlessly deliver reliable services, adapt to changing demands, and ensure minimal downtime. As part of the chapter, we will learn the considerations that are required to be taken in the application design to handle the scale of events. ECS Services will be enhanced scaled using target tracking policies, RDS database to be deployed in multi-AZ deployment, etc. Also, the active – passive **disaster recovery** (**DR**) strategy will be implemented using Amazon Route 53 configurations.

Auto scalability

Automatic scalability (**AS**), also known as **auto-scaling**, is a pivotal concept in modern computing architectures that enables applications and systems to dynamically adjust their resources based on changing workloads. This dynamic resource allocation allows organizations to optimize performance, reduce operational costs, and maintain consistent user experiences, regardless of fluctuating demand.

At its core, automatic scalability revolves around the principle of elasticity. It involves deploying additional resources, such as servers or containers, when demand increases and scaling down when demand decreases. This process is automatic and driven by predefined rules and thresholds, allowing the system to adapt without requiring manual intervention.

Automatic scalability is particularly valuable in cloud computing environments, where resources are provisioned and managed programmatically. Cloud platforms like **Amazon Web Services** (**AWS**), Microsoft Azure, and Google Cloud offer tools and services that facilitate auto-scaling. These platforms enable organizations to design and implement rules that trigger scaling actions based on various metrics, such as CPU utilization, memory usage, network traffic, or response times.

One common approach to auto-scaling involves setting up scaling policies that dictate when and how resources should be added or removed. For instance, if the CPU utilization of a web server reaches a certain threshold, a scaling policy might instruct the system to launch additional instances of that server. Once the demand decreases, the policy can also trigger the removal of excess instances to conserve resources and cost.

In addition to reactive auto-scaling, where resources are scaled in response to changing conditions, predictive auto-scaling involves using historical data and forecasting algorithms to anticipate future demand spikes. This approach aims to proactively provision resources to handle anticipated traffic, ensuring a smooth user experience during peak periods.

Auto-scaling brings a range of benefits to organizations. It enhances application availability by preventing overload-induced crashes, improves performance during traffic surges, and helps optimize operational costs by avoiding over-provisioning of resources. Furthermore, it aligns with agile development practices by enabling organizations to iterate quickly and launch new features without being constrained by fixed resource capacities.

However, it is essential to design auto-scaling strategies carefully. Over scaling can lead to unnecessary costs, while under scaling can result in degraded performance and user dissatisfaction. Regular monitoring and fine-tuning of scaling policies based on real-world performance data are crucial to achieving the full benefits of automatic scalability.

Automatic ECS scaling

The ability to automatically raise or reduce the desired task count in the Amazon ECS service is known as automatic scaling in ECS. For this functionality, Amazon ECS makes use of the Application Auto Scaling service. The average CPU and memory usage for the application service is published by Amazon ECS in CloudWatch metrics, which can be used in conjunction with other CloudWatch metrics to horizontally scale out the service, i.e., increase the number of tasks to handle the increased load, or scale in the service, i.e., decrease the number of tasks to lower costs during the time of reduced load. Types of ECS scaling:

- Target tracking scaling policies
- Scheduled scaling

Recipe 61: Auto scaling ECS services with target tracking policies

A target value is set for a metric from a list of metrices provided by AWS. Auto scaling ECS publishes the values of these metrices to CloudWatch, which triggers a CloudWatch alarm if the value is breached. The scaling policy then adjusts the number of tasks based on the target value, so that the value of the metric remains on or around the target value.

Update the ECS services customer-enquiry-service, enquiry-broadcast-service, and config service to set the auto scaling logic using target tracking policies. First, set the desired number of tasks as required. Refer to *Figure 8.1* for reference:

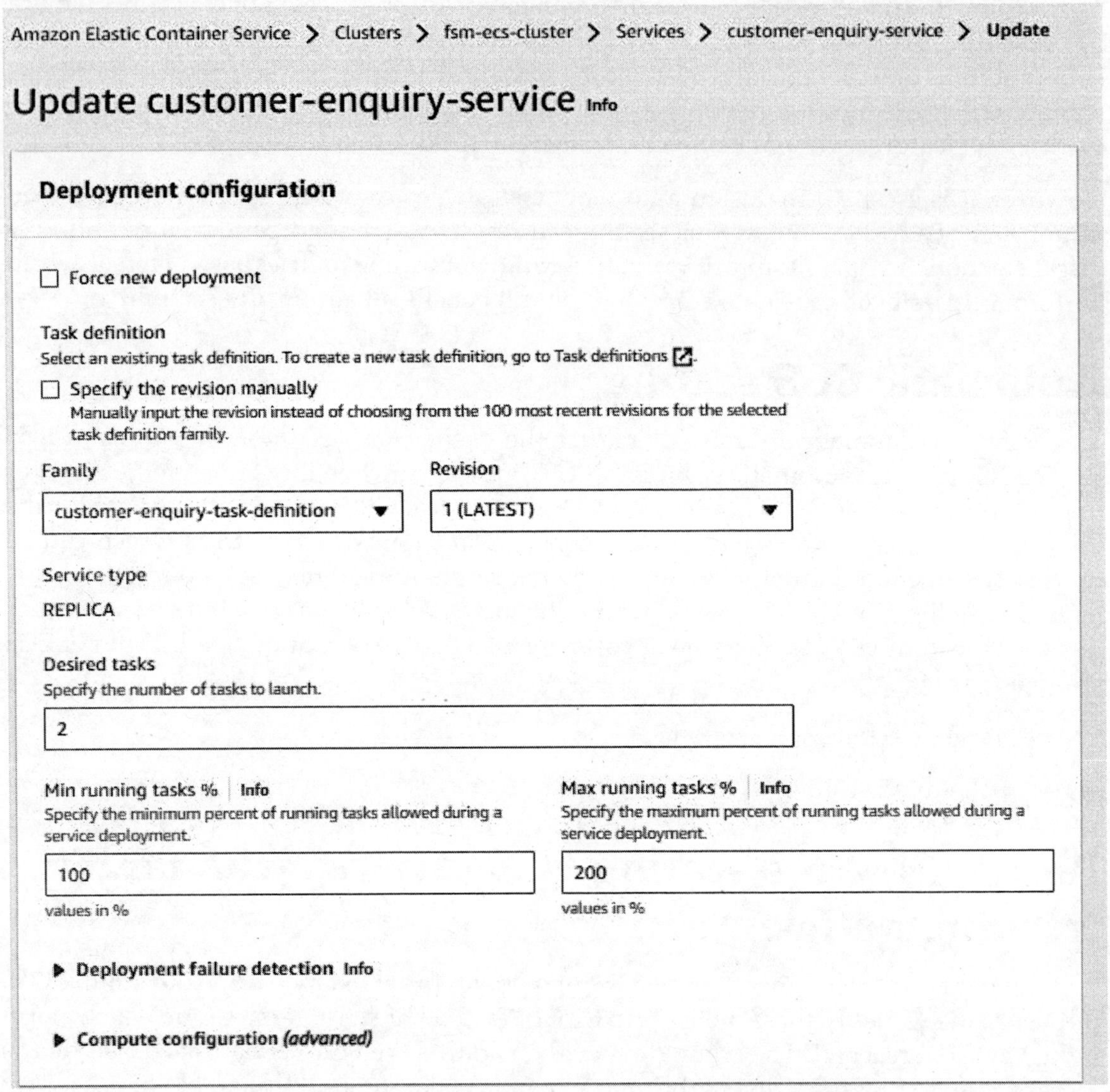

Figure 8.1: Updated customer-enquiry-service Desired tasks

In the section, **Service auto scaling**, enable **Use service auto scaling**, set minimum and the maximum number of tasks, and add a scaling policy. Refer to *Figure 8.2* for reference:

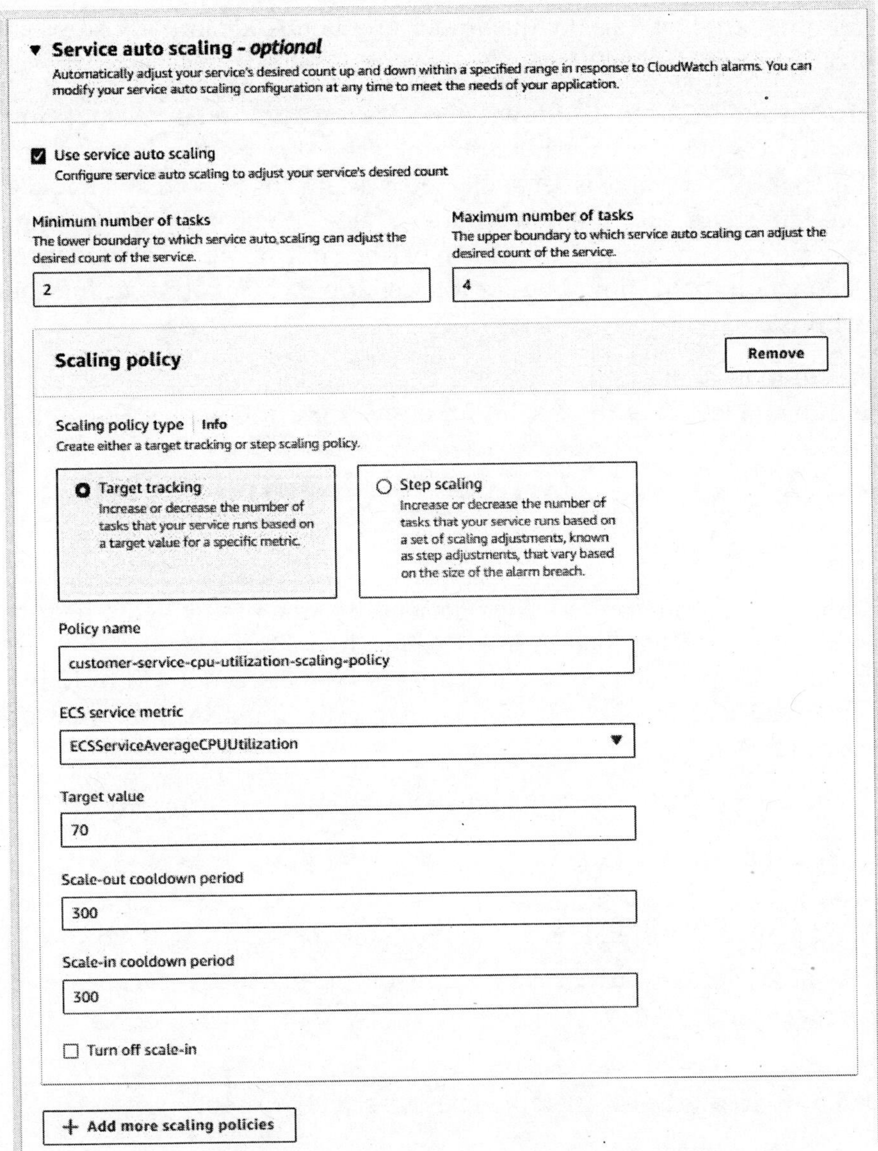

Figure 8.2: *Configuring target tracking auto scaling policy*

Here,

- **ECS service metric** is the performance metrics associated with the ECS service and average CPU utilization has been set as its value.
- **Target value** a is a specific metric that the auto-scaling policy aims to maintain or reach. Its value is set as 70%, which means if the average CPU utilization of the running tasks is 70% or more than start a new task till the count of total number

of running tasks reaches the maximum number. And similarly stops a task if the utilization drops below 70%

- **Scale-out** and **Scale-in cooldown period** is the duration in seconds during which Amazon ECS will not launch additional tasks after a scale-out or a scale-in event respectively. Their value is set as 300 seconds, means ECS will wait for 300 seconds before launching additional tasks after scale-out event or terminating any tasks after scale-in event. Longer cooldown periods may be appropriate for services that have longer initialization times or for scenarios where rapid scaling could lead to instability.

Also, as clear from the above figures the desired task count should be greater than or equal to the minimum and less than the maximum number of configured tasks.

Recipe 62: Auto scaling ECS services with schedule scaling

Schedule scaling allows an application to scale as per the predefined schedule, which is created based on predictable load changes using the historical data. For example, if an application witnesses peak load in the morning hours between 9 AM to 12 PM on every day than scheduled scaling can be used to scale out the application service at 9 AM and scale in back at 12 PM.

Follow the following steps for setting up the schedule scaling using AWS CLI:

1. **Register the scalable target**

   Before registering the scalable target with the Application Auto Scaling check whether any ECS resource is already registered by running the below command:

   ```
   aws application-autoscaling describe-scalable-targets --service-namespace ecs
   ```

   If the output is as below then there are no scalable targets:

   ```
   {
       "ScalableTargets": []
   }
   ```

   Use the following command to register the count of tasks for the ECS services:

   ```
   aws application-autoscaling register-scalable-target \
       --service-namespace ecs \
       --scalable-dimension ecs:service:DesiredCount \
       --resource-id service/fsm-ecs-cluster/customer-enquiry-service \
       --min-capacity 2 --max-capacity 2
   ```

Here,

- **scalable-dimension** defines what is to be scaled, **ecs:service:DesiredCount** is to be used for scaling the task count of **ecs** services.
- **resource-id** is the resource that needs to be scaled, for ECS service resource is service followed by the cluster name and the service name, example, **service/fsm-ecs-cluster/customer-enquiry-service** where **fsm-ecs-cluster** is the name of the cluster and **customer-enquiry-service** is the name of the ECS service.
- **min-capacity** and **max-capacity** are used to set the desired capacity of the target.

Verify the registered targets by re running the first command:

```
aws application-autoscaling describe-scalable-targets --service-namespace ecs
```

This time the output should be like:


```
{
    "ScalableTargets": [
        {
            "ServiceNamespace": "ecs",
            "ResourceId": "service/fsm-ecs-cluster/customer-enquiry-service",
            "ScalableDimension": "ecs:service:DesiredCount",
            "MinCapacity": 2,
            "MaxCapacity": 2,
            "RoleARN": "arn:aws:iam::746797604555:role/aws-service-role/ecs.application-autoscaling.amazonaws.com/AWSServiceRoleForApplicationAutoScaling_ECSService",
            "CreationTime": "2023-08-09T17:53:20.508000+05:30",
            "SuspendedState": {
                "DynamicScalingInSuspended": false,
                "DynamicScalingOutSuspended": false,
                "ScheduledScalingSuspended": false
            }
        }
    ]
}
```

2. **Create scheduled actions**

   A scheduled action is created by providing following details, what resource needs to be scheduled, when to be scheduled that is, what time and what should be the maximum and minimum number of instances. Then at the scheduled time, the values of minimum and maximum possible instances of that resource are set to the defined value in the scheduled action by the Application Auto Scaling. Now, if the existing number of instances for that resource is lying outside the updated minimum and maximum, it leads scaling of the resource as per the new values.

   Two scheduled actions need to be created, run the following commands to create them:

```
aws application-autoscaling put-scheduled-action \
  --service-namespace ecs \
  --scalable-dimension ecs:service:DesiredCount \
  --resource-id service/fsm-ecs-cluster/customer-enquiry-service \
  --scheduled-action-name peak-load-start-scheduled-action \
  --schedule "rate(1 day)" \
  --start-time 2023-08-30T9:00:00 \
  --end-time 2023-09-30T22:00:00 \
  --scalable-target-action MinCapacity=6,MaxCapacity=10

aws application-autoscaling put-scheduled-action \
  --service-namespace ecs \
  --scalable-dimension ecs:service:DesiredCount \
  --resource-id service/fsm-ecs-cluster/customer-enquiry-service \
  --scheduled-action-name peak-load-end-scheduled-action \
  --schedule "rate(1 day)" \
  --start-time 2023-08-30T12:00:00 \
  --end-time 2023-09-30T22:00:00 \
  --scalable-target-action MinCapacity=2,MaxCapacity=2
```

   Here,

   - `Schedule rate` schedules the action to be run every day.
   - `start-time` and `end-time` set the date and time since when the action is to be run and until what date and time. Hours are in 24-hour format in UTC.
   - `scalable-target-action` updates the desired range of min and max capacity.

Run the following command to view the list of scheduled actions:

```
aws application-autoscaling describe-scheduled-actions --service-namespace ecs
```

The output would be like:


```
{
    "ScheduledActions": [
        {
            "ScheduledActionName": "peak-load-end-scheduled-action",
            "ScheduledActionARN": "arn:aws:autoscal-
ing:us-east-1:746797604555:scheduledAction:d04ac097-e6b0-4be7-b36c-f7
13dab29b72:resource/ecs/service/fsm-ecs-cluster/customer-enquiry-ser-
vice:scheduledActionName/peak-load-end-scheduled-action",
            "ServiceNamespace": "ecs",
            "Schedule": "rate(1 day)",
            "ResourceId": "service/fsm-ecs-cluster/customer-enquiry-ser-
vice",
            "ScalableDimension": "ecs:service:DesiredCount",
            "StartTime": "2023-08-30T17:30:00+05:30",
            "EndTime": "2023-10-01T03:30:00+05:30",
            "ScalableTargetAction": {
                "MinCapacity": 2,
                "MaxCapacity": 2
            },
            "CreationTime": "2023-08-09T19:31:47.749000+05:30"
        },
        {
            "ScheduledActionName": "peak-load-start-scheduled-action",
            "ScheduledActionARN": "arn:aws:autoscal-
ing:us-east-1:746797604555:scheduledAction:d04ac097-e6b0-4be7-b36c-f7
13dab29b72:resource/ecs/service/fsm-ecs-cluster/customer-enquiry-ser-
vice:scheduledActionName/peak-load-start-scheduled-action",
            "ServiceNamespace": "ecs",
            "Schedule": "rate(1 day)",
            "ResourceId": "service/fsm-ecs-cluster/customer-enquiry-ser-
vice",
            "ScalableDimension": "ecs:service:DesiredCount",
            "StartTime": "2023-08-30T14:30:00+05:30",
            "EndTime": "2023-10-01T03:30:00+05:30",
            "ScalableTargetAction": {
```

```
                "MinCapacity": 6,
                "MaxCapacity": 10
            },
            "CreationTime": "2023-08-09T19:30:46.212000+05:30"
        }
    ]
}
```

3. **Clean up**

   Run the following commands to delete the scheduled actions:

```
aws application-autoscaling delete-scheduled-action \
  --service-namespace ecs \
  --scalable-dimension ecs:service:DesiredCount \
  --resource-id service/fsm-ecs-cluster/customer-enquiry-service \
  --scheduled-action-name peak-load-start-scheduled-action

aws application-autoscaling delete-scheduled-action \
  --service-namespace ecs \
  --scalable-dimension ecs:service:DesiredCount \
  --resource-id service/fsm-ecs-cluster/customer-enquiry-service \
  --scheduled-action-name peak-load-end-scheduled-action
```

   Run the following commands to deregister the scalable target:

```
aws application-autoscaling deregister-scalable-target \
  --service-namespace ecs \
  --scalable-dimension ecs:service:DesiredCount \
  --resource-id service/fsm-ecs-cluster/customer-enquiry-service
```

Similarly, **enquiry-broadcast-service** and **config-service** are enhanced to auto scale as and when needed. Scheduled scaling in conjunction with scaling policies together on the same resource can be used to get the advantages of both and provide greater flexibility for managing application loads.

Handling scale-in events gracefully

Auto scalability is a boon in keeping the application running hardware costs under control as it allows application to horizontally scale-out (add more running instances in parallel) in situations of peak load and scale-in (reduce the number of running instances) when the hardware requirement decreases. However, this requires applications to be enhanced to handle scale-in events for smooth running. Think of a scenario where a particular application node is processing some data or is in a transaction and the orchestrator decides to shut that application node as part of scale-in activity. In order to avoid user-facing errors or other issues, it is crucial to manage these terminations graciously. As an illustration, a container might shut down before the load balancer stops feeding its requests, which would result in HTTP 5xx errors being returned. Like this, a job processor that is linked to a work queue may be shut off before it has completed a time-consuming task, causing lengthy delays in reprocessing. In the worst-case scenario, the task might not even be retried, resulting in lost work or a failure of the business process.

Graceful shutdown refers to the controlled and systematic process of stopping a software application, service, or system in a way that ensures data integrity, minimizes disruptions, and maintains user satisfaction. Rather than abruptly halting processes or cutting off connections, a graceful shutdown involves completing ongoing tasks, saving data, and notifying users or clients about the impending shutdown. This approach allows for the orderly conclusion of transactions, prevents data loss, and enables users to make informed decisions based on the shutdown notification. By considering ongoing operations and providing a smooth transition, a graceful shutdown contributes to a positive user experience and ensures that the shutdown process does not lead to errors, inconsistencies, or negative impacts on the overall system.

Recipe 63: Handling graceful shutdown in container

The task started by the ECS agent oversees creating the working environment for each container involved in the job. Each container's entry process receives a SIGTERM signal when a task is terminated. A SIGKILL signal will be delivered to the process once a timeout has passed. The interval between the transmission of the SIGTERM and SIGKILL signals is 30 seconds by default and can be altered by using the *stopTimeout* task parameter. Processes will be abruptly terminated upon receiving the SIGKILL signal if they do not shut down before the timeout expires. And this is the way in which all OCI compliant orchestrators handle graceful shutdown. They also make sure that once the termination signal has been sent, the container will no longer receive new requests from the load balancer.

The application running in the container should be smart enough to catch these signals from the orchestrator and should gracefully shutdown itself on receiving the termination signal. The three microservice Config Server, Customer Enquiry and Config Server containers are started via a respective entry point script. The script is the first process that receives the signals from an orchestrator and needs to forward the signals to the child process, which in this case is a Spring Boot application. All three entry point scripts are to be enhanced to include this logic:

ConfigServerEntryPoint.sh

```
#!/bin/sh

## Sigterm Handler
sigterm_handler() {
  echo "Gracefully stopping the process with Id = $pid"
  if [ "$pid" -ne 0 ]; then
    # the above if statement is important because it ensures
    # that the application has already started. without it you
    # could attempt cleanup steps if the application failed to
    # start, causing errors.
    kill -15 "$pid"
    wait "$pid"
  fi
  exit 0;
}

## Setup signal trap
# on callback execute the specified handler
trap 'sigterm_handler' SIGTERM

execution_handler(){

 # Existing code

 nohup java -jar config-server.jar ${EXTERNAL_PARAMS} ${HEAP_OPTS} > log/nohup.out &
 pid="$!"
}

# Existing code
```

The above code is responsible for catching the termination signal from outside, which in this case is an orchestrator, and once the SIGTERM is caught **`sigterm_handler`** is invoked, refer to *line 19* in the above code. The **`sigterm_handler`** is responsible for forwarding the termination signal to the child process, the id of which is captured on starting the process, refer to *line 26* in the above code.

Similarly, the scripts **`CustomerEnquiryEntryPoint.sh`** and **`EnquiryBroadcastEntry-Point.sh`** are to be enhanced to handle the termination signal.

High availability

High availability (**HA**) is a fundamental architectural concept that focuses on ensuring uninterrupted access to services, applications, or systems, even in the presence of hardware failures, software issues, or other unexpected disruptions. In today's interconnected and digitally-driven landscape, where downtime can result in substantial financial losses and damage to reputation, high availability has become a crucial requirement for organizations across various industries.

At its core, high availability revolves around redundancy, fault tolerance, and seamless failover mechanisms. Redundancy involves deploying multiple instances of critical components, such as servers, databases, or network paths so that if one fails, the workload can be shifted to another without noticeable interruption. This ensures that even if a single point of failure occurs, the overall system remains operational.

To achieve fault tolerance, systems are designed to detect faults automatically and respond proactively. This might involve rerouting traffic, reallocating resources, or switching to backup components. The goal is to minimize the impact of failures on end-users, often without requiring human intervention.

In addition to redundancy and fault tolerance, high availability incorporates efficient failover mechanisms. Failover refers to the seamless transition from a failed component or system to a healthy backup, without affecting the user experience. This could include shifting traffic from one data center to another, switching to a standby server, or utilizing a redundant network path. The key is to execute these transitions swiftly and transparently.

High availability architectures are often deployed in conjunction with load balancing. Load balancers distribute incoming traffic evenly across multiple instances, ensuring that no single instance is overwhelmed, and allowing systems to handle increased demand without compromising performance. Load balancers also play a pivotal role in rerouting traffic during failover events, preventing disruptions.

Incorporating high availability into a system's design requires careful planning, thorough testing, and ongoing monitoring. It is a multifaceted approach that considers hardware, software, network topology, and user experience. By adopting high availability practices, organizations can minimize downtime, enhance user satisfaction, and maintain business continuity, even in the face of unexpected challenges.

Highly available database

Highly available Amazon **Relational Database Service** (**RDS**) is an advanced database deployment configuration designed to ensure continuous availability, durability, and resilience of critical databases. This approach involves deploying RDS instances in a **multi-availability zone** (**Multi-AZ**) setup, where the primary database instance is replicated synchronously to a standby instance located in a separate data center within the same region. In the event of a hardware failure, software issue, or maintenance event affecting the primary instance, Amazon RDS automatically promotes the standby instance to the primary role, seamlessly redirecting database traffic to the standby without noticeable downtime. This failover process, coupled with automated backups and automated software patching, ensures that data remains accessible, and operations continue without disruption, even during unplanned outages. Highly Available Amazon RDS configurations provide organizations with the confidence that their critical databases can endure unexpected challenges while maintaining data integrity and application availability.

Recipe 64: Amazon RDS for database high availability

While creating an RDS database Amazon provides an option to deploy into multi-AZ mode in which one instance will be a **primary instance** and all DB operations happen over this database instance. Other instances called **secondary instances** are also created in other AZs in the same region, they are kept up to date with the primary instance and are used only in case the primary instance goes down. Refer to *Figure 8.3* for reference:

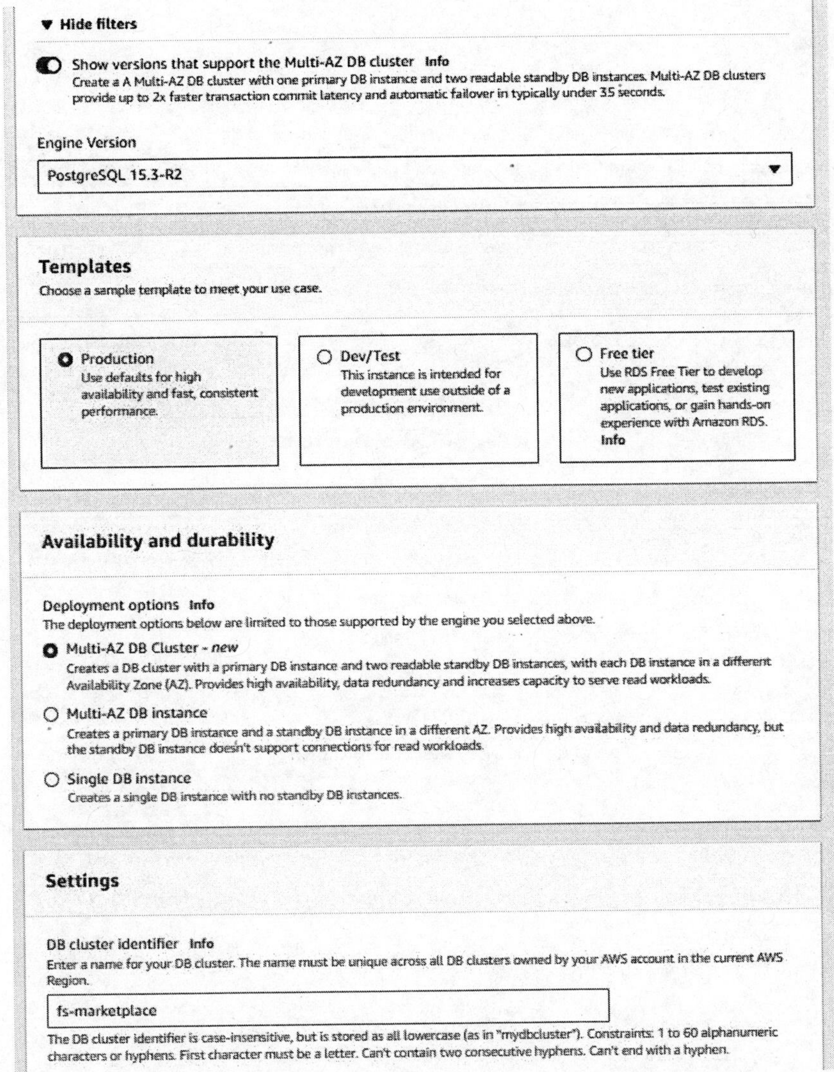

***Figure 8.3:** Multi-AZ mode selected while creating an RDS database*

Existing RDS instances can also be converted into a multi-AZ deployment mode from a single instance mode. Select the `fs-marketplace` database in the RDS console and there is an option in the **Actions** menu to convert to multi-AZ deployment, refer to *Figure 8.4* and *Figure 8.5* for reference:

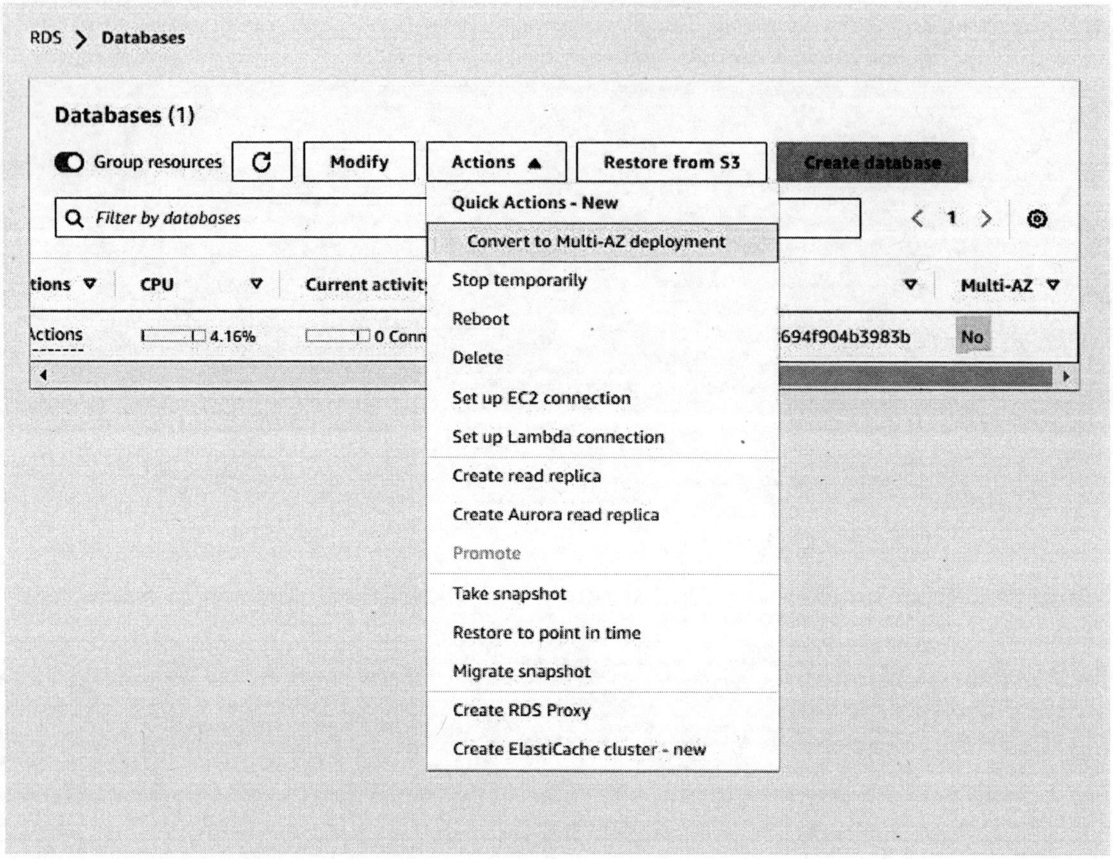

***Figure 8.4**: Converting existing fs-marketplace database from single instance to multi-AZ deployment mode*

Refer to following *Figure 8.5*:

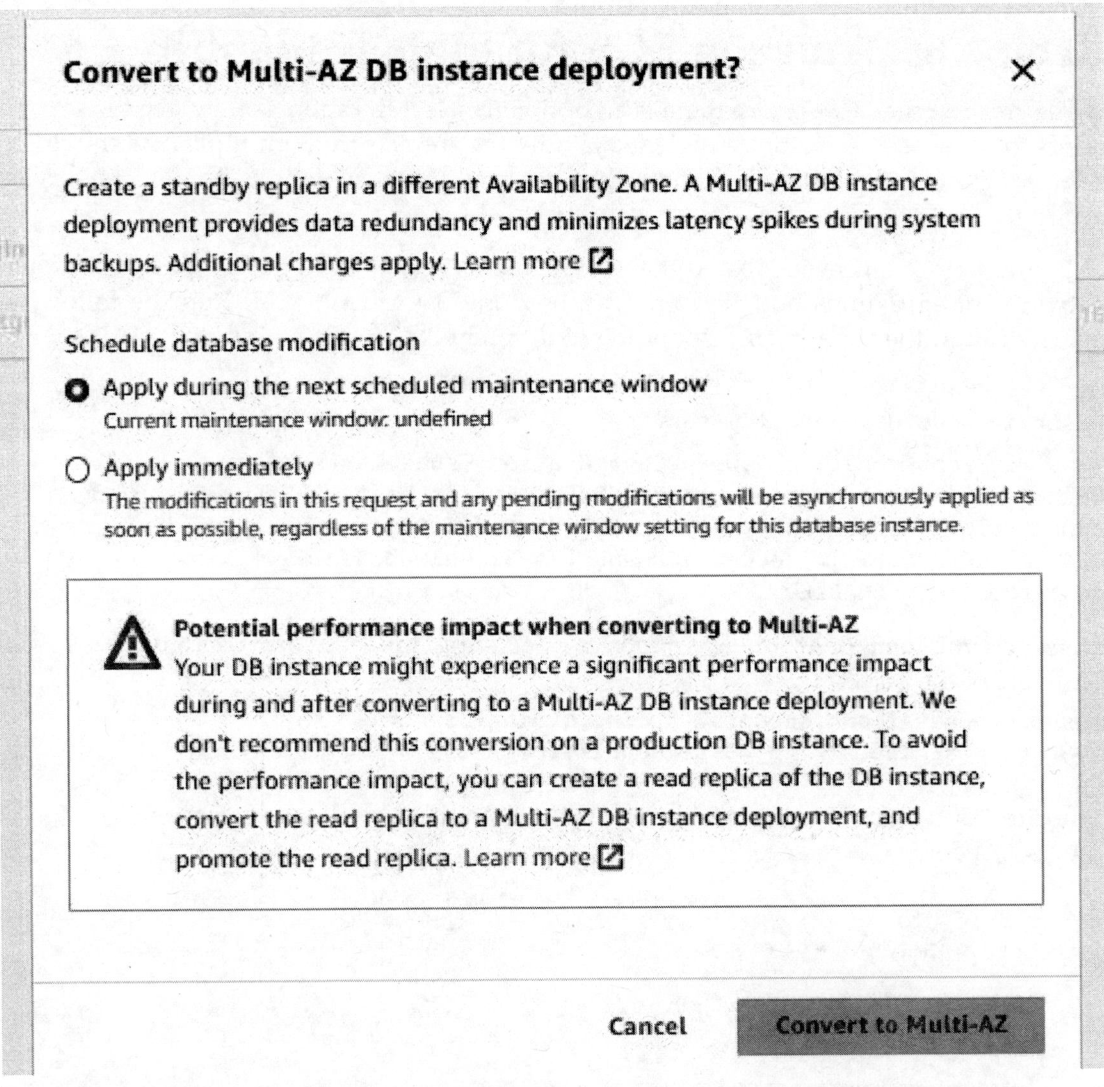

Figure 8.5: *Conforming when to apply the multi-AZ deployment mode changes*

Highly available ECS service

A highly available database is complimented by a highly available ECS service, and this is achieved by configuring multiple AZs for the ECS service. Once this is done tasks belonging to an ECS service will be spawned in multiple availability zones and if by chance one or more availability zone goes down then the tasks running in those availability zones are started in other healthy availability zones. This makes an ECS service fault tolerant and highly available.

Recipe 65: Amazon ECS for high availability

While creating the ECS service there is an option to select the subnets in which the service needs to be associated with, for high availability the subnets from multiple AZs should be selected. The only limitation is that the subnets should be part of the same VPC the service is part of.

Once the service has been created the management console does not support editing the network configurations but the same can be done using AWS CLI. Run the following queries to add the subnets corresponding to different AZs in the region of the VPC.

```
aws ecs update-service --cluster fsm-ecs-cluster \
--service customer-enquiry-service \
--network-configuration "awsvpcConfiguration={subnets=[subnet-05cb20f57875d70eb, subnet-0c4370a5045d8c9e7, subnet-0695f59e05eac57c3, subnet-07535426beb85245f, subnet-00529825a6a2e98f1, subnet-054d98b404fb28ca9 ], securityGroups=[sg-06eae19abc4de7696], assignPublicIp=ENABLED}"
```

Here, **`awsvpcConfiguration`** is an object specifying the network configurations. The structure of the object is:

```
awsvpcConfiguration={subnets=[string,string],securi-tyGroups=[string,string],assignPublicIp=string}
```

The effect of the above command can be viewed on the console under the network tab of the specified service, refer to *Figure 8.6* for reference:

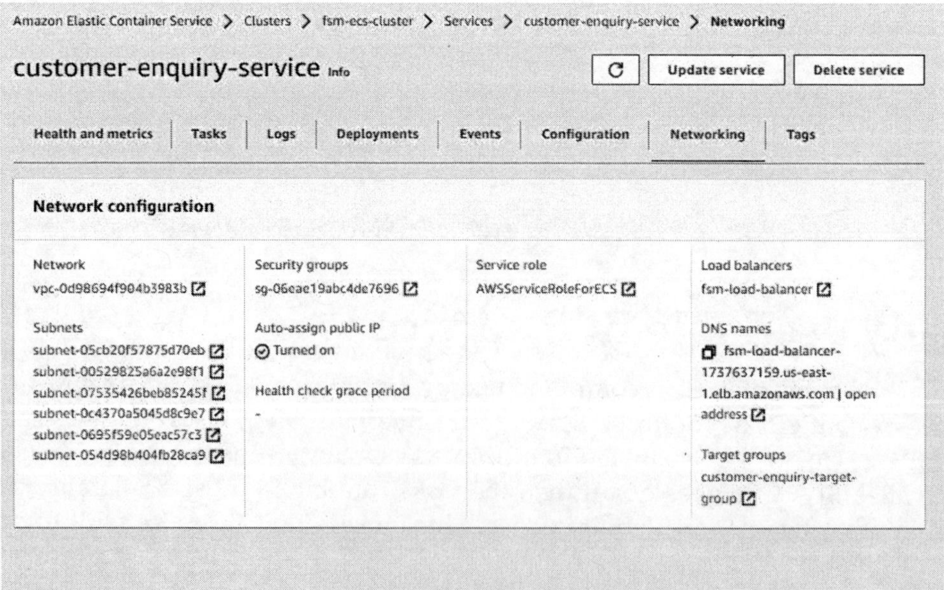

***Figure 8.6**: customer-enquiry-service configured to run in multiple subnets*

Similarly, **enquiry-broadcast-service** and **config-service** are enhanced to run in multiple subnets in different availability zones.

Recipe 66: Enhance load balancer to support multi-AZs

Running Amazon ECS services in multiple availability zones will not work until the network traffic can be routed to those running tasks. For this the load balancer needs to be enhanced to support the AZs in which the ECS tasks are running. The load balancer routes the traffic to only those AZs which are attached to the load balancer. So, make sure that all the configured subnets in the ECS service should be attached to the load balancer. Run the following queries using AWS CLI to set the subnets on the **Application Load Balancer (ALB)**:

```
aws elbv2 set-subnets --load-balancer-arn arn:aws:elasticloadbalancing:us-east-1:746797604555:loadbalancer/app/fsm-load-balancer/f1d95f36f6d5a99e --subnets subnet-05cb20f57875d70eb subnet-0c4370a5045d8c9e7 subnet-0695f59e05eac57c3 subnet-07535426beb85245f subnet-00529825a6a2e98f1 subnet-054d98b404fb28ca9
```

All previously enabled subnets, with their current configurations, as well as any additional subnets, must be included as the specified subnets replace the previously enabled subnets. The changes can be validated by viewing the load balancer details on the console, refer to *Figure 8.7* for reference:

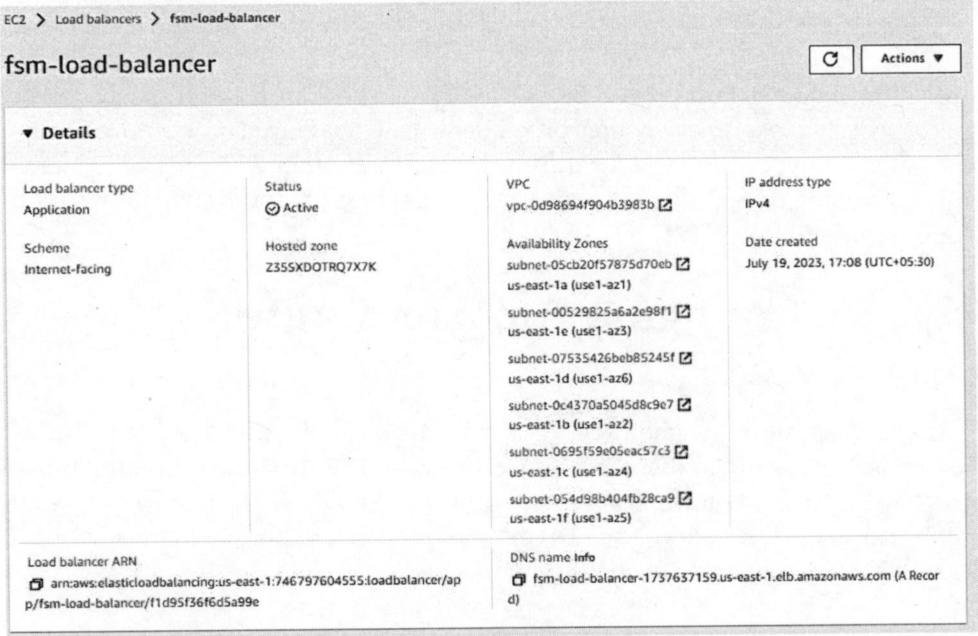

Figure 8.7: *fsm-load-balancer supporting multiple subnets*

The subnets can be added to an Application Load Balancer via AWS Management Console as well.

When using Amazon ECS Fargate, the distribution of traffic across availability zones is handled by the underlying infrastructure managed by AWS. AWS automatically distributes tasks across multiple availability zones for high availability.

Disaster recovery

Though multi-AZ services and database deployments provide high availability to the application but what if the complete region goes down, how can the application be made available quickly in such scenarios? All this is catered to as part of the organization's disaster recovery strategy and the application architecture.

Disaster recovery (**DR**) is a critical component of any robust IT strategy, aimed at minimizing the impact of catastrophic events on an organization's data, systems, and operations. Such events could include natural disasters, cyberattacks, hardware failures, or human errors. The goal of disaster recovery is to swiftly restore essential services and data to normal operations, reducing downtime and ensuring business continuity.

Amazon Route 53, a scalable **domain name system** (**DNS**) web service offered by AWS, plays a pivotal role in disaster recovery strategies. Route 53 not only manages domain names and directs internet traffic to resources, but it can also be leveraged to enhance the resilience and recovery capabilities of applications and services.

One of the primary ways Route 53 aids in disaster recovery is through its DNS failover functionality. By configuring health checks on resources, such as Amazon EC2 instances or **Application Load Balancers** (**ALBs**), Route 53 can continuously monitor the health of these resources. If a resource becomes unavailable due to a disaster or failure, Route 53 can automatically redirect traffic to a healthy resource in another AWS region or data center, thereby minimizing downtime. This failover process is swift and transparent to end-users, ensuring a seamless transition.

Recipe 67: Configure Amazon Route 53 for disaster recovery

Assuming corresponding to the existing architectural deployment in the primary region that is, US East (N. Virginia) there is a disaster recovery setup done very similar in another AWS region Europe (Ireland). The entry point for the DR setup is an AWS Application Load Balancer in the DR region, `fsm-load-balancer-dr`, as shown in the *Figure 8.8* which shows load balancers in the Europe (Ireland) region:

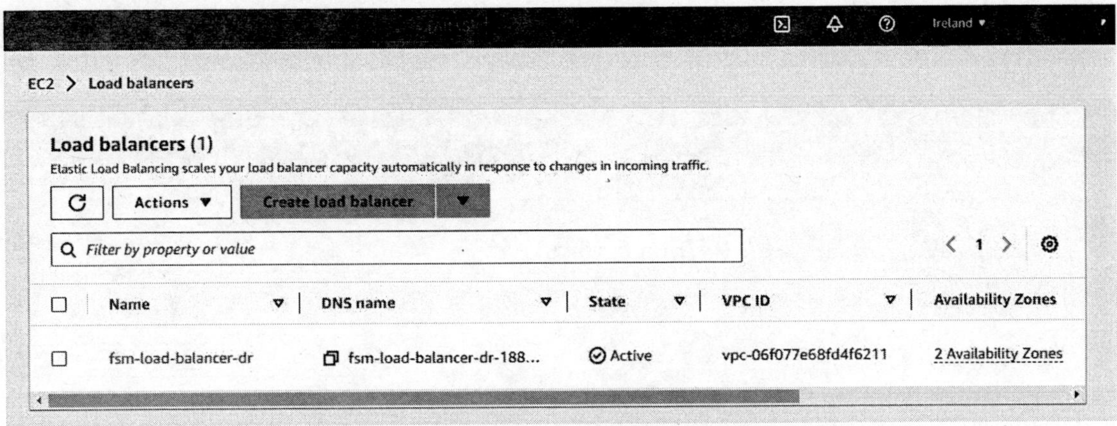

Figure 8.8: fsm-load-balancer-dr created in AWS Ireland region

Now, as part of configuring Route 53, a hosted zone needs to be created first. In the AWS management console, go to **Hosted zones** under **Route 53** and click **Create hosted zone** and create it by adding the domain name. This book refers to the domain **`financial-service-marketplace.com`** as a domain that will be publicly accessed and has been already registered with Route 53. Refer to *Figure 8.9* for reference:

Route 53 > Hosted zones > Create hosted zone

Create hosted zone Info

Hosted zone configuration

A hosted zone is a container that holds information about how you want to route traffic for a domain, such as example.com, and its subdomains.

Domain name Info

This is the name of the domain that you want to route traffic for.

financial-service-marketplace.com

Valid characters: a-z, 0-9, ! " # $ % & ' ( ) * + , - / : ; < = > ? @ [\ ] ^ _ ` { | } . ~

Description - *optional* Info

This value lets you distinguish hosted zones that have the same name.

The hosted zone is used for...

The description can have up to 256 characters. 0/256

Type Info

The type indicates whether you want to route traffic on the internet or in an Amazon VPC.

Public hosted zone — A public hosted zone determines how traffic is routed on the internet.

Private hosted zone — A private hosted zone determines how traffic is routed within an Amazon VPC.

Tags Info

Apply tags to hosted zones to help organize and identify them.

No tags associated with the resource.

Add tag

You can add up to 50 more tags.

Cancel   Create hosted zone

Figure 8.9: Creating a hosted zone for Route 53

Once created the domain name is visible under the *Hosted zones*, also as part of the creation of hosted zone few records get automatically created, also visible in *Figure 8.10*:

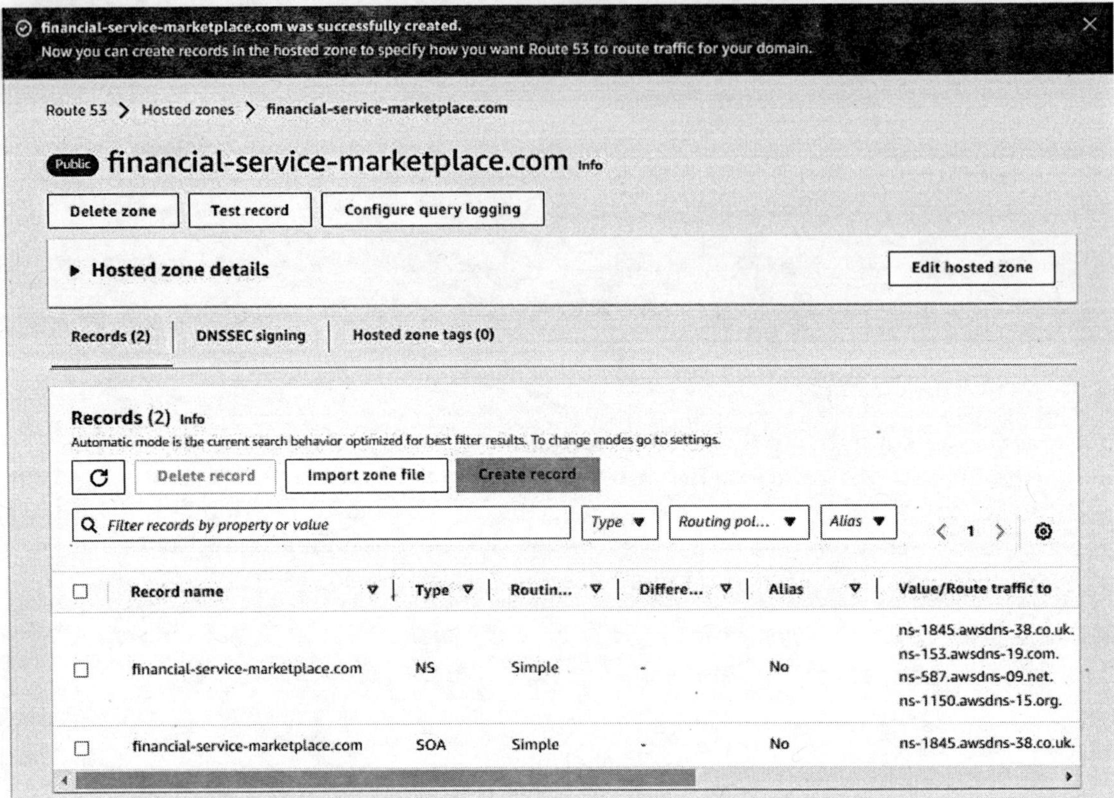

***Figure 8.10**: Created financial-service-marketplace.com hosted zone for Route 53*

Once done an active-passive failover strategy can be implemented. In this setup, a primary resource or group of resources is typically available, while a secondary resource or group of resources is prepared to take over if all the primary resources become unavailable. As part of this, two new records need to be created with routing policy **Failover**, explained in the following steps:

1. Select **Routing policy** to **Failover**.
2. Provide subdomain if required.
3. Select **Record type** as **A**, which is for routing traffic to an IPV4 and some AWS resources.
4. Enable **Alias**
5. Under **Route traffic to**, select **Alias to Application and Classic Load Balancer**.
6. The select the **region**, in this case the primary region.

7. Then select the name of the load balancer from the primary region.
8. Select **Primary** in the failover record type drop down.
9. Give a logical name to the record id, for example *Primary Load Balancer*.

Refer to *Figure 8.11* for reference:

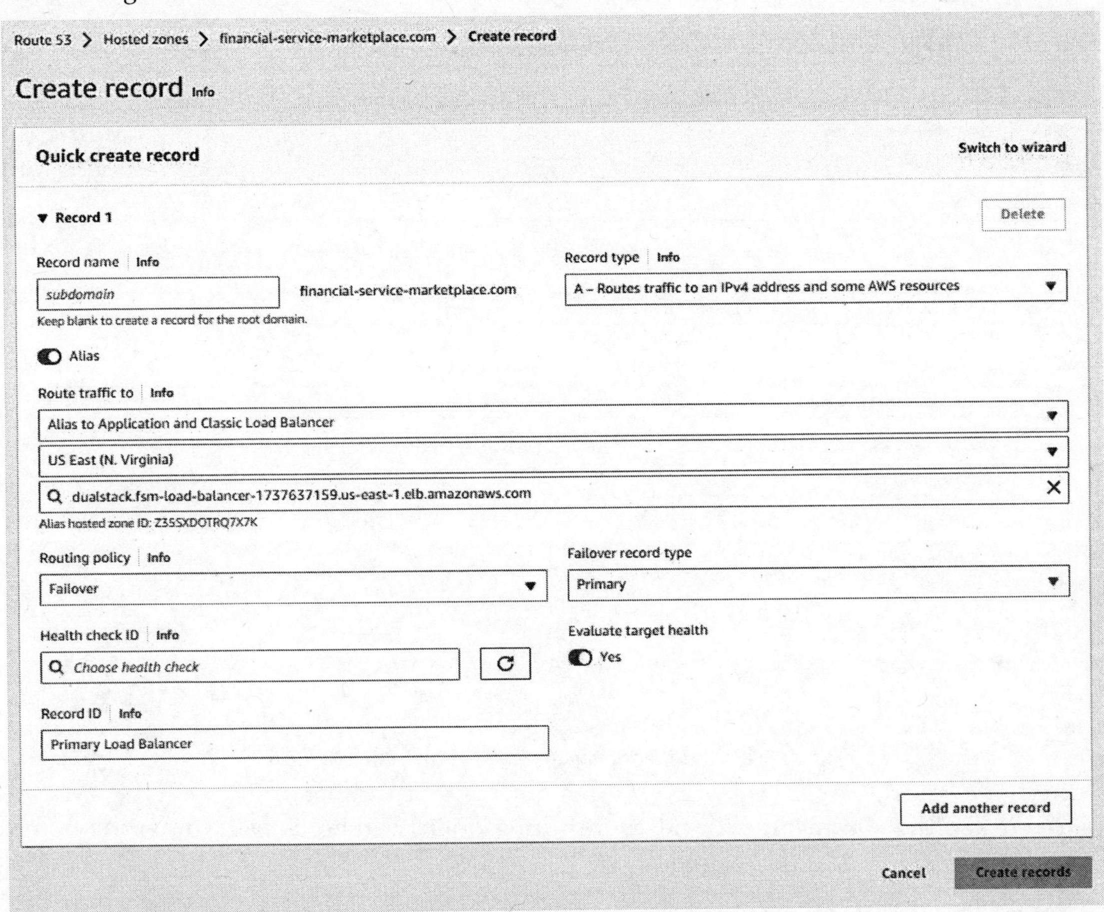

Figure 8.11: *Creating primary failover record for Route 53*

Like the above record a second record needs to be created with failover record type as secondary that routes the traffic to the DR application load balancer on failover. Refer to the *Figure 8.12* for reference:

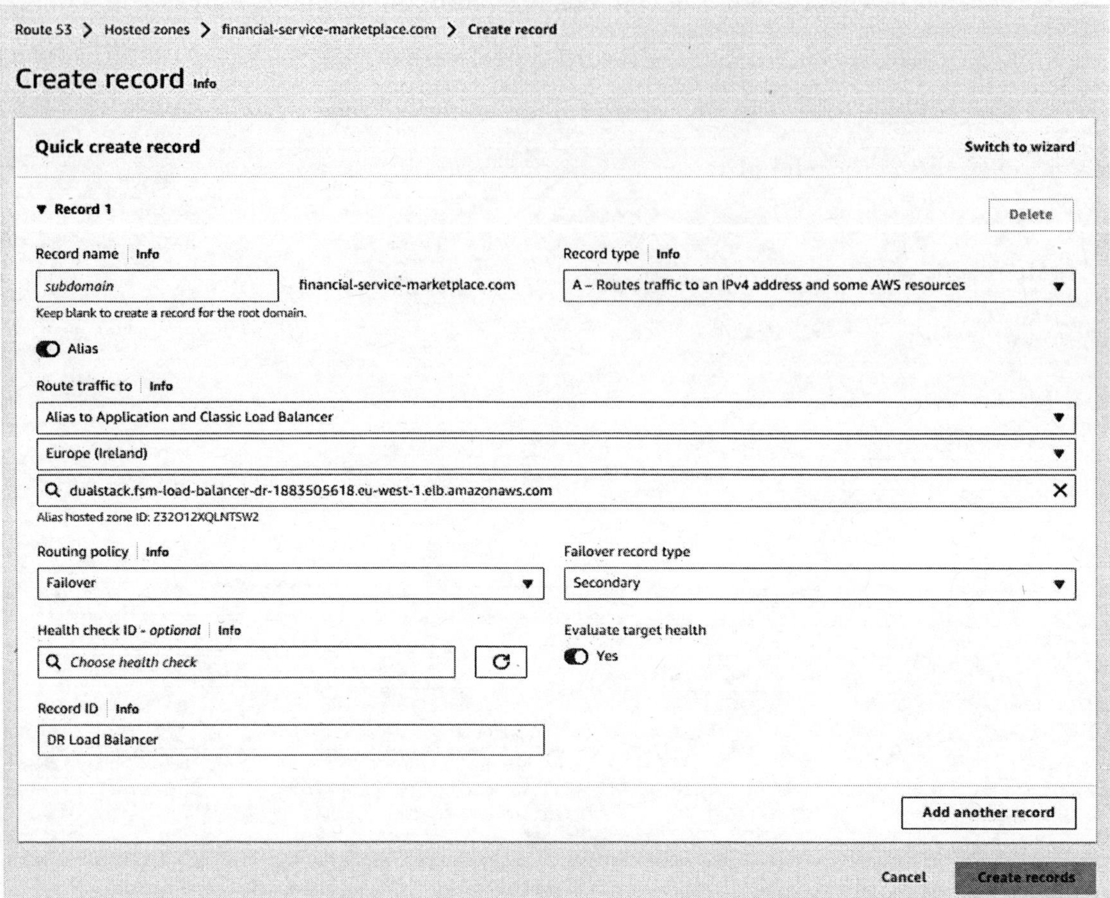

Figure 8.12: Creating Secondary failover record for Route 53

Once created the two records for failover routing policy can be viewed under the hosted zone, refer to *Figure 8.13* for reference:

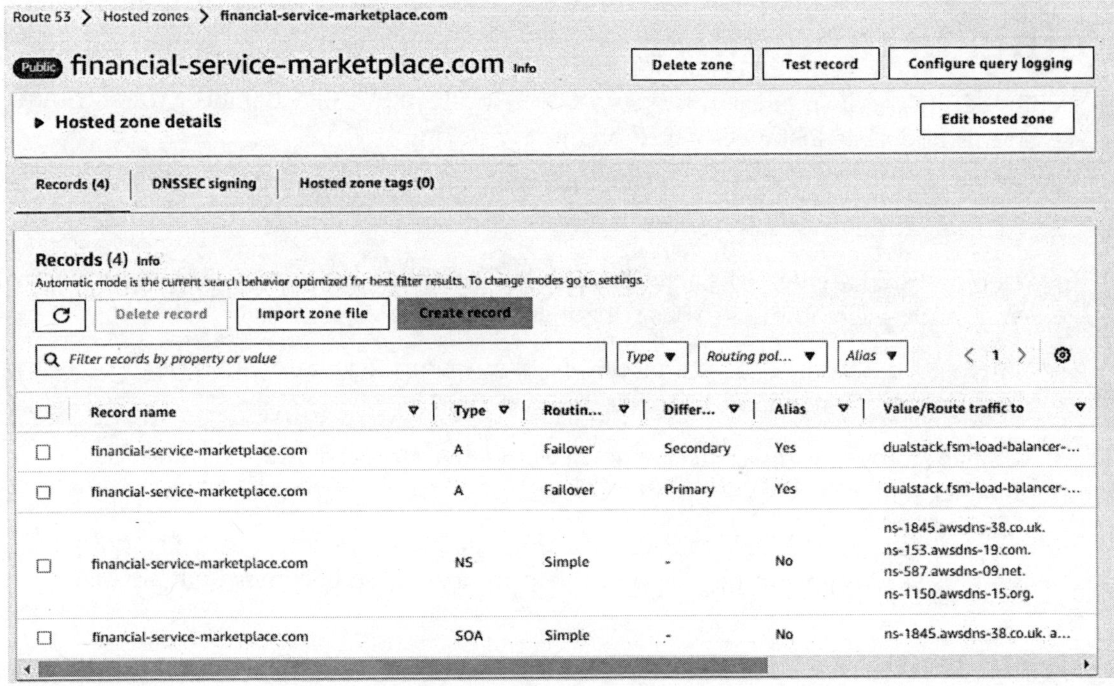

***Figure 8.13**: Failover routing policy records*

Once complete, the Route 53 will forward all the requests to the primary load balancer but in case the resources of the primary region are unhealthy it will route the traffic to the secondary load balancer.

Develop well-documented disaster recovery runbooks outlining step-by-step procedures to restore the ECS Fargate services in case of a major outage.

Conclusion

In this chapter, we have learnt the fundamentals of auto scalability, high availability and disaster recovery and have implemented them in financial service marketplace application for the underlying microservices. We have also demonstrated the changes that need to be done in the application to handle scale-in events that are triggered as part of auto scalability.

In the next chapter, we will learn about the cloud security measures, the offerings by Amazon in this space and the ways to implement them as part of the application deployment architecture.

Points to remember

- Integrate the ECS Fargate tasks with an Application Load Balancer to distribute traffic and scale instances based on target tracking.
- Make sure the load balancer supports all the subnets which have been configured for the underlying tasks to run.
- Deploy ECS Fargate tasks across multiple availability zones to ensure redundancy and failover capabilities in case of zone-specific issues.
- If using a database, choose an RDS Multi-AZ setup to ensure database availability across multiple availability zones.
- Consider replicating critical resources, such as task definitions and container images, to another AWS region for disaster recovery purposes.
- Configure Route 53 DNS failover to automatically redirect traffic to a standby ECS Fargate service in another region if the primary region becomes unavailable.

Questions

1. What are the key metrics that you should consider when setting up auto scaling policies for ECS Fargate tasks?
2. What is the significance of CloudWatch Alarms in the context of auto scaling for ECS Fargate, and how do they trigger scaling actions?
3. What code changes need to be done in the Spring Boot application to handle termination signal graceful shutdown?
4. What are the different ways of database replication across AWS regions?
5. How does an orchestrator know that a particular task is unhealthy and needs to be replaced with a new task?
6. What are the different types of routing policies supported by Route 53?

CHAPTER 9
Cloud Security

Introduction

In the last chapter, we talked about attaining auto scalability and high availability of the application by leveraging the elasticity of the **Amazon Web Services** (**AWS**) cloud and demonstrated the changes that need to be done at the application level to attain the same. We also talked about the importance of disaster recovery and ways to implement it in the AWS environment.

Security carries considerable significance and is paramount for any organization. In this chapter, we will discuss methods for implementing security in the cloud environment. Additionally, we will explore the tools provided by the AWS cloud that can be utilized to secure our application.

Structure

In this chapter, we will discuss about following topics:

- Identity and access management
  - IAM policy
  - IAM group
  - IAM user
  - IAM role

- Data protection
  - AWS Key Management Service
  - AWS Secret Manager
- Network security
  - Virtual private cloud
  - Security groups
  - AWS Web Application Firewall

Objectives

By the end of this chapter, we will have a comprehensive understanding of core security principles and practices within **Amazon Web Services** (**AWS**). Readers will explore essential topics related to **identity and access management** (**IAM**), **data protection**, and **network security** in the cloud. As part of the chapter, we will create IAM policy, groups, users, and roles to provide selective access to the AWS resources, use AWS KMS to encrypt data within AWS, and store and use secrets in and from an AWS Secret Manager. We will also go through the fundamentals of network security and learn ways to create and configure VPCs, Security Groups and WAF to improve the security posture for the application. By the end of this chapter, readers will be equipped with the knowledge and practical insights necessary to establish robust security measures and protect sensitive data in their AWS environments.

Identity and access management

Identity and access management (**IAM**) is a foundational service provided by **Amazon Web Services** (**AWS**) that enables organizations to manage user identities and control access to their AWS resources in a secure and organized manner. IAM serves as a crucial component of cloud security, allowing administrators to define and enforce fine-grained permissions for users, groups, roles, and resources across their AWS infrastructure.

At its core, IAM provides a centralized mechanism to create and manage identities, including users and their associated credentials, roles for cross-account access, and groups for easier permission management. Each IAM identity is associated with a set of permissions, which determine what actions an identity can perform on specific AWS resources. By adhering to the principle of least privilege, IAM ensures that identities are only granted the minimal necessary permissions to carry out their tasks, reducing the risk of unauthorized access and accidental data exposure.

IAM plays a pivotal role in enforcing the concepts of authentication and authorization within AWS environments. Authentication involves verifying the identity of users or applications attempting to access AWS resources. IAM supports various authentication mechanisms, including AWS Management Console passwords, access keys, and federated identity providers such as Active Directory or SAML-based providers. Authorization, on the other hand, determines the actions an authenticated identity is allowed to perform on specific resources. IAM policies are used to define these authorizations, providing a powerful and flexible way to specify permissions based on actions, resources, and conditions.

IAM also enables the principle of shared responsibility, where organizations maintain control over their AWS environment while allowing individual users or teams to manage specific subsets of resources. This is achieved through the delegation of permissions via IAM roles. IAM roles allow identities to assume temporary permissions, facilitating secure cross-account access and minimizing the exposure of long-term credentials.

IAM policy

An IAM policy is a crucial component of AWS Identity and Access Management that defines permissions for identities, such as users, groups, and roles, to interact with specific AWS resources. IAM policies are essentially JSON documents that articulate what actions an identity is allowed or denied on which resources. These policies act as rule sets that dictate the level of access an identity has within an AWS environment. AWS provides many AWS managed policies which can be used as is to provide permissions but they are not specific to a particular resource.

IAM policies are structured to include information about the actions (API operations), resources (such as Amazon S3 buckets or EC2 instances), and conditions (optional constraints) that determine whether a request is permitted or denied. Policies can be attached directly to IAM users, groups, or roles, or they can be associated with resources like Amazon S3 buckets to control access at the resource level. IAM policies follow the principle of least privilege, which means that identities are granted only the minimum permissions required to perform their tasks, reducing the attack surface and risk of unintended actions.

IAM policies are normally created in the JSON format and has the following structure:

```
{
  "Version": "",
  "Statement": [
    {
      "Sid": "",
      "Effect": "",
      "Action": "",
      "Resource": ""
    }
```

```
  ]
}
```

Please verify the JSON as mentioned below with respective parameters:

```
{
  "Version": "2012-10-17",
  "Statement": [
    {
      "Sid": "StatementID",
      "Effect": "Allow or Deny",
      "Action": [
        "service:action",
        "service:action"
      ],
      "Resource": "arn:aws:service:region:account-id:resource-id",
      "Condition": {
        "ConditionKey": "ConditionValue"
      }
    },
    {
      "Effect": "Allow or Deny",
      "Action": "service:action",
      "Resource": [
        "arn:aws:service:region:account-id:resource-type/resource-id",
        "arn:aws:service:region:account-id:resource-type/resource-id"
      ]
    }
  ]
}
```

Here,

- **`Version`**: The version field specifies the language version of the policy. It should always be set to **`"2012-10-17"`**, which represents the current version of the policy language.

- `Statement`: The `"Statement"` field contains an array of one or more policy statements, each representing a permission or denial. Each statement has its own `"Effect"`, `"Action"`, `"Resource"`, and optional `"Condition"` fields, the usage of the fields has been explained below:
    - o `Sid`: It is a statement Id an optional field, can hold any value and acts as a unique identifier for a statement within the policy document.
    - o `Effect`: Specifies whether the statement allows (`"Allow"`) or denies (`"Deny"`) the defined actions on the specified resources.
    - o `Action`: Lists the AWS service API actions that the policy statement grants or denies permission to.
    - o `Resource`: Defines the specific **AWS resources** (**ARNs**) to which the actions apply. This field helps to scope the permissions to specific resources.
    - o `Condition` (optional): Allows for further restrictions on the statement based on context, such as time of day, IP address, or other contextual factors.

Understanding these components is essential for crafting IAM policies that accurately reflect the desired permissions and security posture within an AWS environment.

Through IAM policies, organizations can exercise granular control over access permissions, allowing them to tailor authorization based on specific use cases or responsibilities. Policies can also be crafted to permit or deny actions based on contextual factors such as time, source IP, or specific conditions, enhancing security by implementing dynamic access control. IAM policies serve as a powerful tool for enforcing the security posture of AWS environments, ensuring that identities have the appropriate level of access and reinforcing the principle of separation of duties.

Recipe 68: Creating IAM policy for accessing S3 bucket

An IAM policy is to be created for accessing fs-marketplace-bucket and all its objects. Follow the given steps to create the IAM policy:

1. Login to the AWS Management Console and search IAM or type in the following URL: **https://console.aws.amazon.com/iam/**.
2. Go to **Policies** under Access management and click **Create policies**.
3. A policy can be created using step-by-step instructions in a GUI, or there is an option to create it via JSON by pressing the **JSON** button.

4. In the policy editor, paste the following JSON and click **Next**:

```
{
  "Version": "2012-10-17",
  "Statement": [
    {
      "Sid": "ListBucketAccess",
      "Effect": "Allow",
      "Action": [
        "s3:ListBucket"
      ],
      "Resource": [
        "arn:aws:s3:::fs-marketplace-bucket"
      ]
    },
    {
      "Sid": "BucketObjectAccess",
      "Effect": "Allow",
      "Action": [
        "s3:PutObject",
        "s3:GetObject",
        "s3:DeleteObject"
      ],
      "Resource": [
        "arn:aws:s3:::fs-marketplace-bucket/*"
      ]
    }
  ]
}
```

Here, there are two statements, one for providing access on the bucket with the ARN **`arn:aws:s3:::fs-marketplace-bucket`** and the other is for all the objects inside that bucket by mentioning the ARN as **`arn:aws:s3:::fs-marketplace-bucket/*`**. For reference, refer *Figure 9.1*:

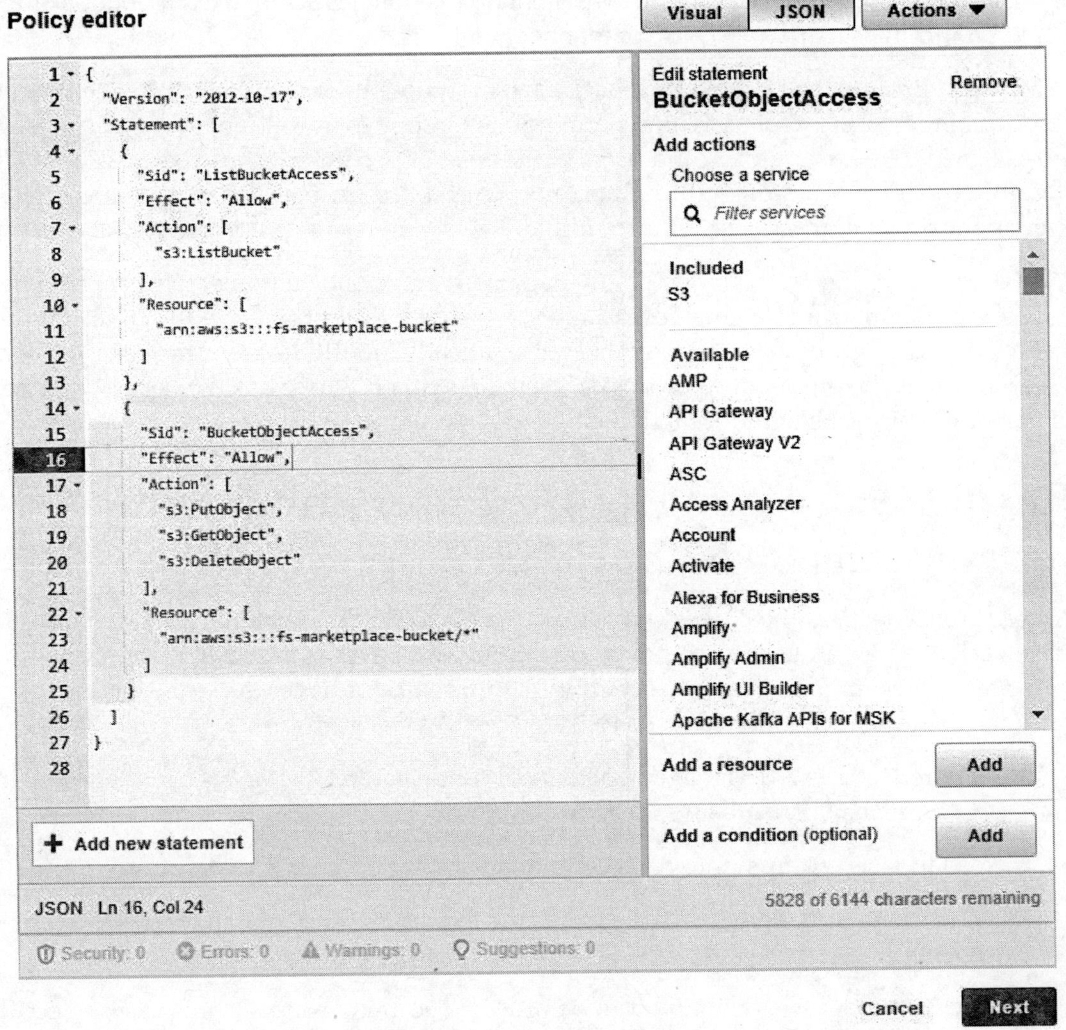

Figure 9.1: Creating policy using JSON policy editor

5. Give a logical name of the policy, for example `fs-marketplace-bucket-policy`, and click **Create policy**.

   Policy with the provided name will be created with type **Customer managed**.

IAM group

An IAM user group is a fundamental organizational structure within AWS that simplifies the process of managing permissions and access control for multiple users with similar roles or responsibilities. IAM user groups provide an efficient way to assign permissions at scale, making it easier to maintain consistent access policies across a team or department while promoting security and ease of management.

IAM user groups bring together IAM users who share similar job functions or responsibilities. Instead of assigning permissions directly to individual users, permissions are assigned to the user group, and users within that group inherit those permissions. This streamlines the process of granting and revoking access, especially in scenarios where users perform similar tasks or require similar levels of access to AWS resources.

IAM user groups also simplify access management and policy enforcement. When a new user joins a team or a role changes, administrators can add or remove the user from the appropriate user group, and the user will automatically inherit the associated permissions. This simplifies the onboarding process and ensures that the user has the necessary access to perform their tasks without manual adjustments.

Recipe 69: Creating an IAM user group with permissions on S3 buckets

A user group needs to be created which has access to the **`fs-marketplace-bucket`** and this is achieved by attaching the policy created in the previous recipe to this group. Now, whoever will be part of this user group will automatically have access to the desired S3 buckets. Follow the mentioned steps to create the IAM user group:

1. Login to the AWS Management Console and search IAM or type in the following URL: **https://console.aws.amazon.com/iam/**.
2. Go to **User groups** under Access management and click **Create group**.
3. Give a logical name to the group, for example **`fs-marketplace-s3-access-group`**.
4. Select the policies that need to be attached to this group. In this case, select the policy **`fs-marketplace-bucket-policy`**. For reference, refer to *Figure 9.2*:

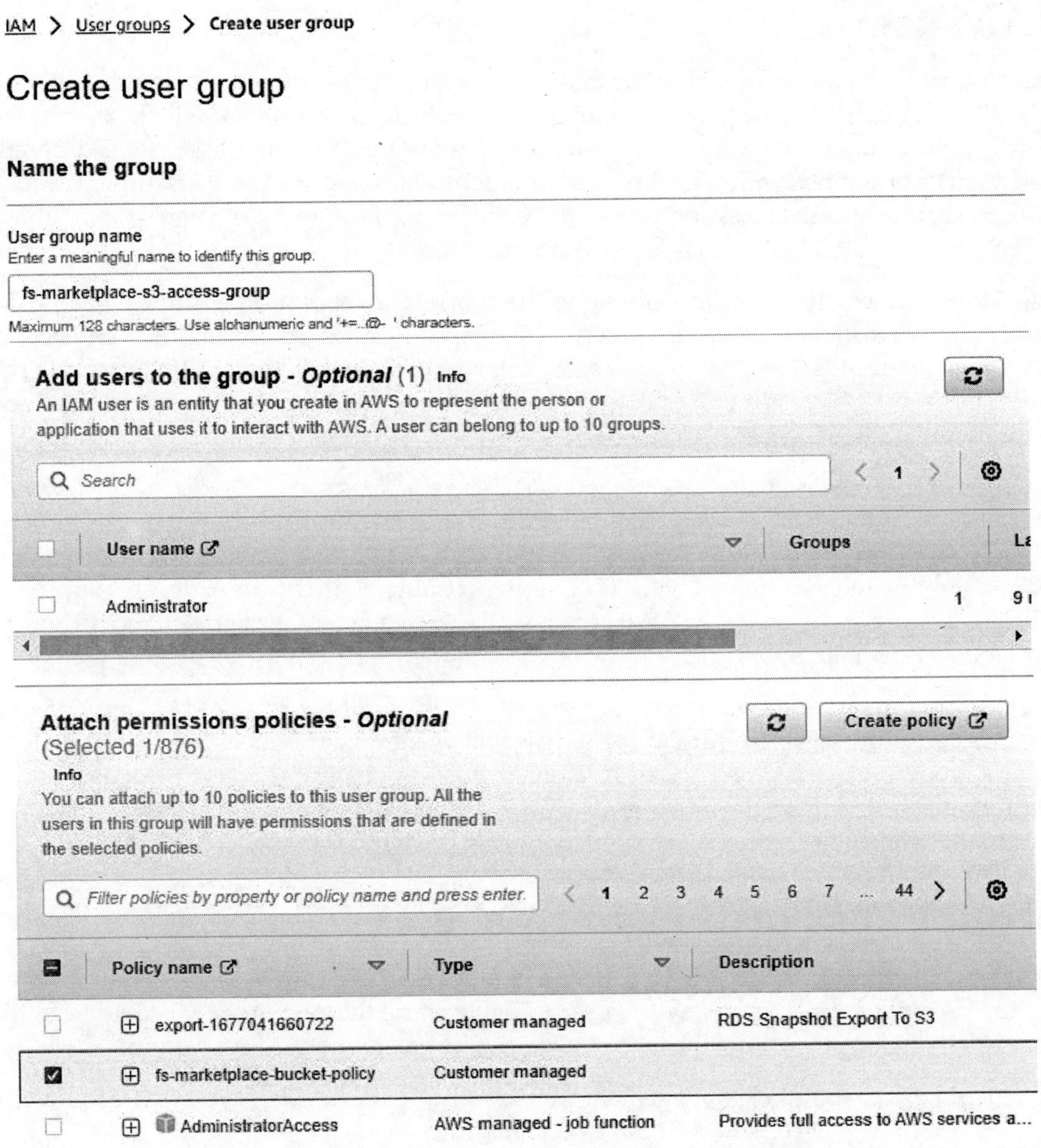

Figure 9.2: Creating user group fs-marketplace-s3-access-group

5. Click *Create group* to create the user group.

In conclusion, IAM user groups are crucial for simplifying access management and permissions allocation in AWS environments. Through the grouping of users based on similar responsibilities and the assignment of permissions at the group level, organizations can establish consistent access policies, bolster security, and effectively handle access control as teams evolve.

IAM user

An IAM user is a foundational entity in AWS that represents an individual with a unique identity who interacts with AWS resources and services. IAM users are distinct from the AWS account root user and provide a way to manage access and permissions for different individuals or entities within an AWS environment. By creating IAM users, organizations can implement strong access controls, enforce the principle of least privilege, and maintain a secure and auditable way to manage AWS resources.

IAM users are essential for implementing the concept of separation of duties. Each IAM user can have distinct permissions based on their specific roles, responsibilities, and needs. By assigning permissions to IAM users, organizations can ensure that users have only the necessary level of access required to perform their tasks, reducing the risk of unauthorized actions and data breaches.

IAM users have their own unique credentials, including a username and password, which they use to authenticate and access the AWS Management Console. For programmatic access, IAM users can also generate access keys that allow applications, scripts, or command-line tools to interact with AWS services using AWS SDKs or APIs. This approach eliminates the need to share the AWS account's root user credentials and enhances security by compartmentalizing access.

IAM users can also be organized into groups, which simplifies the process of managing permissions for users with similar roles. This allows administrators to apply permissions at the group level, making it easier to manage access policies for teams or departments. Additionally, IAM users can be assigned IAM roles, enabling temporary access to resources across AWS accounts without exposing long-term credentials.

Recipe 70: Creating an IAM user

A user needs to create and link to a group **`fs-marketplace-s3-access-group`** created in the previous recipe. This way the user will inherit all the permissions provided to the group automatically. Follow the mentioned steps to create the IAM user group.

1. Login to the AWS Management Console and search IAM or type in the following URL: **https://console.aws.amazon.com/iam/**.
2. Go to **Users under** Access management and click **Create user**.
3. Give a user name that you want to generate, for example **`fsm-varun`**.
4. Select **Provide user access to the AWS Management Console**.
5. Select **I want to create an IAM user**.
6. Choose the console password and click **Next**.

Select **Add user to group** and select the groups to which the user needs to be added. In this case, select the group **`fs-marketplace-s3-access-group`**. For reference, refer to *Figure 9.3*:

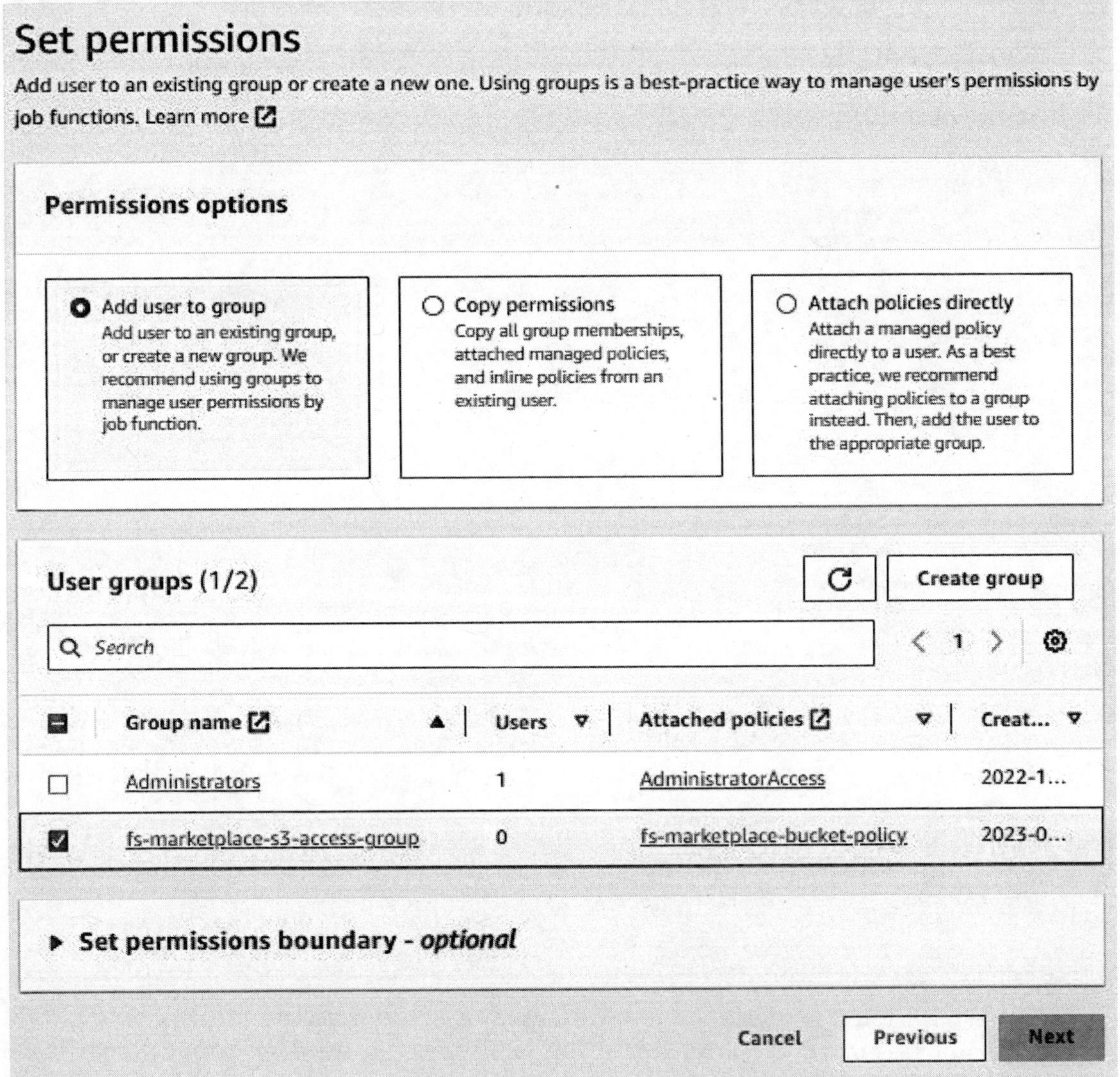

Figure 9.3: *Creating user and attaching it to a group*

7. Click **Next** and review the details.
8. If all is fine, click **Create user** to create the user.

   The user **`fsm-varun`** has been created, refer to *Figure 9.4* for reference:

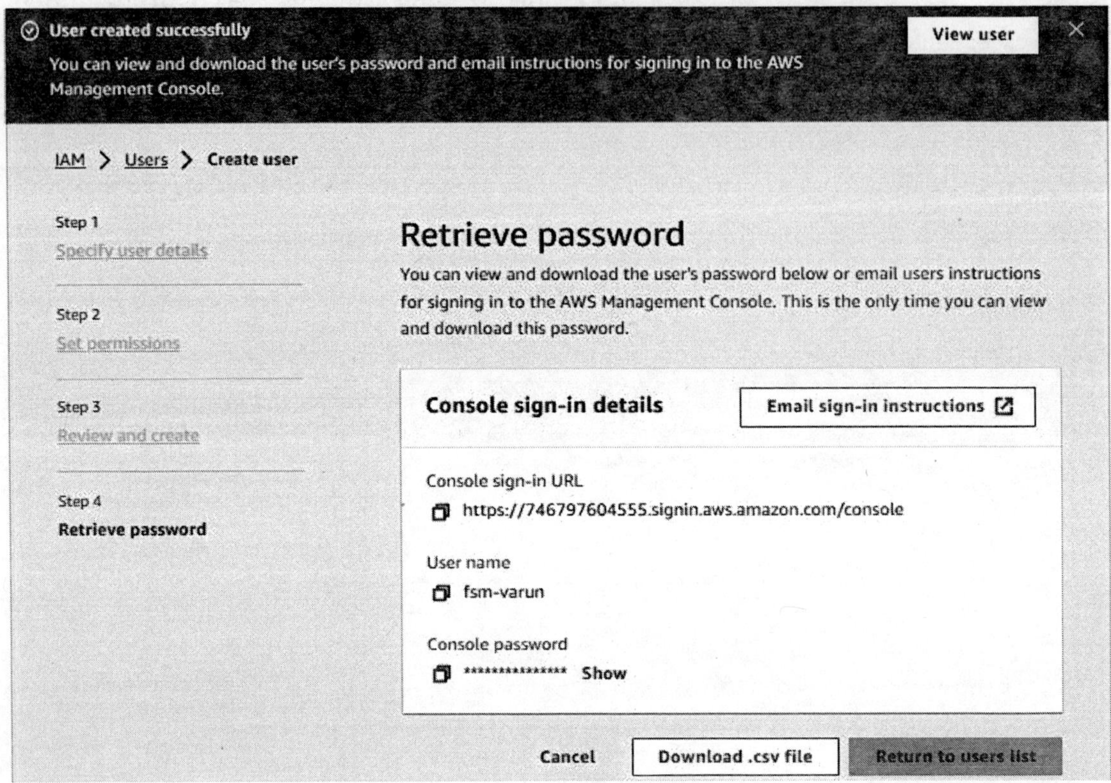

Figure 9.4: *User fsm-varun has been created*

The user can be used to log in to the AWS console and access the S3 buckets on which it has permission.

IAM role

An IAM role is a fundamental concept in AWS that enables secure and controlled access to AWS resources without the need to share long-term credentials, such as access keys or passwords. IAM roles are designed to facilitate cross-account access and are widely used to grant temporary permissions to entities like AWS services, users, or applications. These roles play a crucial role in maintaining security, adhering to the principle of least privilege, and ensuring separation of duties within AWS environments.

IAM roles provide a mechanism for delegating permissions effectively and securely. Rather than directly attaching permissions to identities, roles allow identities to assume the permissions defined by the role when needed. Roles are particularly useful in scenarios where granting long-term credentials could pose security risks, such as in serverless applications, EC2 instances, or AWS Lambda functions.

One of the key advantages of IAM roles is the ability to facilitate cross-account access. Organizations frequently collaborate across multiple AWS accounts, and IAM roles enable controlled access between these accounts. By defining a role in one account and granting that role permissions to another account, resources in the second account can assume the role and inherit the permissions. This minimizes the complexity of sharing credentials while maintaining security boundaries.

Recipe 71: Creating an IAM role for accessing S3 bucket

An IAM role needs to be created for granting access on an S3 bucket to a different AWS account. Follow the mentioned steps to create the IAM role:

1. Login to the AWS Management Console and search IAM or type in the following URL: **https://console.aws.amazon.com/iam/.**
2. Go to **Roles** under Access management and click **Create role.**
3. Select **AWS account** under **Trusted entity type**. Select **Another AWS account** and enter the 12-digit AWS account id of the account to whom the access needs to be given, also called the trusted account and click **Next**. Refer to *Figure 9.5* for reference:

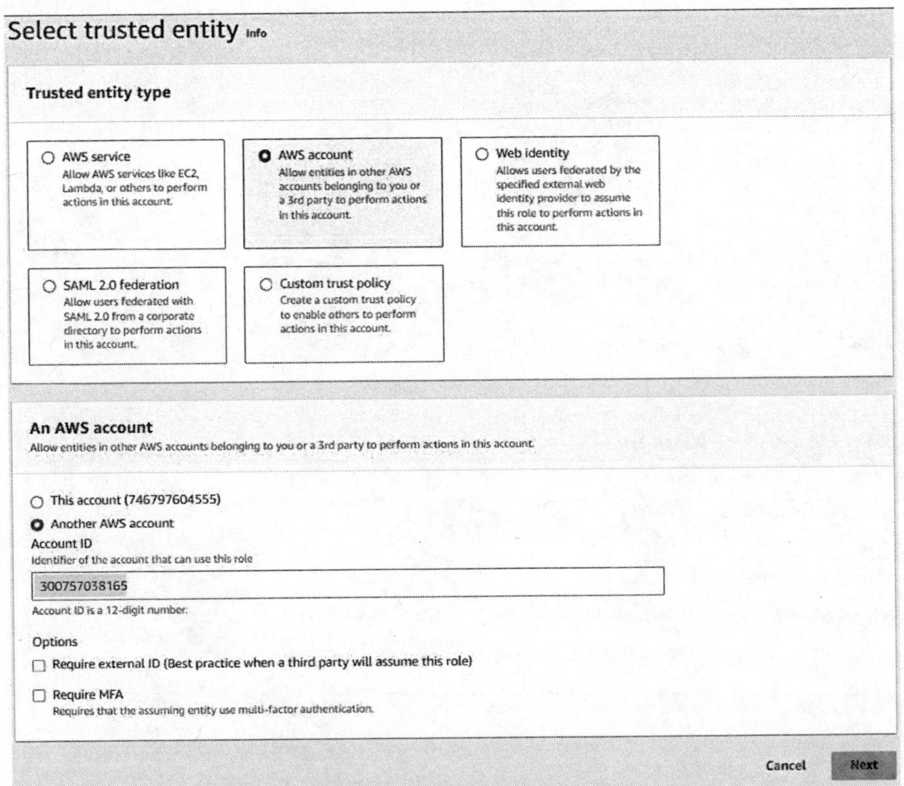

Figure 9.5: *Granting access to another AWS account*

4. Add permissions to the role. Search and select the policy **`fs-marketplace-bucket-policy`** and click **Next**. Refer to *Figure 9.6* for reference:

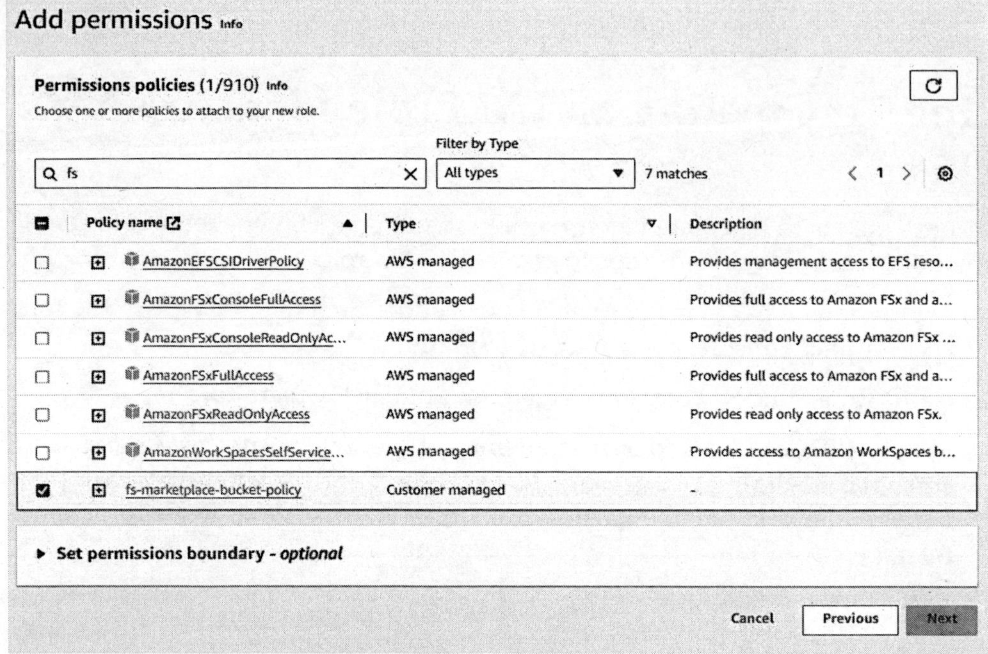

Figure 9.6: Adding permissions to the role

5. Enter name and description for the role, refer to *Figure 9.7* for reference:

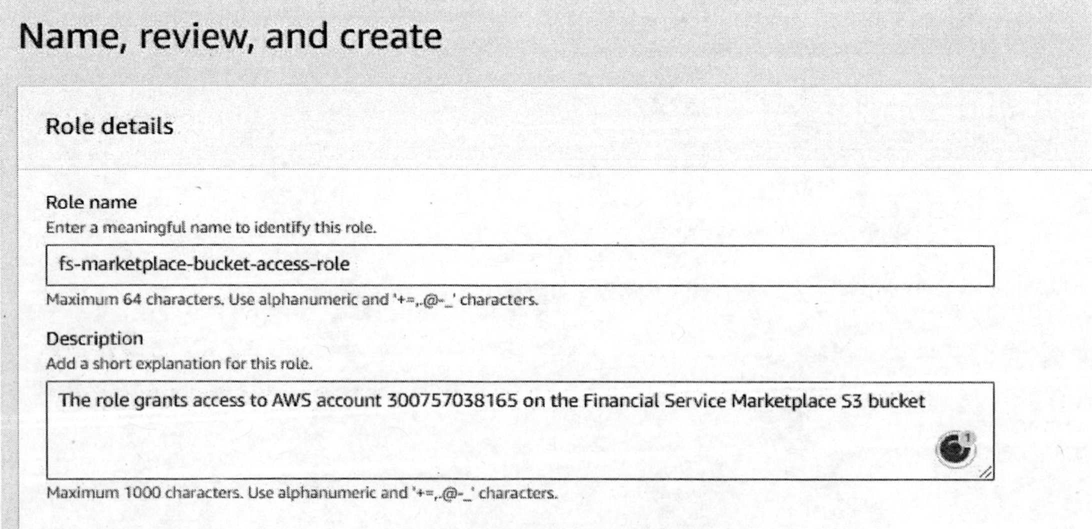

Figure 9.7: Providing role name and description

6. Review the configurations and click **Create role** to create the role.

Once the role has been created, individual users in the trusted account needs to be given permissions to switch to or assume this role. This permission needs to be given by the administrator of the trusted account.

Data protection

Data protection is a paramount concern for organizations operating in the cloud, and AWS offers a comprehensive suite of services and tools to safeguard data throughout its lifecycle. AWS places a strong emphasis on security, privacy, and compliance, and it provides customers with the building blocks needed to implement robust data protection strategies.

One of the fundamental principles of data protection in AWS is encryption. AWS offers encryption solutions for data at rest and data in transit. Amazon S3, for instance, allows customers to enable server-side encryption, ensuring that data stored in S3 buckets is automatically encrypted using keys managed by AWS **Key Management Service** (**KMS**). For data in transit, AWS provides **Transport Layer Security** (**TLS**) for secure communication between clients and services. To enable encrypted transport between systems for the workloads, one can generate, manage, and deploy private and public certificates via the **AWS Certificate Manager** (**ACM**) service.

AWS also offers encryption options for data stored in databases, block storage, and file systems. Amazon RDS, EBS volumes, and EFS all support encryption, allowing organizations to protect sensitive information from unauthorized access. AWS KMS, a fully managed encryption key management service, plays a central role in controlling access to encryption keys, ensuring that only authorized users and services can decrypt protected data.

Data protection extends to identity and access management as well. AWS IAM enables organizations to implement fine-grained access controls, ensuring that users, applications, and services only have access to the data and resources they require to perform their tasks. IAM policies, role-based access control, and temporary security credentials contribute to the principle of least privilege, reducing the risk of data breaches resulting from excessive permissions.

Furthermore, AWS provides AWS Secrets Manager, which is a fully managed service that helps organizations securely protect sensitive information, such as passwords, API keys, and database credentials. It centralizes the storage and management of secrets, eliminating the need to hardcode or manually manage sensitive data in applications. Secrets Manager integrates seamlessly with other AWS services, ensuring secure access to secrets for applications and services, and it supports automatic rotation of credentials, enhancing security by regularly changing secrets without disrupting operations. By providing a secure and convenient way to handle secrets, AWS Secrets Manager simplifies security best practices and helps organizations maintain strong data protection measures in their AWS environments.

AWS Key Management Service

Amazon Web Services Key Management Service (AWS KMS) is a fully managed encryption service that allows organizations to create, control, and manage cryptographic keys for securing their data and applications, generate and verify **message authentication codes (MACs)** in the AWS cloud. in the AWS cloud. AWS KMS plays a pivotal role in enhancing the security and privacy of sensitive data by providing robust encryption capabilities.

At its core, AWS KMS allows organizations to generate and manage encryption keys used for data encryption at rest and in transit. It integrates seamlessly with various AWS services, enabling users to encrypt data in Amazon S3, Amazon EBS volumes, Amazon RDS databases, and more. Additionally, KMS can be used for encrypting and decrypting data within applications running on AWS infrastructure. KMS offers two types of keys: Customer managed keys and AWS managed keys. Customer managed keys are created, owned, and managed by the customer. On the other hand, AWS managed keys are created and managed by AWS on behalf of the customer. Refer to *Figure 9.8* for better understanding AWS KMS and its usage for different operations and integration with different AWS services:

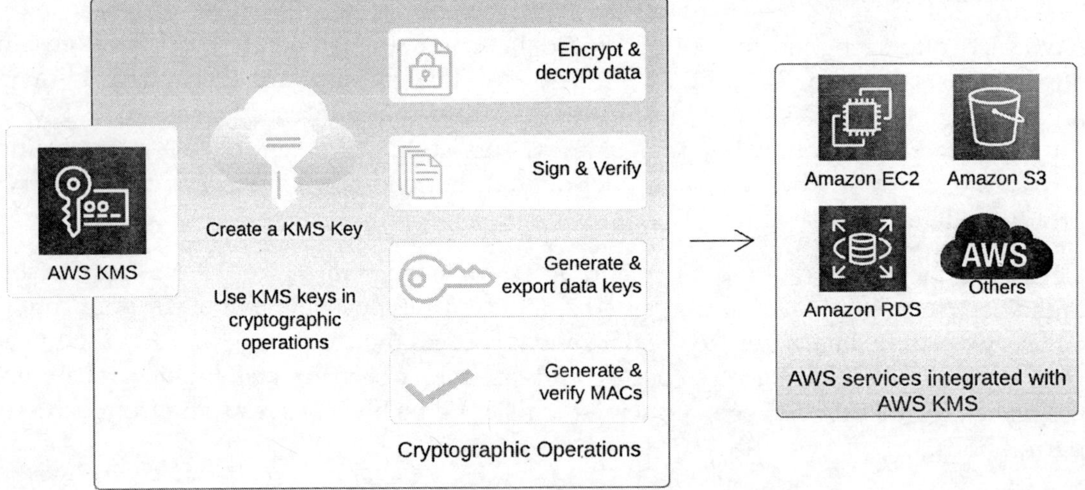

Figure 9.8: *AWS KMS usage and integration with AWS services*

One of the standout features of AWS KMS is its centralization of key management. It eliminates the need for organizations to build and maintain their own key management infrastructure, reducing operational complexity and security risks. KMS also provides fine-grained access controls, allowing organizations to define who can create, manage, and use encryption keys. Moreover, KMS provides automatic key rotation, which enhances security by regularly replacing old encryption keys with new ones without any manual intervention. AWS KMS is a critical component of the AWS security ecosystem, contributing significantly to data protection, compliance, and overall security posture in the cloud.

Recipe 72: Creating customer managed key

Customer managed keys (**CMKs**) in **AWS Key Management Service** (**KMS**) are encryption keys created and managed by customers, giving them full control over key policies and lifecycles. CMKs are used to encrypt data in various AWS services and can be rotated, audited, and customized to meet specific security and compliance requirements. The AWS Management Console for AWS KMS displays customer managed keys on the customer controlled keys page.

Follow the steps to create a customer managed key:

1. Login to the AWS Management Console and search KMS or type in the following URL: **https://us-east-1.console.aws.amazon.com/kms/home.**
2. Go to customer managed keys and click **Create key**.
3. Select **Systematic** in key type, **Encrypt and decrypt** for key usage, and click **Next**.
4. Give a logical alias, for example, `fs-marketplace-s3-key`.
5. Select administrators for this key, in this case only **Administrator** has been selected.
6. Select users of this key and click **Next**. The following users and roles need to be selected in this case:
    - `Administrator`
    - `fsm-varun`
    - `AWServiceRoleForECS`
    - `ecsTaskExecutionRole`

   Refer *Figure 9.9* for reference:

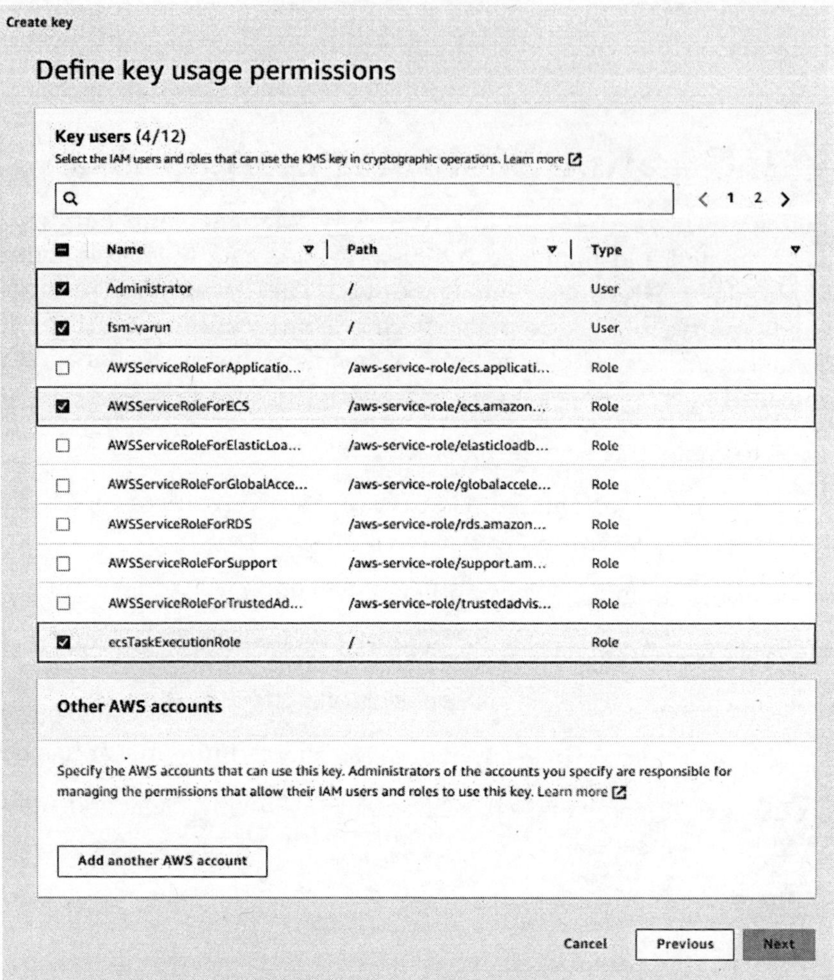

Figure 9.9: *Users and roles that can use the fs-marketplace-s3-key*

7. Review and validate the key policy and click **Finish** to create the key.

Recipe 73: Using KMS key to encrypt S3

Encryption types supported by AWS S3 are:

- **SSE-S3** (Server-side encryption with Amazon S3 managed keys) is the default encryption provided by AWS for S3 and uses the strongest block ciphers.
- **SSE-KMS** (Server-side encryption with AWS Key Management Service keys) provides more control over the keys and provides an option to choose from default AWS managed (`aws/s3`) or customer managed keys. This also has a feature which can be used to view who has accessed the KMS key and when.

- **DSSE-KMS** (Dual-layer server-side encryption with AWS Key Management Service keys) provides an additional layer of encryption, mainly to be used in cases that have high compliance requirements from the regulations' perspective.
- **SSE-C** (SSE with customer provided keys) is a server-side encryption option in AWS S3. It allows you to provide your own encryption keys, giving you more control over the security of your S3 data.

Follow the steps for encrypting the S3 bucket using KMS keys that is, SSE-KMS:

1. Login to the AWS Management Console and search S3 or type in the following URL: **https://s3.console.aws.amazon.com/s3/buckets**
2. Select **`fs-marketplace-bucket`** and go to the **Properties** tab.
3. Edit the **Default Encryption** section.
4. Select the **SSE-KMS** encryption type and select one of the following two available KMS keys:
   - **`fs-marketplace-s3-key`**
   - **`aws/s3`**

   Refer *Figure 9.10* for reference:

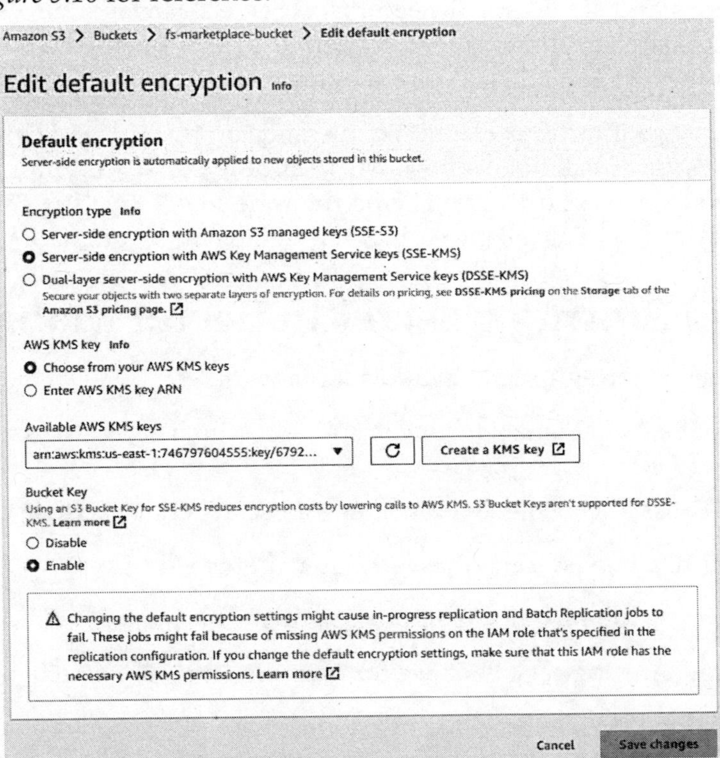

***Figure 9.10**: Setting encryption type to SSE-KMS for fs-marketplace-bucket*

5. Click **Save changes** to update the encryption.

AWS Secrets Manager

AWS Secrets Manager is a fully managed service provided by **Amazon Web Services (AWS)** that simplifies the management of sensitive information, such as API keys, database credentials, and passwords. It offers a secure and centralized solution for storing, retrieving, and rotating secrets used by applications, services, and AWS resources.

One of the primary advantages of AWS Secrets Manager is its role in enhancing security practices. Secrets, such as database passwords or API keys, are often considered high-value targets for attackers. Secrets Manager helps mitigate security risks by enabling organizations to store these sensitive credentials securely, reducing the likelihood of accidental exposure or misuse. Secrets are encrypted both at rest and in transit, and they can be automatically rotated on a predefined schedule, ensuring that even if a secret is compromised, it remains valid for only a limited time.

Furthermore, Secrets Manager offers a seamless integration with various AWS services and applications. Users can easily retrieve secrets programmatically through API calls, making it effortless to access credentials securely during runtime. It integrates with AWS Lambda, AWS RDS, and other AWS services, ensuring that secrets are readily available to the applications and services that need them. Secrets Manager also supports custom rotation scripts, enabling organizations to define their own logic for rotating secrets, including updating application configurations or certificates when a secret is rotated.

AWS Secrets Manager improves overall security and compliance, makes managing secrets easier, and lowers the possibility of data breaches brought on by compromised credentials. Organizations may increase operational efficiency and maintain a strong security posture in their AWS settings by centralizing secret management and automating rotation.

Recipe 74: Storing a secret in Secret Manager

Follow the steps for storing a secret in a Secret Manager:

1. Login to the AWS Management Console and search Secret Manager or type in the following URL:

   https://us-east-1.console.aws.amazon.com/secretsmanager/listsecrets

2. Click **Store a new secret** and select others in the secret type.

3. In the **Key/value** pair add the following details:

   a. **Key**: Any logical key name, for example **`CONFIG_SERVER_SECRET_KEY`**

   b. **Value**: Provide the value of the secret. The key would be used to store the config server password, so provide the password that has been hardcoded in the AWS ECS Task definition.

4. Add more **Key/value** pair if required, refer to *Figure 9.11* for reference:

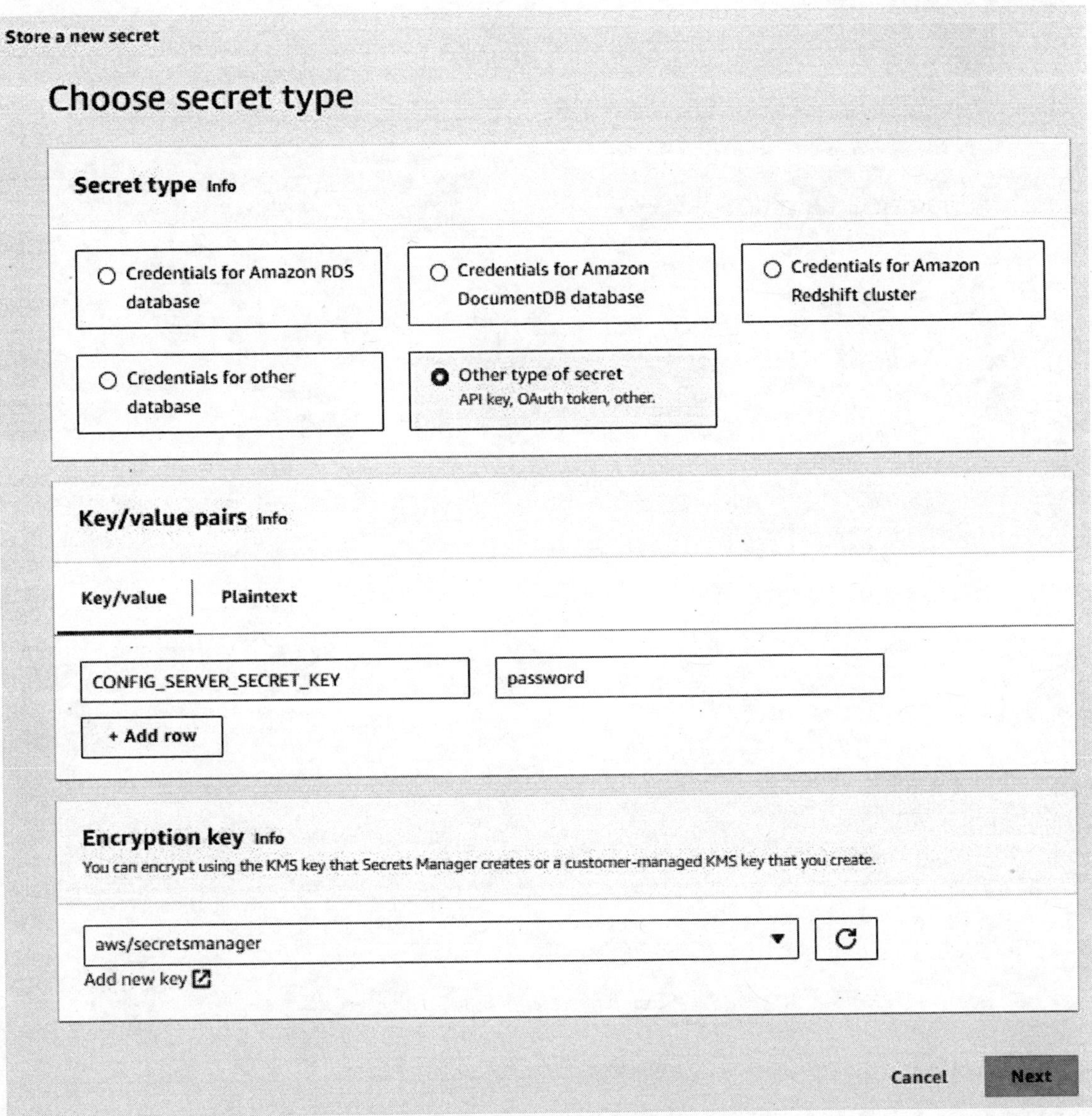

Figure 9.11: Storing Config Server password as secret in Secret Manager

5. Select the default encryption key and click **Next**.
6. Give a logical name to the secret, for example, `fsm-marketplace-secret` and click **Next**.
7. Review and click **Store**. The secret will be created, click on it to view the details, refer to *Figure 9.12* for reference:

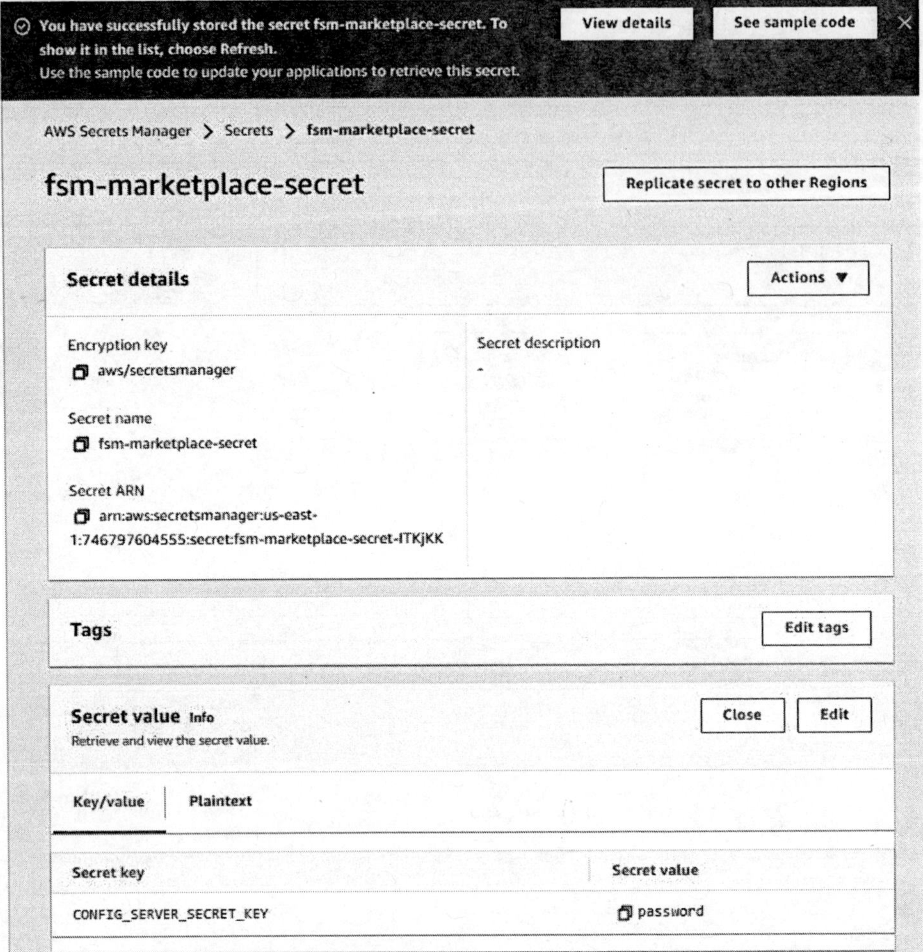

Figure 9.12: Detail of secret fsm-marketplace-secret

8. Copy the ARN, as it will be used to access the secret.

ARN is **`arn:aws:secretsmanager:us-east-1:746797604555:secret:fsm-marketplace-secret-ITKjKK`**

Recipe 75: Accessing secret from Secrets Manager in AWS ECS

While creating task definitions for running docker images, some of the secrets have been hardcoded in the task definition itself, but it is a security rick as the secrets will be exposed to anyone having access to the task definitions. The ideal way is to fetch these secrets from the secret manager, follow the mentioned steps to update task definitions to pick secrets such as Config Server password from the secret manager:

1. Go to task definitions in the ECS cluster and, select **`customer-enquiry-task-definition`** and click **Create new revision**.
2. Go to the **Environment variable** section and update the **value type** and **value** follows, for key **`CONFIG_SERVER_PASSWORD`**:
   a. **Value type**: **`ValueFrom`**
   b. **Value**: The format of the value is **`<arn>:<json-key>:<version-stage>:<version-id>`**.

   So the value in our case would be,

   `arn:aws:secretsmanager:us-east-1:746797604555:secret:fsm-marketplace-secret-ITKjKK:CONFIG_SERVER_SECRET_KEY::`

   Here, **`CONFIG_SERVER_SECRET_KEY`** is the **`json-key`** in secret, and **`version-stage`** and **`version-id`** are blank.

Refer to *Figure 9.13* for reference:

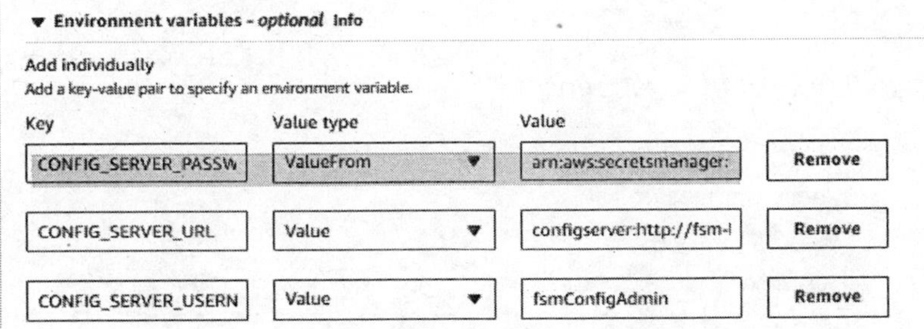

***Figure 9.13**: Environment variable value is set using Secret Manager*

3. Click **Create** to create a new revision.

Once done, the ECS service needs to be updated to use the latest revision of the task definition.

Recipe 76: Enhance ECS execution role to access Secret Manager

ECS services cannot access the secret manager until it has been given access permissions and this is done by adding an inline policy to the **`ecsTaskExecutionRole`** using the following steps:

1. Go to **Roles** and select **`ecsTaskExecutionRole`**.
2. Click **Add permissions** and select **Create inline policy**.
3. Go to the JSON view and, paste the following policy in the policy editor and click **Next**:

```
{
    "Version": "2012-10-17",
    "Statement": [
        {
            "Effect": "Allow",
            "Action": [
                "secretsmanager:GetSecretValue"
            ],
            "Resource": [
           "arn:aws:secretsmanager:us-east-1:746797604555:secret:fsm-
marketplace-secret-ITKjKK"
            ]
        }
    ]
}
```

Refer to *Figure 9.14* for reference:

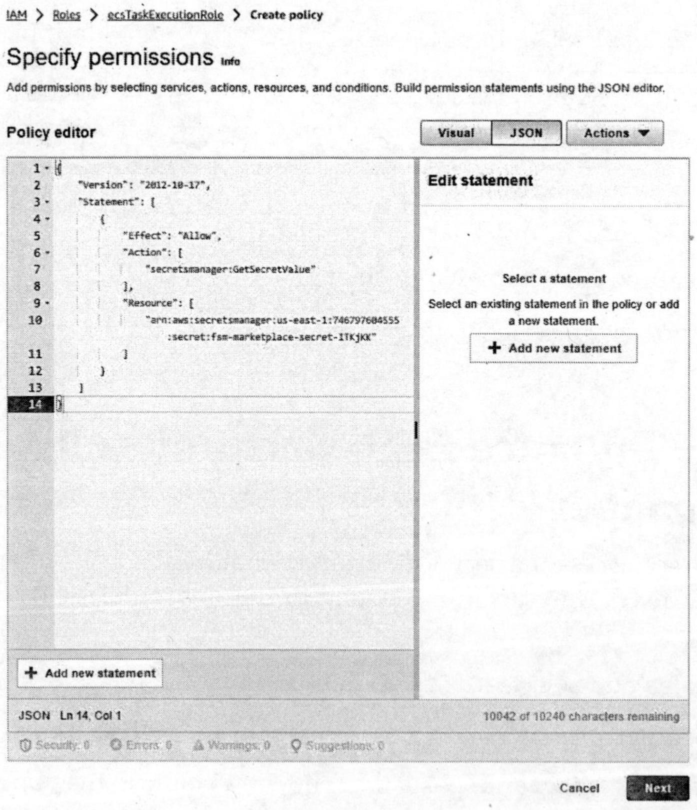

Figure 9.14: *Adding inline policy to ecsTaskExecutionRole*

4. Provide a logical policy name, for example **`access-fsm-marketplace-secrets`** and click **Create policy**.

A policy that gives permissions to access secrets from the Secret Manager has been added to the ECS task execution role and is visible in the *Figure 9.15*:

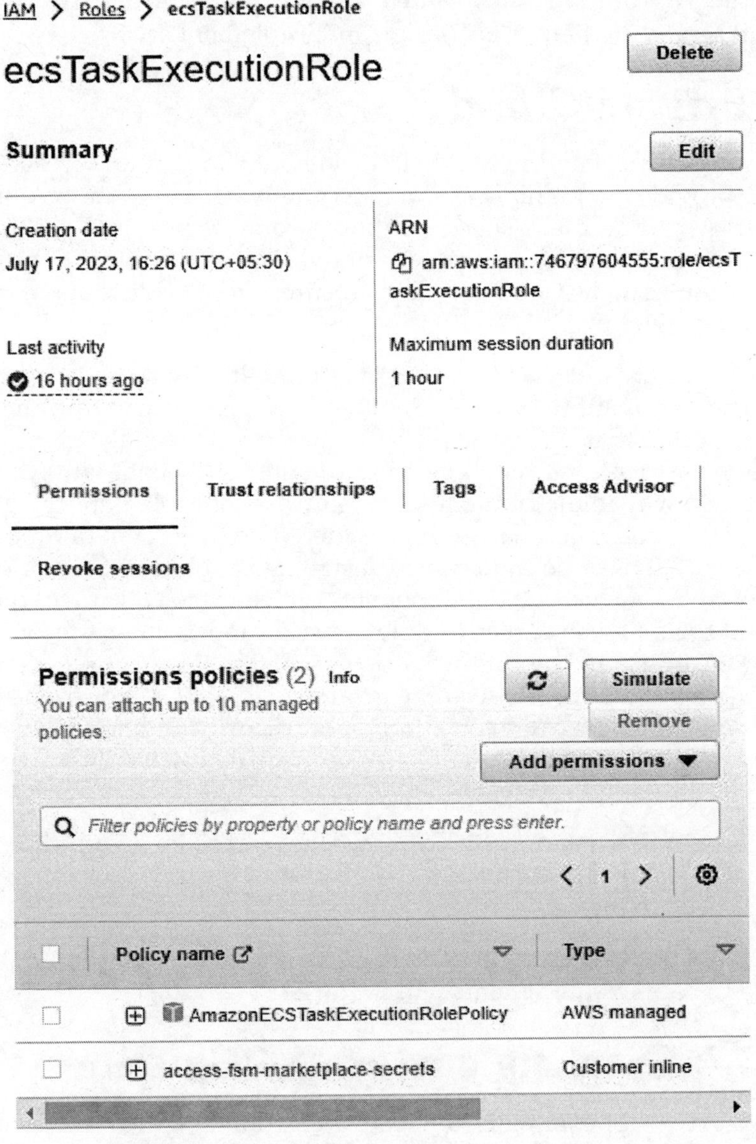

***Figure 9.15:** Inline policy added to ecsTaskExecutionRole*

Once the role has been enhanced AWS ECS services can access the secret from Secret Manager and can inject its value into the containers as environment variables on startup.

Network security

Network security refers to the set of practices, technologies, and policies implemented to protect an organization's digital assets, data, and communication pathways within computing environments. In the AWS cloud environment network security helps in ensuring the integrity, confidentiality, and availability of resources. AWS provides a robust set of tools and services to help users design and implement secure network architectures.

Virtual Private Cloud

AWS users can create isolated network environments known as **Virtual Private Clouds** (**VPCs**). VPC provides a highly customizable network environment and allow users to define their own IP address space, configure route tables, and control inbound and outbound traffic using security groups and **network access control lists** (**NACLs**). It acts as a virtual data center in the cloud, offering a secure and scalable foundation for deploying applications and services.

One of the key features of AWS VPC is its ability to create isolated and segmented environments known as **subnets**. In AWS, subnets are segments within an Amazon **Virtual Private Cloud** (**VPC**) that enable users to organize and manage their cloud resources effectively. Subnets are created within a VPC and are associated with specific availability zones, providing a way to distribute resources across multiple data centers for enhanced availability and fault tolerance. Each subnet is identified by its own unique **Classless Inter-Domain Routing** (**CIDR**) block and can be designated as either public or private based on its accessibility from the internet. Public subnets typically host resources that require direct internet access, such as web servers, while private subnets house resources that should not be directly exposed to the internet, such as databases or application servers. AWS users can configure **route tables**, **security groups**, and **NACLs** for each subnet, allowing for fine-grained control over network traffic and security. Subnets play a crucial role in designing a well-architected and secure AWS infrastructure, facilitating the deployment of diverse applications and services within a VPC.

There is a concept of VPC Peering which allows the connection of multiple VPCs, enabling seamless communication between them. This is useful for scenarios where resources from different VPCs need to interact securely.

By leveraging AWS VPC, users can build secure and isolated network environments tailored to their specific requirements within the AWS Cloud.

Recipe 77: Creating custom VPC using AWS CLI

Run the below AWS CLI command to create a custom VPC with the defined IP address range:

```
aws ec2 create-vpc \
--cidr-block 10.0.0.0/16 \
--instance-tenancy default \
--tag-specification 'ResourceType=vpc,Tags=[{Key=Name,Value=FSM-VPC}]'
```

Here,

- **`cidr-block`** defines the IP range to be associated with the VPC.
- **`instance-tenancy`** defines the tenancy of the instances that will be launched inside the VPC, by default the instances will be launched with the shared tenancy. Possible values are *default, dedicated* and *host*.
- **`tag-specification`** is a list of tags to be associated with the resource. Resource type needs to be mentioned while specifying the tags for a particular resource.

Output is as shown in *Figure 9.16*, new VPC created with id **`vpc-0f2bc18038166e4ae`**:

```
$ aws ec2 create-vpc \
> --cidr-block 10.0.0.0/16 \
> --instance-tenancy default \
>    --tag-specification 'ResourceType=vpc,Tags=[{Key=Name,Value=FSM-VPC}]'
{
    "Vpc": {
        "CidrBlock": "10.0.0.0/16",
        "DhcpOptionsId": "dopt-0f3327b1b76bd2336",
        "State": "pending",
        "VpcId": "vpc-0f2bc18038166e4ae",
        "OwnerId": "746797604555",
        "InstanceTenancy": "default",
        "Ipv6CidrBlockAssociationSet": [],
        "CidrBlockAssociationSet": [
            {
                "AssociationId": "vpc-cidr-assoc-049701482ddbcbc4c",
                "CidrBlock": "10.0.0.0/16",
                "CidrBlockState": {
                    "State": "associated"
                }
            }
        ],
        "IsDefault": false,
        "Tags": [
            {
                "Key": "Name",
                "Value": "FSM-VPC"
            }
        ]
    }
}
```

Figure 9.16: Output of create VPC command

Recipe 78: Creating subnets in a VPC using AWS CLI

Run the below AWS CLI command to create a subnet with the defined IP address range in above created VPC:

```
aws ec2 create-subnet --vpc-id vpc-0f2bc18038166e4ae --cidr-block
10.0.1.0/20
--availability-zone us-east-1a \
--tag-specifications 'ResourceType=subnet,Tags=[{Key=Name,Value=FSM-ipv4-
subnet}]'
```

Here,

- **`vpc-id`** is the id of the VPC in which the subnet is to be created.
- **`cidr-block`** defines the IP range to be associated with the subnet, the range should be withing the range of IP addresses for the VPC.
- **`availability-zone`** defines the availability zone in which subnet is to be created. The availability zone should be from the region in which the VPC is created.
- **`tag-specifications`** is a list of tags to be associated with the resource. Resource type needs to be mentioned while specifying the tags for a particular resource.

Output is as shown in Figure 9.17:

```
$ aws ec2 create-subnet \
> --vpc-id vpc-0f2bc18038166e4ae \
> --cidr-block 10.0.1.0/20 \
> --availability-zone us-east-1a \
> --tag-specifications 'ResourceType=subnet,Tags=[{Key=Name,Value=FSM-ipv4-subnet}]'
{
    "Subnet": {
        "AvailabilityZone": "us-east-1a",
        "AvailabilityZoneId": "use1-az1",
        "AvailableIpAddressCount": 4091,
        "CidrBlock": "10.0.0.0/20",
        "DefaultForAz": false,
        "MapPublicIpOnLaunch": false,
        "State": "available",
        "SubnetId": "subnet-08a17ffd0a583d342",
        "VpcId": "vpc-0f2bc18038166e4ae",
        "OwnerId": "746797604555",
        "AssignIpv6AddressOnCreation": false,
        "Ipv6CidrBlockAssociationSet": [],
        "Tags": [
            {
                "Key": "Name",
                "Value": "FSM-ipv4-subnet"
            }
        ],
        "SubnetArn": "arn:aws:ec2:us-east-1:746797604555:subnet/subnet-08a17ffd0a583d342",
        "EnableDns64": false,
        "Ipv6Native": false,
        "PrivateDnsNameOptionsOnLaunch": {
            "HostnameType": "ip-name",
            "EnableResourceNameDnsARecord": false,
            "EnableResourceNameDnsAAAARecord": false
        }
    }
}
```

Figure 9.17: Output of create subnet command

Security groups

In AWS, security groups serve as virtual firewalls that control inbound and outbound traffic for Amazon **Elastic Compute Cloud** (**EC2**) instances within an Amazon **Virtual Private Cloud** (**VPC**). Security groups act as a first line of defense, allowing users to define rules that permit or deny traffic based on protocols, ports, and source or destination IP addresses. These rules are stateful, meaning that if you allow inbound traffic, the corresponding outbound traffic is automatically permitted, and vice versa. They only have **`"allow"`** rules, not **`"deny"`** rules and by default every port is closed. This simplifies the management of network security, as users can specify the desired access controls without the need to create separate rules for incoming and outgoing traffic. This granular control over network traffic, combined with the ability to dynamically adjust rules, makes security groups a fundamental component for securing AWS resources and building a robust and scalable network infrastructure.

Recipe 79: Creating security group using AWS CLI

Run the below AWS CLI command to create a security group in above created VPC:

```
aws ec2 create-security-group \
--group-name FSM-sg \
--description "Financial service marketplace security group" \
--vpc-id vpc-0f2bc18038166e4ae
```

Here,

- **`group-name`** is the name of the security group.
- **`Description`** is a description for the security group. This is a required parameter.
- **`vpc-id`** is the id of the VPC for which the security group is to be created.

Output is as shown in *Figure 9.18*, security group with group id **`sg-076373510fab850f2`** has been created:

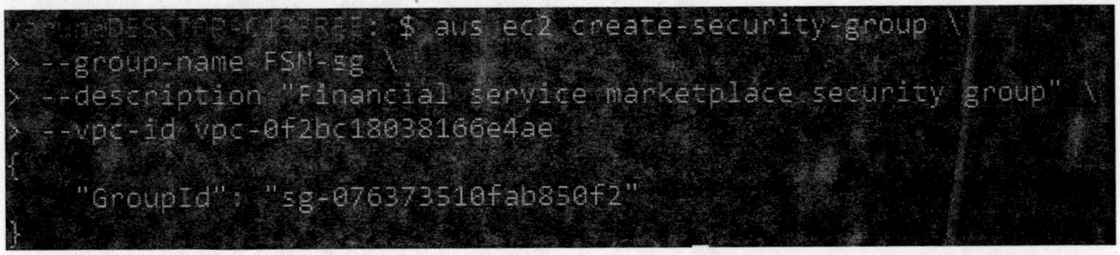

```
$ aws ec2 create-security-group \
> --group-name FSM-sg \
> --description "Financial service marketplace security group" \
> --vpc-id vpc-0f2bc18038166e4ae
{
    "GroupId": "sg-076373510fab850f2"
}
```

Figure 9.18: Output of create security group command

Recipe 80: Describing security group using AWS CLI

View the above created security group using the below command:

`aws ec2 describe-security-groups --group-ids sg-076373510fab850f2`

Output is as shown in *Figure 9.19:*

```
varun@DESKTOP-C133REE: $ aws ec2 describe-security-groups --group-ids sg-076373510fab850f2
{
    "SecurityGroups": [
        {
            "Description": "Financial service marketplace security group",
            "GroupName": "FSM-sg",
            "IpPermissions": [],
            "OwnerId": "746797604555",
            "GroupId": "sg-076373510fab850f2",
            "IpPermissionsEgress": [
                {
                    "IpProtocol": "-1",
                    "IpRanges": [
                        {
                            "CidrIp": "0.0.0.0/0"
                        }
                    ],
                    "Ipv6Ranges": [],
                    "PrefixListIds": [],
                    "UserIdGroupPairs": []
                }
            ],
            "VpcId": "vpc-0f2bc18038166e4ae"
        }
    ]
}
```

Figure 9.19: *Output of describe security group command*

Here,

- **`Description`** is the description of the security group.
- **`GroupName`** is the name of the security group.
- **`OwnerId`** is the AWS account ID of the owner of the security group.
- **`GroupId`** is the ID of the security group.
- **`VpcId`** is the ID of the VPC for the security group.
- **`IpPermissions`** is a list off inbound traffic rules. It is empty, means no traffic from outside can reach a resource used with this security group.

- **`IpPermissionEgress`** is a list of outbound traffic rules. There is 1 rule with **`IpProtocol`** as **`-1`** which means **`All`** and CIDR range **`0.0.0.0/0`**, so no restriction on any traffic going out.

Recipe 81: Adding a rule to a security group

Run the below command to add an inbound rule to a security group via AWS CLI:

```
aws ec2 authorize-security-group-ingress \
--group-id sg-076373510fab850f2 \
--protocol tcp --port 5432 --cidr 10.0.1.0/20
```

Here,

- **`group-id`** is the security group to which the rule is to be added.
- **`protocol`** defines the protocol for the incoming traffic.
- **`port`** defines the port on which the incoming traffic is allowed.
- **`cidr`** defines the CIDR range of the **`source`** from where the traffic is allowed.

Output is as shown in *Figure 9.20*:

```
varun@DESKTOP-C133REE: $ aws ec2 authorize-security-group-ingress \
> --group-id sg-076373510fab850f2 \
> --protocol tcp \
> --port 5432 \
> --cidr 10.0.1.0/20
{
    "Return": true,
    "SecurityGroupRules": [
        {
            "SecurityGroupRuleId": "sgr-020abf1f39a045ccb",
            "GroupId": "sg-076373510fab850f2",
            "GroupOwnerId": "746797604555",
            "IsEgress": false,
            "IpProtocol": "tcp",
            "FromPort": 5432,
            "ToPort": 5432,
            "CidrIpv4": "10.0.0.0/20"
        }
    ]
}
```

***Figure 9.20**: Output of add incoming rule command*

Here,

- **`Return`** returns true if the request succeeds; otherwise, returns an error.
- **`SecurityGroupRules`** provides information about the inbound (ingress) security group rules that were added.
- **`SecurityGroupRuleId`** is the ID of the security group rule.
- **`GroupId`** is the ID of the security group.
- **`GroupOwnerId`** is the ID of the AWS account that owns the security group.
- **`IsEgress`** indicates whether the security group rule is an outbound rule.
- **`IpProtocol`** is the IP protocol name (**`tcp`**, **`udp`**, **`icmp`**, **`icmpv6`**) or number.
- **`FromPort`**, if the protocol is TCP or UDP, this is the start of the port range. If the protocol is ICMP or ICMPv6, this is the type number.
- **`ToPort`**, if the protocol is TCP or UDP, this is the end of the port range. If the protocol is ICMP or ICMPv6, this is the type number.
- **`CidrIpv4`** is the IPv4 CIDR range.
- **`Description`** is the security group rule description.

The security groups rules can also be viewed on AWS management console, refer to *Figure 9.21* for reference:

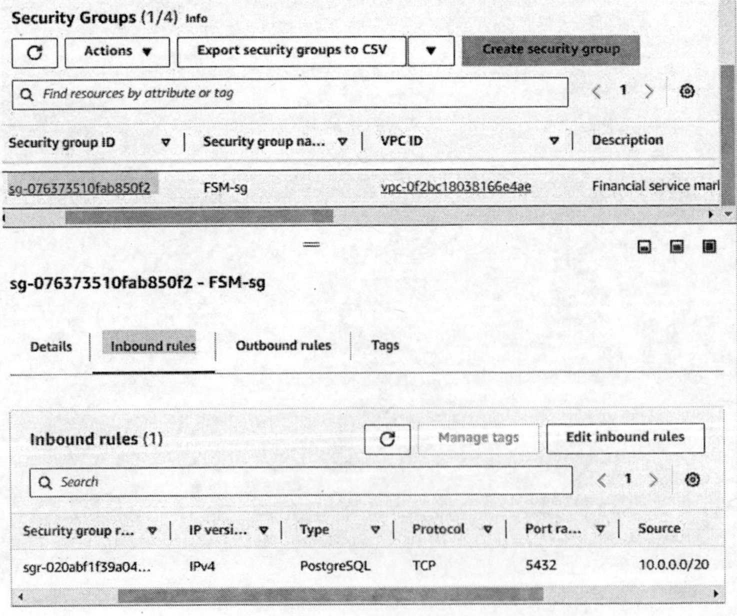

***Figure 9.21:** Inbound rule for a security group*

Here, type as *PostgresSQL* is being populated by the system as the port is port *5432*, which is the default port on which the PostgreSQL DB listens.

AWS Web Application Firewall

The **AWS Web Application Firewall (WAF)** is a security service that helps protect web applications from common web exploits and malicious traffic. AWS WAF allows users to define customizable web security rules along with web **access control lists (ACLs)**, that filter and monitor HTTP and HTTPS traffic to applications hosted on Amazon CloudFront, Application Load Balancer, or Amazon API Gateway. Users can create rules to block specific IP addresses, prevent SQL injection attacks, mitigate **cross-site scripting (XSS)**, and safeguard against other application layer vulnerabilities.

AWS WAF integrates with AWS CloudWatch, providing real-time visibility into web traffic and allowing users to monitor the effectiveness of their security rules. When a web ACL detects suspicious or malicious activity, it can trigger CloudWatch Alarms or be integrated with AWS Lambda functions for automated responses.

Additionally, AWS WAF provides protection against **Distributed Denial of Service (DDoS)** attacks. When used in conjunction with **AWS Shield**, it helps mitigate DDoS threats, ensuring the availability and performance of web applications.

The main components of AWS WAF are:

- **Web ACLs**: Web ACLs are central to AWS WAF and serve as a container for the rules that define how to inspect and control web requests. A Web ACL consists of one or more rules that can be customized to match specific conditions, such as IP addresses, country origins, or patterns found in the request.
- **Rules**: Rules are the building blocks of Web ACLs. They define the conditions under which AWS WAF acts on web requests. Rules can target various aspects of the request, including headers, query strings, IP addresses, and more. Users can create rules to block, allow, or count web requests based on specific criteria.
- **Rule groups**: There is an option to specify rules directly within a web ACL or within reusable rule groups. Managed rule groups are offered by AWS, as well as by AWS Marketplace sellers, and these can be utilized for your requirements.

AWS WAF is highly scalable, allowing users to deploy it across multiple environments and web applications. With its managed service model, users benefit from automatic updates to the rulesets, providing protection against emerging threats without manual intervention. AWS WAF is a valuable tool for organizations looking to enhance the security posture of their web applications and protect against a wide range of cyber threats.

Recipe 82: Creating Web ACL with rules

Follow the given steps to create an ECS cluster via AWS ECS Management Console:

1. Login to the AWS Management Console and search WAF or type in the following URL: **https://us-east-1.console.aws.amazon.com/wafv2/homev2/web-acls**.

   The region can be changed as per your preference.

2. Click **Create web ACL** and provide following details:

   a. Select resource type as **Regional resources** as ACL needs to be associated with Application Load Balancer.

   b. Name and description, enter a logical name, for example **`FSM_ACL`**. The same name can be used as CloudWatch metric name.

   Refer to *Figure 9.22* for reference:

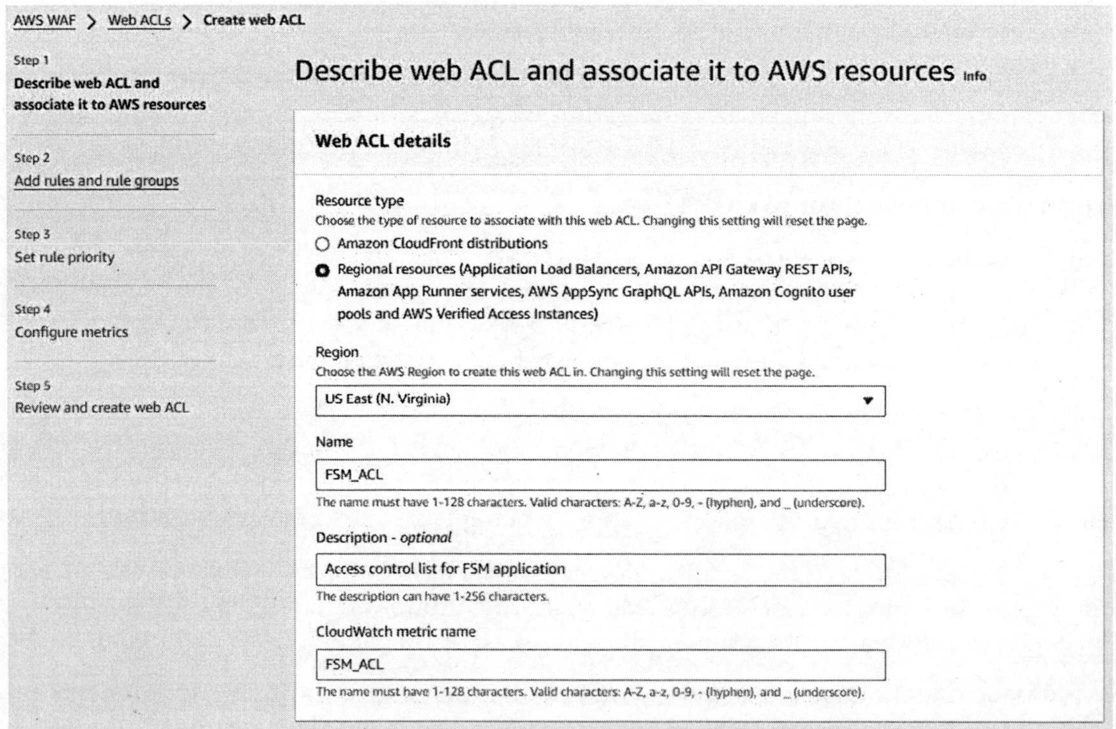

Figure 9.22: *Creating web ACL with the name FSM_ACL*

3. Click **Next** to add rules and rule groups to the ACL. Both custom rules and manages rules can be added.

4. Select **Add managed rule groups** from **Add rules**. Select the rule groups as per the requirements:

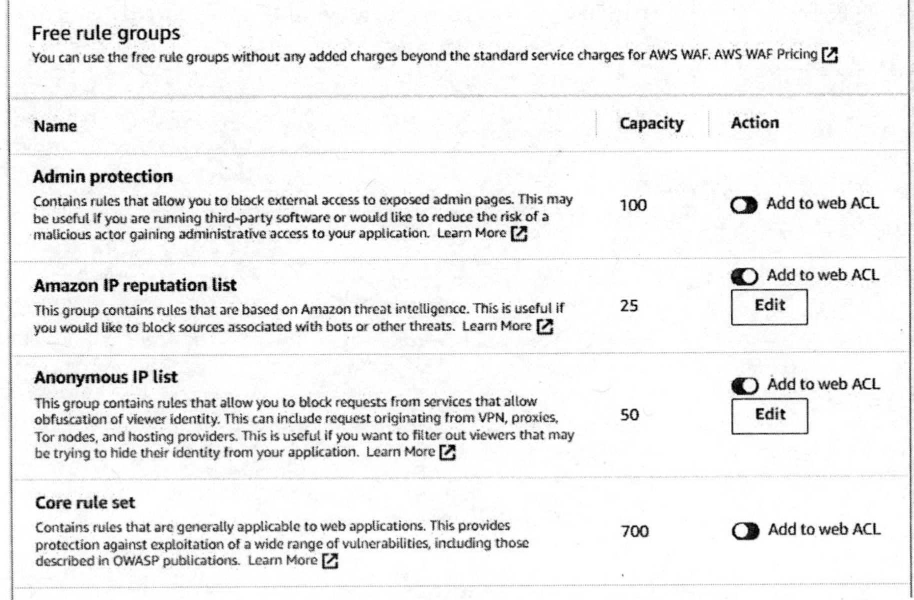

Figure 9.23: Selecting managed rules for the web ACL

The following figure shows manages rules added to the web ACL:

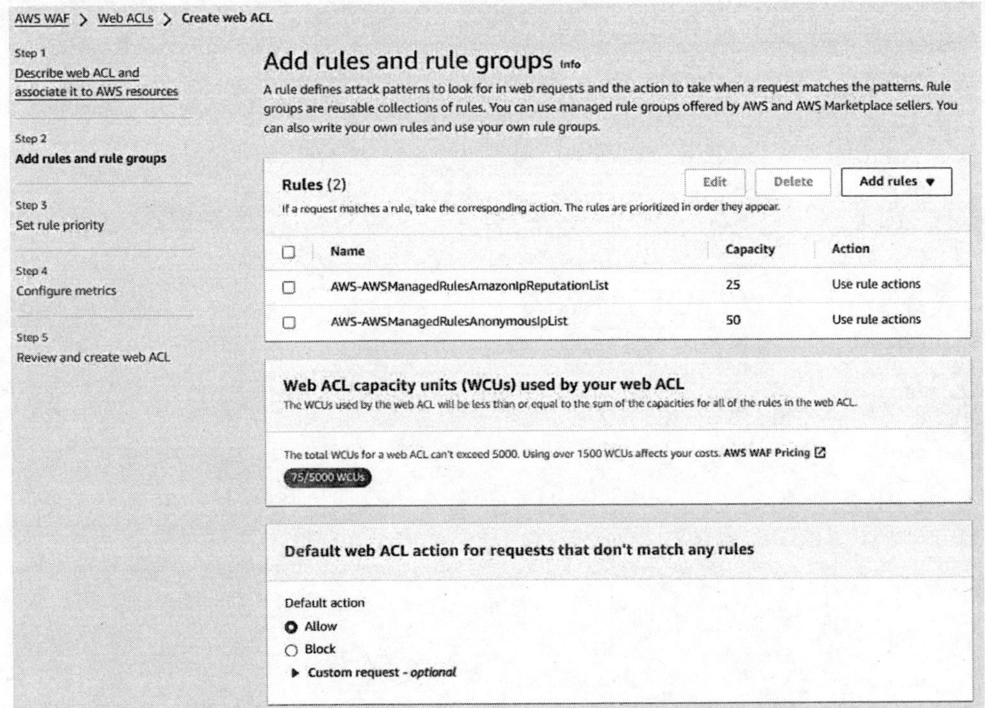

Figure 9.24: Managed rules added to the web ACL

5. Click **Next** to set the priority of the rules, refer to *Figure 9.25* for reference:

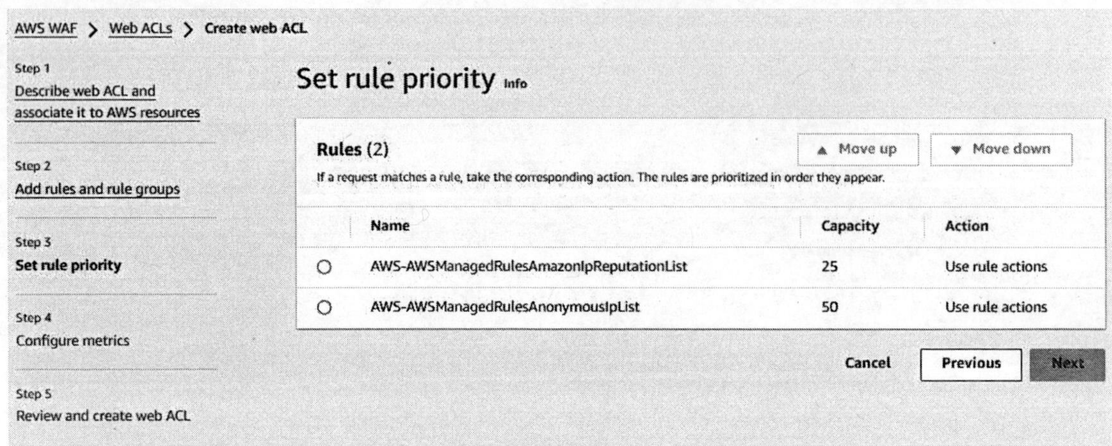

***Figure 9.25**: Setting priority for the rules*

6. Click **Next** to set the CloudWatch metrics names for the for the above rules.
7. Click **Next** again to review the settings and create the new web ACL. Refer to *Figure 9.26* for reference:

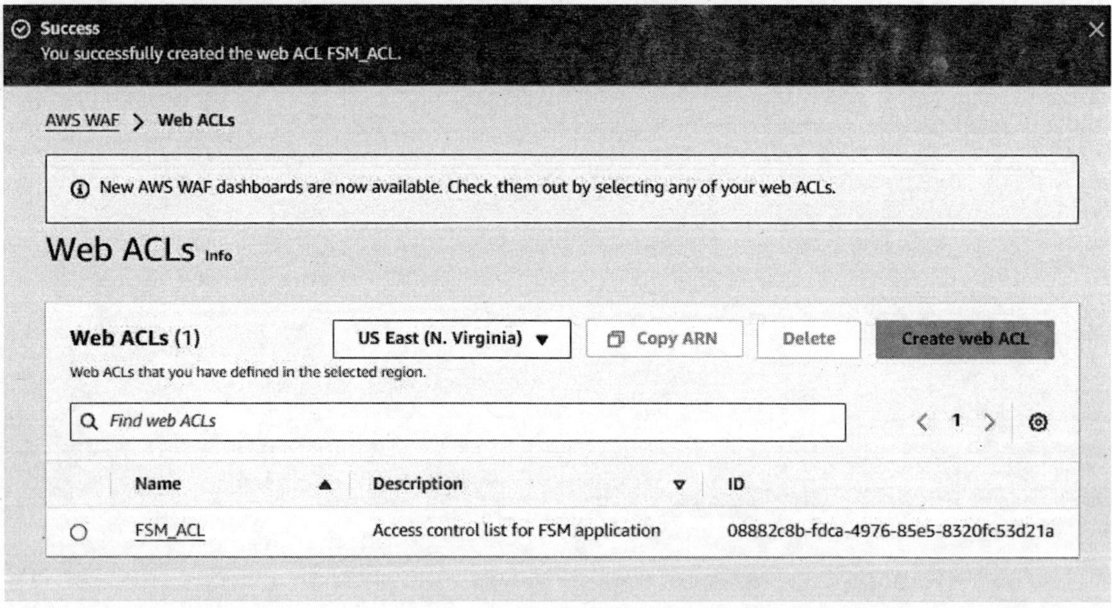

***Figure 9.26**: New web ACL with the name FSM_ACL has been created*

For ACL to work it needs to be associated with an AWS resource. Following recipe explains how to associate the ACL with and AWS resource.

Recipe 83: Associating Web ACL with ALB

Follow the given steps to associate the web **`ACL FSM_ACL`** with **AWS Application Load Balancer** (ALB) **`fsm-load-balancer`**:

1. Login to the AWS Management Console and search WAF or type in the following URL: **https://us-east-1.console.aws.amazon.com/wafv2/homev2/web-acls.**

   The region can be changed as per your preference.

2. Click on the **`ACL FSM_ACL`** to open the ACL configurations.

3. Click on the tab **Associated AWS resources** and click **Add AWS resources.**

4. Select **Application Load Balancer** and then select the **`fsm-load-balancer`** in the search resource section, refer to *Figure 9.27* and *Figure 9.28* for reference:

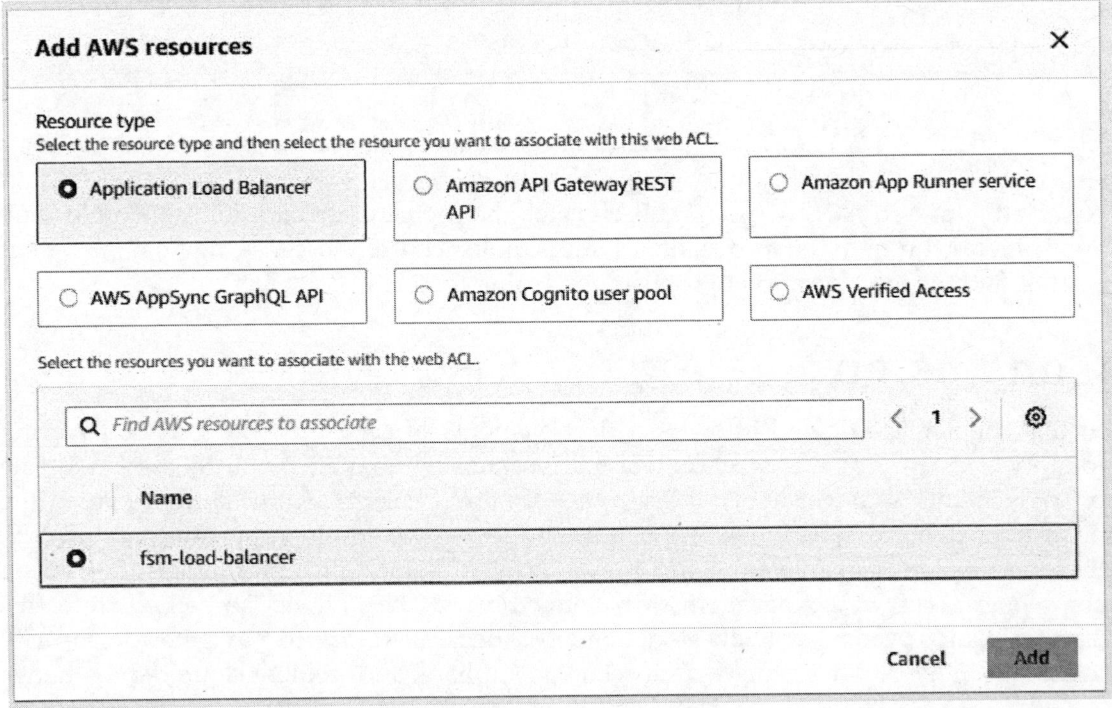

Figure 9.27: *Associating FSM_ACL with fsm-load-balancer*

The following figure shows **FSM_ACL** has been associated with **fsm-load-balancer**:

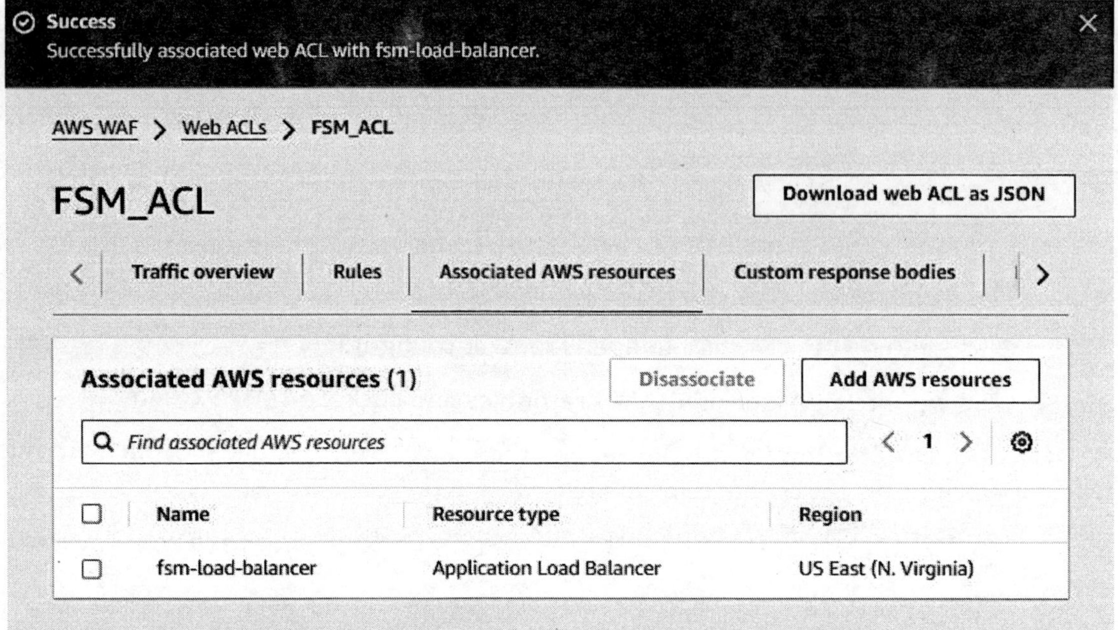

***Figure 9.28**: FSM_ACL has been associated with fsm-load-balancer*

Associating a Web ACL with an ALB elevates the security and durability of your web applications through the provision of meticulous control, defense against prevalent threats, and the incorporation of robust monitoring features.

Conclusion

In this chapter, we delved into the critical elements of security within AWS, covering Identity and IAM, data protection, encryption and key management, the essential role of AWS Secrets Manager and fundamentals of network security. These topics are at the heart of any robust security strategy in the cloud. As we continue our journey in AWS, these security fundamentals will remain essential in maintaining data integrity, ensuring compliance, and protecting against evolving threats. The knowledge gained from this chapter equips readers with the tools and practices necessary to navigate the security landscape in AWS, paving the way for secure, compliant, and resilient cloud deployments.

In the next chapter, we will learn about the observability paradigm of an application. It will detail out the tools available in the AWS environment that can be used to build a complete logging and monitoring system for an application that is used to provide real-time insights on the application to its administrators.

Points to remember

- Policies can be attached to IAM users, groups, or roles.
- Policies have an `"Effect"` field, which can be `"Allow"` or `"Deny"`.
- Permissions in policies are based on actions and resources.
- IAM groups are logical collections of IAM users.
- Groups simplify permission management by allowing policies to be attached to groups rather than individual users.
- Users can belong to multiple groups, streamlining access control for various roles.
- IAM users represent individuals or entities that interact with AWS resources.
- Each IAM user has a unique set of credentials for authentication.
- Users can be assigned permissions through policies attached to them directly or via group membership.
- IAM roles are entities that grant permissions to AWS resources.
- Roles are used for cross-account access, allowing temporary permissions for identities from other accounts.
- VPCs provide isolation for resources in the AWS Cloud, allowing users to segment the infrastructure logically. VPC should be designed to separate public and private resources.
- Use multiple subnets within a VPC, spread across different availability zones, for high availability and fault tolerance. Public and private subnets can be created to control access to resources.
- VPC peering allows communication between different VPCs. Use it to enable resource sharing and collaboration between isolated environments.
- Follow the principle of least privilege. Only allow necessary traffic and access to resources. Regularly review and refine security group rules based on changing requirements.
- AWS WAF offers Managed Rule Groups created by AWS security experts. Integrate these rule groups into your Web ACLs to benefit from pre-configured protections against common threats.

Questions

1. What are managed policies, and how do they differ from inline policies?
2. What is the principle of least privilege, and how does it relate to IAM policies?
3. What is an IAM user, and how does it differ from the AWS account's root user?
4. How can IAM users access AWS services programmatically?
5. How are IAM roles used to grant temporary permissions in AWS?
6. Can IAM roles be used for cross-account access, and if so, how does it work?
7. What types of encryption keys are supported by KMS?
8. How does KMS facilitate key rotation, and why is it important for security?
9. What is AWS Secrets Manager, and what problem does it solve for organizations?
10. What types of secrets can be stored in AWS Secrets Manager?
11. Explain the concept of subnets within a VPC and their importance in terms of availability and fault tolerance.
12. Describe the role of Security Groups in a VPC and how they differ from NACLs.
13. How does AWS handle data encryption at rest and in transit?
14. What are the best practices for securing AWS access credentials?
15. Describe the features of AWS WAF and how it enhances application security?

Join our book's Discord space

Join the book's Discord Workspace for Latest updates, Offers, Tech happenings around the world, New Release and Sessions with the Authors:

https://discord.bpbonline.com

CHAPTER 10
Observability

Introduction

The previous chapter explained about cloud security and discussed **identity and access management** (**IAM**), data protection and network security in detail. It covered the importance of IAM policy, IAM group, IAM user, and IAM role and showed how to create and use them for fine-grained access management. The chapter also talked about the importance and use of AWS **Key Management Service** (**KMS**), AWS Secret Manager, AWS Security Groups and AWS WAF service in improving the application's security posture.

In this chapter, we will talk about the observability paradigm of the application, its importance, and the tools available in the AWS ecosystem for implementing observability for an application. We will explore logging and monitoring aspects of an application in detail and build an observability system that can be used by the application administrators to get key insights about the running application from both technical and business perspectives.

Structure

In this chapter, we will discuss the following topics:

- Observability
- Logging

  - Container logging
  - AWS CloudWatch Logs
  - AWS CloudTrail
- Monitoring
  - CloudWatch metrics
  - CloudWatch alarms
  - CloudWatch dashboards
- Tagging

Objectives

The objective of this chapter is to CloudWatch logging and monitoring to equip readers with the essential knowledge and practical skills to establish a robust observability strategy for their AWS-based applications and services. This chapter aims to offer insights into how CloudWatch's suite of tools, including metrics, logs, alarms, and dashboards, can be leveraged to gain a comprehensive understanding of system behavior and performance. Readers will learn how to set up and configure CloudWatch to capture, store, and analyze log data, as well as to collect and visualize metrics in real-time. Readers will also learn the importance of tags and their association with AWS resources. By the end of the chapter, readers will be empowered to proactively monitor, troubleshoot, and optimize their AWS resources, ultimately enhancing the reliability, security, and performance of their cloud-based applications.

Observability

Observability is a critical aspect of managing and maintaining microservices architectures effectively. In the context of microservices, observability refers to the ability to gain insights into the behavior, performance, and health of individual microservices and the overall system. It encompasses logging, monitoring, and other practices that enable teams to understand what is happening within their distributed systems.

One of the key challenges in microservices environments is the inherent complexity of the architecture. With numerous interconnected services communicating over networks, it becomes challenging to identify and diagnose issues quickly. Observability provides the necessary tools and practices to address this challenge.

Benefits of observability

In the world of microservices, observability offers several significant benefits that are crucial for maintaining the reliability, performance, and overall health of complex distributed systems. Here are some of the key advantages:

- **Early issue detection**: Observability tools and practices allow for real-time monitoring of microservices, enabling teams to detect issues, anomalies, and errors as they occur. This proactive approach allows for rapid response and issue mitigation, reducing downtime and minimizing the impact on users.
- **Efficient troubleshooting**: When issues do arise, observability provides a wealth of data, including metrics, logs, and traces, that can be used for troubleshooting. Developers and operations teams can pinpoint the root cause of problems more quickly, reducing **mean time to resolution** (MTTR) and improving system reliability.
- **Performance optimization**: With observability, organizations gain insights into the performance of individual microservices and the interactions between them. This data helps in identifying and addressing bottlenecks, latency issues, and resource constraints, leading to improved system performance.
- **Scalability and resource management**: Observability tools can help monitor resource utilization (CPU, memory, network, and so on) of microservices, allowing for informed decisions on scaling strategies.
- **Enhanced security**: Monitoring and logging help detect and respond to security incidents and anomalies. Observability can assist in identifying unauthorized access, unusual patterns, or potential security breaches, strengthening the overall security posture of microservices.
- **Compliance and auditing**: Observability helps organizations meet compliance requirements by providing a detailed audit trail of system activities. This is especially important in regulated industries where data tracking and reporting are mandatory.

Observability is an indispensable practice for organizations operating in a microservices architecture. It empowers teams with the data and insights needed to ensure the reliability, performance, and security of their microservices-based applications, ultimately leading to a better competitive edge in the market.

Logging

Logging is a critical aspect; microservices generate logs that capture crucial information about their operations, such as requests, responses, errors, and events. Centralized logging systems assist in aggregating and storing these logs, facilitating easier search, analysis, and issue troubleshooting. Logs provide a detailed history of microservices' activities, enabling developers and operations teams to understand the events leading up to a problem.

Logging is a fundamental practice in **Amazon Web Services** (**AWS**) that plays a pivotal role in ensuring the operational health, security, and performance of cloud-based applications and services. AWS logging involves capturing and storing various data types, including events, errors, and informational messages generated by AWS resources and applications in the cloud. This data is crucial for monitoring, diagnosing issues, detecting anomalies, and meeting compliance and auditing requirements.

AWS offers multiple logging solutions and services, and understanding how to leverage them effectively is essential for maintaining a robust and reliable cloud infrastructure:

- Container logging
- AWS CloudWatch Logs
- AWS CloudTrail

Container logging

Handling logs generated inside a containerized application is different compared to a non-containerized application. The reason for the different log handling requirement is that the logs written to console or on a file system by default are ephemeral and only exist until the container is up and running. Moreover, with autoscaling in picture, various instances of these containers are consistently in operation, each generating logs within its own scope only. AWS provides direct connectors to ship console logs generated inside a container to AWS CloudWatch and Splunk but requires different design patterns like **Sidecar** to ship logs from containers to any other service or if logs need to be fetched from a file system.

For Amazon ECS with Fargate, AWS supports multiple destinations where logs can be shipped directly or indirectly:

- Amazon CloudWatch (directly)
- Splunk (directly)
- Firehose (via AWS FireLens)
- Kinesis (via AWS FireLens)
- OpenSearch (via AWS FireLens)
- Elasticsearch
- S3 (via AWS FireLens)
- Custom destination (via AWS FireLens)

Here, CloudWatch and Splunk are the monitoring and log management offerings, in which Splunk is a third-party solution well integrated with AWS. Others are services which are used to feed logs to or are part of a complex and advanced logging ecosystem.

AWS FireLens is a powerful container log router and enhancer that simplifies log management for containerized applications running on services like Amazon ECS with AWS Fargate. With FireLens, you can easily route container logs to various destinations, such as Amazon CloudWatch Logs, Amazon Kinesis Data Firehose, and Amazon Elasticsearch. It provides a flexible and extensible way to configure log routing and enrich log data by using fluentd or Fluent Bit as the log router. FireLens runs as a Sidecar container to the main container, collects the logs, and pushes them to the desired destination.

AWS CloudWatch Logs

AWS CloudWatch Logs is a central logging service that allows to collect, store, and analyze log data generated by AWS resources and applications. Log groups and log streams can be created to organize and categorize the log data. CloudWatch Logs provides powerful querying and alerting capabilities, enabling the setup of alarms based on specific log events or patterns. It integrates seamlessly with other AWS services, making it a fundamental component of AWS observability. Logs and metrics from an application running on EC2 instances or even on-prem servers can be collected and sent to the CloudWatch using CloudWatch agents. These agents run in parallel to the application, collect and stream the details back to the configured CloudWatch service.

An overview of AWS CloudWatch logs has already been provided as a step while creating Amazon ECS task definition. Follow the mentioned steps for configuring the CloudWatch log service from scratch:

1. Creating a log group
2. Instrumenting applications to push logs to CloudWatch
3. Viewing logs in CloudWatch

Recipe 84: Creating a log group

Log groups help in organizing the logs by grouping the logs from logically similar sources together. Log groups can be created as mentioned:

1. Login to the AWS Management Console and search **CloudWatch** or type in the following URL: **https://console.aws.amazon.com/cloudwatch/.**
2. Go to **Log groups** under **Logs** and click **Create log group**.
3. Give a logical group name, for example **`/ecs/customer-enquiry-task-definition`**. The name has been chosen as one of the sources of logs for the microservice Customer Enquiry running under an ECS service as a task. The intension is to group all the logs from this source under the above-mentioned log group.
4. Select the desired retention setting, after the selected period the logs will no longer be available. Refer to *Figure 10.1* for reference:

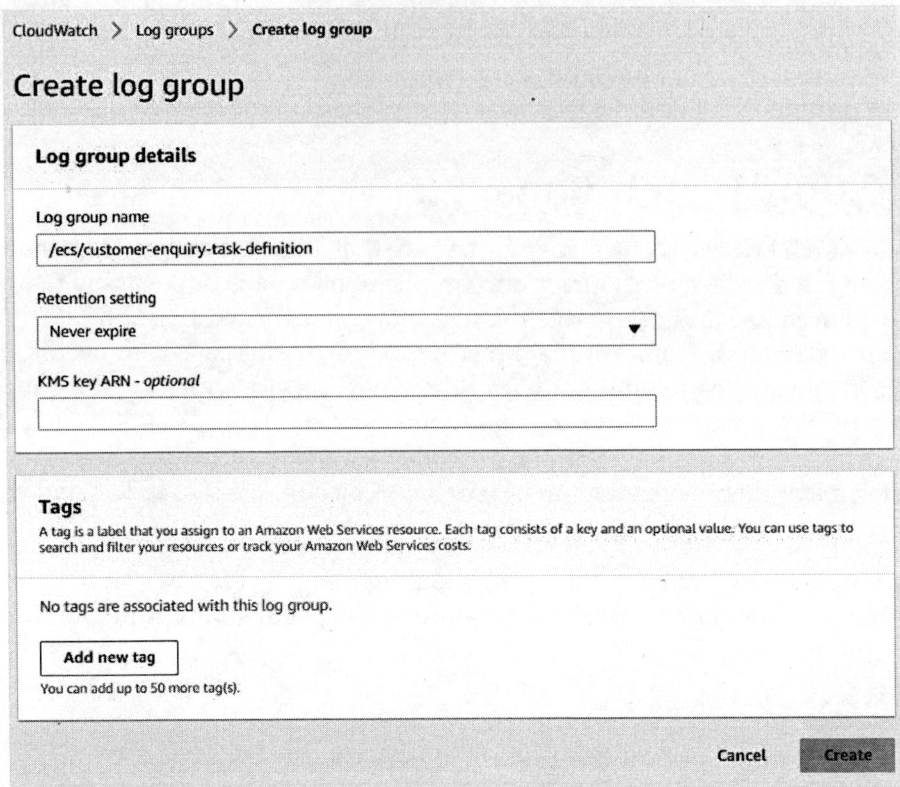

Figure 10.1: Creating a log group for an ECS task

5. Click **Create** to create the **Log group**.

Similarly, create **Log groups** corresponding to all the microservices. Refer to *Figure 10.2* for reference:

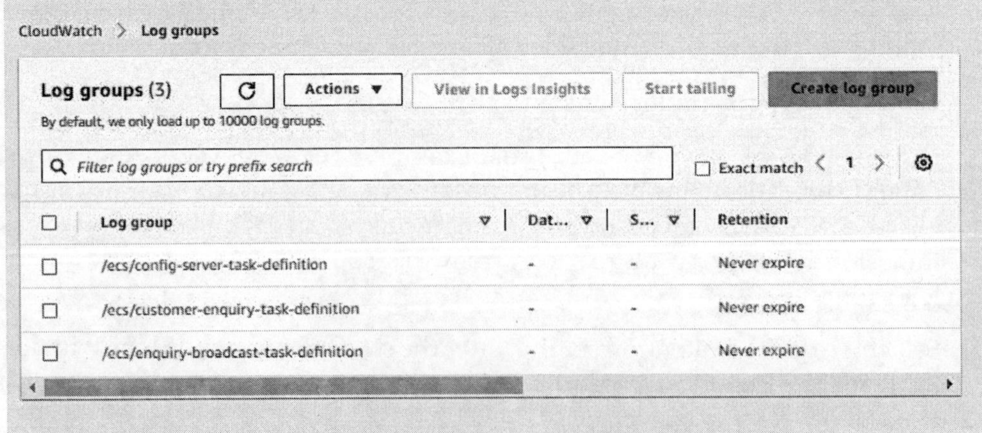

Figure 10.2: List of log groups

Under these **Log groups** are **Log Streams**, which represent individual streams of log data within a log group. Each log stream typically corresponds to a source of log events, such as an application, service, or instance. Log streams are uniquely identified within a log group by their names.

Recipe 85: Instrumenting applications to push logs to CloudWatch

CloudWatch has seamless connectivity with AWS services, and the services can be configured to push logs directly to AWS CloudWatch. As already mentioned before, if the applications are running on EC2 or on-prem servers then CloudWatch agents can be configured to push the logs to CloudWatch.

In this case, Amazon ECS service is being used for running the microservices, which has a direct connectivity with AWS CloudWatch. Follow the mentioned steps to enhance ECS task definition to use CloudWatch for log collection:

1. Log in to the AWS Management Console and search **ECS** or type in the following URL: **https://us-east-1.console.aws.amazon.com/ecs/v2/task-definitions**
2. The region can be changed as per your preference.
3. Select the desired task definition, for example **`customer-enquiry-task-definition`** and click **Create new revision**.
4. Go to the **Logging** section and enable the check box **Use log collection**.
5. Select **Amazon CloudWatch** from the drop down.
6. There are a few properties that need to be set as mentioned in *Table 10.1*:

Key	Value	Usage
`awslogs-group`	Example: **`/ecs/customer-enquiry-task-definition`**	It is the log group under which the logs will be collected
`awslogs-region`	Example: **`us-east-1`**	Identifies the region where the log needs to be collected, it will be the same region where log groups also exist.
`awslogs-stream-prefix`	Example: **`ecs`**	It is a prefix for log streams that will be created for the logs generated by the tasks corresponding to this Task definition.

Key	Value	Usage
`awslogs-create-group`	True/ False	If set to true the log group gets created if not already present

***Table 10.1**: Key and value for configuring CloudWatch in ECS Task definition*

Refer to *Figure 10.3* for reference:

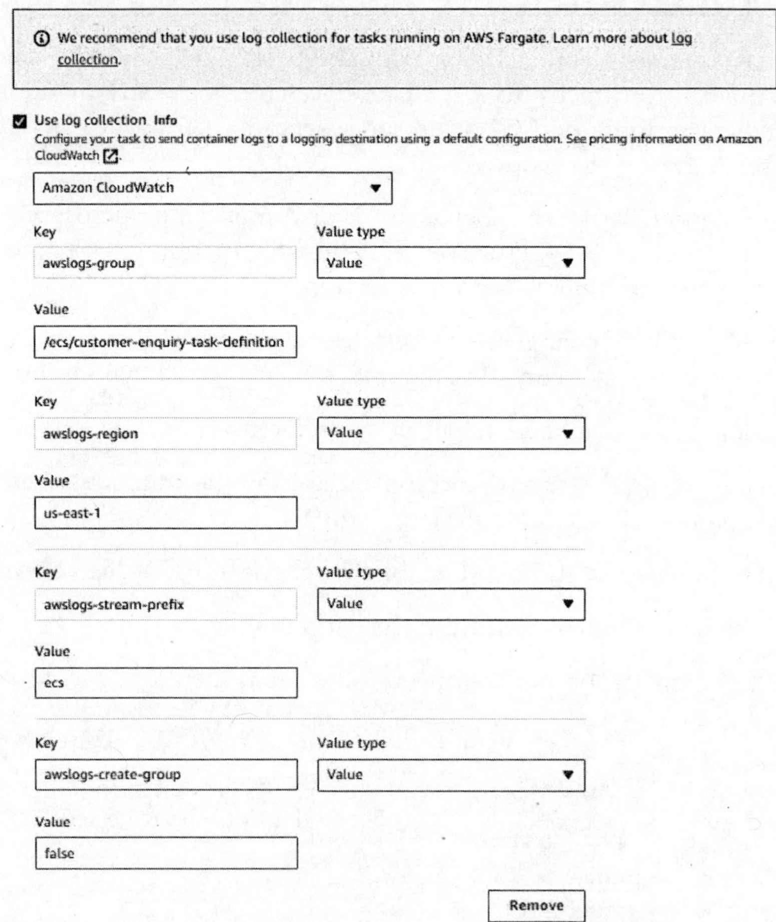

***Figure 10.3**: Configuring CloudWatch in ECS task definition*

7. Click Create to create a new version of the task definition

Recipe 86: Viewing logs in CloudWatch

Once the above configuration is done, the logs generated by microservices on execution as ECS tasks inside docker containers get shipped to the CloudWatch. Different log streams are formed inside a log group, each of which corresponds to a job that is executed as part of an ECS service. To access the logs produced in AWS CloudWatch, adhere to the following steps:

1. Login to the AWS Management Console and search **CloudWatch** or type in the following URL: **https://console.aws.amazon.com/cloudwatch/**.

2. Click on the desired log group, for example **`/ecs/customer-enquiry-task-definition`**. Inside the **Log group**, one to many **Log streams** will be available, refer to *Figure 10.4* for reference:

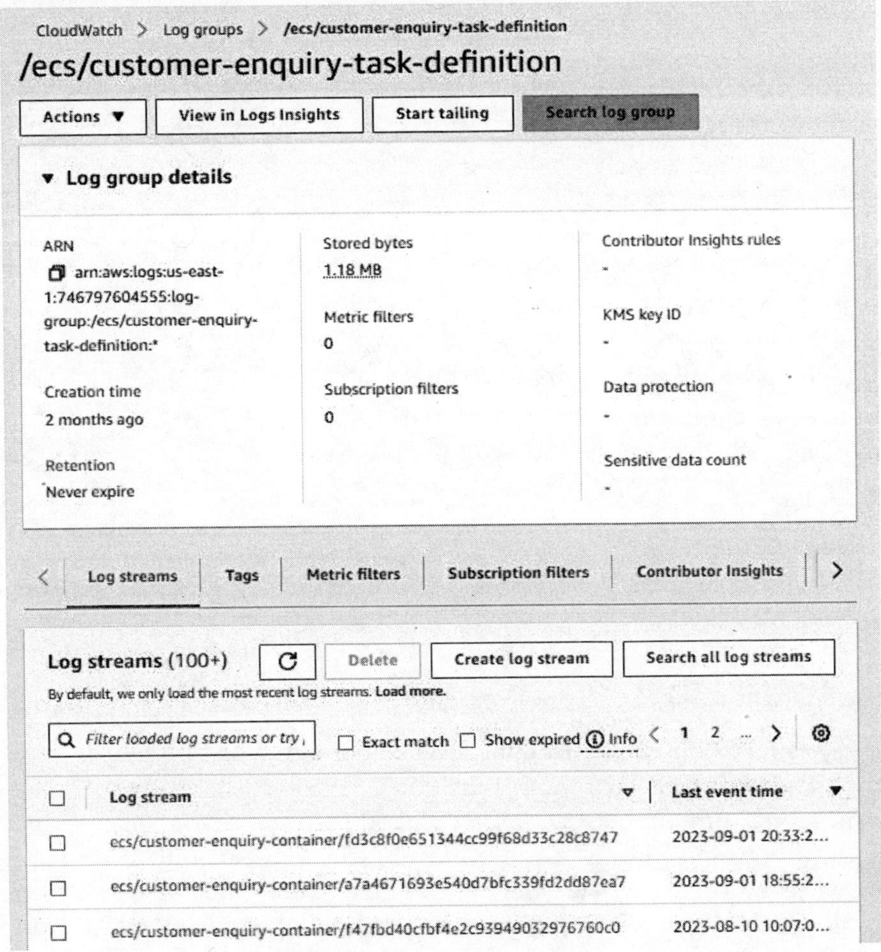

Figure 10.4: *Log streams inside a Log group /ecs/customer-enquiry-task-definition*

3. The Log stream names are all prefixed with **`ecs`** as set in the property **`awslogs-stream-prefix`**, followed by the container name that is **`customer-enquiry-container`** and container id. Click on one of the **Log streams** to view the corresponding logs, refer to *Figure 10.5* for reference:

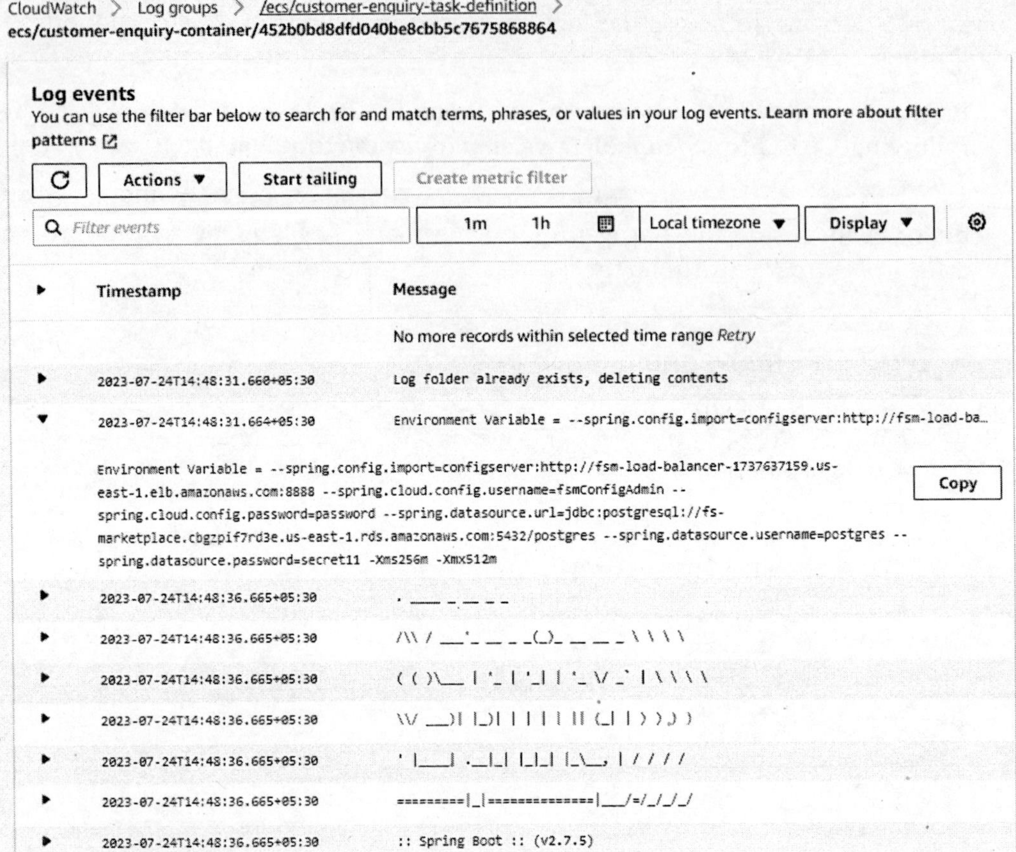

Figure 10.5: Log from a Log stream under Log group /ecs/customer-enquiry-task-definition

AWS CloudTrail

AWS CloudTrail is a robust and essential service that offers comprehensive visibility into the activities and actions occurring within your AWS infrastructure. It functions as an auditing and monitoring tool, capturing a detailed record of API calls, resource changes, and configuration modifications made within your AWS account. CloudTrail provides valuable insights into who, what, when, and where specific actions took place, enabling organizations to enhance security, maintain compliance, troubleshoot issues, and optimize their AWS environment.

CloudTrail operates by recording events, which include AWS Management Console sign-ins, AWS SDKs or CLI usage, and actions initiated by AWS services. These events are collected and stored in a secure and durable manner, ensuring the integrity and tamper resistance of the log data. Users can access CloudTrail logs via the AWS Management Console, AWS CLI, or programmatically through the CloudTrail API.

One of the significant advantages of CloudTrail is its ability to create an audit trail that simplifies security analysis and forensics. Organizations can track changes to critical resources, detect unauthorized access or suspicious activities, and gain deep insights into operational patterns. Furthermore, CloudTrail integrates seamlessly with Amazon CloudWatch Logs and AWS Lambda, allowing for real-time monitoring, alerting, and automated responses to specific events, enhancing the overall security and operational integrity of AWS environments. It is an indispensable tool for security and compliance-conscious organizations seeking to maintain a robust and well-governed cloud infrastructure.

Recipe 87: Creating trail with AWS CloudTrail

CloudTrail logs are generated in encrypted files and are stored in the Amazon S3 bucket. Follow the below steps for creating a trail with AWS CloudTrail:

1. Login to the AWS Management Console and search **CloudTrail** or type in the following URL: **https://console.aws.amazon.com/cloudtrail**.
2. Click **Create a trail**.
3. Provide a logical trail name, for example, `fsm-management-events`. Refer to *Figure 10.6* for reference:

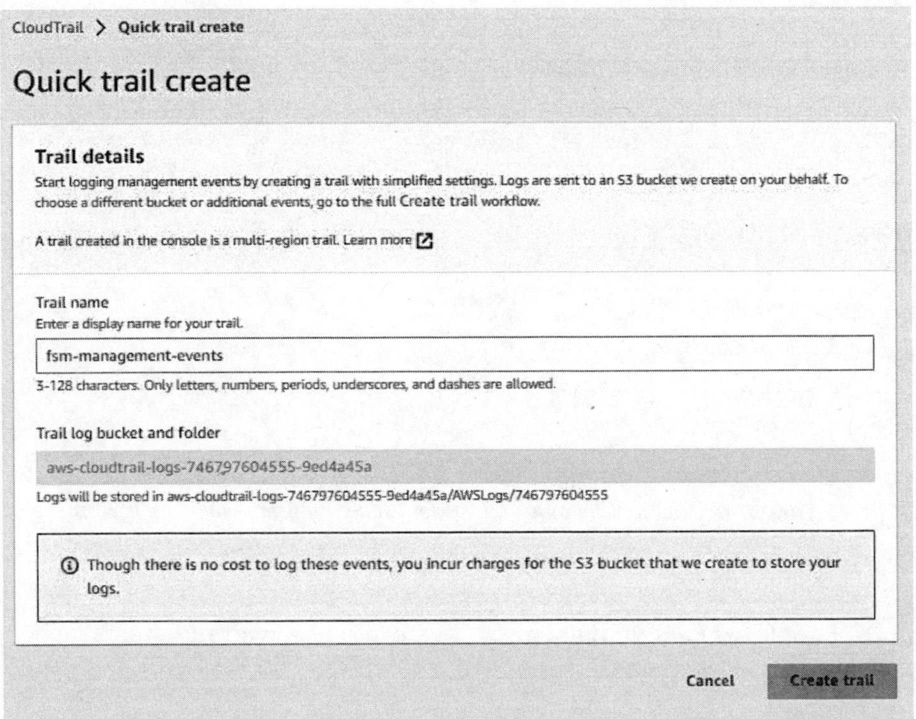

Figure 10.6: *Creating a trail with the name fsm-management-events using CloudTrail*

4. Click **Create trail** to create the trail.
5. Click on the newly created trail, for example **`fsm-management-events`**.
6. Edit CloudWatch Logs and enable the logs. Give a logical **Log group name** and **Role name**. Refer to *Figure 10.7* for reference:

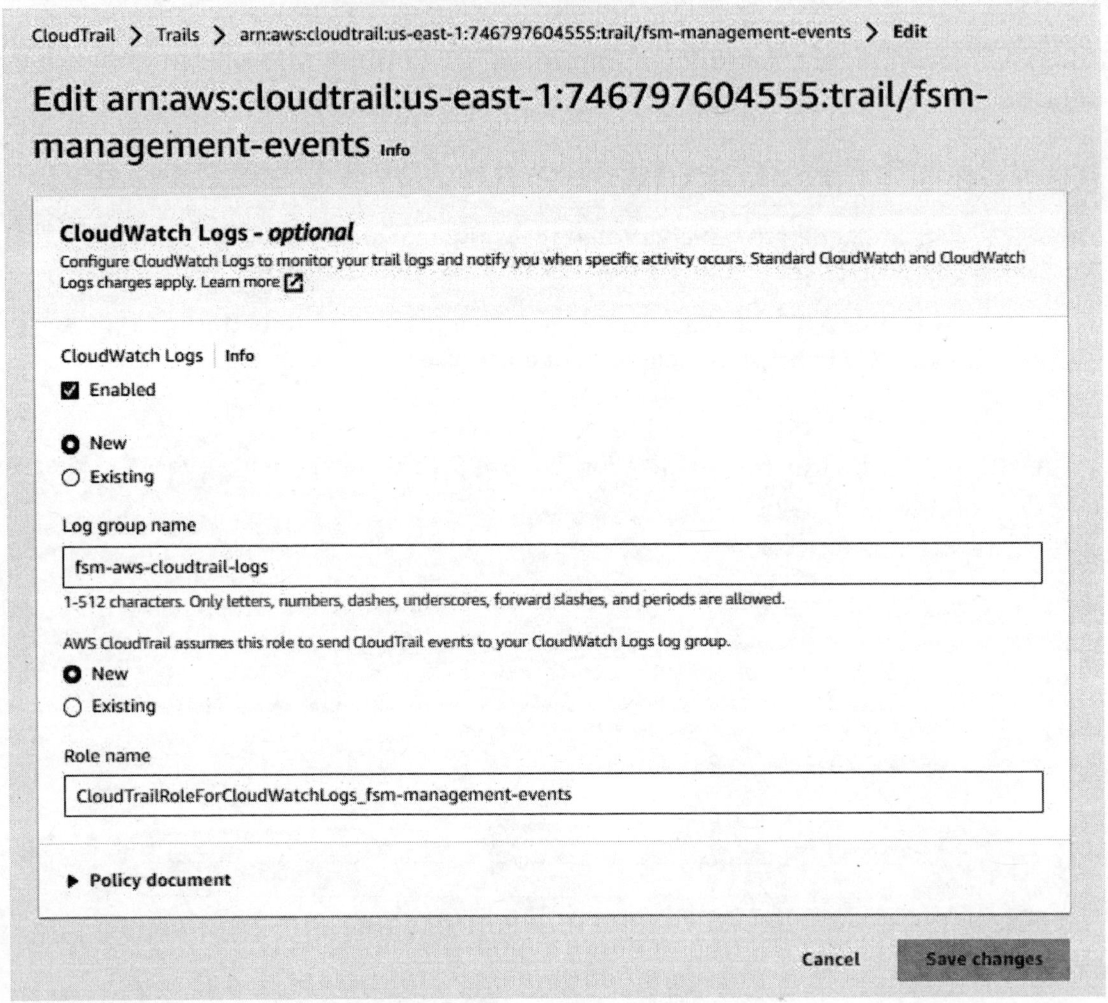

CloudTrail > Trails > arn:aws:cloudtrail:us-east-1:746797604555:trail/fsm-management-events > Edit

Edit arn:aws:cloudtrail:us-east-1:746797604555:trail/fsm-management-events Info

CloudWatch Logs - *optional*

Configure CloudWatch Logs to monitor your trail logs and notify you when specific activity occurs. Standard CloudWatch and CloudWatch Logs charges apply. Learn more

CloudWatch Logs | Info

Enabled

New

Existing

Log group name

fsm-aws-cloudtrail-logs

1-512 characters. Only letters, numbers, dashes, underscores, forward slashes, and periods are allowed.

AWS CloudTrail assumes this role to send CloudTrail events to your CloudWatch Logs log group.

New

Existing

Role name

CloudTrailRoleForCloudWatchLogs_fsm-management-events

Policy document

Cancel Save changes

Figure 10.7: Enabling CloudWatch Logs for CloudTrail fsm-management-events

7. Click **Save changes**.

The CloudTrail **`fsm-management-events`** logs can be viewed in CloudWatch under the log group **`fsm-aws-cloudtrail-logs`**.

Recipe 88: Viewing CloudTrail Events

AWS CloudTrail Event History is a feature that provides a comprehensive, time-ordered record of all API events and management actions within an AWS account for the past 90 days. It offers a historical view of activities, allowing users to search and analyze events, investigate security incidents, and track changes to resources. Follow the below steps for viewing event history in AWS CloudTrail:

1. Log in to the AWS Management Console and search **CloudTrail** or type in the following URL: **https://console.aws.amazon.com/cloudtrail.**
2. Click **Event history** to view the history of events. It is evident from the *Figure 10.8* that every event gets captured from AWS Login to AWS Service call:

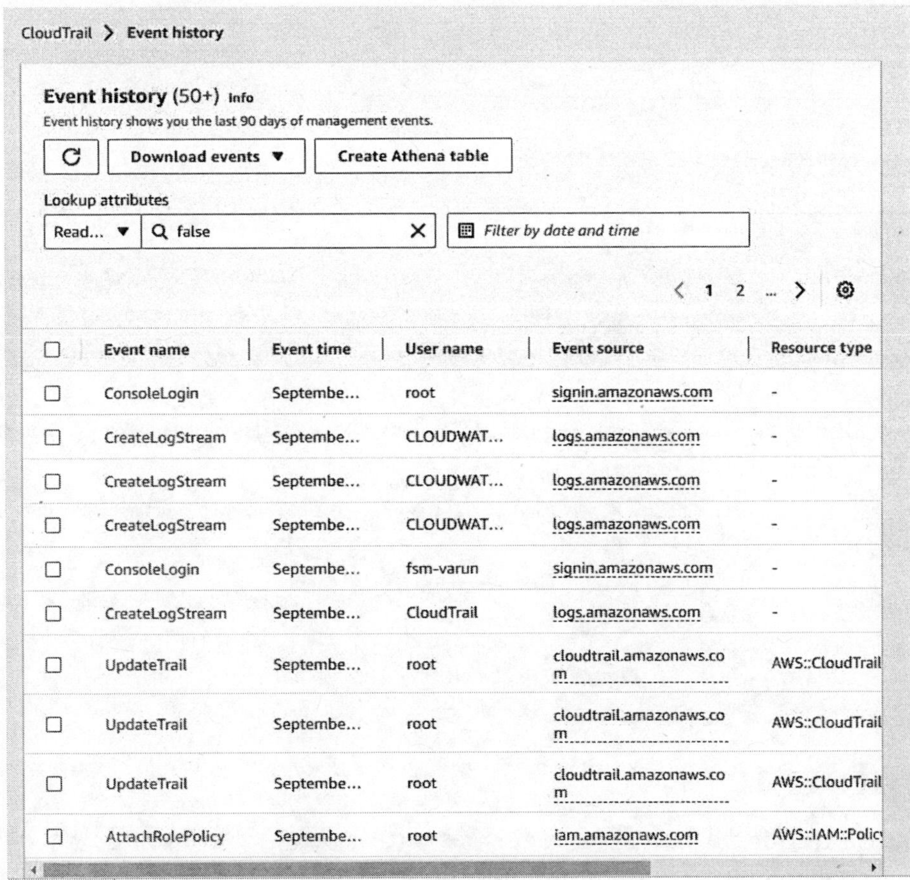

Figure 10.8: *Event history in CloudTrail*

3. Click the event **UpdateTrail** to view the details. Refer to *Figure 10.9* to validate the CloudTrail name as well as the IAM role and log group name:

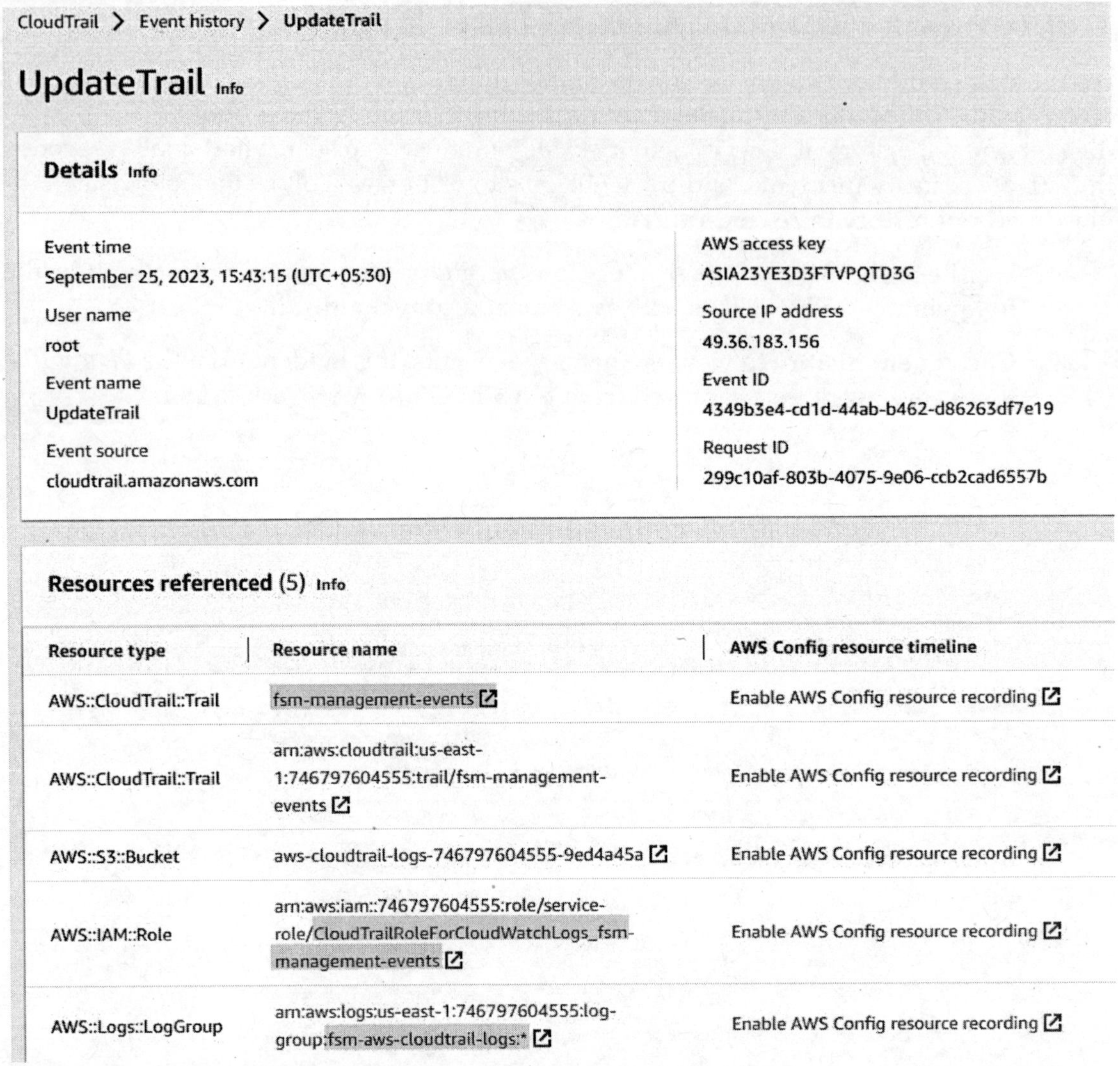

CloudTrail > Event history > **UpdateTrail**

UpdateTrail Info

Details Info

Event time
September 25, 2023, 15:43:15 (UTC+05:30)
User name
root
Event name
UpdateTrail
Event source
cloudtrail.amazonaws.com

AWS access key
ASIA23YE3D3FTVPQTD3G
Source IP address
49.36.183.156
Event ID
4349b3e4-cd1d-44ab-b462-d86263df7e19
Request ID
299c10af-803b-4075-9e06-ccb2cad6557b

Resources referenced (5) Info

Resource type	Resource name	AWS Config resource timeline
AWS::CloudTrail::Trail	fsm-management-events	Enable AWS Config resource recording
AWS::CloudTrail::Trail	arn:aws:cloudtrail:us-east-1:746797604555:trail/fsm-management-events	Enable AWS Config resource recording
AWS::S3::Bucket	aws-cloudtrail-logs-746797604555-9ed4a45a	Enable AWS Config resource recording
AWS::IAM::Role	arn:aws:iam::746797604555:role/service-role/CloudTrailRoleForCloudWatchLogs_fsm-management-events	Enable AWS Config resource recording
AWS::Logs::LogGroup	arn:aws:logs:us-east-1:746797604555:log-group:fsm-aws-cloudtrail-logs:*	Enable AWS Config resource recording

Figure 10.9: *UpdateTrail Event details*

Monitoring

Monitoring is a critical aspect of managing resources and applications in AWS. AWS offers a comprehensive suite of monitoring and observability services and tools that enable users to gain insights into the performance, health, and operational aspects of their AWS resources and workloads.

Amazon CloudWatch is the core monitoring service in AWS. Apart from allowing users to collect logs and track metrics CloudWatch allows to set alarms and provides a unified view of the operational health of AWS resources and applications, making it easier to troubleshoot issues and maintain system performance. It offers features like dashboards, customizable alarms, and automated actions through CloudWatch Events, making it a central hub for monitoring and alerting.

CloudWatch Metrics

Amazon CloudWatch Metrics are the foundation of AWS monitoring and observability, providing a wealth of data that helps users gain insights into the performance and behavior of their AWS resources and applications. These metrics are numerical data points that represent various aspects of the AWS environment, such as the CPU utilization of an EC2 instance, the latency of an API Gateway, or the number of requests processed by an S3 bucket. AWS services automatically collect and publish these metrics at regular intervals, typically in 1-minute or 5-minute intervals, allowing them to track changes and trends over time.

CloudWatch Metrics offer a comprehensive view of the AWS infrastructure's operational health. Users can create customized dashboards and visualizations, set up alarms based on metric thresholds, and perform in-depth analysis of the performance of their resources. With a wide array of pre-built metrics and the ability to create custom metrics, one can tailor his monitoring strategy to meet specific needs. These metrics play a crucial role in AWS autoscaling, where they inform decisions about resource provisioning and scaling actions based on changes in demand. Whether the need is to track the performance of a single resource or monitor an entire application stack, CloudWatch metrics provide the data foundation necessary to maintain the reliability and performance of the AWS workloads.

Custom CloudWatch metrics

Creating custom AWS CloudWatch metrics is essential when the standard set of pre-defined metrics provided by AWS services does not fully address the specific monitoring and operational needs. There are several scenarios in which creating a custom AWS metric is advisable:

- **Application-specific metrics**: Custom metrics allow to collect data that is specific to the application's functionality and performance. For example, someone might want to track the number of user sign-ups, the processing time for specific application tasks, or custom error rates that are unique to the application.
- **Business metrics**: In addition to technical metrics, custom metrics enable us to monitor business-related metrics, such as revenue, conversion rates, or customer engagement. These metrics help bridge the gap between technical performance and business outcomes.

- **Non-AWS resources**: If the application relies on non-AWS resources, like on-premises servers or third-party services, one can create custom metrics to monitor the performance and health of these resources within the same CloudWatch environment.
- **Application logs and events**: By instrumenting the code to emit custom metrics based on specific events or log data, one can gain insights into application behavior that is not captured by standard CloudWatch metrics. For example, metrics can be created based on specific log patterns, errors, or anomalies.
- **Fine-grained monitoring**: Custom metrics allow for fine-grained monitoring of specific aspects of the application or infrastructure that may not be covered by standard AWS metrics. This granularity is crucial for identifying performance bottlenecks and optimizing resource utilization.
- **Integration with third-party tools**: Custom metrics can be used to integrate CloudWatch with third-party monitoring and analytics tools, enabling a unified view of the infrastructure and applications.

Custom AWS metrics helps to gain deeper insights into the AWS environment, tailor monitoring to the specific needs, and bridge the gap between technical performance metrics and the broader objectives of the business and applications. Custom metrics empower application owners to monitor, troubleshoot, optimize, and make data-driven decisions that align with the unique operational requirements.

Recipe 89: Creating a custom metric

It could be necessary to capture unsuccessful attempts to log into the AWS Management Console. Using the CloudTrail logs, a custom metric may be created to measure this. Take these steps to create a custom metric:

1. Login to the AWS Management Console and search **CloudWatch** or type in the following URL: **https://console.aws.amazon.com/cloudwatch/.**
2. Go to **Log groups** and select the **Log group** that has been created for collecting CloudTrail logs, for example, in our case, it is `fsm-aws-cloudtrail-logs`.
3. Click **Create metric filter** under **Actions** menu. Refer to *Figure 10.10* for reference:

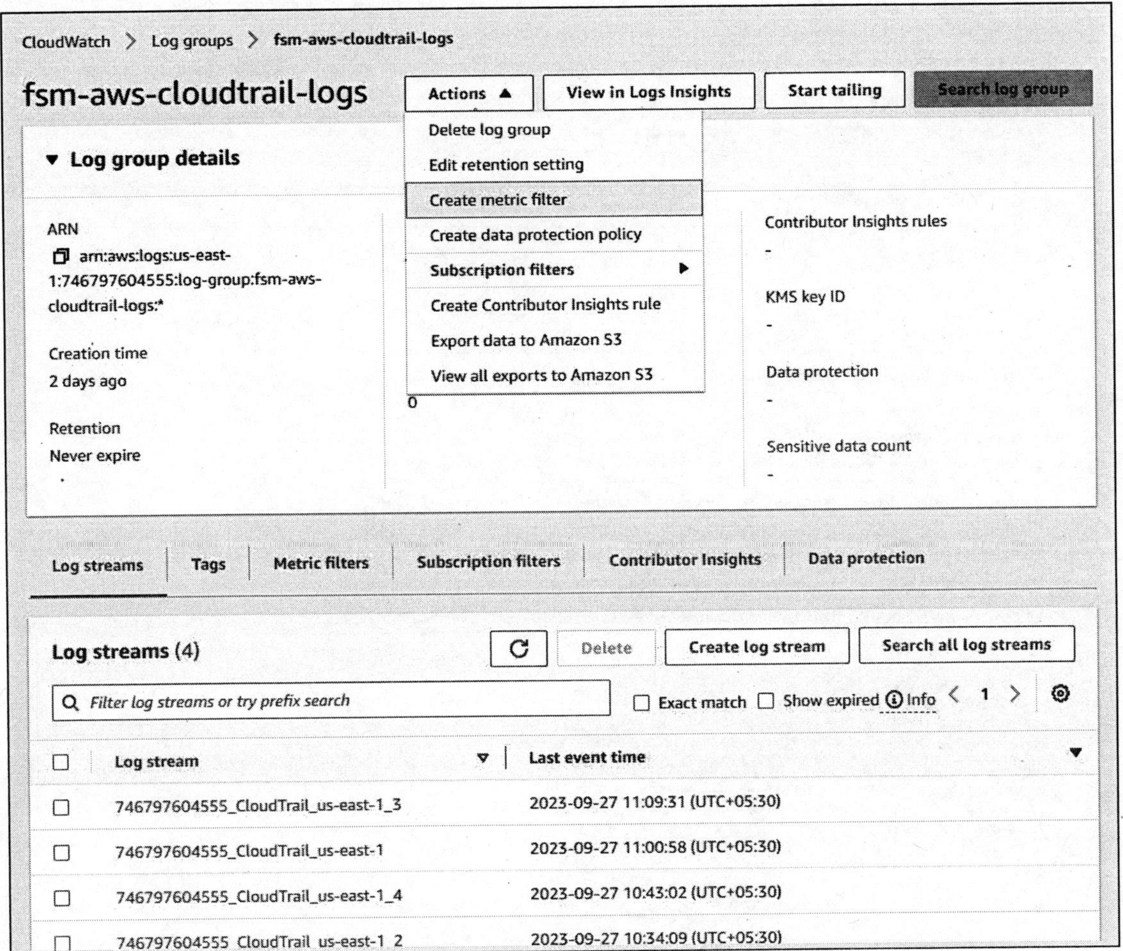

***Figure 10.10**: Creating custom metric using CloudTrail logs*

4. Paste the following pattern in the Filter pattern:

```
{ ($.eventName = ConsoleLogin) && ($.errorMessage = "Failed
authentication") }
```

5. Pattern can be optionally tested if any failed logins have already been captured. Select the **Log stream** in which failed logins have been captured from the drop down Select **Log data** to test and click Test pattern. Refer to *Figure 10.11* for reference:

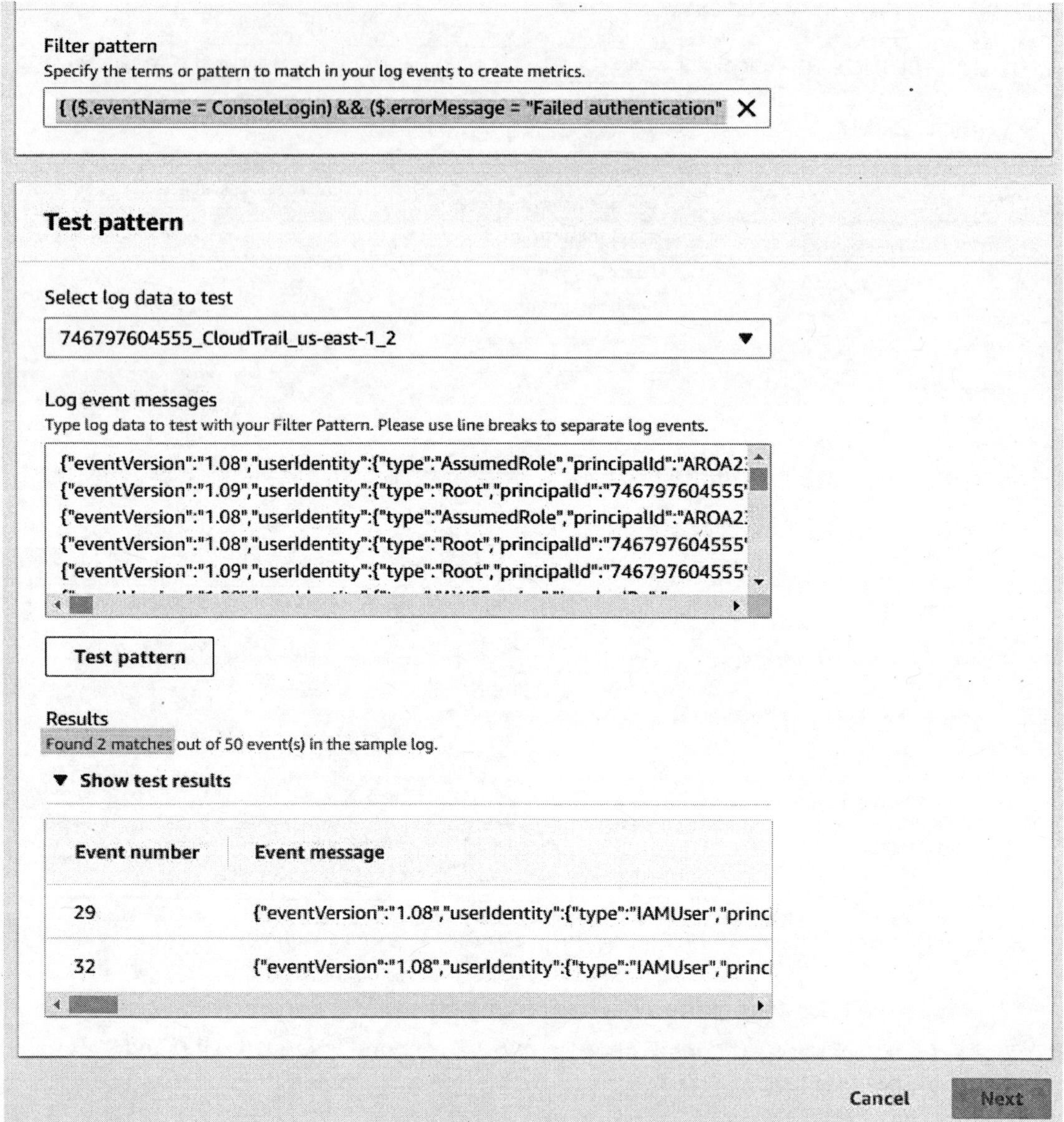

Figure 10.11: Defining filter pattern and testing it on CloudTrail Logs

In this case, the results show two instances of failed authentication events, which validate that the pattern is correct.

6. Click **Next** and provide the logical filter name, for example, **fsm-console-sign-in-failure**.
7. In **Metric details** section, give a logical metric namespace, for example, **fsm-metrics**, enable **Create new** and provide a logical metric name, for example, **fsm-**

console-sign-in-failure-count. Set Metric value as **1**, it is a value that is published to the metric name in case of an occurrence of filter pattern match. Refer to *Figure 10.12* for reference:

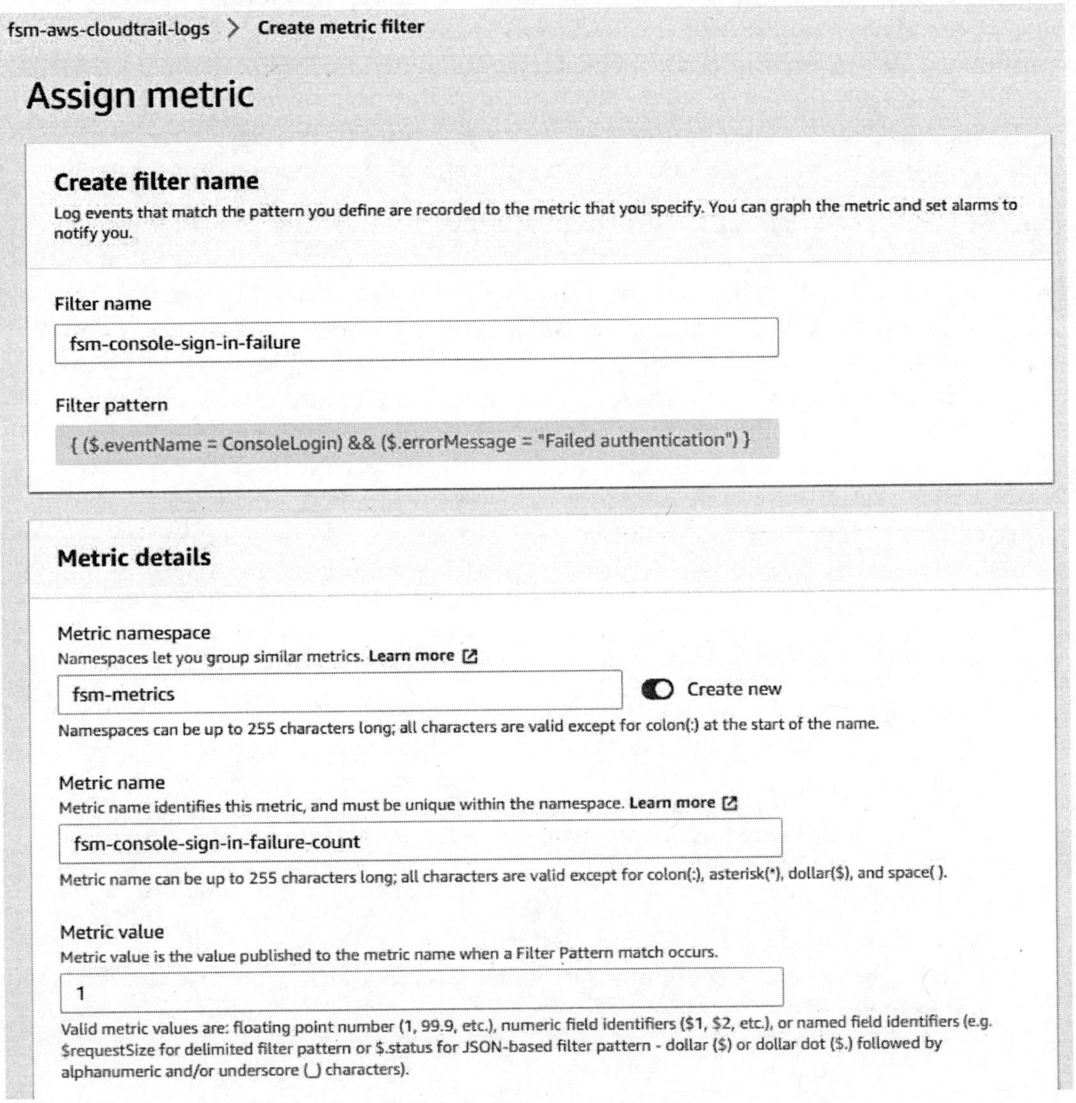

fsm-aws-cloudtrail-logs > **Create metric filter**

Assign metric

Create filter name

Log events that match the pattern you define are recorded to the metric that you specify. You can graph the metric and set alarms to notify you.

Filter name

fsm-console-sign-in-failure

Filter pattern

{ ($.eventName = ConsoleLogin) && ($.errorMessage = "Failed authentication") }

Metric details

Metric namespace

Namespaces let you group similar metrics. **Learn more**

fsm-metrics

Create new

Namespaces can be up to 255 characters long; all characters are valid except for colon(:) at the start of the name.

Metric name

Metric name identifies this metric, and must be unique within the namespace. **Learn more**

fsm-console-sign-in-failure-count

Metric name can be up to 255 characters long; all characters are valid except for colon(:), asterisk(*), dollar($), and space( ).

Metric value

Metric value is the value published to the metric name when a Filter Pattern match occurs.

1

Valid metric values are: floating point number (1, 99.9, etc.), numeric field identifiers ($1, $2, etc.), or named field identifiers (e.g. $requestSize for delimited filter pattern or $.status for JSON-based filter pattern - dollar ($) or dollar dot ($.) followed by alphanumeric and/or underscore (_) characters).

***Figure 10.12**: Configuring filter name and metric details for metric filter*

8. Click **Next**, review all the details and if all is fine again click **Create metric filter** to create the filter. The filter will be visible under the **Metric filters** tab of the log group.

Once the metric has been created, it can be used as an input for creating CloudWatch alarms.

CloudWatch alarms

Amazon CloudWatch alarms is a pivotal feature within AWS CloudWatch that enables users to proactively monitor and respond to the performance of their AWS resources and applications. These alarms act as automated triggers, allowing one to set specific thresholds for metrics and take predefined actions when those thresholds are breached. By defining alarms, one can detect issues, bottlenecks, or irregularities in the AWS environment, and promptly address them to maintain the reliability and performance of the services.

Setting up CloudWatch alarms is a straightforward process. First, select a metric to monitor, such as CPU utilization, request latency, or error rates, from the extensive list of available metrics in AWS CloudWatch. Apart from the default metrics, **custom metrics** can also be created and used in CloudWatch alarms. Next, specify the threshold values or conditions that, when met or exceeded, will trigger the alarm. These conditions can be as simple as **greater than** or **less than** a certain value, or more complex, involving multiple metrics and time periods. Once the alarm is triggered, CloudWatch can automatically initiate actions like sending notifications through Amazon **Simple Notification Service** (**SNS**), stopping, or terminating instances, or invoking AWS Lambda functions, depending on the predefined actions. This automation ensures that one can respond to issues swiftly, minimizing potential downtime and performance degradation in the AWS environment.

Recipe 90: Creating a CloudWatch Alarm

Follow the steps for creating a CloudWatch Alarm, as part of this recipe, the custom metric will be leveraged for creating the alarm:

1. Login to the AWS Management Console and search **CloudWatch** or type in the following URL: **https://console.aws.amazon.com/cloudwatch/**.
2. Go to **Log groups** and select the **Log group** that contains the custom metric filter.
3. Select the **checkbox** against the metric filter from the **Metric filters** tab that is to be used for creating the alarm and click **Create alarm**. Refer to *Figure 10.13* for reference:

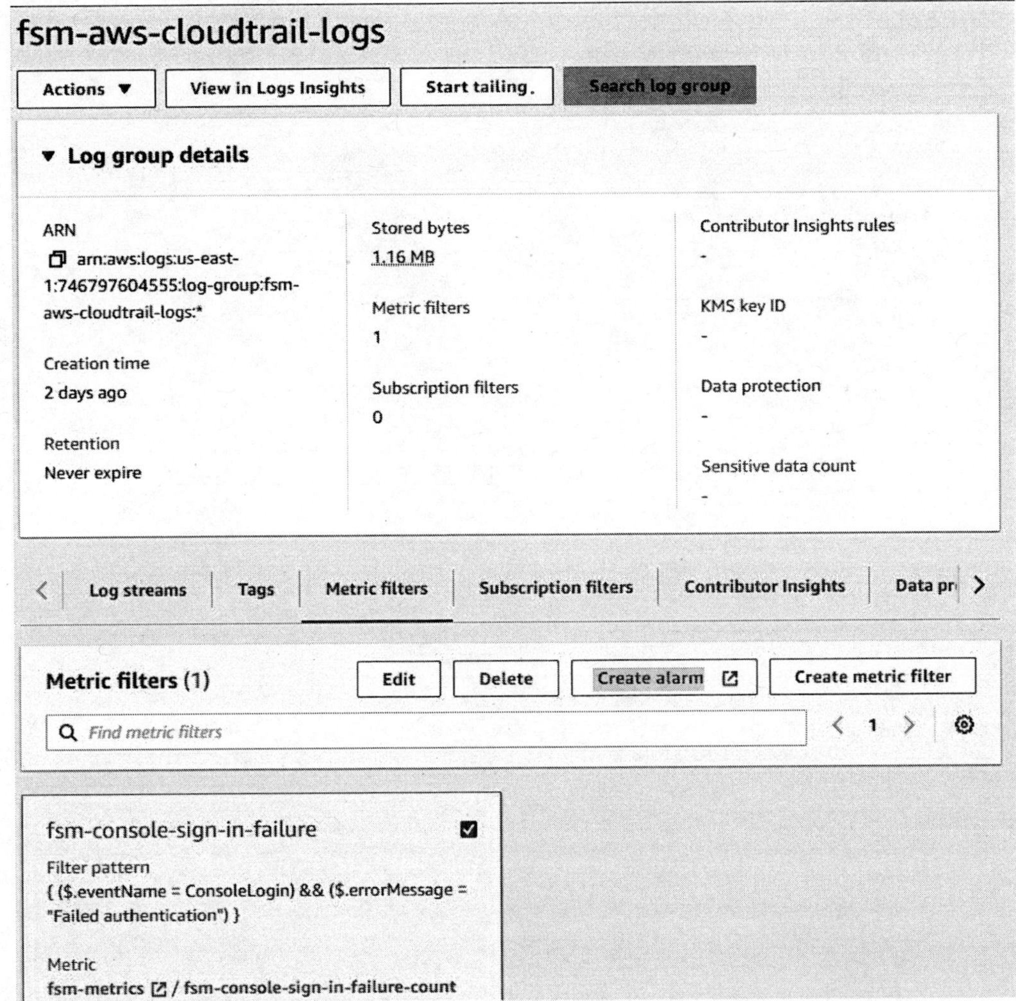

***Figure 10.13:** Creating CloudWatch alarm using custom metric filter fsm-console-sign-in-failure-count*

4. In the **Metric** section, the graph on the y-axis has the number of instances of failure events and on the x-axis is the time. Set the values as:

   a. **Statistic**: Set the value as Sum

   b. **Period**: Set the value to 1 minute

   In the **Conditions** section, set the values as:

   a. **Threshold type**: Select **Static**

   b. **Whenever fsm-console-sign-in-failure-count is**: Select **Greater | threshold**

   c. **Threshold value**: Set to **1**

The alarm will trigger if the metric value goes above the threshold value that is **`1`** in the configured period, which is **`1 minute`**. Refer to *Figure 10.14* for referencing the preceding configurations:

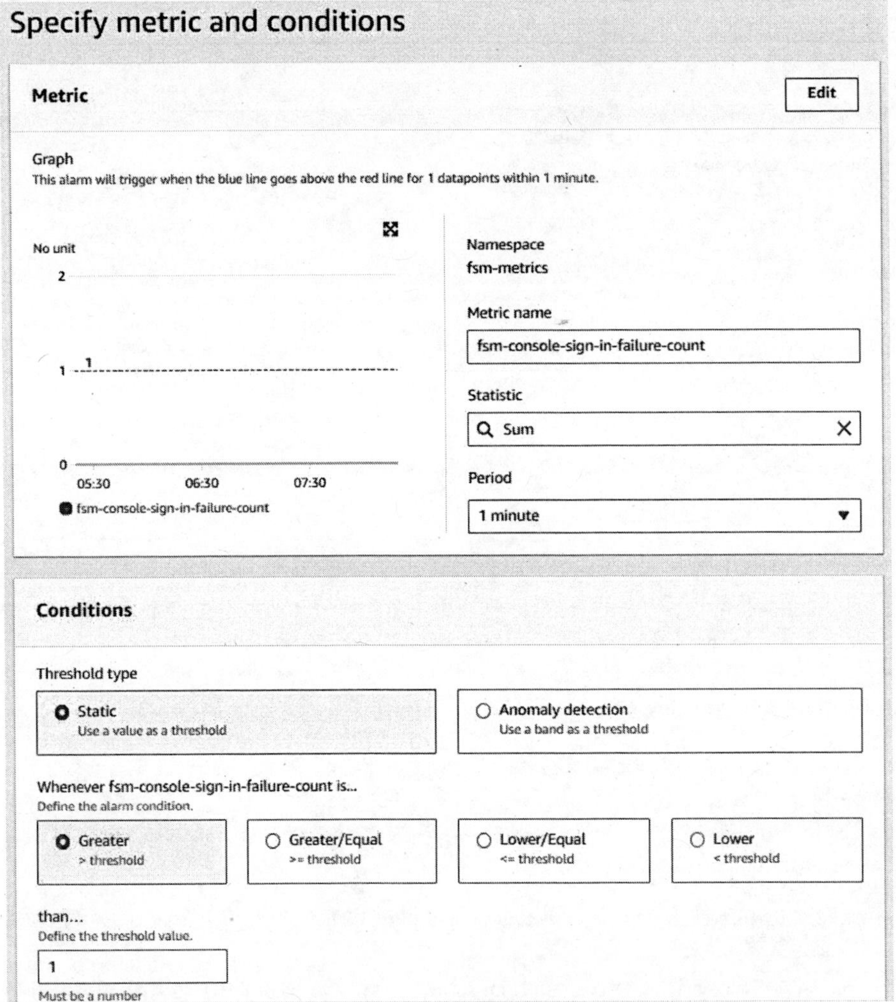

Figure 10.14: Configuring metricsand conditions for the CloudWatch alarm

5. Click **Next** and then configure the actions by setting the following values:
    a. **Alarm state trigger**: Select **In alarm**, which means that the action is to be taken when the **`fsm-console-sign-in-failure-count`** is in an alarm state.
    b. **Send a notification to the following SNS topic**: Select **Create new topic**, this is the topic to which the notification using Amazon **Simple Notification Service** (**SNS**) will be sent in case of an alarm.
    c. Provide a logical name for the topic, for example, **`fsm-alarm-topic`**.

d. Provide email endpoints that will receive the notification, add comma separated email addresses, each recipient needs to confirm the subscription request for the topic sent to them over email.

e. Click **Create topic** to create the topic, refer to *Figure 10.15* for reference:

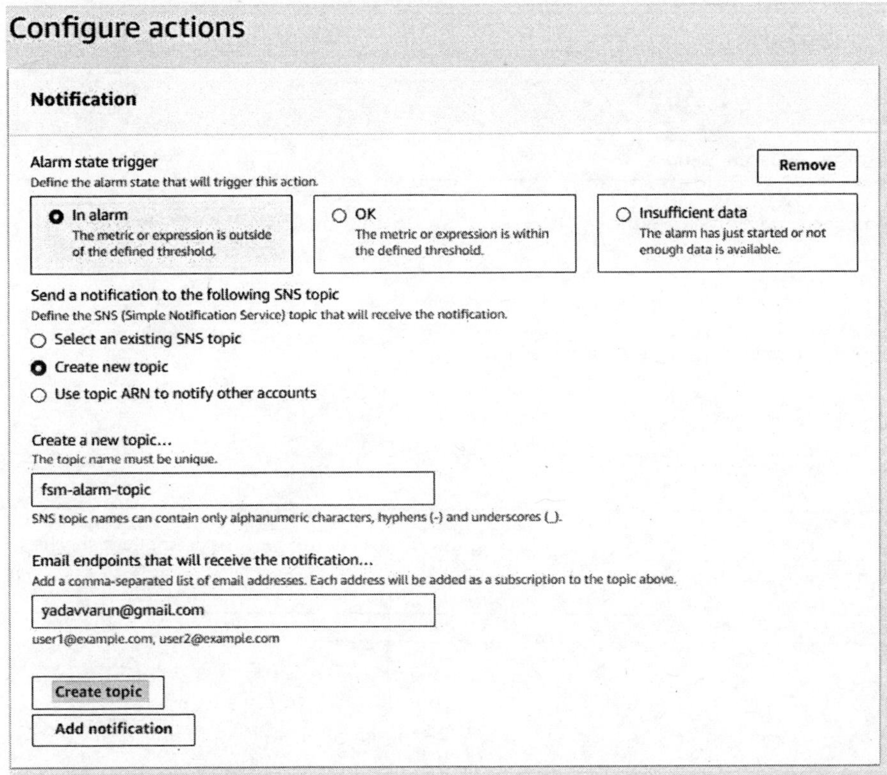

***Figure 10.15**: Configuring actions for the CloudWatch alarm*

f. Click the conformation link on the email that has been received on the above-mentioned email address. Refer to *Figure 10.16* to get the reference of the email containing the **Confirm subscription** link:

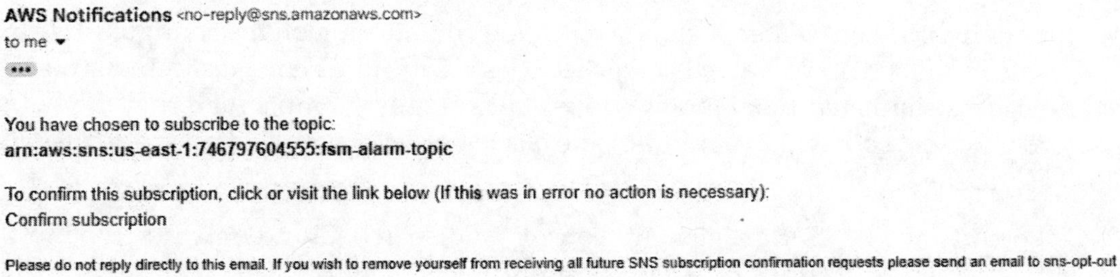

AWS Notifications <no-reply@sns.amazonaws.com>
to me ▾

You have chosen to subscribe to the topic:
arn:aws:sns:us-east-1:746797604555:fsm-alarm-topic

To confirm this subscription, click or visit the link below (If this was in error no action is necessary):
Confirm subscription

Please do not reply directly to this email. If you wish to remove yourself from receiving all future SNS subscription confirmation requests please send an email to sns-opt-out

***Figure 10.16**: SNS topic subscription confirmation email*

6. Click **Next** and provide a logical name of the alarm, for example **`fsm-console-sign-in-failure-alarm`**. Refer to *Figure 10.17* for reference:

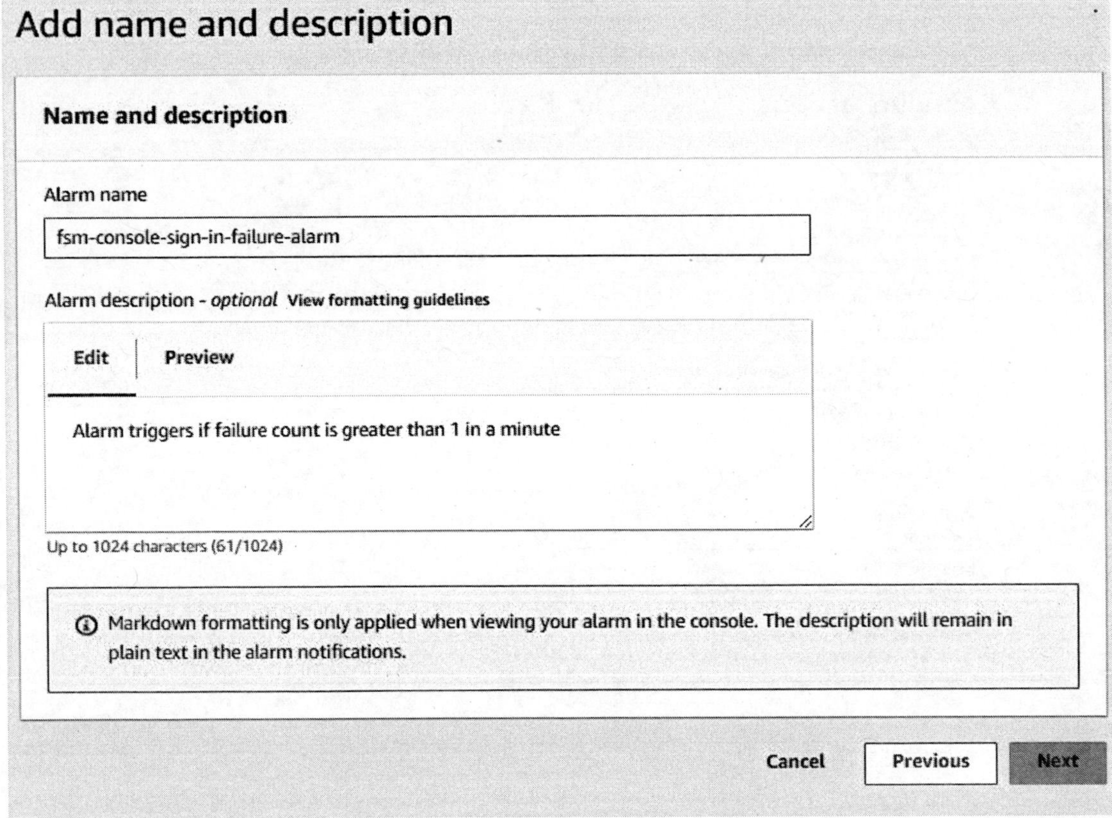

Figure 10.17: *Setting alarm name and description for the CloudWatch alarm*

7. Click **Next** to review all the configurations and then finally click **Create alarm** to create the alarm.

Recipe 91: Triggering and viewing an alarm

Once the alarm has been created, there is continuous monitoring on the configured metric, and whenever the threshold value is breached, the alarm status changes to **In alarm**. The scenario can be simulated by manually doing failed login attempts (entering the wrong password twice or more within a minute), the alarm gets triggered and can be accessed by following the steps:

1. Login to the AWS Management Console and search **CloudWatch** or type in the following URL: **https://console.aws.amazon.com/cloudwatch/**.

2. Go to **All alarms** and select `fsm-console-sign-in-failure-alarm`.

3. The graph shows the number of occurrences of failure as 3 and its status changes to **In alarm**. Refer to *Figure 1.18* for reference:

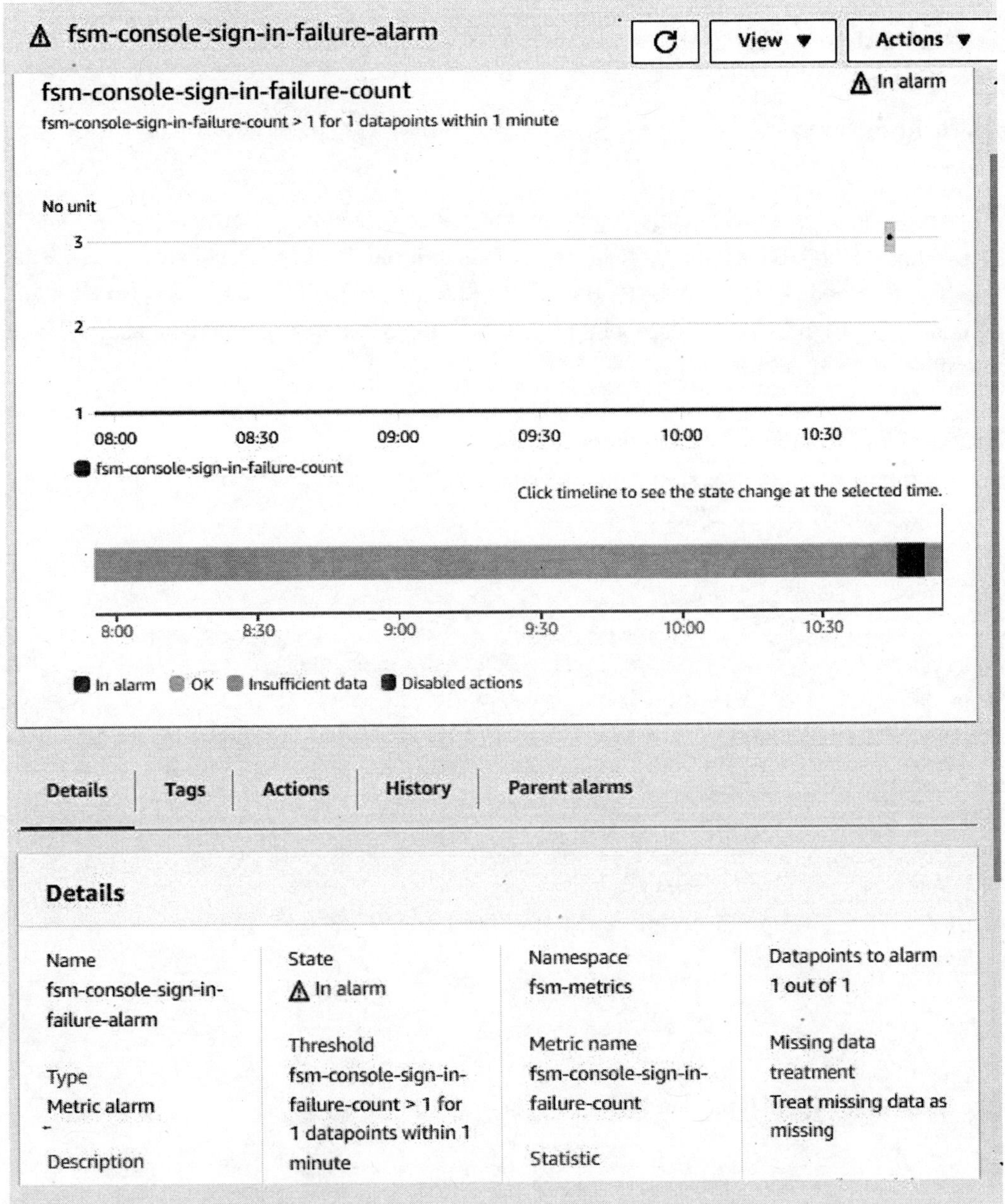

Figure 10.18: *fsm-console-sign-in-failure-alarm is in state In alarm*

4. The configured alarm action to send an email to subscribed recipients can be validated by viewing the email from **AWS Notifications** in the mail box. Refer to *Figure 19.19* to get the reference of the email:

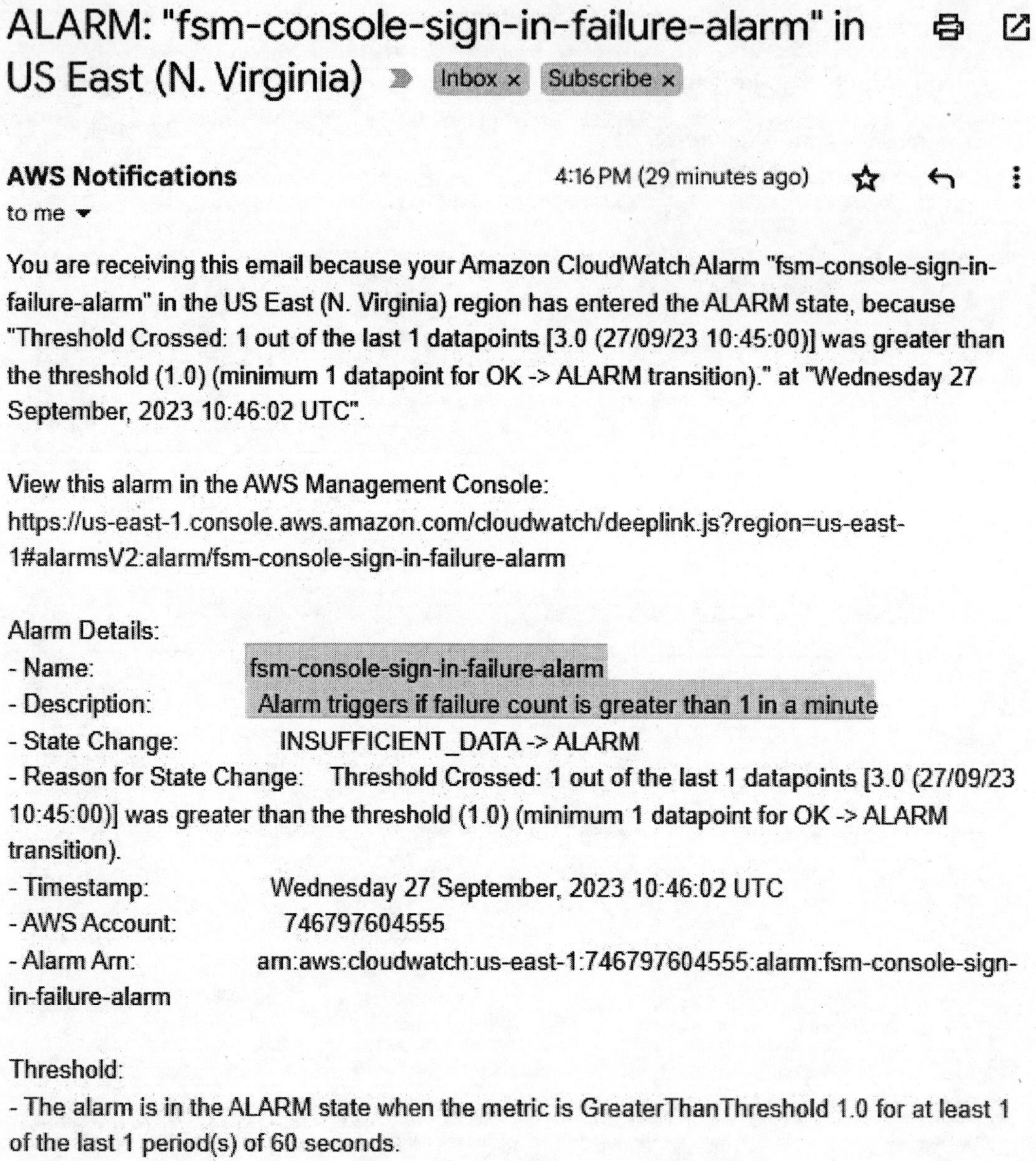

ALARM: "fsm-console-sign-in-failure-alarm" in US East (N. Virginia) Inbox × Subscribe ×

AWS Notifications 4:16 PM (29 minutes ago)

to me

You are receiving this email because your Amazon CloudWatch Alarm "fsm-console-sign-in-failure-alarm" in the US East (N. Virginia) region has entered the ALARM state, because "Threshold Crossed: 1 out of the last 1 datapoints [3.0 (27/09/23 10:45:00)] was greater than the threshold (1.0) (minimum 1 datapoint for OK -> ALARM transition)." at "Wednesday 27 September, 2023 10:46:02 UTC".

View this alarm in the AWS Management Console:
https://us-east-1.console.aws.amazon.com/cloudwatch/deeplink.js?region=us-east-1#alarmsV2:alarm/fsm-console-sign-in-failure-alarm

Alarm Details:
- Name: fsm-console-sign-in-failure-alarm
- Description: Alarm triggers if failure count is greater than 1 in a minute
- State Change: INSUFFICIENT_DATA -> ALARM
- Reason for State Change: Threshold Crossed: 1 out of the last 1 datapoints [3.0 (27/09/23 10:45:00)] was greater than the threshold (1.0) (minimum 1 datapoint for OK -> ALARM transition).
- Timestamp: Wednesday 27 September, 2023 10:46:02 UTC
- AWS Account: 746797604555
- Alarm Arn: arn:aws:cloudwatch:us-east-1:746797604555:alarm:fsm-console-sign-in-failure-alarm

Threshold:
- The alarm is in the ALARM state when the metric is GreaterThanThreshold 1.0 for at least 1 of the last 1 period(s) of 60 seconds.

***Figure 10.19**: AWS alarm notification email*

CloudWatch dashboards

Amazon CloudWatch dashboards provide a powerful and customizable way to visualize and monitor the AWS resources and applications in real-time. These dashboards enable users to aggregate and display CloudWatch metrics, logs, and alarms in a single, interactive view. They serve as a central hub for monitoring and troubleshooting, allowing administrators to gain immediate insights into the operational health of the AWS environment.

With CloudWatch dashboards customized, multi-widget views can be created that are tailored to specific monitoring needs. One can choose from a wide range of available widgets, including line charts, stacked area charts, text, and alarms, to build comprehensive dashboards that provide a holistic view of the infrastructure and applications. Dashboards also support the embedding of custom HTML and image widgets to include external content or diagrams to enhance the monitoring experience.

These dashboards are especially valuable for DevOps teams and system administrators who need to track **key performance indicators (KPIs)** and critical metrics in real-time. By visualizing metrics and alarms on a single dashboard, teams can respond quickly to issues, troubleshoot effectively, and ensure the optimal performance and availability of their AWS resources and applications. CloudWatch dashboards contribute to improved operational efficiency and the ability to make data-driven decisions in AWS environments.

Recipe 92: Creating custom CloudWatch dashboard

Though AWS CloudWatch provides a default dashboard with multiple widgets, each showing a different CloudWatch metric. The dashboard is available on the home screen on Amazon CloudWatch.

Amazon CloudWatch also has a provision to create custom dashboards, follow the steps for creating the same:

1. Login to the AWS Management Console and search **CloudWatch** or type in the following URL: **https://console.aws.amazon.com/cloudwatch/.**

2. Go to **Dashboards** and click **Create dashboard**.

3. Give a logical name to the dashboard, for example, `fsm-admin-dashboard`.

4. Add a widget from the available widgets, for example **Alarm status** and click **Next**. Refer to *Figure 10.20* for reference:

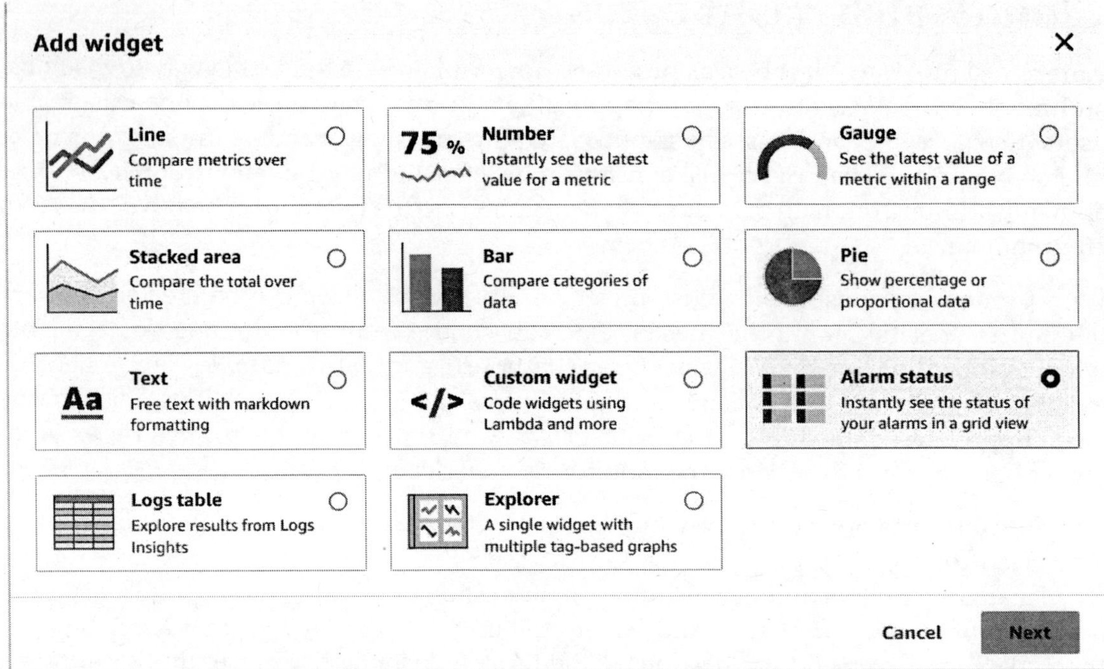

Figure 10.20: Selecting an Alarm status widget for the custom dashboard

5. Select the alarm `fsm-console-sign-in-failure-alarm` and click the **Create widget**.
6. Give a logical title of the widget, for example, Console Failed Login Alarm, and click **Add to dashboard**.
7. Add more widgets by clicking the + or **Add** button. This time, select the **Bar widget** and **Metrics** as the data source.
8. From the available metrics category, choose **ECS metric** and select `MemoryUtilization` metric. Refer to *Figure 10.21* for reference:

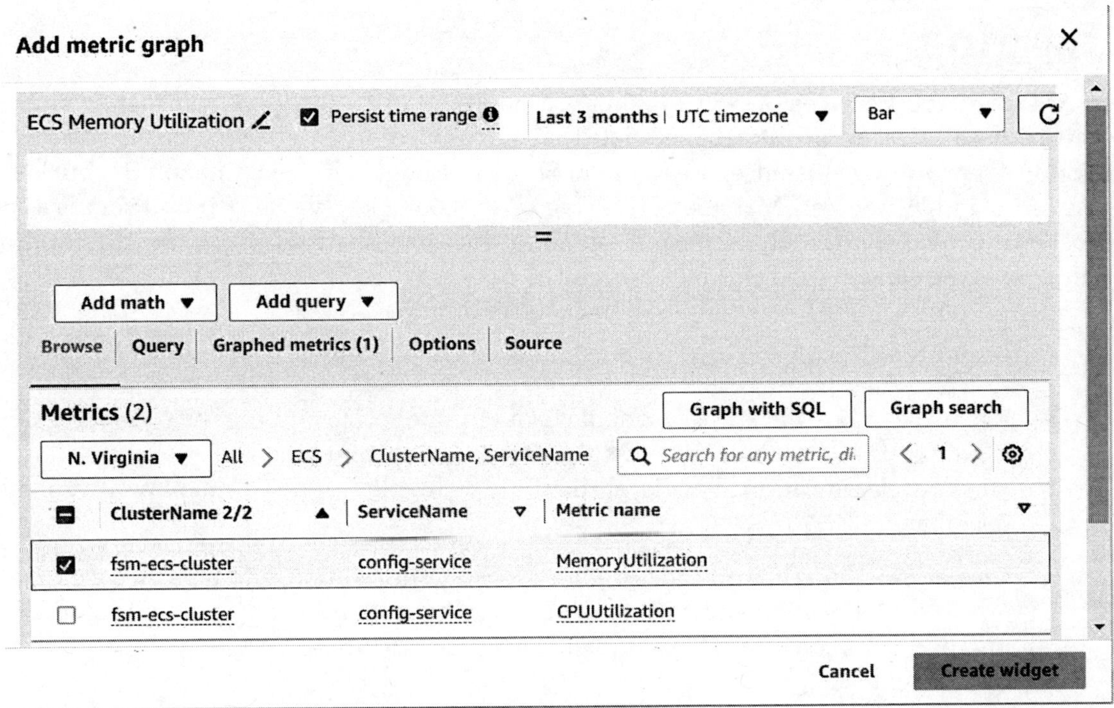

Figure 10.21: Adding a Bar widget with MemoryUtilization metric

9. Click **Create widget** to create the widget. Similarly, more widgets can be added with different CloudWatch metrics or logs

10. Click **Save** to save the dashboard. *Figure 10.22* refers to the **`fsm-admin-dashboard`**:

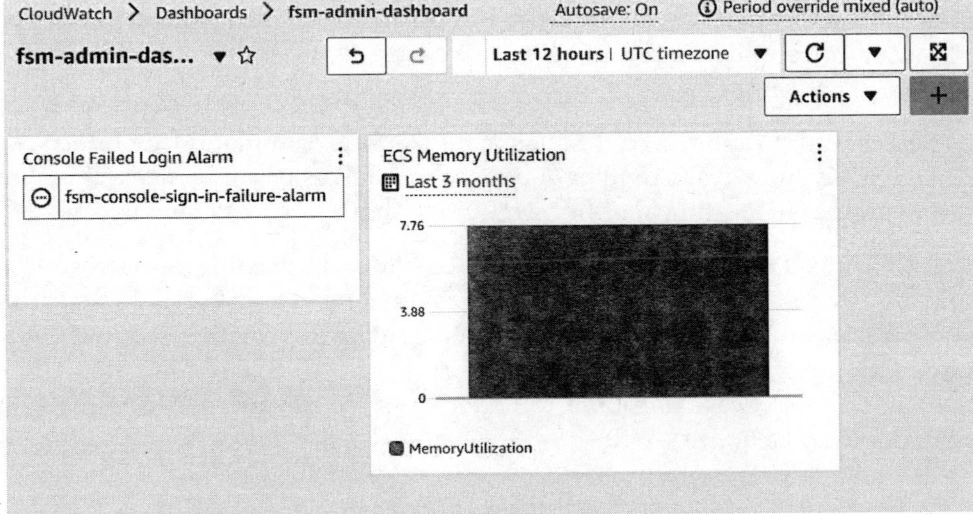

Figure 10.22: fsm-admin-dashboard

Tagging

In **Amazon Web Services (AWS)**, tagging is a powerful organizational and management feature that allows users to attach metadata to AWS resources like Amazon Elastic Compute Cloud (Amazon EC2) instance, an Amazon Simple Storage Service (Amazon S3) bucket, or a secret in AWS Secrets Manager, etc. A tag consists of a key-value pair and serves as a label that provides additional information about the associated resource; tag keys & tag values are case sensitive. Tags can be applied to a wide range of AWS resources, including instances, volumes, security groups, S3 buckets, and more.

Tags are immensely useful for several purposes:

- **Resource organization**: Tags enable users to categorize and organize resources in a way that reflects their business structure, application architecture, or any other relevant classification. This is particularly valuable in environments with many resources.
- **Cost allocation**: AWS provides detailed billing information, and tags play a crucial role in cost allocation and budgeting. By tagging resources with specific identifiers, organizations can easily track and allocate costs to different projects, departments, or cost centers.
- **Automation and resource management**: Tags are often used in automation scripts and policies. For instance, AWS IAM policies can be configured to grant or restrict permissions based on tags. This allows for fine-grained control over resource access.
- **Operational Insights**: Tags contribute to operational insights by providing additional context about resources. Tags can include information such as application version, environment (for example, production or development), owner, or compliance status. This makes it easier to understand the purpose and state of each resource.
- **Search and filtering**: AWS Management Console, **command line interface (CLI)**, and SDKs allow users to filter and search resources based on tags. This simplifies the process of locating specific resources within a large AWS environment.

Tags can be applied when creating resources or added to existing resources, providing flexibility and adaptability to changing organizational needs. AWS services such as AWS Resource Groups and AWS Cost Explorer leverage tags to provide users with enhanced visibility and management capabilities across their AWS environment. Ultimately, effective tagging practices contribute to better resource governance, cost management, and operational efficiency in AWS.

Recipe 93: Adding tag to S3 bucket using AWS CLI

Run the below AWS CLI command for adding tags to the S3 bucket *fs-marketplace-bucket* to mark it as part of the production environment:

```
aws s3api put-bucket-tagging --bucket fs-marketplace-bucket \
--tagging 'TagSet=[{Key=Environment,Value=production},{Key=CostCenter,Val-
ue=123}]'
```

Here,

- **bucket** defines the name of the bucket to which the tags need to be added.
- **tagging** is a container for **TagSet** and **Tags**.
- **TagSet** is a list of sets of tags. 2 tags have been added with key **Environment** and value **production**; and key **CostCenter** and value **123.**

Refer to *Figure 10.23* for the effect of the above command:

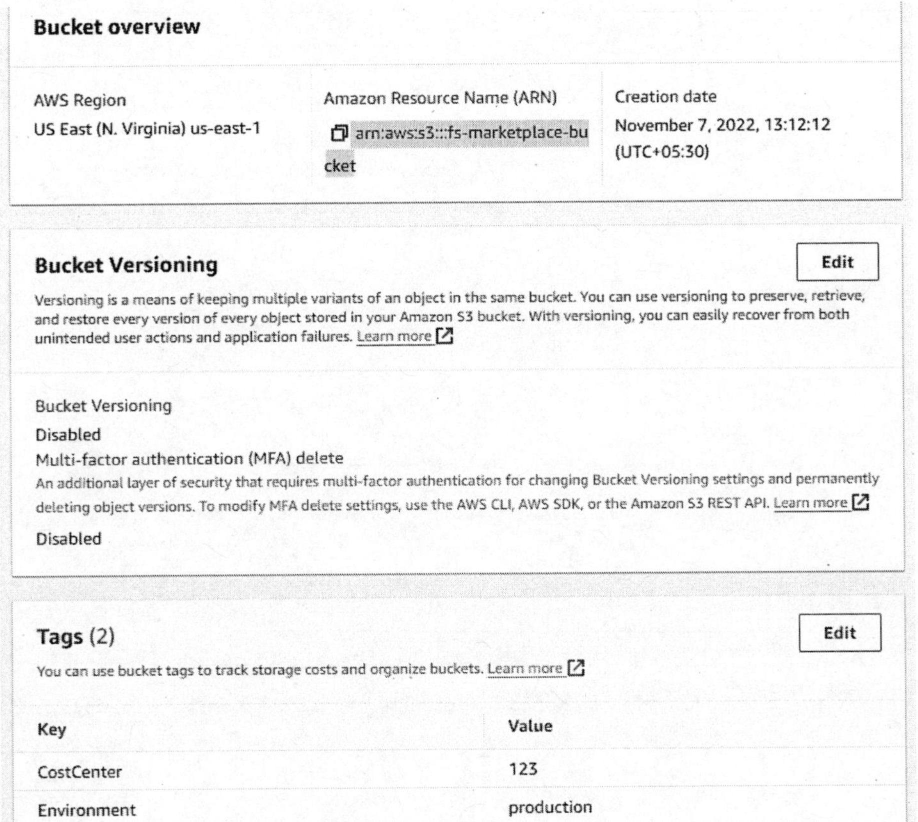

Figure 10.23: *Tags added to fs-marketplace-bucket*

Recipe 94: Adding tag to ECS cluster using AWS CLI

Run the below AWS CLI command for adding tags to the ECS cluster **`fsm-ecs-cluster`** to mark it as part of the production environment:

```
aws ecs tag-resource \
--resource-arn arn:aws:ecs:us-east-1:746797604555:cluster/fsm-ecs-cluster \
--tags key=Environment,value=production key=CostCenter,value=123
```

Here,

- **`resource-arn`** is the **Amazon Resource Name** (**ARN**) of the resource to which the tags need to be added.
- **`tags`** hold a list of key and value pair. 2 tags have been added with key **`Environment`** and value **`production`**; and key **`CostCenter`** and value **`123`**.

Refer to *Figure 10.24* for the response to the above command:

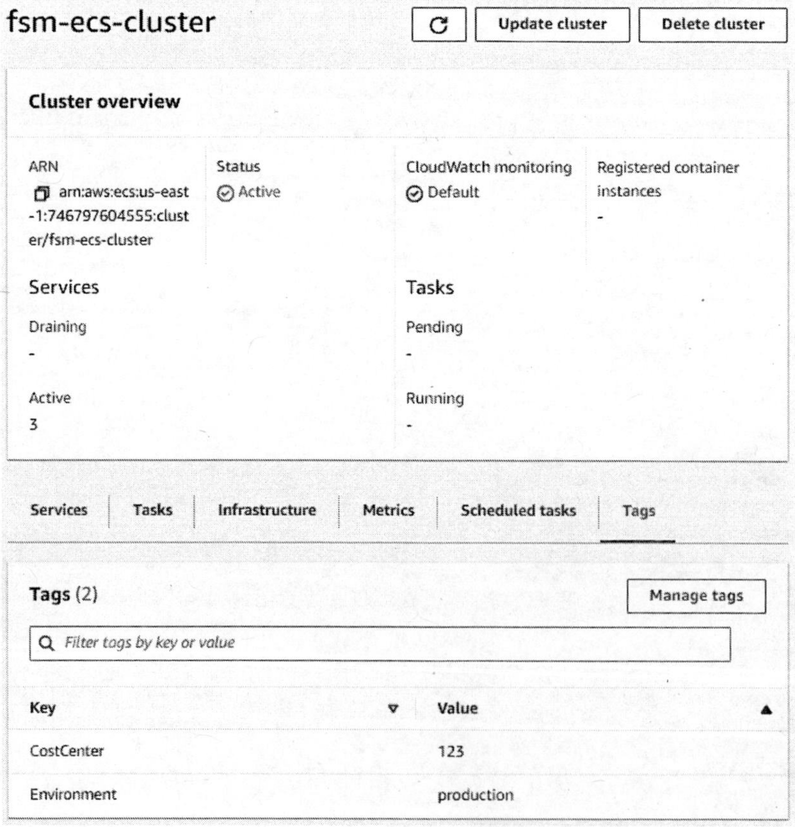

Figure 10.24: *Tags added to fsm-ecs-cluster*

Recipe 95: Adding tag to AWS RDS using AWS CLI

Run the below AWS CLI command for adding tags to the RDS instance **`fs-marketplace`** to mark it as part of the production environment:

```
aws rds add-tags-to-resource \
--resource-name arn:aws:rds:us-east-1:746797604555:db:fs-marketplace \
--tags '[{"Key": "Environment","Value": "production"},{"Key":
"CostCenter","Value": "123"}]'
```

Here,

- **`resource-name`** is the name **Application Resource Name (ARN)** of the resource to which the tags need to be added.
- **`Tags`** hold list of tags that are key value pair. The tags can be provided in the simple *Key=string,Value=string* format or in the JSON format as shown in the above command. 2 tags have been added with key **`Environment`** and value **`production`**; and key **`CostCenter`** and value **`123`**.

Refer to *Figure 10.25* for the response of the above command:

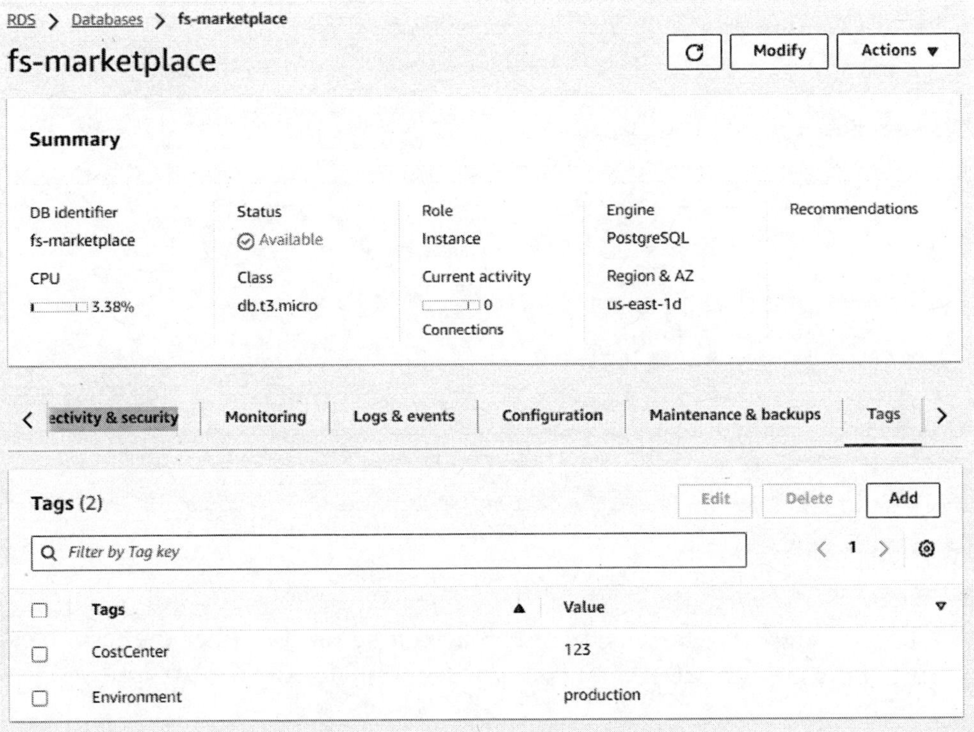

Figure 10.25: *Tags added to RDS fs-marketplace*

Recipe 96: Creating cost report for production resources

The tags added in the previously recipes are very helpful in generating the cost and usage reports for a group of resources. Follow the below steps for generating the report for production resources:

1. Login to the AWS Management Console and search **billing** or type in the following URL: **https://console.aws.amazon.com/billing/**.
2. Click on **Cost allocation tags** from the left menu.
3. Select the tag **Environment** and click **Activate**. Refer to *Figure 10.26* for reference:

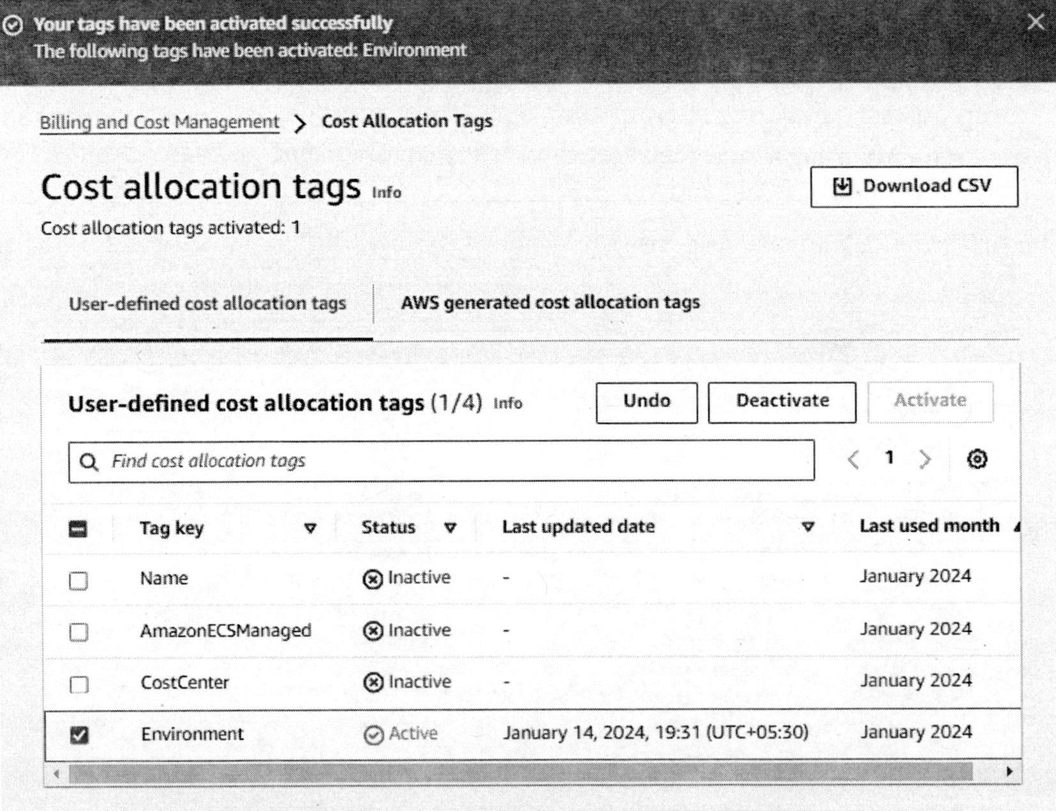

***Figure 10.26**: Environment has been activated as a cost allocation tag*

Once the tags have been activated, they can be used to filter the resources in the cost and usage report. It can take up to 24 hours for the tags to appear in the tag's filter.

4. Click on **Cost Explorer** from the left menu.

5. There are many filters available on the right-hand side, look for a filter with the name tag. Choose tag **Environment** from the drop down. On selecting the **Environment** tag a new filter appears for the selected tag, that is, **Environment.**
6. Open the drop down of the new filter, select includes and then select **production,** refer to *Figure 10.27* for reference:

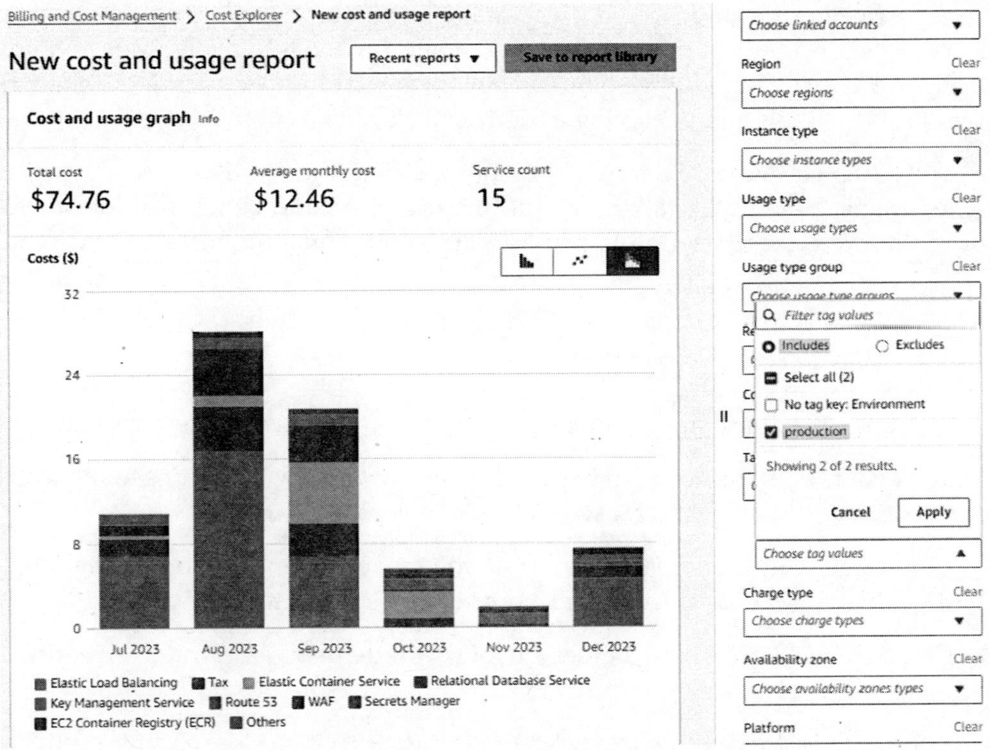

Figure 10.27: *Using cost allocation tags to filter cost reports*

7. Click **Apply** to apply the filter and view the cost report only for the resources used in the production environment.

The report can also be saved to the library if required.

Conclusion

In this chapter, we explored the concept of observability and equipped readers with practical skills and insights into harnessing CloudWatch Logs, CloudTrail, alarms, dashboards, and AWS tags for comprehensive observability and operational excellence. By implementing these recipes, readers are empowered to maintain the reliability, security, and performance of their AWS-based applications and services while proactively responding to evolving operational needs. The knowledge gained is instrumental in maximizing the potential of AWS observability tools and achieving operational excellence in the cloud.

In the next chapter, we will learn about automating the infrastructure setup using **Infrastructure as Code** (**IaC**), talking about the principles and benefits of IaC, including tools and best practices for defining, provisioning, and managing infrastructure through code.

Points to remember

- Log data can be organized into log groups and log streams for effective management.
- Log agents or SDKs are used to send log data to CloudWatch Logs for analysis and retention.
- CloudTrail trails are created to define the resources and regions to monitor, and they deliver logs to an Amazon S3 bucket or CloudWatch Logs.
- CloudWatch alarms can be set on both predefined AWS metrics and custom metrics.
- Actions triggered by CloudWatch alarms can include sending notifications via Amazon SNS, invoking AWS Lambda functions, or stopping/terminating instances.
- Dashboards support a variety of widgets, including line charts, text, alarms, and custom HTML.
- Dashboards can be shared across to monitor critical resources and performance metrics.
- Tags in AWS provide a means to add contextual information to resources.
- Tags enable efficient search and filtering of resources based on specific criteria. This capability is invaluable for observability as it allows users to quickly locate and focus on relevant resources within a large AWS environment.

Questions

1. What are managed policies, and how do they differ from inline policies?
2. What is the primary purpose of AWS CloudWatch Logs, and how does it contribute to observability in AWS?
3. Why and how can custom log data be integrated with CloudWatch Logs?
4. What is the role of AWS CloudTrail in AWS observability? How does it differ from CloudWatch Logs?
5. How do CloudWatch alarms contribute to real-time monitoring and proactive issue resolution?
6. What is the purpose of CloudWatch dashboards in AWS, and how can they be used to enhance observability?
7. How can observability tools like CloudWatch Logs, CloudTrail, alarms, and dashboards contribute to security analysis and compliance monitoring in AWS?
8. Describe a situation where you might need to create a custom CloudWatch metric, and how would you set it up?
9. How do AWS observability tools enable data-driven decision-making and optimization of AWS resources and applications?
10. How can AWS tags be effectively utilized to enhance cost allocation and provide organizational insights in a large and dynamic cloud environment?
11. Are there any third-party tools available for AWS observability?
12. How can serverless applications be monitored in AWS?

Join our book's Discord space

Join the book's Discord Workspace for Latest updates, Offers, Tech happenings around the world, New Release and Sessions with the Authors:

https://discord.bpbonline.com

CHAPTER 11

Infrastructure Automation with IaC

Introduction

The previous chapter explained the importance of observability in the world of microservices. It explained the logging and monitoring of applications and how they can be achieved by using different services offered by cloud providers like AWS. The chapter also demonstrated how to leverage these services to gain crucial insights on cloud-based applications and supporting systems.

In this chapter, we will cover an important concept of automatically provisioning the application infrastructure via **Infrastructure as Code** (**IaC**). The chapter lays down the foundation of the most widespread used IaC tool in the industry, that is **Terraform**. We will walk through step-by-step with examples for creating Terraform scripts and executing them for provisioning of the infrastructure in the AWS cloud. Finally, it will demonstrate a very useful feature of importing the existing infrastructure into Terraform and using them in creating infrastructure provisioning scripts.

Structure

In this chapter, we will discuss following topics:

- Introduction to Infrastructure as Code
- Terraform

- Getting started with Terraform
- Writing Terraform scripts
- Provisioning infrastructure with Terraform
- Importing existing infrastructure in Terraform

Objectives

The objective of this chapter is to provide a comprehensive guide to IaC by covering essential topics and hands-on lab exercises. Readers will learn how to get started with Terraform, from installing it to writing their first Terraform script. They will gain proficiency in provisioning infrastructure in the AWS cloud using Terraform, exploring key concepts. The chapter will also demonstrate how to import current infrastructure into Terraform, giving readers the ability to efficiently manage both new and legacy resources. By the end of the chapter, readers will have a strong foundation in IaC principles and the practical skills needed to manage infrastructure with Terraform in AWS.

Introduction to Infrastructure as Code

Infrastructure as Code (**IaC**) represents a transformative approach to managing and provisioning infrastructure in the world of modern software development and IT operations. At its core, Infrastructure as a Code is the process of treating servers, networks, databases, and other resources as code, enabling code to be used for definition, creation, and management of these resources instead of manual processes or configuration files. This paradigm shift, rooted in principles borrowed from software development, has brought unprecedented efficiency, reliability, and scalability to infrastructure management, making it an integral part of DevOps practices and cloud computing.

In traditional IT operations, provisioning and managing infrastructure often involved time-consuming, error-prone, and manual tasks. IaC, however, flips this model by introducing automation, version control, and consistency. With IaC, infrastructure is defined using code, written in languages like **HashiCorp Configuration Language** (**HCL**), YAML, or JSON. This code serves as a blueprint for the infrastructure's desired state. IaC tools, such as Terraform, Ansible, and AWS CloudFormation, interpret this code and automatically create and configure resources accordingly. This not only accelerates the provisioning process but also ensures that infrastructure remains consistent and repeatable across environments. It allows for tracking changes, reviewing code, and applying testing and quality assurance principles to infrastructure, bringing it in line with software development practices.

One of the primary benefits of IaC is its ability to deliver infrastructure agility. In a rapidly changing technology landscape, IaC enables organizations to adapt quickly to evolving requirements and to scale resources up or down as needed. Moreover, IaC fosters collaboration between development and operations teams, as they work together to define, manage, and evolve infrastructure code. This convergence is a hallmark of DevOps, where infrastructure and application development are tightly integrated, leading to smoother releases and more reliable systems. As a result, IaC has become a fundamental pillar of efficient, reliable, and scalable infrastructure management in the age of cloud computing and digital transformation.

Following are a few popular IaC tools:

- **Terraform**: Terraform by HashiCorp is an open-source IaC tool that enables the provisioning and management of infrastructure resources across various cloud providers and platforms using declarative code.
- **AWS CloudFormation**: It a service from **Amazon Web Services** (**AWS**) for defining and provisioning AWS infrastructure as code. It uses JSON or YAML templates to create and manage AWS resources.
- **Ansible**: Ansible is an open-source automation tool that focuses on configuration management and application deployment.
- **Puppet**: Puppet is a configuration management tool that allows to define and enforce the desired state of infrastructure and applications. It is particularly useful for managing large server fleets.
- **Chef**: Chef is another popular configuration management tool that provides infrastructure automation using recipes and cookbooks. It enables you to define, deploy, and manage Infrastructure as Code.
- **SaltStack**: SaltStack is an event-driven automation and orchestration tool that uses YAML for defining infrastructure states. It excels in remote execution and configuration management tasks.
- **Google Cloud Deployment Manager**: It is **Google Cloud Platform's** (**GCP**) IaC tool, allowing users to define and deploy GCP resources using YAML or Python templates.
- **Azure Resource Manager**: It is designed for Microsoft Azure and enable the definition and deployment of Azure infrastructure using JSON templates.
- **Pulumi**: It is an IaC tool that empowers developers to use familiar programming languages for cloud infrastructure deployment, bridging the gap between software development and infrastructure provisioning.
- **Juju**: It is an IaC tool that abstracts complexity, streamlining the modeling and management of services across various cloud and container environments

Amongst above **Terraform** is one of the most widely used IaC tools in the industry because of its multi-cloud support, declarative language, integration with version control systems, compliance, and governance.

Terraform

Terraform, developed by HashiCorp, is a highly versatile and widely adopted IaC tool that has transformed the way infrastructure is provisioned and managed in modern IT environments. It empowers organizations to define, create, and maintain their infrastructure through code, enabling a more efficient, repeatable, and scalable approach to managing resources in the cloud, on-premises, or across hybrid environments.

At the heart of Terraform is its declarative configuration language, HCL, which allows users to express the desired state of their infrastructure. Terraform users can define resources such as virtual machines, networks, databases, and security groups, as well as their interdependencies by describing infrastructure in a readable and easy-to-understand manner. This code-based approach replaces manual, error-prone infrastructure setup with automated and consistent provisioning, greatly reducing the risk of misconfigurations.

One of Terraform's standout features is its multi-cloud and multi-provider support. Organizations can use a single Terraform configuration to manage resources across various cloud providers, including AWS, Azure, Google Cloud, and more. This versatility is especially valuable for businesses with diverse infrastructure requirements or those transitioning to a multi-cloud strategy. Terraform's rich ecosystem of providers and modules extends its capabilities, enabling users to interact with a broad spectrum of services and resources.

Terraform's infrastructure definitions are versioned and stored in a version control system, typically Git. This not only facilitates collaboration among development and operations teams but also enables infrastructure as code to be managed just like application code. The inclusion of infrastructure code in the same version control system as application code fosters DevOps practices, streamlines collaboration, and supports best practices in **continuous integration** and **continuous deployment** (**CI/CD**).

Terraform's extensive community and vibrant ecosystem provide users with a wealth of resources, from community-contributed modules to official documentation. Additionally, HashiCorp offers commercial products like Terraform Enterprise for larger organizations, delivering advanced features and enhanced support. All these aspects combine to make Terraform a powerful, versatile, and user-friendly tool for automating and managing infrastructure at scale.

Terraform lifecycle

Terraform follows a lifecycle that consists of several key phases: init, plan, apply, and destroy. These phases help users define, create, update, and potentially remove infrastructure resources using Terraform configurations:

init

The **init** phase is the first step in the Terraform lifecycle. It is primarily responsible for initializing a new or existing Terraform project. During this phase, Terraform initializes the working directory and downloads any provider plugins and modules specified in your configuration. terraform init is run when a new project is set up or changes are made to the provider configurations. This command ensures that Terraform has all the necessary dependencies to manage your infrastructure. Below is the syntax for this command:

```
terraform init
```

plan

The **plan** phase is where Terraform examines the configuration and the existing infrastructure to determine what changes, if any, are required to achieve the desired state defined in the Terraform code. Running terraform plan generates a plan that outlines the actions Terraform will take, such as creating new resources, updating existing ones, or destroying resources. It provides an opportunity to review and validate the expected changes before applying them. Below is the syntax for this command:

```
terraform plan
```

apply

In the **apply** phase, Terraform executes the actions outlined in the plan created during the previous phase. Running terraform apply instructs Terraform to create, update, or delete resources based on the plan. It interacts with the target infrastructure and makes the necessary changes to align it with the desired state. This phase is where the actual infrastructure provisioning or modification occurs. Below is the syntax for this command:

```
terraform apply
```

destroy

The **destroy** phase is used when the resources managed by Terraform are to be decommissioned and removed. Running terraform destroy instructs Terraform to delete all the resources specified in the configuration. This phase is particularly useful when one needs to tear down temporary environments, save costs, or clean up resources that are no longer needed. As the implications are irreversible, be cautious when using destroy to avoid unintentional data loss or resource removal. Below is the syntax for this command:

```
terraform destroy
```

These four phases make up the core lifecycle of Terraform, providing a structured approach to managing infrastructure.

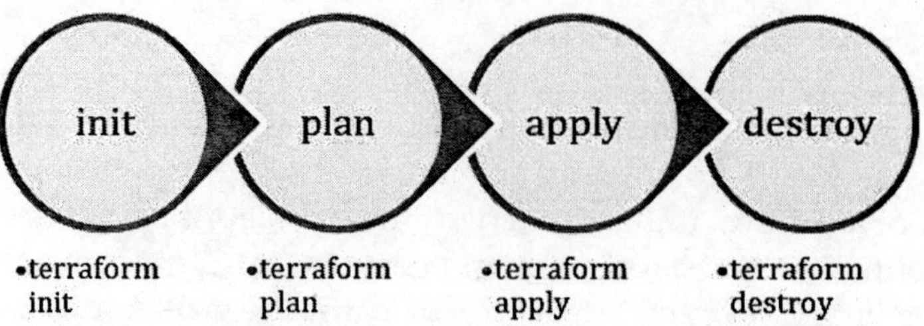

Figure 11.1: *Terraform lifecycle*

By following this lifecycle, one can ensure that the infrastructure remains in the desired state and changes are applied consistently and safely.

Terraform provider

Terraform providers play an important role in facilitating the interaction of Terraform with diverse infrastructure platforms and services. In Terraform, a provider is essentially a plugin that allows the tool to communicate with a specific platform or service, such as a cloud provider, database system, or networking equipment. These providers bridge the gap between Terraform configurations and the underlying infrastructure, making it possible to manage and provision resources in a declarative manner.

Providers abstract the complexity of interacting with specific platforms. They define a set of resource types that you can include in your Terraform configurations, encapsulating the necessary API calls and configurations. Terraform supports a wide range of providers, including cloud providers like AWS, Azure, and Google Cloud, as well as providers for databases, networking equipment, and more. This multi-provider support allows users to create and manage infrastructure across various platforms using a single, consistent language. Each provider requires specific configuration details, such as access keys, secrets, and endpoints, which are typically set in the Terraform configuration. These configuration parameters are essential for authenticating and authorizing Terraform to manage resources on the platform.

Each provider specifies a set of resource types (such as virtual machines, databases, and network security groups) that can be utilized in Terraform configurations. For example, using an AWS provider grants access to a variety of AWS resources such as EC2, RDS, IAM, and so on. Users reference these resource types in their code to specify the desired infrastructure components.

Providers are versioned independently from Terraform itself. This allows providers to evolve and add new features or resource types without necessitating an update to the Terraform core. Terraform providers can be developed and maintained by both HashiCorp (the organization behind Terraform) and the community. This extensibility allows providers to be created for custom or niche platforms and services.

Terraform configuration files

Terraform configuration files are at the core of the Terraform IaC approach and have the file extensions `.tf` and `.tf.json`, enabling users to define, provision, and manage infrastructure resources in a declarative and repeatable manner. They use HCL, a human-readable language that provides a clear and concise way to express infrastructure components and their relationships. HCL syntax allows one to define resource types, attributes, and configuration parameters in a straightforward format.

Terraform configurations are declarative, meaning only how the desired infrastructure should look like need to be specified rather than the step-by-step process of how to achieve it. This approach simplifies the management of infrastructure by abstracting the complexity of resource provisioning and management. It uses key-value pair for **input** and **output variables**, input variables are utilized as arguments to input values at run time and output variables are used to return values that can be used by other configurations.

Terraform uses various file types to structure and define infrastructure configurations. Here is a list of different types of Terraform files:

- **Terraform configuration files (.tf)**: These files contain the main infrastructure definitions, they define providers, resources, data sources, variables, outputs, and other configuration elements. Terraform uses these files to create and manage infrastructure.
- **Variable declaration files (variables.tf or variables.tf.json)**: Variable declaration files specify input variables used in the configuration. They define the variable name, type, and optional default values. Variables make the configurations more flexible and customizable.
- **Variable definition files (.tfvars)**: These files provide values for the input variables declared in the configuration. They allow to assign specific values to variables without modifying the main configuration files. Variables declared at the root level can be assigned values using these files apart from assigning values using environment variables.
- **Terraform state files (.tfstate)**: State files store the current state of the infrastructure managed by Terraform. They keep track of resource attributes, dependencies, and the relationship between your configuration and the real-world infrastructure.
- **Terraform ignore files (.terraformignore)**: These files define patterns of files and directories that should be excluded from upload to Terraform Cloud and can better the time for Terraform Cloud to prepare a remote plan.
- **Module files (modules/*.tf)**: Encapsulate reusable sets of resources, promoting modular and maintainable code.
- **Provider configuration files (provider.tf)**: Specify provider-specific settings and credentials.

- **Backend configuration files (backend.tf)**: Define settings for remote backends where Terraform state is stored.
- **Output files (output.tf)**: Declare values to be exposed after Terraform applies changes, aiding in sharing information with other systems or users.
- **Override files (override.tf or similar)**: Custom configuration files that override settings in other files.

Terraform module

A module is any group of Terraform configuration files contained within a folder. There is a single module, referred to as the root module, in every Terraform configuration. Terraform modules enhances the reusability, maintainability, and organization of infrastructure code. Modules allows to encapsulate a collection of Terraform resources into a single, self-contained unit. This means one can define and manage complex components of the infrastructure, such as virtual networks, web applications, or databases, as reusable modules.

Modules typically accept **input variables** that customize their behavior. Users can provide values for these variables when instantiating a module, allowing for configuration flexibility. Modules also define **output variables** that expose information about the resources created by the module.

Terraform state

Terraform state is used to keep track of the current state of the managed infrastructure. In essence, it serves as a record of the relationship between your Terraform configuration and the real-world resources it manages.

Terraform maintains a state file, typically named **`terraform.tfstate`**, which contains a snapshot of the attributes and metadata of the managed resources. This file is generated and updated with each terraform apply. While state files contain valuable information about your infrastructure, they may also include sensitive data like credentials or keys. It is crucial to secure state files properly and avoid storing sensitive data in plain text within them.

Getting started with Terraform

As part of the book AWS has been used as a cloud provider for hosting the Financial Services Marketplace application comprising of multiple microservices run as **Elastic Container Services** (**ECS**), connecting internally to RDS PostgresSQL database, and accessed using an **application load balancer** (**ALB**).

The required infrastructure on AWS can be built, modified, or destroyed using Terraform.

Terraform installation

Installing Terraform is the initial step in getting started with this IaC tool. Terraform is designed to be versatile and can be installed on various operating systems.

Recipe 97: Installing Terraform

Before installing Terraform, make sure one has a system that meets the prerequisites. Terraform is available for Windows, macOS, and Linux, and one will need a system with an appropriate OS. To install Terraform, visit the official Terraform website (**https://www.terraform.io/downloads.html**). On this page, download links for different operating systems will be available. Choose the appropriate version for the system and follow the instructions.

Installing Terraform on Windows

Download the zip file containing the **`terraform.exe`**, extract the binary and place it in a directory that is included in your system's PATH variable. This enables one to run Terraform from the command prompt.

Run the command **`terraform --version`** to display the installed Terraform version, confirming a successful installation, as shown in *Figure 11.2*:

Command Prompt

```
Microsoft Windows [Version 10.0.21996.1]
(c) Microsoft Corporation. All rights reserved.

C:\Users\This>terraform --version
Terraform v1.6.2
on windows_386

Your version of Terraform is out of date! The latest version
is 1.7.0. You can update by downloading from https://www.terraform.io/downloads.html
```

Figure 11.2: *Terraform version is 1.6.2*

Installing Terraform on Linux (Ubuntu 20.04 LTS)

Run the following commands on Linux shell:

```
sudo wget -O- https://apt.releases.hashicorp.com/gpg | sudo gpg --dearmor -o /usr/share/keyrings/hashicorp-archive-keyring.gpg

sudo echo "deb [signed-by=/usr/share/keyrings/hashicorp-archive-keyring.gpg] https://apt.releases.hashicorp.com $(lsb_release -cs) main" | sudo tee /etc/apt/sources.list.d/hashicorp.list

sudo apt update && sudo apt install terraform
```

It is a combination of three commands which downloads the signing key to a new keyring, adds the HarsiCorp repo and finally update packages and install the Terraform product, as shown in *Figure 11.3*:

```
varun@DESKTOP-C133REE: ~
varun@DESKTOP-C133REE:~$ sudo wget -O- https://apt.releases.hashicorp.com/gpg | sudo gpg --dearmor
 -o /usr/share/keyrings/hashicorp-archive-keyring.gpg
--2024-01-17 17:50:35--  https://apt.releases.hashicorp.com/gpg
Resolving apt.releases.hashicorp.com (apt.releases.hashicorp.com)... 108.158.221.60, 108.158.221.8
9, 108.158.221.87, ...
Connecting to apt.releases.hashicorp.com (apt.releases.hashicorp.com)|108.158.221.60|:443... conne
cted.
HTTP request sent, awaiting response... 200 OK
Length: 3980 (3.9K) [binary/octet-stream]
Saving to: 'STDOUT'

-                         100%[===================================>]   3.89K  --.-KB/s    in 0.01s

2024-01-17 17:50:39 (403 KB/s) - written to stdout [3980/3980]

varun@DESKTOP-C133REE:~$ sudo echo "deb [signed-by=/usr/share/keyrings/hashicorp-archive-keyring.g
pg] https://apt.releases.hashicorp.com $(lsb_release -cs) main" | sudo tee /etc/apt/sources.list.d
/hashicorp.list
deb [signed-by=/usr/share/keyrings/hashicorp-archive-keyring.gpg] https://apt.releases.hashicorp.c
om focal main
varun@DESKTOP-C133REE:~$ sudo apt update && sudo apt install terraform
Get:1 http://security.ubuntu.com/ubuntu focal-security InRelease [114 kB]
Get:2 https://download.docker.com/linux/ubuntu focal InRelease [57.7 kB]
Get:3 https://download.docker.com/linux/ubuntu focal/stable amd64 Packages [34.2 kB]
Hit:4 http://archive.ubuntu.com/ubuntu focal InRelease
Get:5 http://archive.ubuntu.com/ubuntu focal-updates InRelease [114 kB]
```

***Figure 11.3**: Installing Terraform on Linux (Ubuntu)*

After installation it can be verified that the terraform has been successfully installed by running the following command on the shell:

```
terraform --version
```

The following output confirms the successful installation:

```
Terraform v1.6.2

on linux_amd64
```

Setting the environment

The prerequisites required for setting the environment are:

- Terraform CLI
- AWS CLI
- AWS account credentials

Installation of Terraform is being shown in the previous recipe, moreover, AWS CLI has already been installed and configured as documented in *Chapter 1, Microservices and Cloud,* of the book. As part of the AWS CLI configuration, AWS access key, AWS secret key and AWS Region has already been set, if their values are not provided otherwise the values set as part of the configuration will be used.

Writing Terraform scripts

Once we are done with setting up the environment, we are good to start writing Terraform scripts.

Recipe 98: Creating first Terraform script

Create a new directory with a name **FSM AWS Infra Terraform**, parallel to the directory structure for financial service marketplace microservices. Move inside the newly created folder, create a new file with the main.tf and paste the following configuration code in that file:

main.tf

```
1.  terraform {
2.    required_providers {
3.      aws = {
4.        source = "hashicorp/aws"
5.        version = "~> 5.23"
6.      }
7.    }
8.
9.    required_version = ">= 1.2.0"
10. }
11.
12. provider "aws" {
13.   region = "${var.region}"
14. }
```

Here,

- *Line 1* begins the *terraform {}* block, which includes the terraform settings like provider information, version of terraform to be used, and so on. The providers are downloaded from the Terraform Registry (**https://registry.terraform.io/**) by default.
- *Line 3* defines the terraform provider **`aws`** whose source is **`hashicorp/aws`** which is a shortform for **`registry.terraform.io/hashicorp/aws`**. The version is optional but recommended to avoid any compatibility issues later.

- *Line 9* declares the version of Terraform to be used.
- *Line 12* begins the provider block and can be used to add configurations for the provider, for example region, access key, secret key, and so on. Multiple provider blocks can be added to manage resources from different providers.
- *Line 13*, the value region is to be picked up from a variable which is declared in a separate file.

In the same folder, create a file for declaring the variables, give a logical name, for example **`var.tf`** and paste the following code in that file:

`var.tf`

```
variable "region" {
      default = "us-east-1"
}
```

Here, a variable with the name **`region`** is declared with a default value **`us-east-1`**.

The value of the variable is to be defined in the **`*.tfvars`** file or passed at run time either as command line argument or as environment variables, if not defined or passed at runtime the default value will be used.

Once a new configuration is written or a configuration is checked out from a version control system, the environment or the folder is initialized using the following command:

`terraform init`

The command used to initialize a Terraform project, preparing it for configuration and provisioning by downloading provider plugins and modules as specified in the configuration files. In this case **`aws`** provider is being downloaded and installed as configured in the main.tf file, refer to *Figure 11.4* for reference:

```
varun@DESKTOP-C133REE:/mnt/d/varun/work/projects/FinancialServicesMarketplace/FSM
 AWS Infra Terraform$ terraform init

Initializing the backend...

Initializing provider plugins...
- Finding hashicorp/aws versions matching "~> 5.23"...
- Installing hashicorp/aws v5.33.0...
- Installed hashicorp/aws v5.33.0 (signed by HashiCorp)

Terraform has created a lock file .terraform.lock.hcl to record the provider
selections it made above. Include this file in your version control repositoryso
that Terraform can guarantee to make the same selections by default when
you run "terraform init" in the future.

Terraform has been successfully initialized!

You may now begin working with Terraform. Try running "terraform plan" to see
any changes that are required for your infrastructure. All Terraform commands
should now work.

If you ever set or change modules or backend configuration for Terraform,
rerun this command to reinitialize your working directory. If you forget, other
commands will detect it and remind you to do so if necessary.
```

Figure 11.4*: Initializing FSM AWS Infra Terraform folder*

.terraform.lock.hcl file also gets created as part of the **init** process which makes sure and is used to maintain consistent module versions in Terraform configurations, ensuring that the same modules are applied across different Terraform runs. It enhances predictability, collaboration, and infrastructure reproducibility, promoting a reliable and controlled provisioning process.

Recipe 99: Enhancing Terraform script to create an S3 resource

The scripts created in the previous recipe will be enhanced to create AWS S3 bucket using a Terraform module that will be created as part of this recipe. As previously mentioned, a module is only a collection of configuration files contained in a directory or folder.

To begin, create a sub directory with the name **s3** in the parent directory that is, **FSM AWS Infra Terraform**. Inside the sub directory create a file with a name **s3Bucket.tf** and paste the below code in that file:

s3Bucket.tf

```
1. resource "aws_s3_bucket" "fsm_bucket" {
2.      bucket = "${var.bucket_name}"
3. }
```

Here,

- *Line 1* has a resource block which is used to define infrastructure components. A resource can be a physical resource like S3 bucket or RDS database which is being used to create an external manage resource or a logical resource like TLS Private Key which only contributes in defining the Terraform state.
- A resource is uniquely identified via an id that is a combination of resource type and resource name which is this case are **aws_s3_bucket** and **fsm_bucket** respectively. The unique id for S3 resource would be **aws_s3_bucket.fsm_bucket**.
- Prefix of the resource type match with the provider's local name which in this case is **aws**, this is being used by Terraform to manage that resource using the defined provider.
- *Line 2* sets the value of an argument **bucket** which is one of the arguments used for the resource type **aws_s3_bucket** and accepts the name of the bucket, it is an optional argument if no value is set, Terraform assigns a random unique name to the bucket. In this case the value is being assigned using a variable which needs to be declared separately in the variables file in the same **s3** module or directory.

In the same **s3** folder create a file for declaring the variables, give a logical name, say **s3Var.tf** and paste the following code in that file:

s3Var.tf

```
variable "bucket_name" {
 type = string
}
```

Here, a variable with the name **bucket_name** is declared which accepts a value of type String.

Now, update main.tf to call the **s3** module by appending the following code:

main.tf

```
# existing code

module "s3" {
      source = "./s3"
      bucket_name = "${var.fsm_bucket_name}"
}
```

Here, **bucket_name** is a variable name used under the module **s3** for assigning the value to an argument bucket as previously defined. The value of **bucket_name** is also assigned using a new variable with the name **fsm_bucket_name**.

In this recipe the bucket to be created is to be created in a different region other than the default region. The value of the region is defined in the **. tfvar** file in the same module where the variable has been declared that is the **root** module. Move back to the parent folder and create a file **values.tfvar** and paste the following code in that file.

values.tfvar

```
region = "us-west-1"
```

Here, the value of the variable region is set to **us-west-1**. Values for multiple variables can be set in the same file each in separate new line.

Now, as a new variable got introduced in **main.tf**, it needs to be defined in the **var.tf** file as below:

var.tf

```
# existing code

variable "fsm_bucket_name" {
      type = string
}
```

Refer the below output of the **tree** command for the structure and relationships between the files:

```
├── main.tf
├── s3
│   ├── s3Bucket.tf
│   └── s3Var.tf
├── values.tfvars
└── var.tf

1 directory, 5 files
```

Once done, the scripts can be used to provision the infrastructure.

Provisioning infrastructure with Terraform

Once the environment is set and the terraform scripts are ready, the scripts can be executed to create the infrastructure in the configured provider.

Recipe 100: Executing Terraform script to provision an S3 resource

Execute the command **terraform init** to initialize the newly created module, refer to *Figure 11.5* for your reference:

```
varun@DESKTOP-C133REE:/mnt/d/varun/work/projects/FinancialServicesMarketplace/FSM
 AWS Infra Terraform$ terraform init

Initializing the backend...
Initializing modules...
- s3 in s3

Initializing provider plugins...
- Reusing previous version of hashicorp/aws from the dependency lock file
- Using previously-installed hashicorp/aws v5.33.0

Terraform has been successfully initialized!

You may now begin working with Terraform. Try running "terraform plan" to see
any changes that are required for your infrastructure. All Terraform commands
should now work.

If you ever set or change modules or backend configuration for Terraform,
rerun this command to reinitialize your working directory. If you forget, other
commands will detect it and remind you to do so if necessary.
```

***Figure 11.5**: Initializing module s3*

After initializing the next step is to view the execution plan before applying the infrastructure changes to make sure things are in place for execution. Run the following command to view the plan:

`terraform plan -var "fsm_bucket_name=fs-marketplace-bucket-dr" -var-file values.tfvars`

Here,

- **`var`** is used to assign values to the variables. Value of variable **`fsm_bucket_name`** is set as **`fs-marketplace-bucket-dr`** as the bucket is to be created for the **disaster recovery** (**DR**) perspective.
- **`var-file`** is used to pass the name of the file containing the variable definitions.

Refer to *Figure 11.6* for the output of the command:

```
varun@DESKTOP-C133REE:/mnt/d/varun/work/projects/FinancialServicesMarketplace/FSM
 AWS Infra Terraform$ terraform plan -var "fsm_bucket_name=fs-marketplace-bucket-
dr" -var-file values.tfvars

Terraform used the selected providers to generate the following execution plan.
Resource actions are indicated with the following symbols:
  + create

Terraform will perform the following actions:

  # module.s3.aws_s3_bucket.fsm_bucket will be created
  + resource "aws_s3_bucket" "fsm_bucket" {
      + acceleration_status         = (known after apply)
      + acl                         = (known after apply)
      + arn                         = (known after apply)
      + bucket                      = "fs-marketplace-bucket-dr"
      + bucket_domain_name          = (known after apply)
      + bucket_prefix               = (known after apply)
      + bucket_regional_domain_name = (known after apply)
      + force_destroy               = false
      + hosted_zone_id              = (known after apply)
      + id                          = (known after apply)
      + object_lock_enabled         = (known after apply)
      + policy                      = (known after apply)
      + region                      = (known after apply)
      + request_payer               = (known after apply)
      + tags_all                    = (known after apply)
      + website_domain              = (known after apply)
      + website_endpoint            = (known after apply)
    }

Plan: 1 to add, 0 to change, 0 to destroy.

────────────────────────────────────────────────────────────────────────────────

Note: You didn't use the -out option to save this plan, so Terraform can't
guarantee to take exactly these actions if you run "terraform apply" now.
```

***Figure 11.6**: Output of terraform plan*

One the plan looks fine run the following command to apply the plan and create an S3 bucket in AWS:

`terraform apply -var "fsm_bucket_name=fs-marketplace-bucket-dr" -var-file values.tfvars`

Pass the same variable values as was done in the previous stage for reviewing the execution plan. The command again displays the plan and asks for the conformation in a prompt as shown below before finally updating the infrastructure in the AWS cloud:

`Do you want to perform these actions?`

Enter the response as **`yes`** for Terraform to start executing the plan. The output of the command is as shown in *Figure 11.7*:

```
varun@DESKTOP-C133REE:/mnt/d/varun/work/projects/FinancialServicesMarketplace/FSM
AWS Infra Terraform$ terraform apply -var "fsm_bucket_name=fs-marketplace-bucket-d
r" -var-file values.tfvars

Terraform used the selected providers to generate the following execution plan.
Resource actions are indicated with the following symbols:
  + create

Terraform will perform the following actions:

  # module.s3.aws_s3_bucket.fsm_bucket will be created
  + resource "aws_s3_bucket" "fsm_bucket" {
      + acceleration_status         = (known after apply)
      + acl                         = (known after apply)
      + arn                         = (known after apply)
      + bucket                      = "fs-marketplace-bucket-dr"
      + bucket_domain_name          = (known after apply)
      + bucket_prefix               = (known after apply)
      + bucket_regional_domain_name = (known after apply)
      + force_destroy               = false
      + hosted_zone_id              = (known after apply)
      + id                          = (known after apply)
      + object_lock_enabled         = (known after apply)
      + policy                      = (known after apply)
      + region                      = (known after apply)
      + request_payer               = (known after apply)
      + tags_all                    = (known after apply)
      + website_domain              = (known after apply)
      + website_endpoint            = (known after apply)
    }

Plan: 1 to add, 0 to change, 0 to destroy.

Do you want to perform these actions?
  Terraform will perform the actions described above.
  Only 'yes' will be accepted to approve.

  Enter a value: yes

module.s3.aws_s3_bucket.fsm_bucket: Creating...
module.s3.aws_s3_bucket.fsm_bucket: Creation complete after 8s [id=fs-marketplace-
bucket-dr]

Apply complete! Resources: 1 added, 0 changed, 0 destroyed.
```

***Figure 11.7**: Output of terraform apply*

After executing the **`apply`** command Terraform creates a file with the name **`terraform.tstate`** to maintain the state of the infrastructure and manage the resources that it has generated. The current state of the infrastructure can be validated by executing the following command:

terraform show

As part of creating the state file Terraform collects the metadata from the AWS provider and persists that information in the file. The above command refers to the state file and displays the resources that are managed by Terraform along with the metadata from the file, refer to *Figure 11.8* for your reference:

```
varun@DESKTOP-C133REE:/mnt/d/varun/work/projects/FinancialServicesMarketplace/FSM
 AWS Infra Terraform$ terraform show
# module.s3.aws_s3_bucket.fsm_bucket:
resource "aws_s3_bucket" "fsm_bucket" {
    arn                         = "arn:aws:s3:::fs-marketplace-bucket-dr"
    bucket                      = "fs-marketplace-bucket-dr"
    bucket_domain_name          = "fs-marketplace-bucket-dr.s3.amazonaws.com"
    bucket_regional_domain_name = "fs-marketplace-bucket-dr.s3.us-west-1.amazonaws
.com"
    force_destroy               = false
    hosted_zone_id              = "Z2F56UZL2M1ACD"
    id                          = "fs-marketplace-bucket-dr"
    object_lock_enabled         = false
    region                      = "us-west-1"
    request_payer               = "BucketOwner"
    tags_all                    = {}

    grant {
        id          = "77b4ccbd88c5e39824c0fb5a9865e871cfd8522b6baf26b8b1bfb741975
42ab3"
        permissions = [
            "FULL_CONTROL",
        ]
        type        = "CanonicalUser"
    }

    server_side_encryption_configuration {
        rule {
            bucket_key_enabled = false

            apply_server_side_encryption_by_default {
                sse_algorithm = "AES256"
            }
        }
    }

    versioning {
        enabled    = false
        mfa_delete = false
    }
}
```

Figure 11.8: Details of AWS S3 bucket

An AWS bucket with the name **`fs-marketplace-bucket-dr`** has been created in the AWS region **`us-west-1`**.

The same can also be validated by visiting AWS Management Console for S3 buckets, refer to *Figure 11.9* for reference:

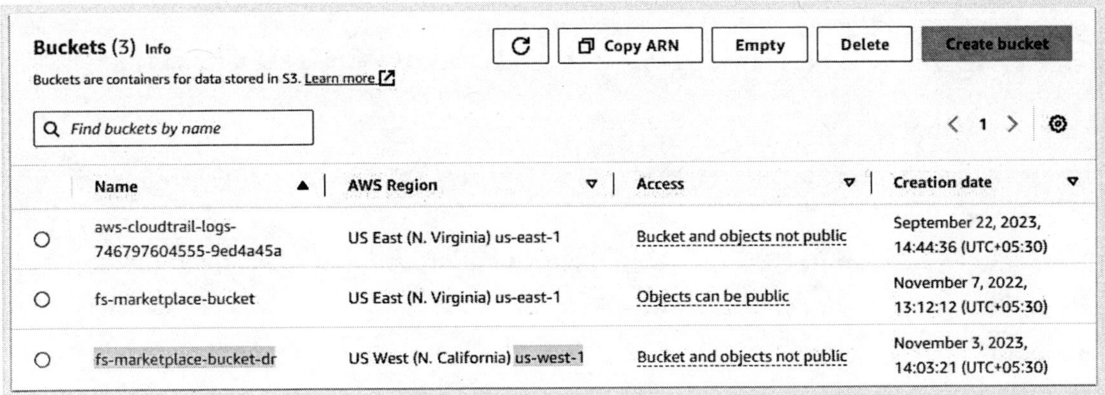

Figure 11.9: Available S3 buckets for the account

Fine-grained properties for a resource can also be configured using Terraform scripts by setting the values for the required arguments while creating a resource.

Importing existing infrastructure in Terraform

Importing existing infrastructure is a very useful and important feature of Terraform, as it allows to manage resources that were created outside of Terraform. To import an existing resource, one need to:

- **Identify the resource**: Determine which resource is to be imported and its associated attributes.
- **Define the resource in the Terraform configuration**: Create a resource block in the Terraform configuration with the same resource type and a placeholder name.
- **Run terraform import**: Use the `terraform import` command with the resource block to associate the existing resource with the Terraform configuration. Terraform will fetch the current state of the resource and record it in the state file. Example:

  ```
  terraform import <Terraform_Resource_Type>.<Resource_Name>
  <Provider_Resource_ID>
  ```

- **Run terraform plan**: After importing, run terraform plan to verify that the configuration matches the imported resource.
- **Use the imported resource attributes**: Copy the imported resource attributes to build the Terraform configuration and use them going forward to manage the infrastructure.

Terraform import is a way to bring existing infrastructure under Terraform's control, making it very easy to script down the infrastructure configurations.

Recipe 101: Importing S3 bucket resource in Terraform

The attributes of the S3 bucket **`fsm-marketplace-bucket`** can be extracted by importing the bucket into Terraform.

Create a separate **`import`** directory with a file **`s3Import.tf`** and paste the following code in that file:

`s3Import.tf`

```
1. terraform {
2.   required_providers {
3.     aws = {
4.       source  = "hashicorp/aws"
5.       version = "~> 5.23"
6.     }
7.   }
8.
9.   required_version = ">= 1.2.0"
10. }
11.
12. provider "aws" {
13.   region = "us-east-1"
14. }
15.
16. resource "aws_s3_bucket" "fsm_bucket_primary" {
17. }
18.
19. resource "aws_s3_bucket_public_access_block" "fsm_bucket_primary" {
20. }
```

Here,

- *Line 16* is a placeholder for capturing the details of the S3 bucket mapped to the local name **`fsm_bucket_primary`**.

- *Line 19* is a placeholder for capturing the details of the access policies of the S3 bucket mapped to the local name **fsm_bucket_primary**.

Once the configuration file has been created run the following commands in the newly created **import** directory:

terraform init

terraform import aws_s3_bucket.fsm_bucket_primary fs-marketplace-bucket

terraform import aws_s3_bucket_public_access_block.fsm_bucket_primary fs-marketplace-bucket

The preceding commands initialize the project and imports the required details from the AWS environment and maps them to the placeholders' names in the Terraform state. Refer *Figure 11.10* for the output of the above import commands:

```
varun@DESKTOP-C133REE:/mnt/d/varun/work/projects/FinancialServicesMarketplace/FSM
 AWS Infra Terraform/import$ terraform import aws_s3_bucket.fsm_bucket_primary fs
-marketplace-bucket
aws_s3_bucket.fsm_bucket_primary: Importing from ID "fs-marketplace-bucket"...
aws_s3_bucket.fsm_bucket_primary: Import prepared!
  Prepared aws_s3_bucket for import
aws_s3_bucket.fsm_bucket_primary: Refreshing state... [id=fs-marketplace-bucket]

Import successful!

The resources that were imported are shown above. These resources are now in
your Terraform state and will henceforth be managed by Terraform.

varun@DESKTOP-C133REE:/mnt/d/varun/work/projects/FinancialServicesMarketplace/FSM
 AWS Infra Terraform/import$ terraform import aws_s3_bucket_public_access_block.f
sm_bucket_primary fs-marketplace-bucket
aws_s3_bucket_public_access_block.fsm_bucket_primary: Importing from ID "fs-marke
tplace-bucket"...
aws_s3_bucket_public_access_block.fsm_bucket_primary: Import prepared!
  Prepared aws_s3_bucket_public_access_block for import
aws_s3_bucket_public_access_block.fsm_bucket_primary: Refreshing state... [id=fs-
marketplace-bucket]

Import successful!

The resources that were imported are shown above. These resources are now in
your Terraform state and will henceforth be managed by Terraform.
```

***Figure 11.10**: Importing existing S3 bucket into Terraform*

The imported configurations can be viewing the Terraform state using the **terraform show** command, refer to *Figure 11.11* for reference:

```
varun@DESKTOP-C133REE:/mnt/d/varun/work/projects/FinancialServicesMarketplace/FSM AWS Inf
ra Terraform/import$ terraform show
# aws_s3_bucket.fsm_bucket_primary:
resource "aws_s3_bucket" "fsm_bucket_primary" {
    arn                         = "arn:aws:s3:::fs-marketplace-bucket"
    bucket                      = "fs-marketplace-bucket"
    bucket_domain_name          = "fs-marketplace-bucket.s3.amazonaws.com"
    bucket_regional_domain_name = "fs-marketplace-bucket.s3.us-east-1.amazonaws.com"
    hosted_zone_id              = "Z3AQBSTGFYJSTF"
    id                          = "fs-marketplace-bucket"
    object_lock_enabled         = false
    region                      = "us-east-1"
    request_payer               = "BucketOwner"
    tags                        = {
        "CostCenter"  = "123"
        "Environment" = "production"
    }
    tags_all                    = {
        "CostCenter"  = "123"
        "Environment" = "production"
    }

    grant {
        id          = "77b4ccbd88c5e39824c0fb5a9865e871cfd8522b6baf26b8b1bfb74197542ab3"
        permissions = [
            "FULL_CONTROL",
        ]
        type        = "CanonicalUser"
    }

    server_side_encryption_configuration {
        rule {
            bucket_key_enabled = true

            apply_server_side_encryption_by_default {
                kms_master_key_id = "arn:aws:kms:us-east-1:746797604555:key/6792dde9-9887
-4341-838d-815e6611fd02"
                sse_algorithm     = "aws:kms"
            }
        }
    }

    versioning {
        enabled    = false
        mfa_delete = false
    }
}

# aws_s3_bucket_public_access_block.fsm_bucket_primary:
resource "aws_s3_bucket_public_access_block" "fsm_bucket_primary" {
    block_public_acls       = false
    block_public_policy     = false
    bucket                  = "fs-marketplace-bucket"
    id                      = "fs-marketplace-bucket"
    ignore_public_acls      = false
    restrict_public_buckets = false
}
```

Figure 11.11: Imported S3 bucket details

Conclusion

In this chapter, we began by understanding the fundamental concepts and importance of IaC, recognizing it as a game-changer for modern infrastructure management. It provided the understanding of Terraform and its life cycle. The installation of Terraform at the beginning of the chapter established the foundation for practical experience in the IaC world. Provisioning infrastructure in AWS using Terraform showcased the power of automation, repeatability, and scalability. It also explored the process of importing existing resources into Terraform, a powerful way to script existing infrastructure. IaC with Terraform is not just a concept; it is a transformative force, enabling one to craft, evolve, and harmonize complex infrastructure seamlessly. As we conclude this chapter, remember that our journey in IaC is just beginning, and Terraform is an indispensable tool for infrastructure mastery. Stay curious, keep experimenting, and let the code shape the future of the infrastructure.

Points to remember

- Terraform uses HCL for configuration files, which is easy to read and write.
- IaC with Terraform is declarative, meaning one needs to define the desired state of the infrastructure in Terraform configuration files (**`.tf`**).
- Terraform configurations define resources, such as EC2 instances, VPCs, and S3 buckets, using resource blocks.
- Use input variables to parameterize the configurations, making them flexible and reusable. Declare variables in separate **`.tf`** files. The values of the variables can be assigned via command line, environment variables or via a **`separate.tfvars`** files.
- Variables used in a module needs to be declared in the same module itself.
- Terraform life cycle phases are init, plan, apply and destroy.
- Organize the code into modules to promote reusability and maintainability.
- Import existing infrastructure to ease the development of configuration files, the attributes from the imported state marks a good starting point for developing the configurations.

Questions

1. How does Terraform ensure consistency and repeatability in infrastructure provisioning?
2. What are the key components of a typical Terraform configuration, and what is the purpose of each?

3. Describe the role of providers in Terraform and provide an example of configuring the AWS provider.
4. Walk through the steps of creating a Terraform script to provision an AWS ECS instance. What resource attributes would you specify?
5. Discuss the concept of Terraform modules and provide an example of creating and using a module.
6. Outline the typical sequence of Terraform commands you would use to provision AWS infrastructure.
7. How do you manage environment-specific configurations, such as AWS region or access credentials, in Terraform scripts?
8. Walk through the steps to import an existing AWS RDS instance into Terraform.
9. How do you destroy resources created by Terraform?
10. How does Terraform maintain state, and why is it important?

Index

A

D

Illegal for sale
or distribution outside
Indian Sub-continent.
Books found outside this
market may be treated as
illegal/ pirated books.